Life of Genghis Khan and The Mongol Invasions

Compiled by
Syed Ramsey

Scribbles

Year of Publication 2018

ISBN : 9789387513303
Price : 795/-

Book Published by

Scribbles

(An Imprint of Alpha Editions)

email - alphaedis@gmail.com

Produced by: PediaPress GmbH
Limburg an der Lahn
Germany
http://pediapress.com/

The content within this book was generated collaboratively by volunteers. Please be advised that nothing found here has necessarily been reviewed by people with the expertise required to provide you with complete, accurate or reliable information. Some information in this book may be misleading or simply wrong. Alpha Editions and PediaPress does not guarantee the validity of the information found here. If you need specific advice (for example, medical, legal, financial, or risk management) please seek a professional who is licensed or knowledgeable in that area.

Sources, licenses and contributors of the articles and images are listed in the section entitled "References". Parts of the books may be licensed under the GNU Free Documentation License. A copy of this license is included in the section entitled "GNU Free Documentation License"

The views and characters expressed in the book are those of the contributors and his/her imagination and do not represent the views of the Publisher.

Contents

Articles	**1**
Timeline of the Mongol Empire	1
Genghis Khan	**17**
Genghis Khan	17
Mongol invasions and conquests	**61**
Central Asia	**63**
Mongol invasion of Central Asia	63
West Asia	**67**
Mongol invasions of the Levant	67
Mongol invasions of Anatolia	79
Mongol conquest of Khwarezmia	84
Siege of Baghdad (1258)	101
East Asia	**111**
Mongol invasions of Korea	111
Mongol conquest of China	116
Mongol invasions of Japan	127
Mongol invasions of Tibet	145
Europe	**155**
Mongol invasion of Europe	155

South Asia — 183
Mongol invasions of India 183

Southeast Asia — 195
First Mongol invasion of Burma 195
Second Mongol invasion of Burma 213
Mongol invasions of Vietnam 215
Mongol invasion of Java 222

Mongol military tactics and organization — 227
Mongol military tactics and organization 227

Appendix — 247
References 247
Article Sources and Contributors 265
Image Sources, Licenses and Contributors 267

Article Licenses — 271

Index — 273

Timeline of the Mongol Empire

This is the **timeline of the Mongol Empire** from from the birth of Temüjin, later Genghis Khan, to the end of the Yuan dynasty in 1368, though the title of Khagan continued to be used by the rulers of the Northern Yuan dynasty, a far less powerful successor entity, until 1634.

12th century

1160s

Year	Date	Event
1162		Temüjin is born in Delüün Boldog near Burkhan Khaldun to the Mongol chieftain Yesugei and Hoelun[1]

1170s

Year	Date	Event
1170		Yesugei takes Temüjin east through Tatar territory to the Khongirad homeland to arrange a future marriage between his son and Börte. Temüjin stays with the Khongirads to learn their ways, however Yesugei is poisoned by the Tatars during his return trip. Temüjin leaves Börte for his father, but arrives too late to see his father alive. His father's followers scatter and Hoelun is left to care for their children by herself.[2] She takes them to the Khentii Mountains, where they live for several years.[3]
1173		Temüjin becomes *anda*, blood brothers, with Jamukha of the Jajirad (Jadaran) clan[4]

1180s

Year	Date	Event
1184		Temüjin leaves to claim Börte. Börte's father gives him a black sable cloak as dowry, which he later gives to Toghrul of the Keraites to gain his favor. Soon after the Merkits abduct Börte and Temüjin flees. Several months later Temüjin assembles an allied force over over 20,000 with his ally Toghrul and sworn blood brother Jamukha, who attack the Merkits and rescue Börte.[3]
1185		Mongols gather at Burkhan Khaldun to throw their support behind Temüjin in fear of the rising power of Jamukha[3]
1187		Temüjin allies himself with the Khongirad to wage war on the Tatars. His blood brother Jamukha refuses to acknowledge his leadership and wages war on him. They clash at the Battle of the Thirteen Wings, which ends inconclusively. However Jamukha's rash and vindictive behavior towards his allies alienates him.[3]

1190s

Year	Date	Event
1192		Jin dynasty starts constructing fortifications in the northwest to prevent depredations by the Mongols[5]
1196		Jin and Mongol troops carry out a punitive expedition against the Tatars[6]

13th century
1200s

Year	Date	Event
1201		Mongols opposing Temüjin promote Jamukha to *gür-khan*[4]
1202		Mongols exterminate the Tatars[7]
1203		Temüjin splits with Toghrul[8]
	spring	The Keraites defeat Temüjin at Qalaqaljid Sands[9]
	autumn	Temüjin defeats Toghrul at Jeje'er Heights[9]
		Temüjin creates the Kheshig, an elite military guard[10]
1204		Temüjin defeats the Naimans, Merkits, and Jamukha; Merkit leaders and Jamukha flee to the Altai Mountains[10]
	fall	Temüjin pursues Jamukha and defeats him in several battles. Eventually Jamukha's allies betray him and turn him over to Temüjin, who kills him by breaking his back.[10]
		The Uyghurs and Ongud submit to Temüjin[11]
1205	spring	*Mongol conquest of Western Xia*: Temüjin of the Mongols raids Western Xia's border settlements[12]
1206	spring	Kokochu, also known as Teb Tengri, chief shaman of the Mongols, bestows upon Temüjin the title of Genghis Khan, "Oceanic Ruler" of the Mongol Empire, at the kurultai of Burkhan Khaldun, sacred mountain of the Mongols[13]
1207		*Mongol conquest of Western Xia*: Genghis Khan sacks Wulahai, a Western Xia garrison along the Yellow River near modern Wuyuan[14]
		Jochi subjugates the 'forest peoples' - Kyrgyz, Oirat, and Buryat[15]
1208		Toq'toa Beki of the Merkits is killed by Mongols and Uyghurs[15]
1209	autumn	*Mongol conquest of Western Xia*: Genghis Khan penetrates Western Xia from Wulahai and defeats a Tangut army before laying siege to Zhongxing, however the Mongols accidentally flood their own camp in the process of breaking the Yellow River dikes and are forced to retreat[16]
		Qocho, Qayaligh, and Almaliq submit to Genghis Khan; Almaliq and the Issyk-Kul region given to Chagatai[17]

1210s

Year	Date	Event
1210		*Mongol conquest of Western Xia*: Emperor Xiangzong of Western Xia submits to the Mongol Empire and hands over a daughter in marriage to Genghis Khan as well as a large supply of camels, falcons, and woven textiles; a Mongol garrison is left at Wulahai[16]
		Kokochu is killed by Qasar in a wrestling match[18]
1211		*Mongol conquest of the Jin dynasty*: Jochi, Ögedei, and Chagatai invade Inner Mongolia[19]
	October	*Mongol conquest of the Jin dynasty*: Jebe takes Juyong Pass from the Jin dynasty[20]
	winter	*Mongol conquest of the Jin dynasty*: Mongol forces retreat from Jin territory[21]
		Karluks rebel against the Qara Khitai and defect to the Mongol Empire[22]
1212	February	*Battle of Yehuling*: Genghis Khan and Muqali crush the Jin army led by Wanyan Jiujin, Duji Sizhong, and Hushahu[21]
1213	5 January	*Mongol conquest of the Jin dynasty*: Jebe takes the Eastern Capital[20]
	July-August	*Mongol conquest of the Jin dynasty*: Genghis Khan crushes a Jin army led by Zhuhu Gaoqi[23]
	autumn	*Mongol conquest of the Jin dynasty*: Jochi, Ögedei, and Chagatai ravage Hebei and Shanxi[24]
	November	*Mongol conquest of the Jin dynasty*: Genghis Khan and Jebe pass through the Zijing Gap[25]
1214	31 March	*Mongol conquest of the Jin dynasty*: Genghis Khan lays siege to the Central Capital[26]
	11 May	*Mongol conquest of the Jin dynasty*: Jin dynasty becomes a tributary and agrees to hand over a daughter of the previous emperor; the Mongols lift the siege[26]
	July	*Mongol conquest of the Jin dynasty*: Khitan and Tatar defectors lay siege to the Central Capital[25]
	December	*Mongol conquest of the Jin dynasty*: Muqali wipes out Jin centers in Liaoning and southern Manchuria[25]
1215	31 May	*Battle of Zhongdu*: Mongol Empire takes the Central Capital and places the Khitan Shimo Ming'an and Jabar Khoja in charge of the city[26]
	23 September	Kublai is born to Tolui and Sorghaghtani Beki[27]
1216		*Mongol conquest of the Qara Khitai*: Jebe seizes Kashgar from the Qara Khitai and Kuchlug flees[28]
		Subutai raids the Kipchaks[29]

1217		*Mongol conquest of the Jin dynasty*: Genghis Khan appoints Muqali as viceroy of North China and leaves for Mongolia[30]
		Mongol conquest of the Jin dynasty: Muqali removes Jin presence in the steppes[25]
1218	autumn	*Mongol conquest of Khwarezmia*: Muhammad II of Khwarezm's forces clash with a Mongol army led by Jochi and Subutai, the battle ending inconclusively[31]
	winter	*Mongol conquest of Khwarezmia*: A Muslim merchant delegation sent by Genghis Khan arrives at Otrar and the governor Inalchuq kills them, seizing their goods for himself; a sole survivor reaches Mongolia and alerts Genghis, who sends three more envoys to demand custody of Inalchuq - they are also killed[31]
		Mongol conquest of Western Xia: Mongol Empire lays siege to Zhongxing and Emperor Xiangzong of Western Xia flees west; his son and officials make peace with the Mongols[32]
		Mongol conquest of the Qara Khitai: Shepherds in Badakhshan capture Kuchlug and hand him over to Jebe, who beheads him; so ends the Qara Khitai[33]
1219	January	Goryeo becomes a tributary of the Mongol Empire[34]
	fall	*Mongol conquest of Khwarezmia*: Ögedei and Chagatai take Otrar and massacres its population; Genghis Khan dispatches Jochi to conquer Syr Darya and another army to conquer Fergana[35]
		Western Xia refuses to send auxiliaries for the Mongol Empire's western campaigns[36]

1220s

Year	Date	Event
1220	15 February	*Mongol conquest of Khwarezmia*: Genghis Khan takes Bukhara and places Yelü Ahai in control of Transoxiana[35]
	16 March	*Mongol conquest of Khwarezmia*: Genghis Khan takes Samarkand and Muhammad II of Khwarezm flees to Nishapur; Genghis Khan dispatches Jebe and Subutai to destroy the sultan[35]
	May	*Mongol conquest of Khwarezmia*: Jebe and Subutai take Balkh and capture Muhammad II of Khwarezm's mother Terken Khatun and family in the Zagros Mountains[37]
	winter	*Mongol conquest of Khwarezmia*: Muhammad II of Khwarezm dies[35]
1221	March	*Mongol conquest of Khwarezmia*: Tolui destroys Merv[35]
	April	*Mongol conquest of Khwarezmia*: Jochi, Chagatai, and Ögedei destroy Urgench while Tolui takes Nishapur and Herat[35]
	spring	*Battle of Parwan*: Jalal ad-Din Mingburnu defeats a Mongol army led by Shikhikhutug in the Hindu Kush[35]
		Mongol conquest of Khwarezmia: Genghis Khan takes Termez[35]

		Siege of Bamyan (1221): Genghis Khan takes Bamyan; Chagatai's son Mutukan dies in the process[19]
	November	*Battle of Indus*: Genghis Khan defeats Jalal ad-Din Mingburnu, who swims across the Indus River and escapes[35]
1222		Subutai and Jebe conquer the Kuban steppe and crush the Cumans[29]
1223		*Mongol conquest of the Jin dynasty*: Muqali dies and the Mongol Empire loses control of Henan, central Shaanxi, and southeast Shandong[25]
	spring	Genghis Khan returns to Mongolia[35]
	31 May	*Battle of the Kalka River*: Subutai and Jebe defeat the forces of Mstislav Mstislavich, Mstislav III of Kiev, Daniel of Galicia, Mstislav II Svyatoslavich, and Köten before sacking Novhorod-Siverskyi and heading back to Mongolia[38]
		Mongol Empire sacks Sudak[39]
1224		Bulgars ambush Subutai and Jebe near Saqsin[40]
		Goryeo stops paying tribute[34]
1226	February	*Mongol conquest of Western Xia*: Mongol Empire seizes Khara-Khoto from Western Xia and sack cities across the Gansu Corridor[36]
	November	*Mongol conquest of Western Xia*: Mongol Empire sacks Lingzhou[32]
	4 December	*Mongol conquest of Western Xia*: Genghis Khan crosses the Yellow River and defeats a Tangut relief column[32]
1227	September	*Mongol conquest of Western Xia*: Emperor Mozhu of Western Xia surrenders to the Mongol Empire and is promptly executed; so ends the Western Xia[41]
		Jochi dies and is succeeded by his son Batu Khan[24]
	August	Genghis Khan dies near the Jing River and Tolui becomes regent[42]
1229	13 September	Ögedei Khan is elected ruler of the Mongol Empire at a kurultai near the Kherlen River[43]
		Mongol invasion of Volga Bulgaria: Sunitay and Kukedey attack Bulgar outposts on the Ural River[40]

1230s

Year	Date	Event
1230		*Mongol conquest of the Jin dynasty*: Doqolqu and Subutai attack Tong Pass and are defeated by Wanyan Heda[25]
	autumn	*Mongol conquest of the Jin dynasty*: Ögedei Khan and Tolui take Fengxiang[25]
1231	August	*Mongol conquest of Khwarezmia*: Chormaqan defeats Jalal ad-Din Mingburnu, who escapes only to be killed by some random Kurd; so ends the Khwarazmian dynasty[37]

		Mongol invasions of Korea: Sartai subjugates Goryeo, however the Mongol overseers are immediately killed afterwards[34]
		"Thunder crash bombs" are employed by Jin troops in destroying a Mongol warship.[44]
1232	spring	*Mongol conquest of the Jin dynasty*: Tolui invades Henan and Ögedei Khan pushes through the Tong Pass[25]
	13 February	*Mongol conquest of the Jin dynasty*: Tolui kills Wanyan Heda[25]
	8 April	*Mongol siege of Kaifeng*: Subutai lays siege to Kaifeng[25]
		Mongol invasions of Korea: Sartai heads back to Goryeo and dies from an arrow[45]
		Mongol invasions of Georgia: Chormaqan subjugates Azerbaijan[46]
		Tolui is struck by sickness and dies[47]
		Mongol conquest of the Jin dynasty: Reusable fire lance barrels made of durable paper are employed by Jin troops during the Mongol siege of Kaifeng.[44]
1233	5 March	*Mongol siege of Kaifeng*: Kaifeng surrenders[25]
	December	*Siege of Caizhou*: Mongol Empire lays siege to Caizhou[25]
1234	9 February	*Siege of Caizhou*: Emperor Aizong of Jin abdicates to a distant relative, Hudun, who becomes Emperor Mo of Jin, and commits suicide; Emperor Mo of Jin is killed by the Mongols; so ends the Jin dynasty[48]
		Ögedei Khan announces his plans to conquer Goryeo, the Song dynasty, and Cumania[49]
1235		Ögedei Khan constructs Karakorum[49]
1236		*Mongol invasion of Volga Bulgaria*: Subutai destroys Bolghar and takes Saqsin[50]
		Mongol invasions of Georgia: Chormaqan subjugates Georgia and Armenia[46]
1237	21 December	*Siege of Ryazan*: Batu, Orda, Güyük, and Möngke sack Ryazan and Suzdal[51]
		Large bombs requiring several hundred men to hurl using trebuchets are employed by Mongols in the siege of Anfeng (modern Shouxian, Anhui Province).[52]
1238	4 March	*Battle of the Sit River*: Mongol Empire kills Yuri II of Vladimir[53]
	spring	*Siege of Kozelsk*: Batu struggles to take Kozelsk for two months before Kadan and Büri take it in three days[54]
		Mongol Empire conquers Crimea[39]
1239	3 March	*Mongol invasion of Rus'*: Mongol Empire sacks Pereiaslav-Khmelnytskyi[51]
	18 October	*Mongol invasion of Rus'*: Mongol Empire sacks Chernihiv[51]

1240s

Year	Date	Event
1240	6 December	*Siege of Kiev (1240)*: Mongol Empire sacks Kiev, Halych, and Vladimir-Suzdal[51]
		Mongol invasions of Tibet: Doorda Darkhan sacks Reting Monastery[55]
1241	9 April	*Battle of Legnica*: Orda defeats the combined force of Henry II the Pious, Mieszko II the Fat, Sulisław of Cracow, and Bolesław Děpoltic[56]
	11 April	*Battle of Mohi*: Boroldai and Subutai defeat a combined army from the Kingdom of Hungary, Croatia, and Knights Templar[56]
	December	*Mongol invasion of Europe*: Kadan crosses the Danube[56]
	11 December	Ögedei Khan dies on a hunting trip after lengthy drinking and his wife Töregene Khatun becomes regent[57]
1242		*Mongol invasion of Europe*: Mongol Empire forces Bulgaria to pay tribute[58]
	spring	*Mongol invasion of Europe*: Mongol forces retreat after receiving news of Ögedei Khan's death; Batu Khan stays at the Volga River and his brother Orda Khan returns to Mongolia[56]
		Chagatai Khan dies and his grandson Qara Hülegü succeeds him[59]
1243	26 June	*Battle of Köse Dağ*: Baiju defeats Kaykhusraw II and subjugates the Armenian Kingdom of Cilicia[60]
1244		Badr al-Din Lu'lu' of Mosul submits to the Mongol Empire[61]
1246		Temüge tries to seize the throne without a kurultai but fails[62]
	24 August	Güyük Khan is elected ruler of the Mongol Empire at a kurultai on the Kherlen River[63]
		Güyük Khan appoints Yesü Möngke as head of the Chagatai Khanate[64]
1248	20 April	Güyük Khan dies on his way to confront Batu Khan and his wife Oghul Qaimish becomes regent[65]

1250s

Year	Date	Event
1251	1 July	Möngke Khan is elected ruler of the Mongol Empire at a kurultai in the Khentii Mountains[66]
	fall	Möngke Khan places his brothers Hulagu Khan and Kublai Khan in charge of West Asia and China, respectively[67]
		Möngke Khan appoints Qara Hülegü as head of the Chagatai Khanate, who dies soon after, and his wife Orghana becomes regent for her young son Mubarak Shah[64]

1252	summer	Möngke Khan places Kublai Khan in charge of the invasion of the Dali Kingdom and Hulagu Khan the invasion of the middle east[68]
	fall	Mongol forces depart from Shanxi and reach the Tao River[68]
		Mongol conquest of the Song dynasty: Mongol forces under the Chinese general Wang Dechen advance into Sichuan and occupy Li Prefecture[68]
		Kublai Khan advances with the main force towards the Dali Kingdom[68]
		Niccolò and Maffeo Polo set off from Venice for China[69]
		Mongol invasions of Tibet: Qoridai invades Tibet as far as Dangquka[70]
1253		Kublai Khan's forces set up headquarters on the Jinsha River in western Yunnan and march on Dali in three columns[68]
	September	*Mongol conquest of the Song dynasty*: Mongol forces occupy Li Prefecture[71]
		Kublai Khan meets Phagpa Lama and promotes the Sakya school of Tibetan Buddhism[72]
1254	January	The Dali Kingdom is conquered, although its dynasty remains in power, and the king, Duan Xingzhi, is later invested with the title of Maharajah by Möngke Khan; so ends the Dali Kingdom[73]
	winter	Kublai Khan returns to Mongolia and leaves Subutai's son Uryankhadai in charge of campaigns against local Yi tribes[73]
		Kublai Khan starts building an independent power base in Henan and Jingzhao where Chinese-style government is implemented[74]
		Mongol conquest of the Song dynasty: Mongol raids on the northern Song border intensify[75]
		Mongol invasions of Korea: Jalairtai Qorchi plunders Goryeo[34]
1255		*Mongol invasions of Korea*: Mongol Empire takes Sinuiju and attacks coastal islands[34]
		Batu Khan dies and is succeeded by his son Sartaq Khan, who dies soon after, and then Ulaghchi[76]
1256	summer	*Mongol conquest of the Song dynasty*: Möngke Khan declares war on the Song dynasty, citing imprisonment of Mongol envoys as casus belli[75]
	20 November	Hulagu Khan takes Alamut from the Assassins[77]
		Daniel of Galicia expels Mongol garrisons from his territory[56]
		Kublai Khan constructs a capital north of the Luan River[78]
1257		Uriyangkhadai, son of Subutai, pacifies Yunnan and returns to Gansu[73]
	winter	*Mongol invasions of Vietnam*: Uriyangkhadai returns to Yunnan and invades the Trần dynasty of Đại Việt[73]
		Möngke Khan launches an investigation into Kublai Khan's activities and subjects officials in Henan and Shanxi to interrogation, executes Kublai's chief pacification officer in Shanxi, and imposes large levies on Shanxi[75]
		Ulaghchi dies and Berke, a Muslim, succeeds him[79]

1258	17 January	*Siege of Baghdad (1258)*: Hulagu Khan sends a Mongol contingent across the Tigris River which suffers a defeat against Aybak[80]
	18 January	*Siege of Baghdad (1258)*: Baiju floods the enemy camp and attacks, driving them back[80]
	29 January	*Siege of Baghdad (1258)*: Hulagu Khan lays siege to Baghdad[80]
	1 February	*Siege of Baghdad (1258)*: Mongol siege weapons breach Baghdad's Ajami tower[81]
	3 February	*Siege of Baghdad (1258)*: Mongol forces take Baghdad's walls[81]
	10 February	*Siege of Baghdad (1258)*: Al-Musta'sim, his sons, and 3,000 dignitaries surrender[81]
	13 February	*Siege of Baghdad (1258)*: Mongols sack Baghdad and Hulagu Khan takes the title of Ilkhan, meaning "obedient khan"[81]
	20 February	*Siege of Baghdad (1258)*: Al-Musta'sim and his family are executed[81]
		Kublai Khan returns to Mongolia to placate his brother[75]
	spring	*Mongol conquest of the Song dynasty*: Möngke Khan's forces reach Gansu[71]
		Mongol invasions of Vietnam: Đại Việt recognizes Mongol suzerainty and Trần Thái Tông sends his son as hostage to the imperial court[73]
	March	*Mongol conquest of the Song dynasty*: Mongols capture Chengdu[82]
		Buqa Temür takes Wasit[77]
	fall	*Mongol conquest of the Song dynasty*: Möngke Khan's forces reach Li Prefecture[71]
		Mongol invasions of Korea: Wonjong of Goryeo goes to the Mongol court as hostage[83]
1259	January	*Mongol conquest of the Song dynasty*: Möngke Khan's forces take Ya Prefecture[71]
	February	*Siege of Diaoyu Castle*: Möngke Khan's forces lay siege to Diaoyu Fortress[84]
	July	*Siege of Diaoyu Castle*: Möngke Khan calls off the siege of Diaoyu Fortress[85]
	August	*Mongol conquest of the Song dynasty*: Taghachar attacks Huainan[71]
	12 August	*Mongol conquest of the Song dynasty*: Möngke Khan dies from dysentry or a wound inflicted by a Song trebuchet, forcing Mongol campaigns throughout Eurasia and China to come to a halt[86]
	September	*Mongol conquest of the Song dynasty*: Kublai Khan's forces cross the Yangtze and lays siege to Ezhou, however he receives news of Möngke Khan's death and Ariq Böke's mobilization, forcing hm to withdraw and deal with his brother[87]
		Wonjong of Goryeo goes back to Goryeo to become ruler - henceforth becoming a Mongol tributary[83]

		Second Mongol invasion of Poland: Berke and Boroldai invade Poland and Daniel of Galicia flees, however his sons and brother Vasilko of Galicia join the Mongols to plunder Lithuania and Polish territories[56]
		Golden Horde elements in Bukhara rebel and Alghu suppresses them[79]

1260s

Year	Date	Event
1260	January	Hulagu Khan takes Aleppo from An-Nasir Yusuf; so ends the Ayyubid dynasty[77]
	2 February	*Sack of Sandomierz (1260)*: Berke and Boroldai sack Sandomierz[56]
	5 May	Kublai Khan convenes a kurultai at Kaiping, which elects him as ruler of the Mongol Empire; so ends the centralized Mongol Empire[88]
	May	*Toluid Civil War*: Ariq Böke proclaims himself great khan of the Mongol Empire at Karakorum[88]
	6 June	Hulagu Khan receives news of Möngke Khan's death and retreats to Ahlat[89]
	26 July	*Battle of Ain Jalut*: Qutuz of the Mamluks advance into Palestine and drive the Mongols from Gaza[89]
	spring	Hulagu Khan's son Yoshmut and commander Elege of the Jalayir take Mayyafaraqin and Mardin[77]
	3 September	*Battle of Ain Jalut*: Qutuz of the Mamluks defeats Mongol forces under Kitbuqa and push them back to the Euphrates[89]
	10 December	*First Battle of Homs*: Baibars defeats a Mongol expedition into Syria[77]
		Toluid Civil War: Berke of the Golden Horde allies with Ariq Böke and declares war on Hulagu Khan[90]
		Toluid Civil War: Alghu, a grandson of Chagatai Khan, deposes Mubarak Shah, an appointee to the Chagatai Khanate of the Mongol Empire[86]
		Mongol conquest of the Song dynasty: Kublai Khan's envoy Hao Jing proposes that the Song dynasty acknowledge Kublai as Son of Heaven in return for autonomy and gets jailed[91]
		Kublai Khan appoints Drogön Chögyal Phagpa as Imperial Preceptor[72]
		Ajall Shams al-Din Omar, from Bukhara, is appointed a commissioner of a district in north China[92]
		Kublai Khan issues three currencies but the paper chao, backed by silver, prevails; total value of paper money amounts to 73,352 silver ingots[93]
1261		*Mongol conquest of the Song dynasty*: Kublai Khan sends funds to Li Tan of Shandong to make war on the Song dynasty[94]
		Badr al-Din Lu'lu' dies and his son Malik Salih kills all the Christians, causing a rebellion in Mosul and Cizre[77]

Timeline of the Mongol Empire

1262	22 February	*Mongol conquest of the Song dynasty*: Mongol-allied warlord of Shandong, Li Tan, defects to the Song dynasty[95]
	August	*Mongol conquest of the Song dynasty*: Kublai Khan's Chinese generals Shi Tianze and Shi Chu crush Li Tan's forces and capture him; Li Tan is trampled to death by horses[94]
	summer	Rebellions in Mosul and Cizre are suppressed[77]
	November	Hulagu Khan kills his vizier Saif-ud-Din Bitigchi and replaces him with Shams al-Din Juvayni[96]
		Berke–Hulagu war: Berke of the Golden Horde allies with the Mamluks and invades Azerbaijan[90]
		Hulagu Khan gives Khorasan and Mazandaran to his son Abaqa and Azerbaijan to his other son Yoshmut[96]
		Kublai Khan prohibits nomads' animals from roaming on farmlands[97]
		Kublai Khan appaoints Ahmad Fanakati to the Central Secretariat to direct state finances[98]
1263	13 January	*Berke–Hulagu war*: Berke defeats Hulagu Khan's army on the Terek River[96]
		Kublai Khan reestablishes the Privy Council to oversee the Imperial Bodyguards and Kheshig[99]
1264		*Toluid Civil War*: Kublai Khan defeats Ariq Böke[90]
		Kublai Khan founds the Supreme Control Commission to administer Tibet and Buddhists[100]
1265	8 February	Hulagu Khan dies and is succeeded by his son Abaqa Khan[101]
		Mongol conquest of the Song dynasty: Song dynasty and Mongol forces clash in Sichuan[91]
		Niccolò and Maffeo Polo arrive at Kublai Khan's court[69]
1266	9 July	Kublai Khan appoints his son Nomukhan *Beiping Wang* (prince of the pacification of the north)[102]
		Berke dies in Tbilisi and is succeeded by his grandnephew Mengu-Timur[101]
		Alghu dies and is succeeded by Mubarak Sha, who is deposed by Ghiyas-ud-din Baraq[79]
		Kublai Khan orders the construction of Daidu, known to the Chinese as Dadu, or Khanbalikh to the Turks[103]
1267		Drikung Kagyu rebels against the Supreme Control Commission and Kublai Khan dispatches forces to crush them[72]
		Kublai Khan orders the construction of an Imperial Ancestral Temple[104]
		Kublai Khan designates Xu Heng as chancellor of the Guozijian[105]
		Mengu-Timur grants Genoa Caffa[106]
1268		*Battle of Xiangyang*: Mongol forces under Aju lay siege to Xiangyang[107]

		The rebellion in Tibet is suppressed and Drogön Chögyal Phagpa is reinstated along with a Mongol pacification commissioner[72]
		Kublai Khan creates the "General Administration for the Supervision of Ortogh" (Muslim merchant association) to lend money at low interest to the ortogh[93]
1269		*Kaidu–Kublai war*: Kaidu, a grandson of Ögedei Khan, rebels against Kublai Khan[90]
		Sambyeolcho Rebellion: Im Yeon engineers a coup against Wonjong of Goryeo and Kublai Khan sends 3,000 troups to vanquish the rebels and reinstate Wonjong[108]
		Drogön Chögyal Phagpa invents the 41 letter 'Phags-pa script, which Kublai Khan designates as the state script[109]
		Niccolò and Maffeo Polo return to Europe[69]

1270s

Year	Date	Event
1270		*Mongol invasions of Tibet*: Mongol forces crush the rebellion in Tibet and implement regular administration[70]
		Ghiyas-ud-din Baraq of the Chagatai Khanate invades the Ilkhanate but suffers defeat[110]
		Kublai Khan founds the Institute of Muslim Astronomy[111]
1271		Ghiyas-ud-din Baraq dies and Kaidu takes control of the Chagatai Khanate, installing Negübei as puppet khan[64]
		Kublai Khan declares himself emperor of the Yuan dynasty and for the first time, annual sacrifices at the altars of Soil and Grain are done in the Chinese style; so ends the unified Mongol Empire[104,112]

- 1274: The second full scale census in the Golden Horde and its vassals Russian principalities. Smolensk, the last of Russian major city-states became subject to the Golden Horde.
- 1287: Third incursion against Poland.
- 1299: The Battle of Wadi al-Khazandar (also known as the Third Battle of Homs). A Mongol victory over the Mamluks.
- 1303: The Battle of Marj al-Saffar. Mongols are defeated by Mamluks. The end of the Mongol invasion to Syria.
- 1305: The yam and trade routes between Mongol Khanates were reopened.
- 1353: Last of the powerful Ilkhanid contender, Togha Temür, was assassinated.
- 1356 Jani Beg conducted a military campaign in Azerbaijan and conquered the city of Tabriz, destroying Chupanid Dynasty and compelled

the Jalayirids to surrender (two successor states of the Ilkhanate). He also asserted Jochid dominance over the Chagatai Khanate, attempting to unite three khanates of the Mongol Empire.
- 1370: Toghon Temür died in Yingchang. His son Ayushiridara retreated to Karakorum in Mongolia, which became known as the Northern Yuan dynasty. Timur became the Emir of Chagatai Khanate.

Gallery

Eurasia on the eve of the Mongol invasions, *c.* 1200.

Mongol Empire in 1227 at Genghis' death

The Mongol Empire, ca. 1300. The gray area is the later Timurid empire.

Bibliography

- Andrade, Tonio (2016), *The Gunpowder Age: China, Military Innovation, and the Rise of the West in World History*, Princeton University Press, ISBN 978-0-691-13597-7.
- Asimov, M.S. (1998), *History of civilizations of Central Asia Volume IV The age of achievement: A.D. 750 to the end of the fifteenth century Part One The historical, social and economic setting*, UNESCO Publishing

- Atwood, Christopher P. (2004), *Encyclopedia of Mongolia and the Mongol Empire*, Facts On File
- Barfield, Thomas (1989), *The Perilous Frontier: Nomadic Empires and China*, Basil Blackwell
- Barrett, Timothy Hugh (2008), *The Woman Who Discovered Printing*, Great Britain: Yale University Press, ISBN 978-0-300-12728-7 (alk. paper)
- Beckwith, Christopher I. (2009), *Empires of the Silk Road: A History of Central Eurasia from the Bronze Age to the Present*, Princeton University Press, ISBN 0-691-13589-4
- Beckwith, Christopher I (1987), *The Tibetan Empire in Central Asia: A History of the Struggle for Great Power among Tibetans, Turks, Arabs, and Chinese during the Early Middle Ages*, Princeton University Press
- Biran, Michal (2005), *The Empire of the Qara Khitai in Eurasian History: Between China and the Islamic World*, Cambridge Studies in Islamic Civilization, Cambridge, England: Cambridge University Press, ISBN 0521842263
- Bregel, Yuri (2003), *An Historical Atlas of Central Asia*, Brill
- Drompp, Michael Robert (2005), *Tang China And The Collapse Of The Uighur Empire: A Documentary History*, Brill
- Ebrey, Patricia Buckley (1999), *The Cambridge Illustrated History of China*, Cambridge: Cambridge University Press, ISBN 0-521-66991-X (paperback).
- Ebrey, Patricia Buckley; Walthall, Anne; Palais, James B. (2006), *East Asia: A Cultural, Social, and Political History*, Boston: Houghton Mifflin, ISBN 0-618-13384-4
- Golden, Peter B. (1992), *An Introduction to the History of the Turkic Peoples: Ethnogenesis and State-Formation in Medieval and Early Modern Eurasia and the Middle East*, OTTO HARRASSOWITZ · WIESBADEN
- Graff, David A. (2002), *Medieval Chinese Warfare, 300-900*[113], Warfare and History, London: Routledge, ISBN 0415239559
- Graff, David Andrew (2016), *The Eurasian Way of War Military Practice in Seventh-Century China and Byzantium*, Routledge, ISBN 978-0-415-46034-7.
- Haywood, John (1998), *Historical Atlas of the Medieval World, AD 600-1492*, Barnes & Noble
- Latourette, Kenneth Scott (1964), *The Chinese, their history and culture, Volumes 1-2*, Macmillan
- Lorge, Peter A. (2008), *The Asian Military Revolution: from Gunpowder to the Bomb*, Cambridge University Press, ISBN 978-0-521-60954-8

- Luttwak, Edward N. (2009), *The Grand Strategy of the Byzantine Empire*, The Belknap Press of Harvard University Press
- Millward, James (2009), *Eurasian Crossroads: A History of Xinjiang*, Columbia University Press
- Mote, F. W. (2003), *Imperial China: 900–1800*, Harvard University Press, ISBN 978-0674012127
- Needham, Joseph (1986), *Science & Civilisation in China*, V:7: *The Gunpowder Epic*, Cambridge University Press, ISBN 0-521-30358-3
- Rong, Xinjiang (2013), *Eighteen Lectures on Dunhuang*, Brill
- Schafer, Edward H. (1985), *The Golden Peaches of Samarkand: A study of T'ang Exotics*, University of California Press
- Shaban, M. A. (1979), *The 'Abbāsid Revolution*[114], Cambridge: Cambridge University Press, ISBN 0-521-29534-3
- Sinor, Denis (1990), *The Cambridge History of Early Inner Asia, Volume 1*, Cambridge University Press
- Sima, Guang (2015), *Bóyángbǎn Zīzhìtōngjiàn 54 huánghòu shīzōng* 柏楊版資治通鑑 54皇后失蹤, Yuǎnliú chūbǎnshìyè gǔfèn yǒuxiàn gōngsī, ISBN 957-32-0876-8
- Skaff, Jonathan Karam (2012), *Sui-Tang China and Its Turko-Mongol Neighbors: Culture, Power, and Connections, 580-800 (Oxford Studies in Early Empires)*, Oxford University Press
- Standen, Naomi (2007), *Unbounded Loyalty Frontier Crossings in Liao China*, University of Hawai'i Press
- Steinhardt, Nancy Shatzman (1997), *Liao Architecture*, University of Hawaii Press
- Twitchett, Denis C. (1979), *The Cambridge History of China, Vol. 3, Sui and T'ang China, 589–906*, Cambridge University Press
- Twitchett, Denis (1994), "The Liao", *The Cambridge History of China, Volume 6, Alien Regime and Border States, 907-1368*, Cambridge: Cambridge University Press, pp. 43–153, ISBN 0521243319
- Twitchett, Denis (2009), *The Cambridge History of China Volume 5 The Sung dynasty and its Predecessors, 907-1279*, Cambridge University Press
- Wang, Zhenping (2013), *Tang China in Multi-Polar Asia: A History of Diplomacy and War*, University of Hawaii Press
- Wilkinson, Endymion (2015). *Chinese History: A New Manual, 4th edition*. Cambridge, MA: Harvard University Asia Center distributed by Harvard University Press. ISBN 9780674088467.
- Xiong, Victor Cunrui (2000), *Sui-Tang Chang'an: A Study in the Urban History of Late Medieval China (Michigan Monographs in Chinese Studies)*, U OF M CENTER FOR CHINESE STUDIES, ISBN 0892641371

- Xiong, Victor Cunrui (2009), *Historical Dictionary of Medieval China*[115], United States of America: Scarecrow Press, Inc., ISBN 0810860538
- Xu, Elina-Qian (2005), *HISTORICAL DEVELOPMENT OF THE PRE-DYNASTIC KHITAN*, Institute for Asian and African Studies 7
- Xue, Zongzheng (1992), *Turkic peoples*, 中国社会科学出版社
- Yuan, Shu (2001), *Bóyángbǎn Tōngjiàn jìshìběnmò 28 dìèrcìhuànguánshídài* 柏楊版通鑑記事本末 *28*第二次宦官時代 , Yuǎnliú chūbǎnshìyè gǔfèn yǒuxiàn gōngsī, ISBN 957-32-4273-7
- Yule, Henry (1915), *Cathay and the Way Thither: Being a Collection of Medieval Notices of China, Vol I: Preliminary Essay on the Intercourse Between China and the Western Nations Previous to the Discovery of the Cape Route*, Hakluyt Society

Genghis Khan

Genghis Khan

<indicator name="pp-default"> 🔒 </indicator> <indicator name="pp-default"> 🔒 </indicator>

Genghis Khan	
1st Khagan of the Mongol Empire *(Supreme Khan of the Mongols)* *King of Kings*	
Genghis Khan as portrayed in a 14th-century Yuan era album, the original version was in black and white. Original size is 47 cm wide and 59.4 cm high. Paint and ink on silk. Now located in the National Palace Museum, Taipei, Taiwan.	
1st Great Khan of the Mongol Empire	
Reign	Spring 1206 – August 18, 1227
Coronation	Spring 1206 in a kurultai at the Onon River, Mongolia
Successor	Ögedei Khan

Born	Temüjin[116] traditional Chinese: 鐵木真 ; simplified Chinese: 铁木真 ; pinyin: *Tiěmùzhēn*; Wade–Giles: *T'ieh³-mu⁴-chen¹*</ref> likely 1162 Khentii Mountains, Mongolia
Died	August 18, 1227 (aged c. 65)
Spouse	Börte Üjin Khatun Yisui Kunju Khatun Khulan Khatun Yesugen Khatun Yesulun Khatun Isukhan Khatun Gunju Khatun Abika Khatun Gurbasu Khatun Chaga Khatun Moge Khatun
Issue	Jochi Chagatai Ögedei Tolui Others
Full name	Genghis Khan Mongol: Чингис хаан *Chinggis Khaan* Mongol script (right): *Chinggis Khagan*[117]
House	Borjigin
Father	Yesügei
Mother	Hoelun

Genghis Khan[118]</ref> (c. 1162 – August 18, 1227), born **Temüjin**, was the Great Khan and founder of the Mongol Empire, which became the largest contiguous empire in history after his death. He came to power by uniting many of the nomadic tribes of Northeast Asia. After founding the Empire and being proclaimed "Genghis Khan", he launched the Mongol invasions that conquered most of Eurasia. Campaigns initiated in his lifetime include those against the Qara Khitai, Caucasus, and Khwarazmian, Western Xia and Jin dynasties. These campaigns were often accompanied by large-scale massacres of the civilian populations – especially in the Khwarazmian and Western Xia controlled lands. By the end of his life, the Mongol Empire occupied a substantial portion of Central Asia and China.

Before Genghis Khan died he assigned Ögedei Khan as his successor. Later his grandsons split his empire into khanates. He died in 1227 after defeating the Western Xia. He was buried in an unmarked grave somewhere in Mongolia. His descendants extended the Mongol Empire across most of Eurasia by conquering or creating vassal states in all of modern-day China, Korea, the Caucasus, Central Asia, and substantial portions of Eastern Europe and Southwest Asia. Many of these invasions repeated the earlier large-scale slaughters of local populations. As a result, Genghis Khan and his empire have a fearsome reputation in local histories.[119]

Beyond his military accomplishments, Genghis Khan also advanced the Mongol Empire in other ways. He decreed the adoption of the Uyghur script as the Mongol Empire's writing system. He also practiced meritocracy and encouraged religious tolerance in the Mongol Empire, and unified the nomadic tribes of Northeast Asia. Present-day Mongolians regard him as the founding father of Mongolia.

Although known for the brutality of his campaigns and considered by many to have been a genocidal ruler, Genghis Khan is also credited with bringing the Silk Road under one cohesive political environment. This brought communication and trade from Northeast Asia into Muslim Southwest Asia and Christian Europe, thus expanding the horizons of all three cultural areas. His name is pronounced /ˈdʒɛŋɡɪs ˈkɑːn/ or usually /ˈɡɛŋɡɪs ˈkɑːn/;[120] Mongolian: Чингис хаан, Çingis hán; Mongolian pronunciation: [tʃʰiŋɡɪs xaːŋ] (◄» listen).

Early life

Lineage

Temüjin was related on his father's side to Khabul Khan, Ambaghai, and Hotula Khan, who had headed the Khamag Mongol confederation and were descendants of Bodonchar Munkhag (c. 900). When the Jurchen Jin dynasty switched support from the Mongols to the Tatars in 1161, they destroyed Khabul Khan.Wikipedia:Verifiability

Temüjin's father, Yesügei (leader of the Borjigin clan and nephew to Ambaghai and Hotula Khan), emerged as the head of the ruling Mongol clan. This position was contested by the rival Tayichi'ud clan, who descended directly from Ambaghai. When the Tatars grew too powerful after 1161, the Jin switched their support from the Tatars to the Keraites.

Figure 1: *Autumn at the Onon River, Mongolia, the region where Temüjin was born and grew up.*

Birth

Little is known about Temüjin's early life, due to the lack of contemporary written records. The few sources that give insight into this period often contradict.

Temüjin's name was derived from the Mongol word *temür* meaning "of iron", while *jin* denotes agency thus *temüjin* means "blacksmith".

Temüjin was probably born in 1162[121] in Delüün Boldog, near the mountain Burkhan Khaldun and the rivers Onon and Kherlen in modern-day northern Mongolia, close to the current capital Ulaanbaatar. *The Secret History of the Mongols* reports that Temüjin was born grasping a blood clot in his fist, a traditional sign that he was destined to become a great leader. He was the second son of his father Yesügei who was a Kiyad chief prominent in the Khamag Mongol confederation and an ally of Toghrul of the Keraite tribe. Temüjin was the first son of his mother Hoelun. According to the *Secret History*, Temüjin was named after the Tatar chief Temüjin-üge whom his father had just captured.

Yesukhei's clan was Borjigin (Боржигин), and Hoelun was from the Olkhunut sub-lineage of the Khongirad tribe.[122] Like other tribes, they were nomads.

Temüjin's noble background made it easier for him to solicit help from and eventually consolidate the other Mongol tribes.Wikipedia:Citation needed

Early life and family

Temüjin had three brothers Hasar, Hachiun, and Temüge, one sister Temülen, and two half-brothers Begter and Belgutei. Like many of the nomads of Mongolia, Temüjin's early life was difficult. His father arranged a marriage for him and delivered him at age nine to the family of his future wife Börte of the tribe Khongirad. Temüjin was to live there serving the head of the household Dai Setsen until the marriageable age of 12.

While heading home, his father ran into the neighboring Tatars, who had long been Mongol enemies, and they offered him food that poisoned him. Upon learning this, Temüjin returned home to claim his father's position as chief. But the tribe refused this and abandoned the family, leaving it without protection.

For the next several years, the family lived in poverty, surviving mostly on wild fruits, ox carcasses, marmots, and other small game killed by Temüjin and his brothers. Temujin's older half-brother Begter began to exercise power as the eldest male in the family and would eventually have the right to claim Hoelun (who was not his own mother) as wife. Temüjin's resentment erupted during one hunting excursion when Temüjin and his brother Khasar killed Begter.

In a raid around 1177, Temujin was captured by his father's former allies, the Tayichi'ud, and enslaved, reportedly with a cangue (a sort of portable stocks). With the help of a sympathetic guard, he escaped from the ger (yurt) at night by hiding in a river crevice.Wikipedia:Citation needed The escape earned Temüjin a reputation. Soon, Jelme and Bo'orchu joined forces with him. They and the guard's son Chilaun eventually became generals of Genghis Khan.

At this time, none of the tribal confederations of Mongolia were united politically, and arranged marriages were often used to solidify temporary alliances. Temüjin grew up observing the tough political climate, which included tribal warfare, thievery, raids, corruption, and revenge between confederations, compounded by interference from abroad such as from China to the south. Temüjin's mother Hoelun taught him many lessons, especially the need for strong alliances to ensure stability in Mongolia.

Wives and children

As previously arranged by his father, Temüjin married Börte of the Onggirat tribe when he was around 16 in order to cement alliances between their two tribes. Soon after the marriage, Börte was kidnapped by the Merkits and reportedly given away as a wife. Temüjin rescued her with the help of his friend and future rival, Jamukha, and his protector, Toghrul of the Keraite tribe. She gave birth to a son, Jochi (1185–1226), nine months later, clouding the issue of his parentage. Despite speculation over Jochi, Börte would be Temüjin's only empress, though he did follow tradition by taking several morganatic wives.

Börte had three more sons, Chagatai (1187–1241), Ögedei (1189–1241), and Tolui (1190–1232). Genghis later took about 500 secondary wives and "consorts", but Börte continued to be his life companion. He had many other children with those other wives, but they were excluded from succession, only Börte's sons being considered to be his heirs. However, a Tatar woman named Yisui, taken as a wife when her people were conquered by the Mongols, eventually came to be given almost as much prominence as Börte, despite originally being only one of his minor wives.[123,124] The names of at least six daughters are known, and while they played significant roles behind the scenes during his lifetime, no documents have survived that definitively provide the number or names of daughters born to the consorts of Genghis Khan.

Uniting the Mongol confederations

In the early 13th century, the Central Asian plateau north of China was divided into several tribes of confederation, including Naimans, Merkits, Tatars, Khamag Mongols, and Keraites, that were all prominent and often unfriendly toward each other, as evidenced by random raids, revenge attacks, and plundering.

Early attempts at power

Temüjin began his ascent to power by offering himself as an ally (or, according to other sources, a vassal) to his father's *anda* (sworn brother or blood brother) Toghrul, who was Khan of the Keraites, and is better known by the Chinese title "Wang Khan", which the Jurchen Jin dynasty granted him in 1197. This relationship was first reinforced when Börte was captured by the Merkits. Temüjin turned to Toghrul for support, and Toghrul offered 20,000 of his Keraite warriors and suggested that Temüjin involve his childhood friend Jamukha, who had himself become Khan of his own tribe, the Jadaran.

Although the campaign recaptured Börte and utterly defeated the Merkits, it also paved the way for the split between Temüjin and Jamukha. Before this, they were blood brothers (*anda*) vowing to remain eternally faithful.

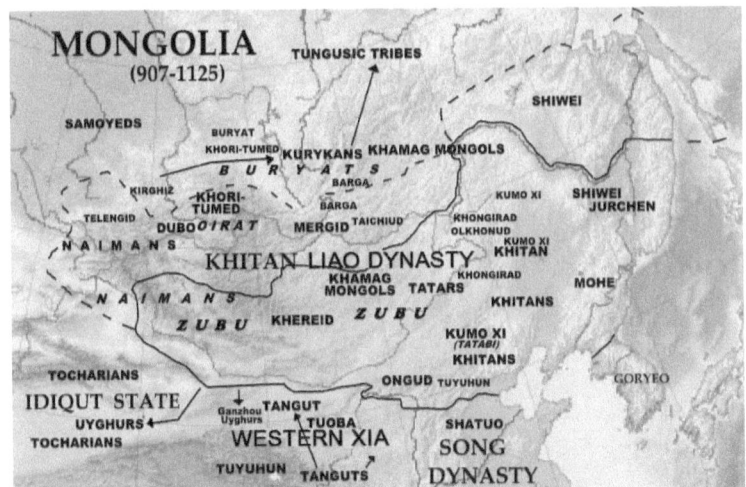

Figure 2: *The locations of the Mongolian tribes during the Khitan Liao dynasty (907–1125)*

Rift with Jamukha and defeat at Dalan Balzhut

As Jamukha and Temüjin drifted apart in their friendship, each began consolidating power, and they became rivals. Jamukha supported the traditional Mongolian aristocracy, while Temüjin followed a meritocratic method, and attracted a broader range and lower class of followers.[125] Following his earlier defeat of the Merkits, and a proclamation by the shaman Kokochu that the Eternal Blue Sky had set aside the world for Temüjin, Temüjin began rising to power.[126] In 1186, Temüjin was elected khan of the Mongols. Threatened by this rise, Jamukha attacked Temujin in 1187 with an army of 30,000 troops. Temüjin gathered his followers to defend against the attack, but was decisively beaten in the Battle of Dalan Balzhut.[127] However, Jamukha horrified and alienated potential followers by boiling 70 young male captives alive in cauldrons. Toghrul, as Temüjin's patron, was exiled to the Qara Khitai.[128] The life of Temüjin for the next 10 years is unclear, as historical records are mostly silent on that period.

Return to power

Around the year 1197, the Jin initiated an attack against their formal vassal, the Tatars, with help from the Keraites and Mongols. Temüjin commanded part of this attack, and after victory, he and Toghrul were restored by the Jin to positions of power. The Jin bestowed Toghrul with the honorable title of Ong Khan, and Temüjin with a lesser title of *j'aut quri*.

Figure 3: *Jurchen inscription (1196) in Mongolia relating to Genghis Khan's alliance with the Jin against the Tatars.*

Around 1200, the main rivals of the Mongol confederation (traditionally the "Mongols") were the Naimans to the west, the Merkits to the north, the Tanguts to the south, and the Jin to the east.

In his rule and his conquest of rival tribes, Temüjin broke with Mongol tradition in a few crucial ways. He delegated authority based on merit and loyalty, rather than family ties. As an incentive for absolute obedience and the Yassa code of law, Temüjin promised civilians and soldiers wealth from future war spoils. When he defeated rival tribes, he did not drive away their soldiers and abandon their civilians. Instead, he took the conquered tribe under his protection and integrated its members into his own tribe. He would even have his mother adopt orphans from the conquered tribe, bringing them into his family. These political innovations inspired great loyalty among the conquered people, making Temüjin stronger with each victory.

Rift with Toghrul

Senggum, son of Toghrul (Wang Khan), envied Temüjin's growing power and affinity with his father. He allegedly planned to assassinate Temüjin. Although Toghrul was allegedly saved on multiple occasions by Temüjin, he gave in to his

Figure 4: *Genghis Khan and Toghrul Khan, illustration from a 15th-century Jami' al-tawarikh manuscript*

son and became uncooperative with Temüjin. Temüjin learned of Senggum's intentions and eventually defeated him and his loyalists.

One of the later ruptures between Temüjin and Toghrul was Toghrul's refusal to give his daughter in marriage to Jochi, Temüjin's first son. This was disrespectful in Mongolian culture and led to a war. Toghrul allied with Jamukha, who already opposed Temüjin's forces. However, the dispute between Toghrul and Jamukha, plus the desertion of a number of their allies to Temüjin, led to Toghrul's defeat. Jamukha escaped during the conflict. This defeat was a catalyst for the fall and eventual dissolution of the Keraite tribe.

The next direct threat to Temüjin was the Naimans (Naiman Mongols), with whom Jamukha and his followers took refuge. The Naimans did not surrender, although enough sectors again voluntarily sided with Temüjin. In 1201, a khuruldai elected Jamukha as Gür Khan, "universal ruler", a title used by the rulers of the Qara Khitai. Jamukha's assumption of this title was the final breach with Temüjin, and Jamukha formed a coalition of tribes to oppose him. Before the conflict, several generals abandoned Jamukha, including Subutai, Jelme's well-known younger brother. After several battles, Jamukha was turned over to Temüjin by his own men in 1206.

According to the *Secret History*, Temüjin again offered his friendship to Jamukha. Temüjin had killed the men who betrayed Jamukha, stating that he did not want disloyal men in his army. Jamukha refused the offer, saying that there can only be one sun in the sky, and he asked for a noble death. The custom was to die without spilling blood, specifically by having one's back broken.

Figure 5: *Genghis Khan proclaimed Khagan of all Mongols. Illustration from a 15th-century Jami' al-tawarikh manuscript.*

Jamukha requested this form of death, although he was known to have boiled his opponents' generals alive.

Sole ruler of the Mongol plains (1206)

The part of the Merkit clan that sided with the Naimans were defeated by Subutai, who was by then a member of Temüjin's personal guard and later became one of Genghis Khan's most successful commanders. The Naimans' defeat left Temüjin as the sole ruler of the Mongol steppe – all the prominent confederations fell or united under his Mongol confederation.

Accounts of Genghis Khan's life are marked by claims of a series of betrayals and conspiracies. These include rifts with his early allies such as Jamukha (who also wanted to be a ruler of Mongol tribes) and Wang Khan (his and his father's ally), his son Jochi, and problems with the most important shaman, who allegedly tried to drive a wedge between him and his loyal brother Khasar. His military strategies showed a deep interest in gathering intelligence and understanding the motivations of his rivals, exemplified by his extensive spy network and Yam route systems. He seemed to be a quick student, adopting new technologies and ideas that he encountered, such as siege warfare from

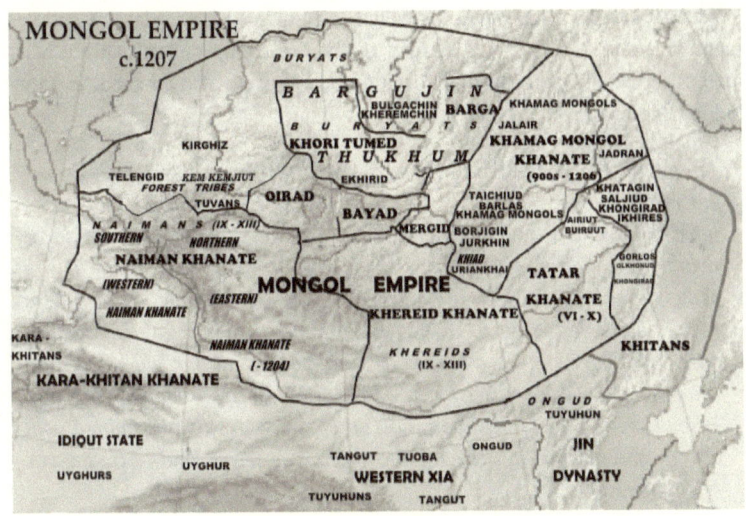

Figure 6: *Mongol Empire circa 1207*

the Chinese. He was also ruthless, demonstrated by his tactic of measuring against the linchpin, used against the tribes led by Jamukha.

As a result, by 1206, Temüjin had managed to unite or subdue the Merkits, Naimans, Mongols, Keraites, Tatars, Uyghurs, and other disparate smaller tribes under his rule. This was a monumental feat. It resulted in peace between previously warring tribes, and a single political and military force. The union became known as the Mongols. At a *Khuruldai*, a council of Mongol chiefs, Temüjin was acknowledged as Khan of the consolidated tribes and took the new title "Genghis Khan". The title Khagan was conferred posthumously by his son and successor Ögedei who took the title for himself (as he was also to be posthumously declared the founder of the Yuan dynasty).

Religion

Genghis Khan was a tengrist, but was religiously tolerant and interested in learning philosophical and moral lessons from other religions. He consulted Buddhist monks, Muslims, Christian missionaries, and the Taoist monk Qiu Chuji.

Genghis Khan, and the following Yuan Emperors forbade Islamic practices like Halal butchering, forcing Mongol methods of butchering animals on Muslims, and other restrictive decrees continued. Muslims had to slaughter sheep in secret. Genghis Khan explicitly called Muslims and Jews "slaves", and demanded that they follow the Mongol method of eating rather than the halal method. Circumcision was also forbidden. Jews were also affected, and forbidden by the Mongols to eat Kosher.

> Among all the [subject] alien peoples only the Hui-hui say 'we do not eat Mongol food". [Cinggis Qa'an replied:] "By the aid of heaven we have pacified you; you are our slaves. Yet you do not eat our food or drink. How can this be right?" He thereupon made them eat. "If you slaughter sheep, you will be considered guilty of a crime." He issued a regulation to that effect ... [In 1279/1280 under Qubilai] all the Muslims say: "if someone else slaughters [the animal] we do not eat". Because the poor people are upset by this, from now on, Musuluman [Muslim] Huihui and Zhuhu [Jewish] Huihui, no matter who kills [the animal] will eat [it] and must cease slaughtering sheep themselves, and cease the rite of circumcision.

Military campaigns

Western Xia Dynasty

During the 1206 political rise of Genghis Khan, the Mongol Empire created by Genghis Khan and his allies shared its western borders with the Western Xia dynasty of the Tanguts. To the east and south was the Jin dynasty, founded by the Manchurian Jurchens, who ruled northern China as well as being the traditional overlords of the Mongolian tribes for centuries.

Genghis Khan organized his people, army, and his state to first prepare for war with Western Xia, or Xi Xia, which was close to the Mongolian lands. He correctly believed that the more powerful young ruler of the Jin dynasty would not come to the aid of Xi Xia. When the Tanguts requested help from the Jin dynasty, they were refused. Despite initial difficulties in capturing its well-defended cities, Genghis Khan managed to force the emperor of Xi Xia to submit to vassal status.

Jin dynasty

In 1211, after the conquest of Western Xia, Genghis Khan planned again to conquer the Jin dynasty. Wanyan Jiujin, the field commander of the Jin army, made a tactical mistake in not attacking the Mongols at the first opportunity. Instead, the Jin commander sent a messenger, Ming'an, to the Mongol side, who defected and told the Mongols that the Jin army was waiting on the other side of the pass. At this engagement fought at Yehuling, the Mongols massacred hundreds of thousands of Jin troops. In 1215, Genghis besieged, captured,

Figure 7: *Battle between Mongol warriors and the Chinese.*

Figure 8: *Genghis Khan entering Beijing.*

and sacked the Jin capital of Zhongdu (modern-day Beijing). This forced the Jin ruler, Emperor Xuanzong, to move his capital south to Kaifeng, abandoning the northern half of his empire to the Mongols. Between 1232 and 1233, Kaifeng fell to the Mongols under the reign of Genghis's third son, Ögedei Khan. The Jin dynasty collapsed in 1234, after the siege of Caizhou.

Qara Khitai

Kuchlug, the deposed Khan of the Naiman confederation that Temüjin defeated and folded into his Mongol Empire, fled west and usurped the khanate of Qara Khitai (also known as the Western Liao, as it was originally established as remnants of the Liao dynasty). Genghis Khan decided to conquer the Qara Khitai and defeat Kuchlug, possibly to take him out of power. By this time the Mongol army was exhausted from ten years of continuous campaigning in China against the Western Xia and Jin dynasty. Therefore, Genghis sent only two tumen (20,000 soldiers) against Kuchlug, under his younger general, Jebe, known as "The Arrow".

With such a small force, the invading Mongols were forced to change strategies and resort to inciting internal revolt among Kuchlug's supporters, leaving the Qara Khitai more vulnerable to Mongol conquest. As a result, Kuchlug's army was defeated west of Kashgar. Kuchlug fled again, but was soon hunted down by Jebe's army and executed. By 1218, as a result of defeat of Qara Khitai, the Mongol Empire and its control extended as far west as Lake Balkhash, which bordered Khwarazmia, a Muslim state that reached the Caspian Sea to the west and Persian Gulf and the Arabian Sea to the south.

Khwarazmian Empire

In the early 13th century, the Khwarazmian dynasty was governed by Shah Ala ad-Din Muhammad. Genghis Khan saw the potential advantage in Khwarazmia as a commercial trading partner using the Silk Road, and he initially sent a 500-man caravan to establish official trade ties with the empire. However, Inalchuq, the governor of the Khwarazmian city of Otrar, attacked the caravan, claiming that the caravan contained spies and therefore was a conspiracy against Khwarazmia. The situation became further complicated because the governor later refused to make repayments for the looting of the caravans and hand over the perpetrators. Genghis Khan then sent a second group of three ambassadors (two Mongols and a Muslim) to meet the Shah himself, instead of the governor Inalchuq. The Shah had all the men shaved and the Muslim beheaded and sent his head back with the two remaining ambassadors. This was seen as an affront and insult to Genghis Khan. Outraged, Genghis Khan planned one of his largest invasion campaigns by organizing together around 100,000 soldiers (10 tumens), his most capable generals and

Figure 9: *Genghis Khan watches in amazement as the Khwarezmi Jalal ad-Din prepares to ford the Indus.*

some of his sons. He left a commander and number of troops in China, designated his successors to be his family members and likely appointed Ögedei to be his immediate successor and then went out to Khwarazmia.

The Mongol army under Genghis Khan, generals and his sons crossed the Tien Shan mountains by entering the area controlled by the Khwarazmian Empire. After compiling intelligence from many sources Genghis Khan carefully prepared his army, which was divided into three groups. His son Jochi led the first division into the northeast of Khwarazmia. The second division under Jebe marched secretly to the southeast part of Khwarazmia to form, with the first division, a pincer attack on Samarkand. The third division under Genghis Khan and Tolui marched to the northwest and attacked Khwarazmia from that direction.

The Shah's army was split by diverse internecine feuds and by the Shah's decision to divide his army into small groups concentrated in various cities. This fragmentation was decisive in Khwarazmia's defeats, as it allowed the Mongols, although exhausted from the long journey, to immediately set about defeating small fractions of the Khwarazmian forces instead of facing a unified defense. The Mongol army quickly seized the town of Otrar, relying on superior strategy and tactics. Genghis Khan ordered the wholesale massacre of

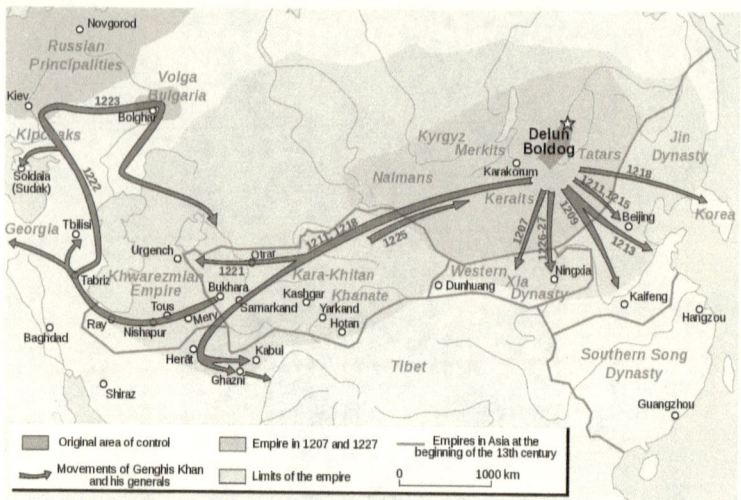

Figure 10: *Significant conquests and movements of Genghis Khan and his generals.*

many of the civilians, enslaved the rest of the population and executed Inalchuq by pouring molten silver into his ears and eyes, as retribution for his actions. Near the end of the battle the Shah fled rather than surrender. Genghis Khan ordered Subutai and Jebe to hunt him down, giving them 20,000 men and two years to do this. The Shah died under mysterious circumstances on a small island within his empire.

The Mongols' conquest, even by their own standards, was brutal. After the capital Samarkand fell, the capital was moved to Bukhara by the remaining men, while Genghis Khan ordered two of his generals and their forces to completely destroy the remnants of the Khwarazmian Empire, including not only royal buildings, but entire towns, populations, and even vast swaths of farmland.

The Mongols attacked Samarkand using captured enemies as body shields. After several days only a few remaining soldiers, loyal supporters of the Shah, held out in the citadel. After the fortress fell, Genghis supposedly reneged on his surrender terms and executed every soldier that had taken arms against him at Samarkand. The people of Samarkand were ordered to evacuate and assemble in a plain outside the city, where they were killed and pyramids of severed heads raised as a symbol of victory.[129] Ata-Malik Juvayni, a high official in the service of the Mongol empire, wrote that in Termez, on the Oxus, "all the people, both men and women, were driven out onto the plain, and divided in accordance with their usual custom, then they were all slain".

The city of Bukhara was not heavily fortified, with a moat and a single wall, and the citadel typical of Khwarazmian cities. The city leaders opened the gates to the Mongols, though a unit of Turkish defenders held the city's citadel for another twelve days. Survivors from the citadel were executed, artisans and craftsmen were sent back to Mongolia, young men who had not fought were drafted into the Mongolian army and the rest of the population was sent into slavery. As the Mongol soldiers looted the city, a fire broke out, razing most of the city to the ground. Genghis Khan had the city's surviving population assemble in the main mosque of the town, where he declared that he was the flail of God, sent to punish them for their sins.

Meanwhile, the wealthy trading city of Urgench was still in the hands of Khwarazmian forces. The assault on Urgench proved to be the most difficult battle of the Mongol invasion and the city fell only after the defenders put up a stout defense, fighting block for block. Mongolian casualties were higher than normal, due to the unaccustomed difficulty of adapting Mongolian tactics to city fighting.

As usual, the artisans were sent back to Mongolia, young women and children were given to the Mongol soldiers as slaves, and the rest of the population was massacred. The Persian scholar Juvayni states that 50,000 Mongol soldiers were given the task of executing twenty-four Urgench citizens each, which would mean that 1.2 million people were killed. The sacking of Urgench is considered one of the bloodiest massacres in human history.

In the meantime, Genghis Khan selected his third son Ögedei as his successor before his army set out, and specified that subsequent Khans should be his direct descendants. Genghis Khan also left Muqali, one of his most trusted generals, as the commander of all Mongol forces in Jin China while he was out battling the Khwarezmid Empire to the west.

Georgia, Crimea, Kievan Rus and Volga Bulgaria

After the defeat of the Khwarazmian Empire in 1220, Genghis Khan gathered his forces in Persia and Armenia to return to the Mongolian steppes. Under the suggestion of Subutai, the Mongol army was split into two forces. Genghis Khan led the main army on a raid through Afghanistan and northern India towards Mongolia, while another 20,000 (two tumen) contingent marched through the Caucasus and into Russia under generals Jebe and Subutai. They pushed deep into Armenia and Azerbaijan. The Mongols destroyed the kingdom of Georgia, sacked the Genoese trade-fortress of Caffa in Crimea and overwintered near the Black Sea. Heading home, Subutai's forces attacked the allied forces of the Cuman–Kipchaks and the poorly coordinated 80,000 Kievan Rus' troops led by Mstislav the Bold of Halych and Mstislav III of Kiev

Figure 11: *Mongol "Great Khans" coin, minted in 1221 at Balk, Afghanistan, AH 618*

who went out to stop the Mongols' actions in the area. Subutai sent emissaries to the Slavic princes calling for a separate peace, but the emissaries were executed. At the Battle of Kalka River in 1223, Subutai's forces defeated the larger Kievan force. They may have been defeated by the neighbouring Volga Bulgars at the Battle of Samara Bend. There is no historical record except a short account by the Arab historian Ibn al-Athir, writing in Mosul some 1100 miles away from the event.[130] Various historical secondary sources – Morgan, Chambers, Grousset – state that the Mongols actually defeated the Bulgars, Chambers even going so far as to say that the Bulgars had made up stories to tell the (recently crushed) Russians that they had beaten the Mongols and driven them from their territory. The Russian princes then sued for peace. Subutai agreed but was in no mood to pardon the princes. As was customary in Mongol society for nobility, the Russian princes were given a bloodless death. Subutai had a large wooden platform constructed on which he ate his meals along with his other generals. Six Russian princes, including Mstislav III of Kiev, were put under this platform and crushed to death.

The Mongols learned from captives of the abundant green pastures beyond the Bulgar territory, allowing for the planning for conquest of Hungary and Europe. Genghis Khan recalled Subutai back to Mongolia soon afterwards, and Jebe died on the road back to Samarkand. The famous cavalry expedition led

Figure 12: *Western Xia dynasty, Jin/Jurchen dynasty, Song dynasty and Kingdom of Dali in 1142.*

by Subutai and Jebe, in which they encircled the entire Caspian Sea defeating all armies in their path, remains unparalleled to this day, and word of the Mongol triumphs began to trickle to other nations, particularly Europe. These two campaigns are generally regarded as reconnaissance campaigns that tried to get the feel of the political and cultural elements of the regions. In 1225 both divisions returned to Mongolia. These invasions added Transoxiana and Persia to an already formidable empire while destroying any resistance along the way. Later under Genghis Khan's grandson Batu and the Golden Horde, the Mongols returned to conquer Volga Bulgaria and Kievan Rus' in 1237, concluding the campaign in 1240.

Western Xia and Jin Dynasty

The vassal emperor of the Tanguts (Western Xia) had earlier refused to take part in the Mongol war against the Khwarezmid Empire. Western Xia and the defeated Jin dynasty formed a coalition to resist the Mongols, counting on the campaign against the Khwarazmians to preclude the Mongols from responding effectively.

In 1226, immediately after returning from the west, Genghis Khan began a retaliatory attack on the Tanguts. His armies quickly took Heisui, Ganzhou,

Figure 13: *Genghis Khan and three of his four sons. Illustration from a 15th-century Jami' al-tawarikh manuscript*

and Suzhou (not the Suzhou in Jiangsu province), and in the autumn he took Xiliang-fu[131]. One of the Tangut generals challenged the Mongols to a battle near Helan Mountains but was defeated. In November, Genghis laid siege to the Tangut city Lingzhou and crossed the Yellow River, defeating the Tangut relief army. According to legend, it was here that Genghis Khan reportedly saw a line of five stars arranged in the sky and interpreted it as an omen of his victory.

In 1227, Genghis Khan's army attacked and destroyed the Tangut capital of Ning Hia and continued to advance, seizing Lintiao-fu, Xining province, Xindu-fu, and Deshun province in quick succession in the spring. At Deshun, the Tangut general Ma Jianlong put up a fierce resistance for several days and personally led charges against the invaders outside the city gate. Ma Jianlong later died from wounds received from arrows in battle. Genghis Khan, after conquering Deshun, went to Liupanshan (Qingshui County, Gansu Province) to escape the severe summer. The new Tangut emperor quickly surrendered to the Mongols, and the rest of the Tanguts officially surrendered soon after. Not happy with their betrayal and resistance, Genghis Khan ordered the entire imperial family to be executed, effectively ending the Tangut lineage.

Succession

The succession of Genghis Khan was already a significant topic during the later years of his reign, as he reached old age. The long running paternity discussion about Genghis's oldest son Jochi was particularly contentious because of the seniority of Jochi among the brothers. According to traditional historical accounts, the issue over Jochi's paternity was voiced most strongly by Chagatai. In *The Secret History of the Mongols*, just before the invasion of the Khwarezmid Empire by Genghis Khan, Chagatai declared before his father and brothers that he would never accept Jochi as Genghis Khan's successor. In response to this tension, and possibly for other reasons, Ögedei was appointed as successor.

Ögedei

Ögedei Khan, born Ögedei (c. 1186 – December 11, 1241) was the third son of Genghis Khan and second Great Khan (Khagan) of the Mongol Empire. He continued the expansion that his father had begun and was a world figure when the Mongol Empire reached its farthest extent west and south during the invasions of Europe and Asia.

Jochi

Genghis Khan was aware of the friction between his sons (particularly between Chagatai and Jochi) and worried of possible conflict between them if he died. He therefore decided to divide his empire among his sons and make all of them Khan in their own right, while appointing one of his sons as his successor. Chagatai was considered unstable due to his temper and rash behavior, because of statements he made that he would not follow Jochi if he were to become his father's successor. Tolui, Genghis Khan's youngest son, was not to be his successor because he was the youngest and in the Mongol culture, youngest sons were not given much responsibility due to their age. If Jochi were to become successor, it was likely that Chagatai would engage in warfare with him and collapse the empire. Therefore, Genghis Khan decided to give the throne to Ögedei. Ögedei was seen by Genghis Khan as dependable in character and relatively stable and down to earth and would be a neutral candidate and might defuse the situation between his brothers.

Jochi died in 1226, during his father's lifetime. Some scholars, notably Ratchnevsky, have commented on the possibility that Jochi was secretly poisoned by an order from Genghis Khan. Rashid al-Din reports that the great Khan sent for his sons in the spring of 1223, and while his brothers heeded the order, Jochi remained in Khorasan. Juzjani suggests that the disagreement arose from a quarrel between Jochi and his brothers in the siege of Urgench. Jochi had attempted to protect Urgench from destruction, as it belonged to territory allocated to him as a fief. He concludes his story with the clearly apocryphal statement by Jochi: "Genghis Khan is mad to have massacred so many people and laid waste so many lands. I would be doing a service if I killed my father when he is hunting, made an alliance with Sultan Muhammad, brought this land to life and gave assistance and support to the Muslims." Juzjani claims that it was in response to hearing of these plans that Genghis Khan ordered

Figure 14: *Mongol Empire in 1227 at Genghis Khan's death*

his son secretly poisoned; however, as Sultan Muhammad was already dead in 1223, the accuracy of this story is questionable.

Death and burial

Genghis Khan died in August 1227, during the fall of Yinchuan, which is the capital of Western Xia. The exact cause of his death remains a mystery, and is variously attributed to being killed in action against the Western Xia, illness, falling from his horse, or wounds sustained in hunting or battle. According to *The Secret History of the Mongols*, Genghis Khan fell from his horse while hunting and died because of the injury. He was already old and tired from his journeys. The *Galician–Volhynian Chronicle* alleges he was killed by the Western Xia in battle, while Marco Polo wrote that he died after the infection of an arrow wound he received during his final campaign. Later Mongol chronicles connect Genghis's death with a Western Xia princess taken as war booty. One chronicle from the early 17th century even relates the legend that the princess hid a small dagger and stabbed him, though some Mongol authors have doubted this version and suspected it to be an invention by the rival Oirads.

Years before his death, Genghis Khan asked to be buried without markings, according to the customs of his tribe. After he died, his body was returned

Figure 15: *The Genghis Khan Mausoleum in the town of Ejin Horo Qi, Inner Mongolia, China*

to Mongolia and presumably to his birthplace in Khentii Aimag, where many assume he is buried somewhere close to the Onon River and the Burkhan Khaldun mountain (part of the Kentii mountain range). According to legend, the funeral escort killed anyone and anything across their path to conceal where he was finally buried. The Genghis Khan Mausoleum, constructed many years after his death, is his memorial, but not his burial site.

In 1939 Chinese Nationalist soldiers took the mausoleum from its position at the 'Lord's Enclosure' (Mongolian: *Edsen Khoroo*) in Mongolia to protect it from Japanese troops. It was taken through Communist-held territory in Yan'an some 900 km (560 mi) on carts to safety at a Buddhist monastery, the Dongshan Dafo Dian, where it remained for ten years. In 1949, as Communist troops advanced, the Nationalist soldiers moved it another 200 km (120 mi) farther west to the famous Tibetan monastery of Kumbum Monastery or Ta'er Shi near Xining, which soon fell under Communist control. In early 1954, Genghis Khan's bier and relics were returned to the Lord's Enclosure in Mongolia. By 1956 a new temple was erected there to house them.[132] In 1968 during the Cultural Revolution, Red Guards destroyed almost everything of value. The "relics" were remade in the 1970s and a great marble statue of Genghis was completed in 1989.[133]

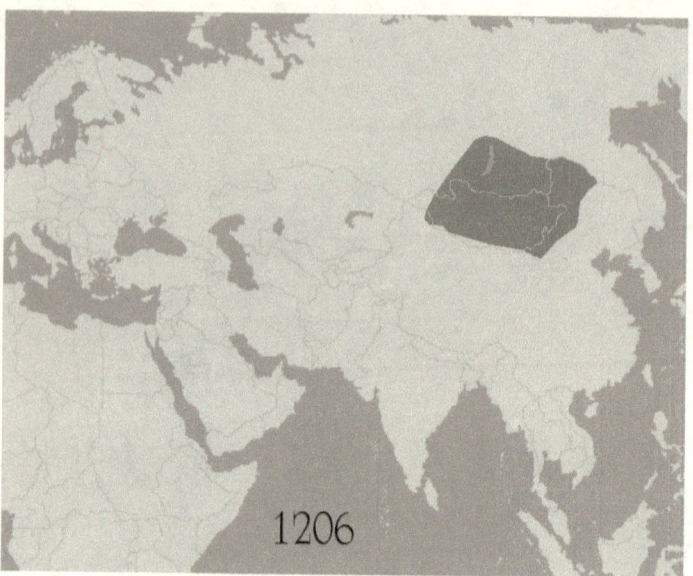

Figure 16: *Mongol Empire*

On October 6, 2004, a joint Japanese-Mongolian archaeological dig uncovered what is believed to be Genghis Khan's palace in rural Mongolia, which raises the possibility of actually locating the ruler's long-lost burial site. Folklore says that a river was diverted over his grave to make it impossible to find (the same manner of burial as the Sumerian King Gilgamesh of Uruk and Atilla the Hun). Other tales state that his grave was stampeded over by many horses, and that trees were then planted over the site, and the permafrost also did its part in hiding the burial site.

Genghis Khan left behind an army of more than 129,000 men; 28,000 were given to his various brothers and his sons. Tolui, his youngest son, inherited more than 100,000 men. This force contained the bulk of the elite Mongolian cavalry. By tradition, the youngest son inherits his father's property. Jochi, Chagatai, Ögedei Khan, and Kulan's son Gelejian received armies of 4,000 men each. His mother and the descendants of his three brothers received 3,000 men each.

Mongol Empire

Politics and economics

The Mongol Empire was governed by a civilian and military code, called the Yassa, created by Genghis Khan. The Mongol Empire did not emphasize the importance of ethnicity and race in the administrative realm, instead adopting an approach grounded in meritocracy. The exception was the role of Genghis Khan and his family. The Mongol Empire was one of the most ethnically and culturally diverse empires in history, as befitted its size. Many of the empire's nomadic inhabitants considered themselves *Mongols* in military and civilian life, including Mongols, Turks and others and included many diverse Khans of various ethnicities as part of the Mongol Empire such as Muhammad Khan.

There were tax exemptions for religious figures and, to some extent, teachers and doctors. The Mongol Empire practiced religious tolerance because Mongol tradition had long held that religion was a personal concept, and not subject to law or interference.Wikipedia:Citation needed Sometime before the rise of Genghis Khan, Ong Khan, his mentor and eventual rival, had converted to Nestorian Christianity. Various Mongol tribes were Shamanist, Buddhist or Christian. Religious tolerance was thus a well established concept on the Asian steppe.

Modern Mongolian historians say that towards the end of his life, Genghis Khan attempted to create a civil state under the Great Yassa that would have established the legal equality of all individuals, including women. However, there is no evidence of this, or of the lifting of discriminatory policies towards sedentary peoples such as the Chinese. Women played a relatively important role in Mongol Empire and in family, for example Töregene Khatun was briefly in charge of the Mongol Empire when next male Khagan was being chosen. Modern scholars refer to the alleged policy of encouraging trade and communication as the Pax Mongolica (Mongol Peace).

Genghis Khan realised that he needed people who could govern cities and states conquered by him. He also realised that such administrators could not be found among his Mongol people because they were nomads and thus had no experience governing cities. For this purpose Genghis Khan invited a Khitan prince, Chu'Tsai, who worked for the Jin and had been captured by the Mongol army after the Jin dynasty was defeated. Jin had captured power by displacing Khitan. Genghis told Chu'Tsai, who was a lineal descendant of Khitan rulers, that he had avenged Chu'Tsai's forefathers. Chu'Tsai responded that his father served the Jin dynasty honestly and so did he; also he did not consider his own father his enemy, so the question of revenge did not apply. This reply impressed Genghis Khan. Chu'Tsai administered parts of the Mongol Empire and became a confidant of the successive Mongol Khans.

Figure 17: *Reenactment of Mongol battle*

Military

Genghis Khan put absolute trust in his generals, such as Muqali, Jebe and Subutai, and regarded them as close advisors, often extending them the same privileges and trust normally reserved for close family members. He allowed them to make decisions on their own when they embarked on campaigns far from the Mongol Empire capital Karakorum. Muqali, a trusted lieutenant, was given command of the Mongol forces against the Jin dynasty while Genghis Khan was fighting in Central Asia, and Subutai and Jebe were allowed to pursue the Great Raid into the Caucasus and Kievan Rus', an idea they had presented to the Khagan on their own initiative. While granting his generals a great deal of autonomy in making command decisions, Genghis Khan also expected unwavering loyalty from them.

The Mongol military was also successful in siege warfare, cutting off resources for cities and towns by diverting certain rivers, taking enemy prisoners and driving them in front of the army, and adopting new ideas, techniques and tools from the people they conquered, particularly in employing Muslim and Chinese siege engines and engineers to aid the Mongol cavalry in capturing cities. Another standard tactic of the Mongol military was the commonly practiced feigned retreat to break enemy formations and to lure small enemy groups away from the larger group and defended position for ambush and counterattack.

Another important aspect of the military organization of Genghis Khan was the communications and supply route or *Yam*, adapted from previous Chinese

Figure 18: *Modern-day location of capital Kharakhorum*

models. Genghis Khan dedicated special attention to this in order to speed up the gathering of military intelligence and official communications. To this end, Yam waystations were established all over the empire.[134]

Khanates

Several years before his death, Genghis Khan divided his empire among his sons Ögedei, Chagatai, Tolui, and Jochi (Jochi's death several months before Genghis Khan meant that his lands were instead split between his sons, Batu and Orda) into several Khanates designed as sub-territories: their Khans were expected to follow the Great Khan, who was, initially, Ögedei.

Following are the Khanates as Genghis Khan assigned them:

- **Empire of the Great Khan**: Ögedei Khan, as *Great Khan*, took most of Eastern Asia, including China; this territory later to comprise the Yuan dynasty under Kublai Khan.
- **Mongol homeland** (present day Mongolia, including Karakorum): Tolui Khan, being the youngest son, received a small territory near the Mongol homeland, following Mongol custom.
- **Chagatai Khanate**: Chagatai Khan, Genghis Khan's second son, was given Central Asia and northern Iran.
- **Blue Horde** to Batu Khan, and **White Horde** to Orda Khan, both were later combined into the Kipchak Khanate, or Khanate of the Golden Horde, under Toqtamysh. Genghis Khan's eldest son, Jochi, had received most of the distant Russia and Ruthenia. Because Jochi died before Genghis Khan, his territory was further split up between his sons. Batu Khan launched an invasion of Russia, and later Hungary and Poland, and crushed several armies before being summoned back by the news of Ögedei's death.

Figure 19: *Genghis Khan's son and successor, Ögedei Khan*

After Genghis Khan

Contrary to popular belief, Genghis Khan did not conquer the whole area of the eventual Mongol Empire. At the time of his death in 1227, the empire stretched from the Caspian Sea to the Sea of Japan. Its expansion continued for one or more generations. Under Genghis's successor Ögedei Khan the speed of expansion reached its peak. Mongol armies pushed into Persia, finished off the Western Xia and the remnants of the Khwarezmids, and clashed with the imperial Song dynasty of China, and eventually took control of all of China in 1279. They also pushed further into Russia and eastern Europe.

Perceptions

Like other notable conquerors, Genghis Khan is portrayed differently by conquered peoples than those who conquered with him. Negative views persist in histories written by many cultures from different geographical regions. They often cite the systematic slaughter of civilians in conquered regions, cruelties and destruction by Mongol armies. Other authors also cite positive aspects of Genghis Khan's conquests.

Figure 20: *Genghis Khan on the reverse of a Kazakhstan 100 Tenge coin. The coin was minted as a collectable to honor the warlord, and is not used in common transactions.*

Positive

Genghis Khan is credited with bringing the Silk Road under one cohesive political environment. This allowed increased communication and trade between the West, Middle East and Asia, thus expanding the horizons of all three cultural areas. Some historians have noted that Genghis Khan instituted certain levels of meritocracy in his rule, was tolerant of religions and explained his policies clearly to all his soldiers.[135] In Turkey, Genghis Khan is considered a great military leader, and it is popular for male children to carry his title as name.

In Mongolia

Genghis Khan had been revered for centuries by Mongols and certain other ethnic groups such as Turks, largely because of his association with Mongol statehood, political and military organization, and his victories in war. He eventually evolved into a larger-than-life figure chiefly among the Mongols and is still considered the symbol of Mongolian culture.

During the communist period in Mongolia, Genghis was often described as a reactionary, and positive statements about him were avoided.[136] In 1962, the

Figure 21: *Portrait on a hillside in Ulaanbaatar, 2006*

erection of a monument at his birthplace and a conference held in commemoration of his 800th birthday led to criticism from the Soviet Union and the dismissal of secretary Tömör-Ochir of the ruling Mongolian People's Revolutionary Party Central Committee.

In the early 1990s, the memory of Genghis Khan underwent a powerful revival, partly in reaction to its suppression during the Mongolian People's Republic period. Genghis Khan became one of the central figures of the national identity. He is considered positively by Mongolians for his role in uniting warring tribes. For example, Mongolians often refer to their country as "Genghis Khan's Mongolia", to themselves as "Genghis Khan's children", and to Genghis Khan as the "father of the Mongols" especially among the younger generation. However, there is a chasm in the perception of his brutality. Mongolians maintain that the historical records written by non-Mongolians are unfairly biased against Genghis Khan and that his butchery is exaggerated, while his positive role is underrated.

In Mongolia today, Genghis Khan's name and likeness appear on products, streets, buildings, and other places. His face can be found on everyday commodities, from liquor bottles to candy, and on the largest denominations of 500, 1,000, 5,000, 10,000, and 20,000 Mongolian tögrög (₮). Mongolia's main international airport in Ulaanbaatar is named Chinggis Khaan International Airport. Major Genghis Khan statues stand before the parliament[137]

Figure 22: *President Elbegdorj's second inauguration on 10 July 2013, in front of the monument to Genghis Khan at the Government Palace in Ulaanbaatar*

and near Ulaanbaatar. There have been repeated discussions about regulating the use of his name and image to avoid trivialization.

Genghis Khan is regarded as one of the prominent leaders in Mongolia's history. He is responsible for the emergence of the Mongols as a political and ethnic identity because there was no unified identity between the tribes that had cultural similarity. He reinforced many Mongol traditions and provided stability and unity during a time of almost endemic warfare between tribes. He is also credited for introducing the traditional Mongolian script and creating the first written Mongolian code of law, the Ikh Zasag ("Great Administration"). Mongolian President Tsakhiagiin Elbegdorj has noted that the Ikh Zasag heavily punished corruption and bribery, and he considers Genghis Khan a teacher for anti-corruption efforts who sought equal protection under the law for all citizens regardless of status or wealth. On the 850th anniversary of Genghis's birth, the President stated "Chinggis ... was a man who deeply realized that the justice begins and consolidates with the equality of law, and not with the distinctions between people. He was a man who knew that the good laws and rules lived longer than fancy palaces." In summary, Mongolians see him as the fundamental figure in the founding of the Mongol Empire and therefore the basis for Mongolia as a country.

As of 2012[138], Elbegdorj issued a decree establishing Genghis Khan's birthday as a national holiday on the first day of winter (according to the Mongolian lunar calendar).

Figure 23: *Genghis Khan Monument in Hohhot, Inner Mongolia, China*

In Japan

Japanese like Kenchō Suyematsu have claimed that the ethnic Japanese Minamoto no Yoshitsune was Genghis Khan.[139]

Mixed

In China

There are conflicting views of Genghis Khan in the People's Republic of China. The legacy of Genghis and his successors, who completed the conquest of China after 65 years of struggle, remains a mixed topic.Wikipedia:Citation needed China suffered a drastic decline in population.[140] The population of north China decreased from 50 million in the 1195 census to 8.5 million in the Mongol census of 1235–36. An unknown number of people migrated to Southern China in this period.[141]

In Inner Mongolia there are a monument and buildings dedicated to him and considerable number of ethnic Mongols in the area with a population of around 5 million, almost twice the population of Mongolia. While Genghis never conquered all of China, his grandson Kublai Khan completed that conquest and established the Yuan dynasty that is often credited with re-uniting China. There has been much artwork and literature praising Genghis as a military leader and political genius. The Mongol-established Yuan dynasty left an indelible imprint on Chinese political and social structures for subsequent generations with literature during the preceding Jin dynasty relatively fewer.

Figure 24: *Invasions like the Battle of Baghdad by his grandson are treated as brutal and are seen negatively in Iraq. This illustration is from a 14th-century Jami' al-tawarikh manuscript.*

Genghis Khan supported the Chinese Daoist sect leader Qiu Chuji and after personally meeting him in what is now Afghanistan, gave him control of all religious affairs in northern China.

Negative

In the Middle East, and particularly in Iran, Genghis Khan is almost universally condemned as a destructive and genocidal warlord who caused enormous destruction to the population of these areas.[142] Steven R. Ward wrote that "Overall, the Mongol violence and depredations killed up to three-fourths of the population of the Iranian Plateau, possibly 10 to 15 million people. Some historians have estimated that Iran's population did not again reach its pre-Mongol levels until the mid-20th century."

In Afghanistan (along with other non-Turkic Muslim countries), he is generally viewed unfavorably, though some groups display ambivalence as it is believed that the Hazara of Afghanistan are descendants of a large Mongol garrison stationed there.[143]

The invasions of Baghdad, Samarkand, Urgench, Kiev, Vladimir among others caused mass murders, such as when portions of southern Khuzestan were completely destroyed. His descendant Hulagu Khan destroyed much of Iran's north and sacked Baghdad, although his forces were halted by the Mamluks of Egypt, but Hulagu's descendant Ghazan Khan returned to beat the Mamluks out of the Levant, Palestine and even Gaza. According to the works of the Persian historian Rashid-al-Din Hamadani, the Mongols killed more than 70,000 people in Merv and more than 190,000 in Nishapur. In 1237, Batu Khan, a grandson of Genghis Khan, launched an invasion into Kievan Rus'. Over the course of three years, the Mongols annihilated all of the major cities of Eastern Europe with the exception of Novgorod and Pskov.

Giovanni de Plano Carpini, the Pope's envoy to the Mongol Great Khan, travelled through Kiev in February 1246 and wrote:

> They [the Mongols] attacked Russia, where they made great havoc, destroying cities and fortresses and slaughtering men; and they laid siege to Kiev, the capital of Russia; after they had besieged the city for a long time, they took it and put the inhabitants to death. When we were journeying through that land we came across countless skulls and bones of dead men lying about on the ground. Kiev had been a very large and thickly populated town, but now it has been reduced almost to nothing, for there are at the present time scarce two hundred houses there and the inhabitants are kept in complete slavery.

Among the Iranian peoples, Genghis Khan, along with Hulagu and Timur are among the most despised conquerors in the region.

Although the famous Mughal emperors were proud descendants of Genghis Khan and particularly Timur, they clearly distanced themselves from the Mongol atrocities committed against the Khwarizim Shahs, Turks, Persians, the citizens of Baghdad and Damascus, Nishapur, Bukhara and historical figures such as Attar of Nishapur and many other notable Muslims. However, Mughal Emperors directly patronized the legacies of Genghis Khan and Timur; together their names were synonymous with the names of other distinguished personalities particularly among the Muslim populations of South Asia.

In much of Russia, Middle East, Korea, China, Ukraine, Poland and Hungary, Genghis Khan and his regime are blamed for considerable destruction and loss of population.

Descent

In addition to most of the Mongol nobility up to the 20th century, the Mughal emperor Babur's mother was a descendant. Timur (also known as Tamerlane), the 14th century military leader, and many other nobilities of central Asian countries claimed descent from Genghis Khan. During the Soviet purge most of the Mongol nobility in Mongolia were purged.

Figure 25: *The Mongol invasion of Hungary. The dismounted Mongols, with captured women, are on the left, the Hungarians, with one saved woman, on the right.*

Figure 26: *Genghis Khan on the Mongolian 1,000 tögrög banknote*

Physical appearance

The closest depiction generally accepted by most historians is the portrait currently in the National Palace Museum in Taipei, Taiwan, which was drawn under the supervision of his grandson Khubilai during the Mongol Yuan dynasty and depicts Genghis Khan with typical Mongol features.

Figure 27: *Statue of Genghis Khan at his mausoleum, China*

Depictions in modern culture

There have been several films, novels and other adaptation works on the Mongolian ruler.

Films

- *Genghis Khan*, a 1950 Philippine film directed by Manuel Conde.
- *Changez Khan*, a 1957 Indian film directed by Kedar Kapoor.
- *Changez Khan*, a 1958 Pakistani film.
- *The Conqueror*, released in 1956 and starring John Wayne as Temüjin and Susan Hayward as Börte.
- *Genghis Khan* starring Omar Sharif.
- *Under The Eternal Blue Sky*, a Mongolian film directed by Baljinnyam, which was released in 1990. Starring Agvaantserengiin Enkhtaivan as Temüjin.
- *Genghis Khan* starring Richard Tyson, Charlton Heston and Pat Morita.
- *Genghis Khan - A Proud Son Of Heaven*, made in Mongolian, with English subtitles.
- *Genghis Khan: To the Ends of the Earth and Sea*, also known as *The Descendant of Gray Wolf*, a Japanese-Mongolian film released in 2007.

Figure 28: *Mural of siege warfare, Genghis Khan Exhibit in San Jose, California, US*

- *Mongol*, a film by Sergei Bodrov released in 2007. (Academy Award nominee for Best Foreign Language Film).
- *No Right to Die - Chinggis Khaan*, a Mongolian film released in 2008.
- *By the Will of Genghis Khan*, a Russian film released in 2009.

Television series

- *Genghis Khan*, a 1987 Hong Kong television series produced by TVB, starring Alex Man.
- *Genghis Khan*, a 1987 Hong Kong television series produced by ATV, starring Tony Liu.
- *Genghis Khan*, a 2004 Chinese-Mongolian co-produced television series, starring Ba Sen, who is a descendant of Genghis Khan's second son Chagatai.

Poetry

- *The End of Genghis*, a poem by F. L. Lucas, in which the dying Khan, attended by his Khitan counsellor Yelü Chucai, looks back on his life.[144]

Novels

- *Jenghiz Khan* and *Batu Khan* by Vasili Yan, trans. L. E. Britton, publisher. Hutchinson
- *The Conqueror* series of novels by Conn Iggulden
- *Steppe* by Piers Anthony
- *Jenghiz Khan* in Telugu (Indian language) by Thenneti Suri
- *Genghis Khan* (Last incarnation) in Metro 2033 by Dmitry Glukhovsky

Short stories

- *The Private Life of Genghis Khan* by Douglas Adams and Graham Chapman

Music

- West German pop band Dschinghis Khan took its name from the German-language spelling of Genghis Khan, "Dschingis Khan". They participated in the Eurovision Song Contest 1979 with their song of the same name.

Video games

- *Age of Empires II: The Age of Kings*
- *Aoki Ookami to Shiroki Mejika IV: Genghis Khan*
- *Crusader Kings 2*
- *Deadliest Warrior: Legends*
- *Sid Meier's Civilization*

Name and title

There are many theories about the origins of Temüjin's title. Since people of the Mongol nation later associated the name with *ching* (Mongolian for strength), such confusion is obvious, though it does not follow etymology.

One theory suggests the name stems from a palatalised version of the Mongolian and Turkic word *tenggis*, meaning "ocean", "oceanic" or "wide-spreading". (Lake Baikal and ocean were called *tenggis* by the Mongols. However, it seems that if they had meant to call Genghis *tenggis* they could have said, and written, "Tenggis Khan", which they did not.) Zhèng (Chinese: 正) meaning "right", "just", or "true", would have received the Mongolian adjectival modifier *-s*, creating "Jenggis", which in medieval romanization would be written "Genghis". It is likely that the 13th century Mongolian pronunciation would have closely matched "Chinggis".

Figure 29: *The gate of Genghis Khan Mausoleum, Ordos, Inner Mongolia*

The English spelling "Genghis" is of unclear origin. Weatherford claims it derives from a spelling used in original Persian reports. Even at this time some Iranians pronounce his name as "Ghengiss". However, review of historical Persian sources does not confirm this.

According to the *Secret History of the Mongols*, Temüjin was named after a powerful warrior of the Tatar tribe that his father Yesügei had taken prisoner. The name "Temüjin" is believed to derive from the word *temür*, Turkic for iron (modern Mongolian: төмөр, *tömör*). The name would imply a blacksmith or a man strong like iron.

No evidence has survived to indicate that Genghis Khan had any exceptional training or reputation as a blacksmith. But the latter interpretation (a man strong like iron) is supported by the names of Genghis Khan's siblings, Temülin and Temüge, which are derived from the same root word.

Name and spelling variations

Genghis Khan, the title is spelled in variety of ways in different languages such as Mongolian Chinggis Khaan, English *Chinghiz*, *Chinghis*, and *Chingiz*, Chinese: 成吉思汗 ; pinyin: *Chéngjísī Hán*, Turkic: *Cengiz Han*, *Çingiz Xan*, *Çingiz Han*, *Chingizxon*, *Çıñğız Xan*, *Chengez Khan*, *Chinggis Khan*, *Chinggis Xaan*, *Chingis Khan*, *Jenghis Khan*, *Chinggis Qan*, *Djingis Kahn*, Russian:

Figure 30: *Monument in Hulunbuir, Inner Mongolia, China*

Чингисхан (*Čingiskhan*) or Чингиз-хан (*Čingiz-khan*), etc. Temüjin is written in Chinese as simplified Chinese: 铁木真 ; traditional Chinese: 鐵木眞 ; pinyin: *Tiěmùzhēn*.

When Kublai Khan established the Yuan dynasty in 1271, he had his grandfather Genghis Khan placed on the official record as the founder of the dynasty or *Taizu* (Chinese: 太祖). Thus, Genghis Khan is also referred to as *Yuan Taizu* (Emperor Taizu of Yuan, Chinese: 元太祖) in Chinese historiography.

Timeline

- Probably 1155, 1162, or 1167: Temüjin was born in the Khentii mountains.
- When Temüjin was nine, his father Yesükhei was poisoned by Tatars, leaving Temüjin and his family destitute.
- c. 1184: Temüjin's wife Börte was kidnapped by Merkits; he called on blood brother Jamukha and Wang Khan for aid, and they rescued her.
- c. 1185: First son Jochi was born; leading to doubt about his paternity later among Genghis's children, because he was born shortly after Börte's rescue from the Merkits.
- 1190: Temüjin united the Mongol tribes, became leader, and devised code of law Yassa.

- 1201: Victory over Jamukha's Jadarans.
- 1202: Adopted as Wang Khan's heir after successful campaigns against Tatars.
- 1203: Victory over Wang Khan's Keraites. Wang Khan himself killed by accident by allied Naimans.
- 1204: Victory over Naimans (all these confederations unite and become the Mongols).
- 1206: Jamukha was killed. Temüjin was given the title *Genghis Khan* by his followers in a Kurultai (around 40 years of age).
- 1207–1210: Genghis led operations against the Western Xia, which comprises much of northwestern China and parts of Tibet. Western Xia ruler submitted to Genghis Khan. During this period, the Uyghurs also submitted peacefully to the Mongols and became valued administrators throughout the empire.
- 1211: After the kurultai, Genghis led his armies against the Jin dynasty ruling northern China.
- 1215: Beijing fell; Genghis Khan turned to west and the Khara-Kitan Khanate.
- 1219–1222: Conquered Khwarezmid Empire.
- 1226: Started the campaign against the Western Xia for forming coalition against the Mongols, the second battle with the Western Xia.
- 1227: Genghis Khan died after conquering the Tangut people. Cause of death is uncertain.

References

Sources

- Hildinger, Erik (1997). *Warriors Of The Steppe: Military History Of Central Asia, 500 BC To 1700 AD*. Cambridge: De Capo Press. ISBN 0-7867-3114-1.
- Lane, George (2004). *Genghis Khan and Mongol Rule*. Westport, Connecticut: Greenwood Publishing Group. ISBN 0-313-32528-6.
- Man, John (2004). *Genghis Khan: Life, Death and Resurrection*. London; New York: Bantam Press. ISBN 0-593-05044-4.
- Ratchnevsky, Paul (1991). *Genghis Khan: His Life and Legacy* [*Čingis-Khan: sein Leben und Wirken*]. tr. & ed. Thomas Nivison Haining. Oxford, UK; Cambridge, Massachusetts, US: B. Blackwell. ISBN 0-631-16785-4.

Further reading

- Brent, Peter (1976). *The Mongol Empire: Genghis Khan: His Triumph and His Legacy*. London: Weidenfeld & Nicholson. ISBN 0-297-77137-X.
- Bretschneider, Emilii (2002). *Mediæval Researches from Eastern Asiatic Sources; Fragments Towards the Knowledge of the Geography & History of Central & Western Asia*. This Elibron Classics book is a facsimile reprint of an 1888 edition by Trübner & Co., London. Adamant Media Corporation. ISBN 978-1-4021-9303-3.
- Cable, Mildred; Francesca French (1943). *The Gobi Desert*. London: Landsborough Publications.
- Chapin, David (2012). *Long Lines: Ten of the World's Longest Continuous Family Lineages*. College Station, Texas: VirtualBookWorm.com. ISBN 978-1-60264-933-0.
- Charney, Israel W. (ed.) (1994). *Genocide: A Critical Bibliographic Review*. New York: Facts on File Publications.
- Farale, Dominique (2002). *De Gengis Khan à Qoubilaï Khan : la grande chevauchée mongole*. Campagnes & stratégies (in French). Paris: Economica. ISBN 2-7178-4537-2.
- Farale, Dominique (2007). *La Russie et les Turco-Mongols : 15 siècles de guerre* (in French). Paris: Economica. ISBN 978-2-7178-5429-9.
- "Genghis Khan"[145]. *Funk & Wagnalls New Encyclopedia*. World Almanac Education Group. 2005. Archived from the original[146] on January 13, 2006. Retrieved May 22, 2008. Via the Internet Archive's copy of the History Channel Web site.
- Smitha, Frank E. "Genghis Khan and the Mongols"[147]. *Macrohistory and World Report*. Retrieved June 30, 2005.
- Kennedy, Hugh (2002). *Mongols, Huns & Vikings*. London: Cassell. ISBN 0-304-35292-6.
- Kradin, Nikolay; Tatiana Skrynnikova (2006). *Imperiia Chingis-khana (Chinggis Khan Empire)* (in Russian). Moscow: Vostochnaia literatura. ISBN 5-02-018521-3. (summary in English)
- Kradin, Nikolay; Tatiana Skrynnikova (2006). "Why do we call Chinggis Khan's Polity 'an Empire'". *Ab Imperio*. **7** (1): 89–118. 5-89423-110-8.
- Lamb, Harold (1927). *Genghis Khan: The Emperor of All Men*[148]. New York: R. M. McBride & company.
- Lister, R. P. (2000). *Genghis Khan*. Lanham, Maryland: Cooper Square Press. ISBN 0-8154-1052-2.
- Man, John (1999). *Gobi: Tracking the Desert*. London; New Haven, Conn: Weidenfeld & Nicolson; Yale University Press. ISBN 0-7538-0161-2.

- Martin, Henry Desmond (1950). *The Rise of Chingis Khan and his Conquest of North China*. Baltimore: Johns Hopkins Press.
- May, Timothy (2001). "Mongol Arms"[149]. *Explorations in Empire: Pre-Modern Imperialism Tutorial: The Mongols*. San Antonio College History Department. Archived from the original[150] on May 18, 2008. Retrieved May 22, 2008.
- Morgan, David (1986). *The Mongols*. The Peoples of Europe. Blackwell Publishing. ISBN 0-631-17563-6.
- Stevens, Keith. "Heirs to Discord: The Supratribal Aspirations of Jamukha, Toghrul, and Temüjin"[151] at the Internet ArchivePDF (72.1 KB) Retrieved May 22, 2008.
- Stewart, Stanley (2001). *In the Empire of Genghis Khan: A Journey among Nomads*. London: Harper Collins. ISBN 0-00-653027-3.
- Turnbull, Stephen (2003). *Genghis Khan & the Mongol Conquests 1190–1400*. Oxford: Osprey Publishing. ISBN 1-84176-523-6.
- Valentino, Benjamin A. (2004). *Final Solutions: Mass Killing and Genocide in the Twentieth Century*. Ithaca, N.Y.: Cornell University Press. ISBN 0-8014-3965-5.

Primary sources

- Juvaynī, Alā al-Dīn Atā Malik, 1226–1283 (1997). *Genghis Khan: The History of the World-Conqueror [Tarīkh-i jahāngushā]*. tr. John Andrew Boyle. Seattle: University of Washington Press. ISBN 0-295-97654-3.
  - Juvaini, 'ala-ad-Din 'Ata-Malik (1958). *History of the World-Conqueror*[152]. tr. John Andrew Boyle. Cambridge, Massachusetts: Harvard University Press. p. 361. Retrieved April 16, 2012.
- Rashid al-Din Tabib (1995). *A Compendium of Chronicles: Rashid al-Din's Illustrated History of the World Jami' al-Tawarikh*. The Nasser D. Khalili Collection of Islamic Art, Vol. XXVII. Sheila S. Blair (ed.). Oxford: Oxford University Press. ISBN 0-19-727627-X.
- Rashid al-Din Tabib (1971). *The Successors of Genghis Khan (extracts from Jami' Al-Tawarikh)*[153]. UNESCO Collection of Representative Works: Persian heritage series. tr. from the Persian by John Andrew Boyle. New York: Columbia University Press. ISBN 0-231-03351-6.
- *The Secret History of the Mongols: A Mongolian Epic Chronicle of the Thirteenth Century [Yuan chao bi shi]*. Brill's Inner Asian Library vol. 7. tr. Igor de Rachewiltz. Leiden; Boston: Brill. 2004. ISBN 90-04-13159-0.

External links

- Genghis Khan[154] on *In Our Time* at the BBC.
- Welcome to The Realm of the Mongols[155]
- Parts of this biography were taken from the Area Handbook series at the Library of Congress[156]
- Estimates of Mongol warfare casualties[157]
- Genghis Khan on the Web[158] (directory of some 250 resources)
- 'Ala' al-Din 'Ata Malik Juvayni[159] A History of the World-Conqueror Ghengis Genghis Khan, Ata-Malik Juvayni and Rashid-al-Din Hamadani
- The History of Genghizcan the Great, First Emperor of the Antient Moguls and Tartars[160]
- "Genghis Khan's Secret Weapon Was Rain"[161], *National Geographic*, Roff Smith, March 10, 2014
- Genghis Khan (Character)[162] on IMDb

Genghis Khan **House of Borjigin (1206–1635)** Born: c. 1162 Died: 1227		
Regnal titles		
Preceded by **Hotula Khan**	**Khagan of Khamag Mongol** 1189–1206	**Khamag Mongol ended** succeeded by Mongol Empire
New title Mongol Empire established	***Khagan* of the Mongol Empire** 1206–1227	Succeeded by **Tolui** **As regent**

Mongol invasions and conquests

Central Asia

Mongol invasion of Central Asia

Mongol invasion of Central Asia0		
Part of the Mongol conquests		
Date	1216-1221	
Location	Central Asia, Iran, Afghanistan, China	
Result	Khwarezmian pyrrhic victory, destruction of the Qara Khitai but Khwarazmian dynasty stays inderpendent	
Territorial changes	Mongol Empire gains control of the most of Qara Khitai	
Belligerents		
Mongol Empire	Qara Khitai Khanate	Khwarazmian dynasty
Commanders and leaders		
Genghis Khan Jochi Chaghatai Ögedei Tolui Subutai Jebe Jelme(POW) Mukali Khubilai Qasar Boorchu(KIA) Sorkin-shara	Kuchlug	Ala ad-Din Muhammad Jalal ad-Din Mingburnu Inalchuq (POW), executed Temur Meliq
Strength		
100,000-150,000	Around 100,000	122,000 men
Casualties and losses		
Around 30-50,000	60-70,000 men	40-50,000

> Mongols were defeated by the Khwarezmanids at Battle of Bukhara, but the city was sacked only weeks later.

The **Mongol invasion of Central Asia** occurred after the unification of the Mongol and Turkic tribes on the Mongolian plateau in 1206. It was finally complete when Genghis Khan conquered the Khwarizmian Empire in 1221.

Siberia (1207-1209)

The conquest of the forest peoples of Siberia was carried out in 1207 by Genghis' eldest son, Jochi. Most of the tribes submitted with little resistance, with the exception of the Yenisei Kyrgyz, who had defeated an expeditionary force in 1204, and took several years to subdue. Tuva was conquered in 1207.

Uyghurs, Qarluqs and Qara Khitai (1216-1218)

The Uyghurs, Qarluqs and local Turkic and Tajik peoples submitted to the Mongolians. The Uyghur state of Kara-Khoja was a vassal of the Qara Khitai, but in 1210, the Uyghur ruler of Kara-Khoja, Idiqut Barchuq appeared before the Khan to declare his allegiance to the Mongolians. He was rewarded with the daughter of Genghis in marriage, and the Uyghurs served under the Mongols as bureaucrats. A leader of the Qarluq and Buzar, the warlord of Chuy Valley, followed the Uyghur example.

The Qara Khitai (Black Khitan) were Khitans of the Liao Dynasty (907–1125) who were driven out of China by the Jurchens of the Jin dynasty. In 1124 some Khitans moved westward under Yeh-lü Ta-shih's leadership and created the Qara Khitai Khanate (Western Liao) between in the Semirechye and the Chu River. They dominated Central Asia in the 12th century after they defeated the Great Seljuk leader Ahmed Sanjar at the Battle of Qatwan in 1141. However, their power was shattered in 1211 through the combined actions of the Khwārezm-Shah 'Alā' ad-Dīn Muḥammad (1200–20), and Küchlüg, a fugitive Naiman prince in flight from Genghis Khan's Mongols. Kuchlug was given shelter by the Qara Khiitai, but he usurped the Gurkhan's throne in 1211.

Kuchlug attacked the city of Almaliq, and the Qarlugs there who were vassals of the Mongols appealed to Genghis Khan for help. In 1216, Genghis dispatched his general Jebe to pursue Kuchlug. The Mongols defeated the Qara Khitai at Balasaghun, Kuchlug fled, but was later killed in 1218.

Khwarezmia (1219-1221)

The Mongols' original conquest of all "people in felt tents", unifying the nomadic tribes in Mongolia and then the Turcomens and other nomadic peoples,Wikipedia:Citation needed had come with relatively little bloodshed, and almost no material loss. It was not originally the intention of the Mongol Empire to invade the Khwarezmid Empire, and according to Juvaini, Genghis Khan had originally sent the ruler of the Khwarezmid Empire, Sultan Muhammad Aladdin, a message seeking trade and greeted him as his neighbor: "I am master of the lands of the rising sun while you rule those of the setting sun. Let us conclude a firm treaty of friendship and peace." or he said "I am Khan of the lands of the rising sun while you are sultan those of the setting sun: Let us conclude a firm agreement of friendship and peace."[163]

However, the Governor of Otrar refused to receive the mission and had all 450 of them killed, with permission from the Sultan. Upon hearing of this atrocity months later, Genghis Khan flew into a rage and used the incident as a pretext for invasion. The Mongol invasion of Central Asia however would entail the utter destruction of the Khwarezmid Empire along with the massacre of much of the civilian population of the region. According to Juvaini, the Mongols ordered only one round of slaughter in Khwarezm and Transoxiana, but systematically exterminated a particularly large portion of the people of the cities of Khorasan. This earned the Mongols a reputation for bloodthirsty ferocity that would mark the remainder of their campaigns.

During the invasion of Transoxania in 1219, along with the main Mongol force, Genghis Khan used a Chinese specialist catapult unit in battle. They were used again in 1220 in Transoxania. The Chinese may have used the catapults to hurl gunpowder bombs, since they already had them by this time While Genghis Khan was conquering Transoxania and Persia, several Chinese who were familiar with gunpowder were serving with Genghis's army. Historians have suggested that the Mongol invasion had brought Chinese gunpowder weapons to Central Asia. One of these was the huochong, a Chinese mortar.

West Asia

Mongol invasions of the Levant

Mongol invasions of the Levant the Mamluk-Ilkhanid War

1260 Mongol offensives in the Levant

Date	1260–1323
Location	Levant and Anatolia
Result	Mongols conquer part of the Abbasid Caliphate and Ayyubid dynasty but fail to conquer the Mamluk Sultanate The Treaty of Aleppo

Belligerents

Ilkhanate of the Mongol Empire
 Armenian Kingdom of Cilicia
 Kingdom of Georgia
Sultanate of Rum
 Principality of Antioch
 County of Tripoli
Yuan Dynasty
 Golden Horde of the Mongol Empire (1259-1264)
 Knights Templar

Mamluk Sultanate
Ayyubids
Golden Horde of the Mongol Empire (after 1264)
Karamanid rebels
Abbasid Caliphate

Commanders and leaders

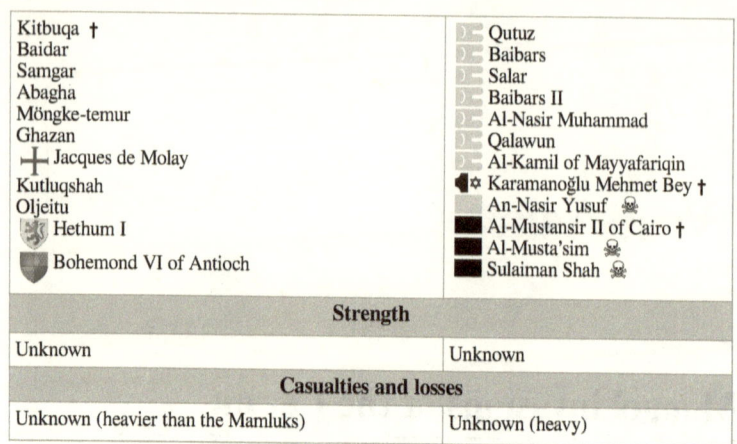

Strength	
Unknown	Unknown
Casualties and losses	
Unknown (heavier than the Mamluks)	Unknown (heavy)

Starting in the 1240s, the Mongols made repeated **invasions of Syria** or attempts thereof. Most failed, but they did have some success in 1260 and 1300, capturing Aleppo and Damascus and destroying the Ayyubid dynasty. The Mongols were forced to retreat within months each time by other forces in the area, primarily the Egyptian Mamluks. Since 1260, it had been described as the **Mamluk-Ilkhanid War**.

First invasion

During the governorship of Bachu in Persia, the Mongolian army under Yisaur attacked Syria in 1244. The reasons for the attack are unclear, but it may have been in retaliation for the Syrian participation on the Seljuk side in the Battle of Köse Dağ.[164] In the autumn 1244, Yisaur concentrated the Mongol forces in the upper Tigris valley where they subjugated the Kurdish province of Akhlat. Moving across, the Mongolian army encountered no resistance and ravaged the area en route. The fortified cities were untaken in his advance because Yisaur was not prepared for siege assault. Passing through the territory of the city of Urfa, he crossed the Euphrates.

He marched directly to Aleppo but went as far as Hailan before the climate impaired his army's movements. Yisaur sent envoys to Aleppo to demand submission of tribute, which Malik agreed to pay. The same demand were sent to Bohemond of Antioch who chose not to fight them instead of defiance.[165]

Yisaur withdrew his force back up the Euphrates valley and received the submission of Malatia. In Egypt, Sultan Saleeh decided to acquiesce to the results and made no attempt to raise an army to encounter the Mongols who had invaded his dominions in Syria.

In 1251, as an expediency to buy peace, Sultan Nasir sent his representatives to Mongolia for the election of Möngke and agreed to make Syria a vassal state of the Mongol Empire.

1260 invasion

In 1255 Hulagu sought to further expand the Empire into the Middle East under orders from his older brother, the Great Khan Möngke. Hulagu's forces subjugated multiple peoples along the way, most notably the center of the Islamic Empire, Baghdad, which was completely sacked in 1258, destroying the Abbasid Caliphate. From there, the Mongol forces proceeded into Syria.

In 1260, Egypt was under the control of the Bahri Mamluks, while most of the Levant (aside from the Crusader states) was still under the control of Ayyubid princes. The Mongols, for their part, had combined their forces with that of their Christian vassals in the region, the Georgians; the army of Cilician Armenia under Hethum I, King of Armenia; and the Franks of Bohemond VI of Antioch. In what is described by the 20th-century historians René Grousset and Lev Gumilev as the "yellow crusade" (*Croisade Jaune*), the combined forces captured the city of Aleppo, and then on March 1, 1260, under the Mongol Christian general Kitbuqa, took Damascus. The last Ayyubid king, An-Nasir Yusuf, was captured by the Mongols near Gaza in 1260. However, Hulagu promised him that he would appoint An-Nasir Yusuf as his viceroy in Syria.[166] With the Islamic power center of Baghdad and Syria gone, the center of Islamic power transferred to the Mamluks in Cairo.

Hulagu's intention at that point was to continue south through Palestine to Egypt, to engage the Mamluks. However, Möngke died in late 1259, requiring Hulagu to return to Karakorum to engage in the councils on who the next Great Khan would be. Hulagu departed with the bulk of his forces, leaving only about 10,000 Mongol horsemen in Syria under Kitbuqa. Some of Kitbuqa's forces engaged in raids southwards towards Egypt, reaching as far as Gaza, where a Mongol garrison was established with 1,000 troops.

The Mamluks took advantage of the weakened state of the Mongol forces, and, negotiating a passive alliance with the remnants of the Crusader forces in Acre, advanced northwards to engage the Mongols at the pivotal Battle of Ain Jalut in September 1260. The Mamluks achieved a decisive victory, Kitbuqa was executed, and the battle established a high-water mark for the Mongol conquests. In previous defeats, the Mongols had always returned later to retake the territory, but they were never able to avenge the loss at Ayn Jalut. The border of the Mongol Ilkhanate remained at the Tigris River for the duration of Hulagu's dynasty. Sultan An-Nasir and his brother were executed after Hulagu heard the news of the defeat of Kitbuqa at Ain Jalut.

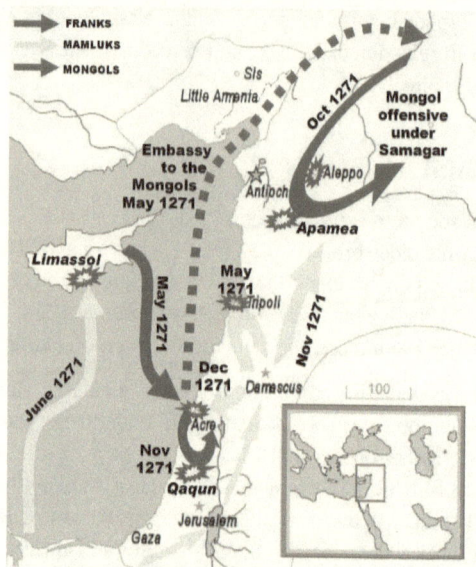

Figure 31: *The Mamluks under Baibars (yellow) fought off the Franks and the Mongols during the Ninth Crusade.*

In December 1260, Hulagu sent 6,000 troops back into Syria, but they were defeated at the First Battle of Homs.

Abbasid Caliphate in Cairo and the rebellion in Mosul

After the fall of Baghdad in 1258, a few of Abbasid princes fled to Syria and Egypt. There, the Abbasids still maintained a feeble show of authority, confined to religious matters, under the Mamluks. But their authority was limited to being figureheads. First of the Caliphs in Cairo, Al-Mustansir II was dispatched to Iraq by Baibars. The Caliph was reinforced with Syrian auxiliaries and the Bedouins. However, he was totally crushed by the Mongol vanguard in South Iraq in 1262. The Mongol protectrate and ruler of Mosul, Badr al-Din's sons sided with the Mamluks and rebelled against the rule of Hulagu. This led to the destruction of the city state and the Mongols finally suppressed the rebellion in 1265.

1271 invasion

The second Mongol invasion of Syria took place in October 1271, when 10,000 Mongols and Seljuk auxiliaries moved southwards from Rûm and captured Aleppo; however they retreated back beyond the Euphrates when the Mamluk leader Baibars marched on them from Egypt.

Area alliances

In the second half of the 13th century, civil war had erupted in the Mongol Empire. In the Middle East, this manifested as conflict between the Mongols of the Golden Horde, and the Mongols of the Ilkhanate, who battled over claims on Georgia and Azerbaijan. Both the Golden Horde and the Ilkhanate sought to strengthen their position via trade agreements or other types of alliances with other powers in the area. In 1261, Berke of the Golden Horde allied with the Mamluk Sultan Baibars,[167,168,169,170,171] against their common enemy the Ilkhanate. This alliance was both strategic, and also in terms of trade exchanges, as the Egyptians had been the Golden Horde's long-standing trade partner and ally in the Mediterranean.[172]

For their part, the Mongols of the Ilkhanate sought (unsuccessfully) an alliance with the Franks of Europe,[173] but did form a Byzantine-Mongol alliance with the Christian Byzantine Empire.

Conflict between the Golden Horde and the Il-Khans

The two Western Mongol realms, the Golden Horde and the Il-Khanate, were already in open war. The roots of the conflict were related to battles between the descendants of Genghis Khan over the control of the Empire. The immediate successor to Genghis Khan was his son Ögedei, but the leadership was then taken by force by the descendants of Genghis' son Tolui. During the reign of Kublai Khan (son of Genghis' son Tolui), descendants of Genghis's other sons Ögedei, Chagatai, and Jochi sought to oppose the rule of Kublai. The Ilkhanate had been founded by Hulagu, another of Tolui's sons, who was therefore loyal to Kublai. The Golden Horde had been founded by Genghis' son Jochi, following the Mongol invasion of Central Asia. Genghis had designated several of the territories south of the Caucasus to Jochi, specifically Georgia, and the Seljukid Sultanate.[174] Hulagu, with the backing of his brother the Great Khan Kublai, invaded and captured these territories in 1256, even installing his capital in the center of the disputed territories, at Maragha. Berke, the leader of the Golden Horde, could not tolerate this infringement of his inheritance, and a drawn-out conflict between the two Mongol realms continued well into the 14th century.[175]

Figure 32: *Mamluks offensive at the Fall of Tripoli in 1289.*

Ethnic and religious affinities

Various affinities led to a more or less natural alliance between the Mongols of the Golden Horde and the Mamluks of Egypt. The Mamluks' Empire had been founded by former slaves bought from the Kipchack territory of southern Russia, which was now an important segment of the Mongol Golden Horde. There were therefore already cultural affinities between large segments of the Mongol Horde and the ruling elite of Egypt.[176] Berke's Turkic subjects also spoke the same Turkic language as the Mamluks.[177] Further, the Golden Horde, under Berke's leadership, was the first of the Mongol states to convert to Islam, which lent to solidarity with the Islamic realms to the south.[178] On the other hand, the Il-Khan rulers were highly favourable to Christianity, and did not commit to Islam until 1295, when the Ilkhan Ghazan, a descendant of Tolui, formerly converted when he took the throne.[179] Even after his conversion though, he continued to battle the Mamluks for control of Syria, while simultaneously seeking an alliance with Christian Europe.

Mongol invasions of the Levant

Figure 33: *The Mamluks defeated the Armenians and captured the prince Leo at the disaster of Mari, 1266: illumination from Le Livre des Merveilles, 15th century.*

Mamluk-Golden Horde rapprochement

The Golden Horde entered into a defensive alliance with the Mamluks in Egypt, with the agreement being that each realm would intervene if the other was attacked by the Ilkhanate.[180,181] This required the Il-khan to devote forces to both his northern and southern borders, and never use all forces in a single battle. On multiple occasions, the forces of the Ilkhanate would start a campaign towards Syria in the south, only to be forced to recall troops within a few months because of attacks from the Golden Horde in the north.[182]

1281 invasion

The third major invasion took place in 1281 under Abaqa Khan. Having crossed the Euphrates and captured Aleppo, the Mongols of the Ilkhanate moved as far south as Homs with 80,000 men before they were beaten back to the Euphrates river at the Second Battle of Homs.

The Il-khan Tekuder (r. 1282-1284) was friendly to Islam, and sent a letter to the Mamluk sultan to broach the subject of peace, but Tekuder's envoy was arrested by the Mamluks. Tekuder's conversion to Islam and attempts to make peace with the Mamluks were not popular with the other nobles of the Ilkhanate. When Tekuder's brother Arghun challenged him for the

Figure 34: *The Mongols and the Armenians were defeated by the Mamluks at the Second Battle of Homs in 1281.*

throne, Tekuder sought assistance in vain from the Mamluks, but was executed. Arghun (1284–91) took power, and as directed by the Great Khan Kublai (r. 1260-94) continued Mongol attempts to conquer Syria.

The Mamluk-Ilkhanid War: 1299–1303

In late 1299, the Mongol Ilkhan Mahmud Ghazan, son of Arghun, took his army and crossed the Euphrates river to again invade Syria. They continued south until they were slightly north of Homs,[183] and successfully took Aleppo. There, Ghazan was joined by forces from his vassal state of Cilician Armenia.[184]

The Mamluk relief force sent from Damascus met the Mongol army northeast of Homs, at the Battle of Wadi al-Khazandar (sometimes called the Battle of Homs) in December 1299. The Mongols had some 60,000 troops, with about 40,000 Georgian and Armenian auxiliaries, and routed the Egyptian Mamluks with their much smaller force of 20,000-30,000 troops. The Mamluks retreated, and were harassed by Maronite and Druze bowmen who wanted independence from the Mamluks. One group of Mongols also split off from Ghazan's army, and pursued the retreating Mamluk troops as far as Gaza,[185] pushing them back to Egypt.

The bulk of Ghazan's forces then proceeded onward towards Damascus. Some of the populace of Damascus upon hearing of the Mongol approach had fled

Mongol invasions of the Levant

Figure 35: *1299, The Battle of Wadi al-Khazandar. The Mongols under Ghazan defeated the Mamluks.*

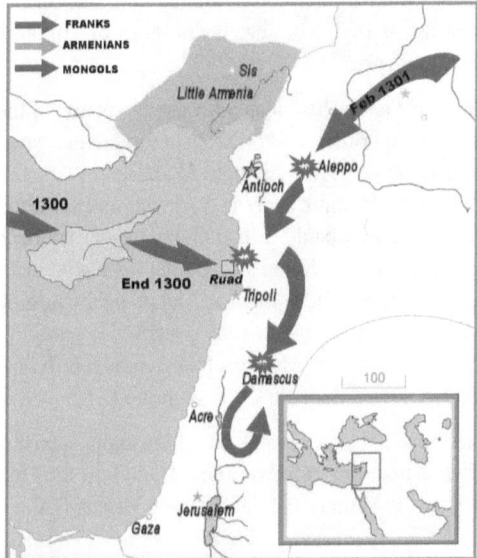

Figure 36: *1300–1301 operations from Ruad and Mongol offensives under Ghazan's general Kutluka.*

to Egypt, and the governor of the city, Arjawash, had entrenched himself deep inside the Citadel of Damascus. The Mongols besieged the city for ten days, which surrendered between December 30, 1299, and January 6, 1300, though its Citadel resisted.[186,187] Ghazan then withdrew most of his forces in February, promising to return in the winter of 1300–1301 to attack Egypt.[188] The reason for the withdrawal is believed to be either the Chagatai Mongols invading their eastern borders, or the need to retreat to areas where there was better grazing room for the horses. The Mamluks had learned that the availability of pastures was important to the Mongols, and so had taken to burning pastureland so as to prevent the rapid advance of the Mongol cavalry. After Ghazan's main force withdrew, only about 10,000 horsemen remained in Syria, under the Mongol general Mulay.

With the retreat of the majority of forces from both sides, for about three months, until the Mamluks returned in May 1300, Mulay's forces were in technical control over Syria,[189] and some Mongols engaged in raids as far south as Jerusalem and Gaza.[190,191,192,193] However, when the Mamluks returned from Egypt, the remaining Mongols retreated with little resistance.

Also in early 1300, two Frankish rulers, Guy d'Ibelin and Jean II de Giblet, had moved in with their troops from Cyprus in response to Ghazan's earlier call. They had established a base in the castle of Nefin in Gibelet (Byblos) on the Syrian coast with the intention of joining him, but Ghazan was already gone.[194,195] They also started to besiege the new city of Tripoli, but in vain,[196] and then returned to Cyprus.

In late 1300, Ghazan's forces had dealt with the distraction of the Chagatai invasion on their northern border, and once again turned their attention to Syria. They crossed the Euphrates river between December 14, 1300 and November 1, 1301. Again, the Mamluk army in Syria withdrew without engaging in combat, which resulted in a panic in Damascus when they heard of the new threat from the Mongols. The Syrians of Hamat were able to achieve a small victory against the Mongols at a battle near Aleppo by the post of Hamat. This created order in Damascus, enough for the governor to send for a larger relief force from Egypt. However, the Mongols had already left Syria due to a death in Ghazan Khan's family.Wikipedia:Citation needed

The Ilkhanate returned to Syria in 1303, travelling unopposed down the Levant until they reached Damascus. However, near Damascus they were once again soundly defeated by the Mamluks at the Battle of Marj al-Saffar in April 1303.

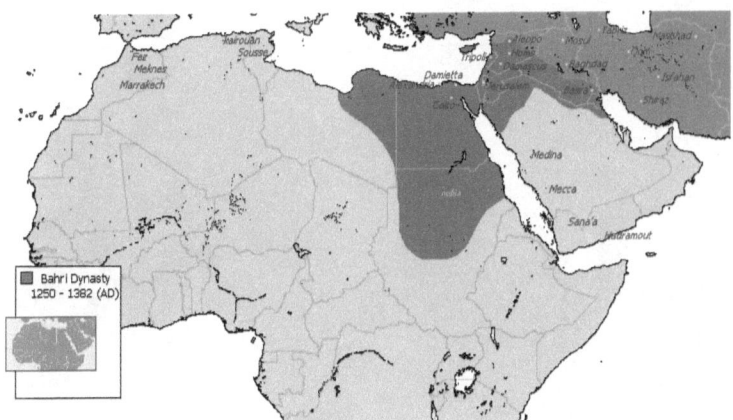

Figure 37: *Dominion of Bahri Mamluks (red)*

Final Stage: 1312

In 1313, the new khan of the Ilkhanate, Öljaitü, pursued an aggressive policy to consolidate his rule, subduing the Caspian Province of Gilan and destroying the autonomous principality of Herat. Encouraged by the defection of some Syrian emirs, Öljaitü decided to cross the Euphrates in 1312 to attack the Mamluk Sultanate. He laid siege to the heavily fortified town of Rahbat. After about a month of fighting in which they suffered heavy casualties, the Mongols ultimately failed to take the fortified place and withdrew. This was to be the last major Mongol incursion into the Levant.[197,198]

Treaty of Aleppo

Following the defeat of the Mongol ruler Ghazan and the progressive conversion of the Il-Khanate to Islam, the Mongols finally were amenable to ceasing hostilities. The first contacts to establish a treaty of peace were communicated via the slave trader al-Majd al-Sallami. After the initial communications, more formal letters and embassies were exchanged.[199] Under the Ilkhanate ruler Abu Sa'id, who was following the advice of his custodian Chupan, the treaty with the Mamluks was ratified in 1322/1323.

Following the treaty and a period of peace, the Il-Khanate further disintegrated, and effectively disappeared during the 14th century.

Figure 38: *The Mongol world, ca. 1300. The gray area is the later Timurid empire.*

References

- Abulafia, David. *The New Cambridge Medieval History*. Cambridge University Press. ISBN 0-521-36291-1.
- Amitai, Reuven (1987). "Mongol Raids into Palestine (AD 1260 and 1300)". *JRAS*: 236–255.
- Grousset, René (1935). *Histoire des Croisades III, 1188-1291* (in French). Editions Perrin. ISBN 2-262-02569-X.
- Demurger, Alain (2007). *Jacques de Molay* (in French). Editions Payot&Rivages. ISBN 2-228-90235-7.
- Jackson, Peter (2005). *The Mongols and the West: 1221-1410*. Longman. ISBN 978-0-582-36896-5.
- Lebédel, Claude (2006). *Les Croisades, origines et conséquences* (in French). Editions Ouest-France. ISBN 2-7373-4136-1.
- Luisetto, Frédéric (2007). Arméniens & autres Chrétiens d'Orient sous la domination Mongole (in French). Librairie Orientaliste Paul Geuthner S.A. ISBN 9782705337919*Maalouf, Amin (1984). *The Crusades Through Arab Eyes*. New York: Schocken Books. ISBN 0-8052-0898-4.
- Maalouf, Amin (1983). *Les croisades vues par les Arabes*. JC Lattes.

- Michaud, Yahia (Oxford Centre for Islamic Studies) (2002). *Ibn Taymiyya, Textes Spirituels I-XVI*[200] (PDF) (in French). "Le Musulman", Oxford-Le Chebec.
- Morgan, David (2007). *The Mongols* (2nd ed.). Blackwell Publishing. ISBN 978-1-4051-3539-9.
- Richard, Jean (1996). *Histoire des Croisades*. Fayard. ISBN 2-213-59787-1.
- Runciman, Steven (1987) [1952-1954]. *A history of the Crusades 3*. Penguin Books. ISBN 978-0-14-013705-7.
- Schein, Sylvia (October 1979). "Gesta Dei per Mongolos 1300. The Genesis of a Non-Event". *The English Historical Review*. **94** (373): 805–819. ISSN 0013-8266[201]. JSTOR 565554[202]. doi: 10.1093/ehr/XCIV.CCCLXXIII.805[203].

External links

- Adh-Dhababi (translated by Joseph Somogyi) (1948). "Record of the Destruction of Damascus by the Mongols in 1299-1301". *Ignace Goldziher Memorial Volume, Part 1*.

Mongol invasions of Anatolia

Mongol invasions of Anatolia occurred at various times, starting with the campaign of 1241–1243 that culminated in the Battle of Köse Dağ. Real power over Anatolia was exercised by the Mongols after the Seljuks surrendered in 1243 until the fall of the Ilkhanate in 1335.[204] Because the Seljuk Sultan rebelled several times, in 1255, the Mongols swept through central and eastern Anatolia. The Ilkhanate garrison was stationed near Ankara.[205,206] Timur's invasion is sometimes considered the last invasion of Anatolia by the Mongols. Remains of the Mongol cultural heritage still can be seen in Turkey, including tombs of a Mongol governor and a son of Hulagu.

By the end of the 14th century, most of Anatolia was controlled by various Anatolian beyliks due to the collapse of the Seljuk dynasty in Rum. The Turkmen Beyliks were under the control of the Mongols through declining Seljuk Sultans.[207,208] The Beyliks did not mint coins in the names of their own leaders while they remained under the suzerainty of the Ilkhanids.[209] The Ottoman ruler Osman I was the first Turkish ruler who minted coins in his own name in the 1320s, for it bears the legend "Minted by Osman son of Ertuğrul".[210] Since the minting of coins was a prerogative accorded in Islamic practice only to be a sovereign, it can be considered that the Ottomans became independent of the Mongol Khans.[211]

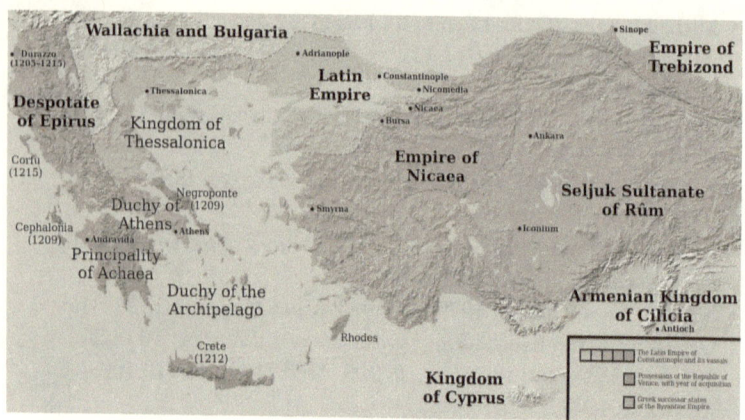

Figure 39: *Map showing the partition of the Byzantine Empire into the Latin Empire, Empire of Nicaea and Despotate of Epirus before the Mongol conquest.*

Early relations

In the 12th century, the Byzantine Empire reasserted control in Western and Northern Anatolia. After the sack of Constantinople in 1204 by Latin Crusaders, two Byzantine successor states were established: the Empire of Nicaea, and the Despotate of Epirus. A third one, the Empire of Trebizond was created a few weeks before the sack of Constantinople by Alexios I of Trebizond. Of these three successor states, Trebizond and Nicaea stood near the Mongolian Empire. Control of Anatolia was then split between the Greek states and the Seljuk Sultanate of Rum, with the Byzantine holdings gradually being reduced.

The Mongol Empire conquered Persia in 1230; Chormaqan became military governor. There were then no hostilities with the Seljuk Turks. 'Ala al-Din Kayqubad I and his immediate successor Giyath al-Din Kaykhusraw II swore an oath of vassalage with the payment of at least token tribute to the Great Khan Ögedei.[212,213] However, in 1238 the Mongols raided part of Greater Armenia, which was a vassal of the Sultan of Rum.

Ögedei died in 1241, and Kaykhusraw took the opportunity to repudiate his vassalage, believing he was strong enough to resist the Mongols. Chormaqan's successor Baiju summoned him to renew his submission: go to Mongolia in person, give hostages, and accept a Mongol darughachi. When the Sultan refused, Baiju declared war. The Seljuks invaded the Kingdom of Georgia, part of the Mongol Empire.

Fall of Karin

Baiju's army attacked Karin in relation to Kaykhusraw's disobedience in 1241. Before attacking, Baiju demanded submission. The inhabitants of the city insulted the Mongol envoy sent by him. Since the city decided to resist and defied Mongol diplomacy, the Mongols besieged it. In two months, the Mongols took Karin and punished its residents. Aware of the Seljuk power in Anatolia, Baiju returned to the Mugan plain without advancing further.

Campaign in Erzurum

Baiju advanced to Erzurum with a contingent of Georgian and Armenian warriors under Awag and Shansheh in 1243. They besieged the city of Erzurum when its governor Yakut refused to surrender it. With the power of twelve catapults, Baiju stormed Erzurum. When the reports of the attack on Erzurum reported to him, Kaykhusraw summoned his armed forces at Konya. He accepted the challenge by sending a war message, defying Baiju that his army took only one of his many cities.

Figure 40: *The Mongolian army chases the Seljuks at the battle of Köse Dağ in 1243.*

Köse Dağ

The Seljuk Sultan made an alliance with all nations surrounding him. The King of Lesser Armenia (Armenian Kingdom of Cilicia) promised him to send a contingent; however, it is not certain they really engaged in his struggle with the Mongols. Kaykhusraw received the military support from the Empire of Trebizond and the Ayyubid Sultan at Aleppo, and the Frankish mercenaries participated in the campaign.[215] Because of little reliable information, it is difficult to measure the opposing troops. But the Seljuk force was larger than the Mongols.

Kaykhusraw advanced from Konya some 200 miles up to Köse Dağ. The Mongolian army entered the area in June 1243 and awaited the march of the Seljuks and their allies. The early stage of the battle was indecisive. The Sultan's forces suffered the greater casualties and he decided to withdraw at night. Pursuing him, Baiju received the submission of Erzinjan, Divrigi and Sivas en route.

The Mongols set up their camp near Sivas. When the Mongols penetrated into Kayseri, it chose to resist them. After a short resistance, it fell to the invaders. Hearing of the disaster at Köse Dağ, Hethum I of Armenian Kingdom of Cilicia quickly made his peace with the Mongols in 1243 and sent his brother Sembat to the Mongol court of Karakorum in 1247 to negotiate an alliance with the Mongolian Emperor Güyük.

Figure 41: *The control of the Mongol Empire over Anatolia in 1265.*[216]

Peace of Sivas

Kaykhusraw sent a delegation headed by his vizier to Baiju, realizing the further resistance would only produce a great disaster. Baiju offered terms based on resubmission and the Sultan was undertaken to pay a tribute tax every year in gold, silk, camel and sheep of uncertain quantities. However, the Turkish realm that had been taken by the military force remained occupied by the Mongols. Almost half of the Sultanate of Rum became an occupied country. The Empire of Trebizond became subject to the Mongolian Qaghan, fearing of the potential punitive expedition because they involved in the battle of Köse Dağ.[217]

In the Empire of Nicaea John III Doukas Vatatzes prepared for the coming Mongol threat. However, Vatatzes had sent envoys to the Qaghans Güyük and Möngke but was playing for time. The Mongol Empire did not cause any harm to his plan to recapture Constantinople from the hands of the Latins who also sent their envoy to the Mongols. Vatatzes' successors, the Palaiologan emperors of the restored Byzantine Empire, made an alliance with the Mongols, giving their princesses in marriage to the Mongol khans.

Mongol conquest of Khwarezmia

Mongol conquest of Khwarezmia	
Part of the Mongol invasion of Central Asia	
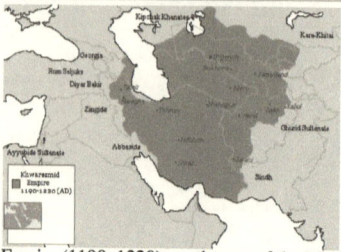 Khwarezmid Empire (1190–1220), on the eve of the Mongol conquests	
Date	1219–1221
Location	Central Asia, Iran, Afghanistan
Result	Decisive Mongol victory
Territorial changes	Khwarezmia annexed to the Mongol Empire
Belligerents	
Mongol Empire	Khwarazmian dynasty
Commanders and leaders	
Genghis Khan Jochi Chaghatai Ögedei Tolui Subutai Jebe Jelme Mukali Khubilai Qasar Bo'orchu Sorkin-shara	Ala ad-Din Muhammad Jalal ad-Din Mingburnu Inalchuq ☠ Temur Meliq
Units involved	
horse archers heavy cavalry lancers auxiliaries, engineers, and specialists siege engines, including Chinese gunpowder weapons Drafted Khwarizmian civilians	Predominantly city garrisons
Strength	
Disputed (see below). Estimates include: • 75,000 • 120,000-200,000 • 700,000 • 150,000 • 800,000	Disputed (see below). Estimates include: • 40,000 • 200,000 • 400,000 • ~400,000

Casualties and losses	
unknown	1.25 million killed including civilians (25% of the population)[218]

The **Mongol conquest of Khwarezmia** from 1219 to 1221[219] marked the beginning of the Mongol conquest of the Islamic states. The Mongol expansion would ultimately culminate in the conquest of virtually all of Asia (as well as parts of Eastern Europe) save for Japan, the Mamluk Sultanate of Egypt and most of the Indian subcontinent and Southeast Asia.

It was not originally the intention of the Mongol Empire to invade the Khwarezmid Empire. According to the Persian historian Juzjani, Genghis Khan had originally sent the ruler of the Khwarezmid Empire, Ala ad-Din Muhammad, a message seeking trade and greeted him as his neighbor: "I am master of the lands of the rising sun while you rule those of the setting sun. Let us conclude a firm treaty of friendship and peace." or he said "I am Khan of the lands of the rising sun while you are sultan those of the setting sun: Let us conclude a firm agreement of friendship and peace."[220] The Mongols' original unification of all "people in felt tents", unifying the nomadic tribes in Mongolia and then the Turcomens and other nomadic peoples, had come with relatively little bloodshed, and almost no material loss. The Mongol wars with the Jurchens however had shown how cruel the Mongols could be. Shah Muhammad reluctantly agreed to this peace treaty, but it was not to last. The war started less than a year later, when a Mongol caravan and its envoys were massacred in the Khwarezmian city of Otrar.

In the ensuing war, lasting less than two years, the Khwarezmid Empire was destroyed.

Origins of the conflict

After the defeat of the Kara-Khitans, Genghis Khan's Mongol Empire gained a border with the Khwarezmid Empire, governed by Shah Ala ad-Din Muhammad. The Shah had only recently taken some of the territory under his control, and he was also busy with a dispute with the caliph in Baghdad, An-Nasir. The Shah had refused to make the obligatory homage to the caliph as titular leader of Islam, and demanded recognition as Shah of his empire, without any of the usual bribes or pretenses. This alone had created problems for him along his southern border. It was at this junction the rapidly expanding Mongol Empire made contact.[221] Mongol historians are adamant that the great khan at that time had no intention of invading the Khwarezmid Empire, and was only interested in trade and even a potential alliance.[222]

The Shah was very suspicious of Genghis' desire for a trade agreement, and messages from the Shah's ambassador at Zhongdu (Beijing) in China described the exaggerated savagery of the Mongols when they assaulted the city during their war with the Jin Dynasty.[223] Of further interest is that the caliph of Baghdad had attempted to instigate a war between the Mongols and the Shah some years before the Mongol invasion actually occurred. This attempt at an alliance with Genghis was made because of a dispute between Nasir and the Shah, but the Khan had no interest in alliance with any ruler who claimed ultimate authority, titular or not, and which marked the Caliphate for an extinction which would come from Genghis' grandson, Hulegu. At the time, this attempt by the Caliph involved the Shah's ongoing claim to be named sultan of Khwarezm, something that Nasir had no wish to grant, as the Shah refused to acknowledge his authority, however illusory such authority was. However, it is known that Genghis rejected the notion of war as he was engaged in war with the Jin Dynasty and was gaining much wealth from trading with the Khwarezmid Empire.Wikipedia:Citation needed

Genghis then sent a 500-man caravan of Muslims to establish official trade ties with Khwarezmia. However Inalchuq, the governor of the Khwarezmian city of Otrar, had the members of the caravan that came from Mongolia arrested, claiming that the caravan was a conspiracy against Khwarezmia. It seems unlikely, however, that any members of the trade delegation were spies. Nor does it seem likely that Genghis was trying to initiate a conflict with the Khwarezmid Empire with the caravan, considering he was making steady progress against a faltering Jin empire in northern China at that very moment.

Genghis Khan then sent a second group of three ambassadors (one Muslim and two Mongols) to meet the shah himself and demand the caravan at Otrar be set free and the governor be handed over for punishment. The shah had both of the Mongols shaved and had the Muslim beheaded before sending them back to Genghis Khan. Muhammad also ordered the personnel of the caravan to be executed. This was seen as a grave affront to the Khan himself, who considered ambassadors "as sacred and inviolable."[224] This led Genghis Khan to attack the Khwarezmian Dynasty. The Mongols crossed the Tian Shan mountains, coming into the Shah's empire in 1219.[225]

Planning and Dispositions

After compiling information from many intelligence sources, primarily from spies along the Silk Road, Genghis Khan carefully prepared his army, which was organized differently from his earlier campaigns.[226] The changes had come in adding supporting units to his dreaded cavalry, both heavy and light.

Figure 42: *Battle of Vâliyân (1221). Jami' al-tawarikh, Rashid al-Din.*

While still relying on the traditional advantages of his mobile nomadic cavalry, Genghis incorporated many aspects of warfare from China, particularly in siege warfare. His baggage train included such siege equipment as battering rams, gunpowder, and enormous siege bows capable of throwing 20-foot arrows into siege works. Also, the Mongol intelligence network was formidable. The Mongols never invaded an opponent whose military and economic will and ability to resist had not been thoroughly and completely scouted. For instance, Subutai and Batu Khan spent a year scouting central Europe, before destroying the armies of Hungary and Poland in two separate battles, two days apart.[227]

In this invasion, the Khan first demonstrated the use of indirect attack that would become a hallmark of his later campaigns, and those of his sons and grandsons. The Khan divided his armies, and sent one force solely to find and execute the Shah – so that he was forced to run for his life in his own country. The divided Mongol forces destroyed the Shah's forces piecemeal, and began the utter devastation of the country which would mark many of their later conquests.

The Shah's army, numbering anywhere from 40,000 to 200,000 (mostly city garrisons), was split among the various major cities, bar an elite unit of cavalry stationed near Samarkand as a reserve force. The empire had just recently conquered much of its territory, and the Shah was fearful that his army, if placed in one large unit under a single command structure, might possibly be turned against him. Furthermore, the Shah's reports from China indicated that the Mongols were not experts in siege warfare, and experienced problems when attempting to take fortified positions. The Shah's decisions on troop deployment would prove disastrous as the campaign unfolded, as the Mongol speed, surprise, and enduring initiative prevented the Shah from effectively maneuvering his forces.

Forces

The estimates for the sizes of the opposing armies are often in dispute. It is certain that all contemporary and near-contemporary sources (or at least those that have survived), consider the Mongols to have been the numerically superior force.[228] Several chroniclers, a notable one being Rashid Al-Din (a historian of the Ilkhanate) provide the figures of 400,000 for the Shah (spread across the whole empire) and 600,000 or 700,000 for the Khan.[229] The Ilkhanate historian Juvayni, in his *Tarikh-i Jahangushay,* also gives a Mongol army size of 700,000. 800,000 for Genghis was claimed by the contemporary Muslim chronicler Minhaj-i-Siraj Juzjani. Modern historians still debate to what degree these numbers reflected reality. David Morgan and Denis Sinor, among others, doubt the numbers are true in either absolute or relative terms, while John Mason Smith sees the numbers as accurate as for both armies (while supporting high-end numbers for the Mongols and their enemies in general, for instance contending that Rashid Al-Din was correct when stating that the Ilkhanate of the 1260s had 300,000 soldiers and the Golden Horde 300,000-600,000).[230] Sinor uses the figure of 400,000 for the Khwarezmians, but puts the Mongol force at 150,000. The Secret History of the Mongols, a Mongol source, states that the Mongols had 105,000 soldiers total (in the whole empire, not just on a campaign) in 1206, 134,500 in 1211, and 129,000 (excluding some far-flung units) in 1227. No similarly reliable source exists for corresponding Kwharezm figures.[231]

Carl Sverdrup, using a variety of sources and estimation methods, gives the number of 75,000 for the Mongol army. Sverdrup also estimates the Khwarezmian army at 40,000 (excluding certain city-restricted militias), and emphasizes that all contemporary sources are in agreement that, if nothing else, the Mongol army was the larger of the two. He states that he came to 40,000 by first calculating the size of the Mongol army based on their historical records, and then assuming the Kwharezmian army was exaggerated by the pro-Mongol historians such as Rashid Al-Din to about the same magnitude as the Mongol army was by both Rashid Al-Din and anti-Mongol chroniclers such as Juzjani.[232] McLynn also says that 400,000 is a massive exaggeration, but considers 200,000 to be closer to the truth (including garrisons).[233] As for the Mongols, he estimates them at 120,000 effectives, out of a total Mongol strength of 200,000 (including troops nominally on the campaign but never engaged, and those in China).[234] Genghis brought along his most able generals, besides Muqali to aid him. Genghis also brought a large body of foreigners with him, primarily of Chinese origin. These foreigners were siege experts, bridge-building experts, doctors and a variety of specialty soldiers.

The only hard evidence of the empire's potential military strength comes from a census ordered by Hulegu Khan of the same regions a few decades later. At that point Hulegu ruled almost all the lands of the former Khwarezmian empire including Persia, modern-day Turkmenistan, and Afghanistan, only missing most of modern-day Uzbekistan and Tajikistan, and the region had had over 40 years to recover population-wise from the initial conquest. These lands were judged to be able to muster five tümens in all.[235] Nominally each tumen was supposed to consist of 10,000 men, but they usually averaged 5,000 men.[236] If Hulegu's census was accurate, then the bulk of the former Khwarezmian lands together could field 25,000 soldiers, lending credence to Sverdrup's estimate of 40,000 troops in total.

During the invasion of Transoxania in 1219, along with the main Mongol force, Genghis Khan used a Chinese specialist catapult unit in battle; they were used again in 1220 in Transoxania. The Chinese may have used the catapults to hurl gunpowder bombs, since they already had them by this time. While Genghis Khan was conquering Transoxania and Persia, several Chinese who were familiar with gunpowder were serving with Genghis's army. Historians have suggested that the Mongol invasion had brought Chinese gunpowder weapons to Central Asia. One of these was the huochong, a Chinese mortar.

Khwarezmian weakness and disunity

In addition to quite possibly outnumbering the force of the Shah, and definitely possessing more horsemen in total and more men at almost every battle, the Mongols were benefited enormously by the fragility of the Khwarezmian empire. While often portrayed as a strong and unified state, most of the Shah's holdings were recent conquests only nominally sworn to him, to the point that the Shah didn't feel like he could trust most of his troops. In the words of historian C.E. Bosworth: "[the dynasty was] highly unpopular and a focus for popular hatred; in none of the provinces they ruled did the Khwarazm Shahs ever succeed in creating a bond of interest between themselves and their subjects."[237] This resulted in him parsing them in garrisons to be commanded by local governors that acted more or less autonomously. There was no attempt to coordinate a grand strategy among the various provinces or unite a significant number of forces in one unified front against the invaders.[238] Additionally, many of the areas that Muhammad charged his troops to defend had been devastated recently by the forces of the Shah himself. For example, in 1220 he

Figure 43: *Madrasah Kukaldash (Tashkent)*

passed through Nishapur and urged the citizens to repair the fortifications he had destroyed when conquering the city years earlier.[239]

The lack of unity in the empire often resulted in large sections of the Shah's army folding with little or no fighting when the Mongols arrived. According to Ibn al-Athir, when Bukhara was attacked most of the Khwarazmian army simply deserted and left the city, leaving the now poorly-defended settlement to seek terms.[240] When Samarkand was subsequently attacked, the Turkic soldiers in the city who felt no loyalty towards the Shah allegedly said of the Mongols: "We are their race. They will not kill us." They surrendered after only four days of fighting before turning the city over to the Mongols on the fifth. However they were executed along with much of the city's population regardless, much to their surprise.[241] Balkh's garrison surrendered without a fight. Merv's garrison surrendered after seven days and a few minor sorties (of only around a couple hundred men each, according to the pro-Mongol Juvayni); they were also all executed, again to their shock.[242] The only major cities known to put up a stout defense were Otrar, which managed to hold out for six months before being captured by the Mongols amidst heavy casualties and a large delay for the Mongol army, and Urgench, where Ibn al-Athir claimed that Mongol losses exceeded those of the defending soldiers for one of the only times in the war.[243,244] The unreliability of the Shah's army was probably most decisive when his son Jalal al-Din's cavalry host simply disintegrated due to desertion as his Afghan and Turkic allies disagreed with him over the distribution of war booty. His forces were reduced heavily which allowed the Mongols to easily overcome them at the Indus River.[245] The Mongols took full advantage of these circumstances with their network of spies, often aided by merchants who had much to gain from Mongol domination and spread rumors imploring the inhabitants of cities to surrender.[246]

Khwarezmian structure

Another advantage for the Mongols was the fact that, compared to most of China, Korea, Central/Western Europe, and many other areas, Khwarezmia was deficient in terms of fortifications. In most of the empire there was no system of forts outside of the walls of major cities, and even the most important cities such as Samarkand and Otrar had their walls constructed out of mud bricks which could be easily reduced by Mongol siege engines.[247] This meant that the Mongols, rather than getting bogged down in dozens of small sieges or single multi-year ones as sometimes happened in China, could simply sweep through large areas of the empire and conquer cities at will in a short time. They had more difficulty in subduing Afghanistan, which had a fortress network, though the relative scarcity of fortresses in the whole of the empire and the ease with which the Mongols subdued large sections of it meant that this didn't matter on a strategic scale. The fortress of Ashiyar held for 15 months of besiegement before falling (requiring the attention of a significant chunk of the Mongol army) while Saif-Rud and Tulak took heavy casualties for the Mongols to subdue. The siege of Bamyan also claimed the life of Chagatai's favorite son, Mötüken.[248]

The urban population of the empire was concentrated in a relatively small number of (by medieval standards) very large cities as opposed to a huge number of smaller towns, which also aided in the Mongols' conquest. The population of the empire is estimated at 5 million people on the eve of the invasion, making it sparse for the large area it covered.[249,250] Historical demographers Tertius Chandler and Gerald Fox give the following estimations for the populations of the empire's major cities at the beginning of the 13th century, which adds up to at least 520,000 and at most 850,000 people:[251]

- Samarkand: 80,000-100,000
- Nipashur: 70,000
- Rayy/Rey: 100,000
- Isfahan: 80,000
- Merv: 70,000
- Balkh: c. 30,000
- Bost: c. 40,000
- Herat: c. 40,000

- Otrar, Urgench, and Bukhara: unknown, but <70,000[252]

The Khwarezmian army consisted of about 40,000 cavalry, mostly of Turkic origin. Militias existed in Khwarezmia's major cities but were of poor quality, and the Shah had trouble mustering them in time.[253] With collective populations of around 700,000, the major cities probably had 105,000 to 140,000 healthy males of fighting age in total (15-20% of the population), but only a fraction of these would be part of a formal militia with any notable measure of training and equipment.

Initial invasion

Though they technically bordered each other, the Mongol and Khwarezm Empires touched far away from the homeland of each nation. In between them was a series of treacherous mountain ranges that the invader would have to cross. This aspect is often overlooked in this campaign, yet it was a critical reason why the Mongols were able to create a dominating position. The Khwarezm Shah and his advisers assumed that the Mongols would invade through the Dzungarian Gate, the natural mountain pass in between their (now conquered) Khara-Khitai and Khwarezm Empires. One option for the Khwarezm defense was to advance beyond the towns of the Syr Darya and block the Dzungarian Gate with an army, since it would take Genghis many months to gather his army in Mongolia and advance through the pass after winter had passed. The Khwarezm decision makers believed they would have time to further refine their strategy, but the Khan had struck first.[254]

Immediately when war was declared, Genghis sent orders for a force already out to the west to immediately cross the Tien Shan mountains to the south and ravage the fertile Ferghana Valley in the eastern part of the Khwarezm Empire. This smaller detachment, no more than 20-30,000 men, was led by Genghis's son Jochi and his elite general Jebe. The Tien Shan mountain passes were much more treacherous than the Dzungarian Gate, and to make it worse, they attempted the crossing in the middle of winter with 5+ feet of snow. Though the Mongols suffered losses and were exhausted from the crossing, their presence in the Ferghana Valley stunned the Khwarezm leadership and permanently stole the initiative away. This march can be described as the Central Asian equivalent of Hannibal's crossing of the Alps, with the same devastating effects. Because the Shah did not know if this Mongol army was a diversion or their main army, he had to protect one of his most fertile regions with force. Therefore, the Shah dispatched his elite cavalry reserve, which prevented him from effectively marching anywhere else with his main army. Jebe and Jochi seem to have kept their army in good shape while plundering the valley, and they avoided defeat by a much superior force. At this point the

Mongols split up and again maneuvered over the mountains: Jebe marched further south deeper into Khwarezm territory, while Jochi took most of the force northwest to attack the exposed cities on the Syr Darya from the east.[255]

Otrar

Meanwhile, another Mongol force under Chagatai and Ogedei descended from either the Altai Mountains to the north or the Dzungarian Gate and immediately started laying siege to the border city of Otrar. Rashid Al-Din stated that Otrar had a garrison of 20,000 while Juvayni claimed 60,000 (horsemen and militia), though like the army figures given in most medieval chronicles, these numbers should be treated with caution and are probably exaggerated by an order of magnitude considering the size of the city.[256] Genghis, who had marched through the Altai mountains, kept his main force further back near the mountain ranges, and stayed out of contact. Frank McLynn argues that this disposition can only be explained as Genghis laying a trap for the Shah. Were the Shah to march his army up from Samarkand to attack the besiegers of Otrar, Genghis could then rapidly encircle the Shah's army from the rear. However, the Shah dodged the trap, and Genghis had to change plans.[257]

Unlike most of the other cities, Otrar did not surrender after little fighting, nor did its governor march its army out into the field to be destroyed by the numerically superior Mongols. Instead the garrison remained on the walls and resisted stubbornly, holding out against many attacks. The siege proceeded for five months without results, until a traitor within the walls (Qaracha) who felt no loyalty to the Shah or Inalchuq opened the gates to the Mongols; the prince's forces managed to storm the now unsecured gate and slaughter the majority of the garrison.[258] The citadel, holding the remaining 1/10 of the garrison, held out for another month, and was only taken after heavy Mongol casualties. Inalchuq held out until the end, even climbing to the top of the citadel in the last moments of the siege to throw down tiles at the oncoming Mongols and slay many of them in close quarters combat. Genghis killed many of the inhabitants, enslaved the rest, and executed Inalchuq.[259]

Sieges of Bukhara, Samarkand, and Urgench

At this point, the Mongol army was divided into five widely separated groups on opposite ends of the enemy Empire. After the Shah did not mount an active defense of the cities on the Syr Darya, Genghis and Tolui, at the head of an army of roughly 50,000 men, skirted the natural defense barrier of the Syr Darya and its fortified cities, and went westwards to lay siege to the city of Bukhara first. To do this, they traversed 300 miles of the seemingly impassable Kyzyl Kum desert by hopping through the various oases, guided most of

Figure 44: *Ruins of Muhammad's palace in Urgench.*

the way by captured nomads. The Mongols arrived at the gates of Bukhara virtually unnoticed. Many military tacticians regard this surprise entrance to Bukhara as one of the most successful maneuvers in warfare.[260] Whatever Mohammed II was intending to do, Genghis's maneuver across his rear completely stole away his initiative and prevented him from carrying out any possible plans. The Khwarezm army could only slowly react to the lightning fast Mongol maneuvers.

Bukhara

Bukhara was not heavily fortified, with a moat and a single wall, and the citadel typical of Khwarezmi cities. The Bukharan garrison was made up of Turkic soldiers and led by Turkic generals, who attempted to break out on the third day of the siege. Rashid Al-Din and Ibn Al-Athir state that the city had 20,000 defenders, though Carl Sverdrup contends that it only had a tenth of this number.[261] A break-out force was annihilated in open battle. The city leaders opened the gates to the Mongols, though a unit of Turkish defenders held the city's citadel for another twelve days. Survivors from the citadel were executed, artisans and craftsmen were sent back to Mongolia, young men who had not fought were drafted into the Mongolian army and the rest of the population was sent into slavery. As the Mongol soldiers looted the city, a fire broke out, razing most of the city to the ground.²⁶² Genghis Khan had the people assemble in the main mosque of the town, where he declared that he was the flail of God, sent to punish them for their sins.Wikipedia:Citation needed

Samarkand

After the fall of Bukhara, Genghis headed to the Khwarezmian capital of Samarkand and arrived in March 1220. During this period, the Mongols also waged effective psychological warfare and caused divisions within their foe. The Khan's spies told him of the bitter fighting between the Shah and his mother, who commanded the allegiance of some of his most senior commanders and his elite Turkish cavalry divisions. Since Mongols and Turks are both steppe peoples, Genghis argued that Tertun Khatun and her army should join the Mongols against her treacherous son. Meanwhile, he arranged for deserters to bring letters that said Tertun Khatun and some of her generals had allied with the Mongols. This further inflamed the existing divisions in the Khwarezm Empire, and probably prevented the senior commanders from unifying their forces. Genghis then compounded the damage by repeatedly issuing bogus decrees in the name of either Tertun Khatun or Shah Mohammed, further tangling up the already divided Khwarezm command structure.²⁶³ As a result of the Mongol strategic initiative, speedy maneuvers, and psychological strategies, all the Khwarezm generals, including the Queen Mother, kept their forces as a garrison and were defeated in turn.

Samarkand possessed significantly better fortifications and a larger garrison compared to Bukhara. Juvayni and Rashid Al-Din (both writing under Mongol auspices) credit the defenders of the city with 100,000-110,000 men, while Ibn Al-Athir states 50,000.²⁶⁴ A more likely number is perhaps 10,000, considering the city itself had less than 100,000 people total at the time.²⁶⁵,²⁶⁶ As Genghis began his siege, his sons Chaghatai and Ögedei joined him after finishing the reduction of Otrar, and the joint Mongol forces launched an assault on the city. The Mongols attacked using prisoners as body shields. On the third day of fighting, the Samarkand garrison launched a counterattack. Feigning retreat, Genghis drew approximately half of the garrison outside the fortifications of Samarkand and slaughtered them in open combat. Shah Muhammad attempted to relieve the city twice, but was driven back. On the fifth day, all but a handful of soldiers surrendered. The remaining soldiers, die-hard supporters of the Shah, held out in the citadel. After the fortress fell, Genghis reneged on his surrender terms and executed every soldier that had taken arms against him at Samarkand. The people of Samarkand were ordered to evacuate and assemble in a plain outside the city, where many were killed.²⁶⁷

About the time of the fall of Samarkand, Genghis Khan charged Subutai and Jebe, two of the Khan's top generals, with hunting down the Shah. The Shah

TERKEN KHATUN, THE MOTHER OF SULTAN MUHAMMAD, BEING LED CAPTIVE BY THE MONGOLS
from a very old MS. of Rashid-ad-Din in the Bibliothèque Nationale

Figure 45: *Terken Khatun, Empress of the Khwarazmian Empire, known as "the Queen of the Turks", held captive by Mongol army.*

had fled west with some of his most loyal soldiers and his son, Jalal al-Din, to a small island in the Caspian Sea. It was there, in December 1220, that the Shah died. Most scholars attribute his death to pneumonia, but others cite the sudden shock of the loss of his empire.Wikipedia:Citation needed

Urgench

Meanwhile, the wealthy trading city of Urgench was still in the hands of Khwarezmian forces. Previously, the Shah's mother had ruled Urgench, but she fled when she learned her son had absconded to the Caspian Sea. She was captured and sent to Mongolia. Khumar Tegin, one of Muhammad's generals, declared himself Sultan of Urgench. Jochi, who had been on campaign in the north since the invasion, approached the city from that direction, while Genghis, Ögedei, and Chaghatai attacked from the south.

The assault on Urgench proved to be the most difficult battle of the Mongol invasion. The city was built along the river Amu Darya in a marshy delta area. The soft ground did not lend itself to siege warfare, and there was a lack of large stones for the catapults. The Mongols attacked regardless, and the city fell only after the defenders put up a stout defense, fighting block for block. Mongolian casualties were higher than normal, due to the unaccustomed difficulty of adapting Mongolian tactics to city fighting.

The taking of Urgench was further complicated by continuing tensions between the Khan and his eldest son, Jochi, who had been promised the city as his prize.

Jochi's mother was the same as his three brothers': Genghis Khan's teen bride, and apparent lifelong love, Borte. Only her sons were counted as Genghis's "official" sons and successors, rather than those conceived by the Khan's 500 or so other "wives and consorts." But Jochi had been conceived in controversy; in the early days of the Khan's rise to power, Borte was captured and raped while she was held prisoner. Jochi was born nine months later. While Genghis Khan chose to acknowledge him as his oldest son (primarily due to his love for Borte, whom he would have had to reject had he rejected her child), questions had always existed over Jochi's true parentage.[268]

Such tensions were present as Jochi engaged in negotiations with the defenders, trying to get them to surrender so that as much of the city as possible was undamaged. This angered Chaghatai, and Genghis headed off this sibling fight by appointing Ögedei the commander of the besieging forces as Urgench fell. But the removal of Jochi from command, and the sack of a city he considered promised to him, enraged him and estranged him from his father and brothers, and is credited with being a decisive impetus for the later actions of a man who saw his younger brothers promoted over him, despite his own considerable military skills.

As usual, the artisans were sent back to Mongolia, young women and children were given to the Mongol soldiers as slaves, and the rest of the population was massacred. The Persian scholar Juvayni states that 50,000 Mongol soldiers were given the task of executing twenty-four Urgench citizens each, which would mean that 1.2 million people were killed. While this is almost certainly an exaggeration, the sacking of Urgench is considered one of the bloodiest massacres in human history.Wikipedia:Citation needed

Then came the complete destruction of the city of Gurjang, south of the Aral Sea. Upon its surrender the Mongols broke the dams and flooded the city, then proceeded to execute the survivors.Wikipedia:Citation needed

The Khorasan campaign

As the Mongols battered their way into Urgench, Genghis dispatched his youngest son Tolui, at the head of an army, into the western Khwarezmid province of Khorasan. Khorasan had already felt the strength of Mongol arms. Earlier in the war, the generals Jebe and Subutai had travelled through the province while hunting down the fleeing Shah. However, the region was far from subjugated, many major cities remained free of Mongol rule, and the region was rife with rebellion against the few Mongol forces present in the region, following rumors that the Shah's son Jalal al-Din was gathering an army to fight the Mongols.

Balkh

Tolui's army consisted of somewhere around 50,000 men, which was composed of a core of Mongol soldiers (some estimates place it at 7,000[269]), supplemented by a large body of foreign soldiers, such as Turks and previously conquered peoples in China and Mongolia. The army also included "3,000 machines flinging heavy incendiary arrows, 300 catapults, 700 mangonels to discharge pots filled with naphtha, 4,000 storming-ladders, and 2,500 sacks of earth for filling up moats." Among the first cities to fall was Termez then Balkh.

Merv

The major city to fall to Tolui's army was the city of Merv. Juvayni wrote of Merv: "In extent of territory it excelled among the lands of Khorasan, and the bird of peace and security flew over its confines. The number of its chief men rivaled the drops of April rain, and its earth contended with the heavens." The garrison at Merv was only about 12,000 men, and the city was inundated with refugees from eastern Khwarezmia. For six days, Tolui besieged the city, and on the seventh day, he assaulted the city. However, the garrison beat back the assault and launched their own counter-attack against the Mongols. The garrison force was similarly forced back into the city. The next day, the city's governor surrendered the city on Tolui's promise that the lives of the citizens would be spared. As soon as the city was handed over, however, Tolui slaughtered almost every person who surrendered, in a massacre possibly on a greater scale than that at Urgench.

Nishapur

After finishing off Merv, Tolui headed westwards, attacking the cities of Nishapur and Herat.[270] Nishapur fell after only three days; here, Tokuchar, a son-in-law of Genghis was killed in battle, and Tolui put to the sword to every living thing in the city, including the cats and dogs, with Tokuchar's widow presiding over the slaughter. After Nishapur's fall, Herat surrendered without a fight and was spared.

Bamian in the Hindukush was another scene of carnage during the 1221 siege of Bamiyan, here stiff resistance resulted in the death of a grandson of Genghis. Next were the cities of Toos and Mashad. By spring 1221, the province of Khurasan was under complete Mongol rule. Leaving garrison forces behind him, Tolui headed back east to rejoin his father.Wikipedia:Citation needed

The final campaign and aftermath

After the Mongol campaign in Khorasan, the Shah's army was broken. Jalal al-Din, who took power after his father's death, began assembling the remnants of the Khwarezmid army in the south, in the area of Afghanistan. Genghis had dispatched forces to hunt down the gathering army under Jalal al-Din, and the two sides met in the spring of 1221 at the town of Parwan. The engagement was a humiliating defeat for the Mongol forces. Enraged, Genghis headed south himself, and defeated Jalal al-Din on the Indus River. Jalal al-Din, defeated, fled to India. Genghis spent some time on the southern shore of the Indus searching for the new Shah, but failed to find him. The Khan returned northwards, content to leave the Shah in India.

After the remaining centers of resistance were destroyed, Genghis returned to Mongolia, leaving Mongolian garrison troops behind. The destruction and absorption of the Khwarezmid Empire would prove to be a sign of things to come for the Islamic world, as well as Eastern Europe. The new territory proved to be an important stepping stone for Mongol armies under the reign of Genghis' son Ögedei to invade Kievan Rus' and Poland, and future campaigns brought Mongol arms to Hungary and the Baltic Sea. For the Islamic world, the destruction of Khwarezmid left Iraq, Turkey and Syria wide open. All three were eventually subjugated by future Khans.

The war with Khwarezmia also brought up the important question of succession. Genghis was not young when the war began, and he had four sons, all of whom were fierce warriors and each with their own loyal followers. Such sibling rivalry almost came to a head during the siege of Urgench, and Genghis was forced to rely on his third son, Ögedei, to finish the battle. Following the destruction of Urgench, Genghis officially selected Ögedei to be successor, as well as establishing that future Khans would come from direct descendants of previous rulers. Despite this establishment, the four sons would eventually come to blows, and those blows showed the instability of the Khanate that Genghis had created.

Jochi never forgave his father, and essentially withdrew from further Mongol wars, into the north, where he refused to come to his father when he was ordered to. Indeed, at the time of his death, the Khan was contemplating a march on his rebellious son. The bitterness that came from this transmitted to his sons, and especially grandsons, Batu and Berke Khan, (of the Golden Horde) who would conquer Kievan Rus. When the Mamluks of Egypt managed to inflict one of history's more significant defeats on the Mongols at the Battle of Ain Jalut in 1260, Hulegu Khan, one of Genghis Khan's grandsons by his son Tolui, who had sacked Baghdad in 1258, was unable to avenge that defeat when Berke Khan, his cousin, (who had converted to Islam) attacked him in the Transcaucasus to aid the cause of Islam, and Mongol battled Mongol for the first time. The seeds of that battle began in the war with Khwarezmia when their fathers struggled for supremacy.

References

- Amitai-Preiss, Reuven. *The Mamluk-Ilkhanid War*, Cambridge University Press, 1996. (ISBN 0-521-52290-0)
- Chambers, James. *The Devil's Horsemen: The Mongol Invasion of Europe*, Atheneum, 1979. (ISBN 0-689-10942-3)
- Greene, Robert. *The 33 Strategies of War*, New York: Viking Penguin, 2006. (ISBN 978-0143112785)
- Hildinger, Erik. *Warriors of the Steppe: A Military History of Central Asia, 500 B.C. to A.D. 1700*, Sarpedon Publishers, 1997. (ISBN 1-885119-43-7)
- Morgan, David. *The Mongols*, 1986. (ISBN 0-631-17563-6)
- Nicolle, David. *The Mongol Warlords: Genghis Khan, Kublai Khan, Hulegu, Tamerlane*, Brockhampton Press, 1998. (ISBN 1-853-14104-6)
- Ratchnevsky, Paul. *Genghis Khan: His Life and Legacy*. Translated and edited by Thomas Nivison Haining. Oxford: Blackwell, 1994. (ISBN 978-0631189497)
- Reagan, Geoffry. *The Guinness Book of Decisive Battles*, New York: Canopy Books, 1992.
- Saunders, J.J. *The History of the Mongol Conquests*, Routledge & Kegan Paul Ltd, 1971. (ISBN 0-8122-1766-7)
- Sicker, Martin. *The Islamic World in Ascendancy: From the Arab Conquests to the Siege of Vienna*, Praeger Publishers, 2000. (ISBN 0-275-96892-8)
- Soucek, Svat. *A History of Inner Asia*, Cambridge, 2000. (ISBN 978-0521657044)
- Stubbs, Kim. Facing the Wrath of Khan." *Military History* (May 2006): 30–37.
- France, John. "Journal of Medieval Military History, Volume 8". Published 18 Nov 2010. ISBN 9781843835967.

External links

- A Map of Events[271] mentioned in this article.

Siege of Baghdad (1258)

Siege of Baghdad (1258)		
Part of the Mongol invasions		
Hulagu's army besieging the walls of Baghdad		
Date	29 January – 10 February 1258 (13 days)	
Location	Baghdad, modern-day Iraq	
Result	Decisive Mongol victory	
Belligerents		
Ilkhanate (Mongol Empire) Armenian Kingdom of Cilicia Kingdom of Georgia Principality of Antioch		Abbasid Caliphate
Commanders and leaders		
Hulagu Khan Arghun Aqa Baiju Buqa-Temür Sunitai Kitbuqa Guo Kan Koke Ilge[272] King David VI King Hethum I		Al-Musta'sim Mujaheduddin Aybak Dwadar Sulaiman Shah Qarasunqur
Units involved		
40,000+ Mongol, Manchurian, Han and Kazakh cavalry[273] 12,000 Armenian cavalry 40,000 Armenian infantry Georgian infantry 1,000 Chinese bombardiers and engineers Chinese, Turkic, Persian infantry		Cavalry Infantry
Strength		
120,000[274]–150,000[275]		50,000
Casualties and losses		

Unknown but believed to be minimal	50,000 soldiers, 200,000–800,000 civilians (Western sources)[276] 2,000,000 civilians (Arab sources)[277]

The **Siege of Baghdad**, which lasted from January 29 until February 10, 1258, entailed the investment, capture, and sack of Baghdad, the capital of the Abbasid Caliphate, by Ilkhanate Mongol forces and allied troops. The Mongols were under the command of Hulagu Khan (or Hulegu Khan), brother of the khagan Möngke Khan, who had intended to further extend his rule into Mesopotamia but not to directly overthrow the Caliphate. Möngke, however, had instructed Hulagu to attack Baghdad if the Caliph Al-Musta'sim refused Mongol demands for his continued submission to the khagan and the payment of tribute in the form of military support for Mongol forces in Iran.

Hulagu began his campaign in Iran with several offensives against Nizari groups, including the Assassins, who lost their stronghold of Alamut. He then marched on Baghdad, demanding that Al-Musta'sim accede to the terms imposed by Möngke on the Abbasids. Although the Abbasids had failed to prepare for the invasion, the Caliph believed that Baghdad could not fall to invading forces and refused to surrender. Hulagu subsequently besieged the city, which surrendered after 12 days. During the next week, the Mongols sacked Baghdad, committing numerous atrocities and destroyed the Abbasids' vast libraries, including the House of Wisdom. The Mongols executed Al-Musta'sim and massacred many residents of the city, which was left greatly depopulated. The siege is considered to mark the end of the Islamic Golden Age, during which the caliphs had extended their rule from the Iberian Peninsula to Sindh, and which was also marked by many cultural achievements.[278]

Background

Baghdad had for centuries been the capital of the Abbasid Caliphate, the third caliphate whose rulers were descendants of Abbas, an uncle of Muhammad. In 751, the Abbasids overthrew the Umayyads and moved the Caliph's seat from Damascus to Baghdad. At the city's peak, it was populated by approximately one million people and was defended by an army of 60,000 soldiers. By the middle of the 13th century, however, the power of the Abbasids had declined and Turkic and Mamluk warlords often held power over the Caliphs. Baghdad still retained much symbolic significance, however, and it remained a rich and cultured city. The Caliphs of the 12th and 13th centuries had begun to develop links with the expanding Mongol Empire in the east. Caliph an-Nasir li-dini'llah, who reigned from 1180–1225, may have attempted an alliance with Genghis Khan when Muhammad II of Khwarezm threatened to attack the Abbasids.²⁷⁹ It has been rumored that some Crusader captives were sent as tribute to the Mongol khagan.²⁸⁰

According to *The Secret History of the Mongols*, Genghis and his successor, Ögedei Khan, ordered their general Chormaqan to attack Baghdad.²⁸¹ In 1236, Chormaqan led a division of the Mongol army to Irbil,²⁸² which remained under Abbasid rule. Further raids on Irbil and other regions of the caliphate became nearly annual occurrences.²⁸³ Some raids were alleged to have reached Baghdad itself,²⁸⁴ but these Mongol incursions were not always successful, with Abbasid forces defeating the invaders in 1238²⁸⁵ and 1245.

Despite their successes, the Abbasids hoped to come to terms with the Mongols and by 1241 had adopted the practice of sending an annual tribute to the court of the khagan. Envoys from the Caliph were present at the coronation of Güyük Khan as khagan in 1246²⁸⁶ and that of Möngke Khan in 1251.²⁸⁷ During his brief reign, Güyük insisted that the Caliph Al-Musta'sim fully submit to Mongol rule and come personally to Karakorum. Blame for the Caliph's refusal and for other resistance offered by the Abbasids to increased attempts by the Mongols to extend their power was placed by the khagans on Chormaqan's lieutenant and successor, Baiju.

Hulagu's expedition

Planning

In 1257, Möngke resolved to establish firm authority over Mesopotamia, Syria, and Iran. The khagan gave his brother, Hulagu, authority over a subordinate khanate and army, the Ilkhanate, and instructions to compel the submission of various Muslim states, including the caliphate. Though not seeking the overthrow of Al-Musta'sim, Möngke ordered Hulagu to destroy Baghdad if the Caliph refused his demands of personal submission to Hulagu and the payment of tribute in the form of a military detachment, which would reinforce Hulagu's army during its campaigns against Iranian Ismaili states.

In preparation for his invasion, Hulagu raised a large expeditionary force, conscripting one out of every ten military-age males in the entirety of the Mongol Empire, assembling what may have been the most numerous Mongol army to have existed and, by one estimate, 150,000 strong. Generals of the army included the Oirat administrator Arghun Agha, Baiju, Buqa Temür, Guo Kan, and Kitbuqa, as well as Hulagu's brother Sunitai and various other warlords.²⁸⁸ The force was also supplemented by Christian forces, including the King of Armenia and his army, a Frankish contingent from the Principality of Antioch,²⁸⁹ and a Georgian force, seeking revenge on the Muslim Abbasids for the sacking of their capital, Tiflis, decades earlier by the Khwarazm-Shahs.²⁹⁰

About 1,000 Chinese artillery experts accompanied the army, as did Persian and Turkic auxiliaries, according to Ata-Malik Juvayni, a contemporary Persian observer.

Early campaigns

Hulagu led his army first to Iran, where he successfully campaigned against the Lurs, the Bukhara, and the remnants of the Khwarezm-Shah dynasty. After subduing them, Hulagu directed his attention toward the Ismaili Assassins and their Grand Master, Imam 'Ala al-Din Muhammad, who had attempted the murder of both Möngke and Hulagu's friend and subordinate, Kitbuqa. Though Assassins failed in both attempts, Hulagu marched his army to their stronghold of Alamut, which he captured. The Mongols later executed the Assassins' Grand Master, Imam Rukn al-Dun Khurshah, who had briefly succeeded 'Ala al-Din Muhammad from 1255-1256.

Capture of Baghdad

Hulagu's march to Baghdad

After defeating the Assassins, Hulagu sent word to Al-Musta'sim, demanding his acquiescence to the terms imposed by Möngke. Al-Musta'sim refused, in large part due to the influence of his advisor and grand vizier, Ibn al-Alkami. Historians have ascribed various motives to al-Alkami's opposition to submission, including treachery and incompetence, and it appears that he lied to the Caliph about the severity of the invasion, assuring Al-Musta'sim that, if the capital of the caliphate was endangered by a Mongol army, the Islamic world would rush to its aid.

Although he replied to Hulagu's demands in a manner that the Mongol commander found menacing and offensive enough to break off further negotiation,[291] Al-Musta'sim neglected to summon armies to reinforce the troops at his disposal in Baghdad. Nor did he strengthen the city's walls. By January 11 the Mongols were close to the city, establishing themselves on both banks of the Tigris River so as to form a pincer around the city. Al-Musta'sim finally decided to do battle with them and sent out a force of 20,000 cavalry to attack the Mongols. The cavalry were decisively defeated by the Mongols, whose sappers breached dikes along the Tigris River and flooded the ground behind the Abbasid forces, trapping them.

Figure 46: *Persian painting (14th century) of Hülegü's army besieging a city. Note use of the siege engine*

Siege of the city

The Abbasid caliphate could supposedly call upon 50,000 soldiers for the defense of their capital, including the 20,000 cavalry under al-Musta'sim. However, hastily assembled these troops were poorly equipped and poorly disciplined. Although the caliph technically had the authority to summon soldiers from other Muslim empires to defend his realm, he either neglected to do so or lacked the ability to. His taunting opposition had lost him the loyalty of the Mamluks, and the Syrian emirs, who he supported, were busy preparing their own defenses.[292]

On January 29, the Mongol army began its siege of Baghdad, constructing a palisade and a ditch around the city. Employing siege engines and catapults, the Mongols attempted to breach the city's walls, and, by February 5, had seized a significant portion of the defenses. Realizing that his forces had little chance of retaking the walls, Al-Musta'sim attempted to open negotiations with Hulagu, who rebuffed the Caliph. Around 3,000 of Baghdad's notables also tried to negotiate with Hulagu but were murdered. Five days later, on February 10, the city surrendered, but the Mongols did not enter the city until the 13th, beginning a week of massacre and destruction.

Figure 47: *Hulagu (left) imprisons Caliph Al-Musta'sim among his treasures to starve him to death. Medieval depiction from Le livre des merveilles, 15th century*

Destruction

Many historical accounts detailed the cruelties of the Mongol conquerors.

- The Grand Library of Baghdad, containing countless precious historical documents and books on subjects ranging from medicine to astronomy, was destroyed. Survivors said that the waters of the Tigris ran black with ink from the enormous quantities of books flung into the river and red from the blood of the scientists and philosophers killed.Wikipedia:Citation needed
- Citizens attempted to flee, but were intercepted by Mongol soldiers who killed in abundance, sparing neither women nor children. Martin Sicker writes that close to 90,000 people may have died.[293] Other estimates go much higher. Wassaf claims the loss of life was several hundred thousand. Ian Frazier of *The New Yorker* says estimates of the death toll have ranged from 200,000 to a million.
- The Mongols looted and then destroyed mosques, palaces, libraries, and hospitals. Grand buildings that had been the work of generations were burned to the ground.
- The caliph Al-Musta'sim was captured and forced to watch as his citizens were murdered and his treasury plundered. According to most accounts, the caliph was killed by trampling. The Mongols rolled the caliph up in a rug, and rode their horses over him, as they believed that the earth would be offended if it were touched by royal blood. But the Venetian traveller

Marco Polo claimed that Al-Musta'sim was locked in a tower with nothing to eat but gold and "died like a dog".[294]
- All but one of Al-Musta'sim's sons were killed, and the sole surviving son was sent to Mongolia, where Mongolian historians report he married and fathered children, but played no role in Islam thereafter (see The end of the Abbasid dynasty).
- Hulagu had to move his camp upwind of the city, due to the stench of decay from the ruined city.

Baghdad was a depopulated, ruined city for several centuries and only gradually recovered some of its former glory.

Comments on the destruction

"Iraq in 1258 was very different from present day Iraq. Its agriculture was supported by canal networks thousands of years old. Baghdad was one of the most brilliant intellectual centers in the world. The Mongol destruction of Baghdad was a psychological blow from which Islam never recovered. With the sack of Baghdad, the intellectual flowering of Islam was snuffed out. Imagining the Athens of Pericles and Aristotle obliterated by a nuclear weapon begins to suggest the enormity of the blow. The Mongols filled in the irrigation canals and left Iraq too depopulated to restore them."[295]

"They swept through the city like hungry falcons attacking a flight of doves, or like raging wolves attacking sheep, with loose reins and shameless faces, murdering and spreading terror...beds and cushions made of gold and encrusted with jewels were cut to pieces with knives and torn to shreds. Those hiding behind the veils of the great Harem were dragged...through the streets and alleys, each of them becoming a plaything...as the population died at the hands of the invaders." (Abdullah Wassaf as cited by David Morgan)

Causes for agricultural decline

SomeWikipedia:Manual of Style/Words to watch#Unsupported attributions historians believe that the Mongol invasion destroyed much of the irrigation infrastructure that had sustained Mesopotamia for many millennia. Canals were cut as a military tactic and never repaired. So many people died or fled that neither the labor nor the organization were sufficient to maintain the canal system. It broke down or silted up. This theory was advanced by historian Svatopluk Souček in his 2000 book, *A History of Inner Asia*.

Other historians point to soil salination as the culprit in the decline in agriculture.[296]

Aftermath

Hulagu left 3,000 Mongol soldiers behind to rebuild Baghdad. Ata-Malik Juvayni was later appointed governor of Baghdad, Lower Mesopotamia, and Khuzistan after Guo Kan went back to Yuan Dynasty to assist Kublai conquest over the Song Dynasty. The Mongol Hulagu's Nestorian Christian wife, Dokuz Khatun successfully interceded to spare the lives of Baghdad's Christian inhabitants.[297,298] Hulagu offered the royal palace to the Nestorian Catholicos Mar Makikha, and ordered a cathedral to be built for him.[299]

Initially, the fall of Baghdad came as a shock to the whole Muslim world, but the city became an economic center where international trade, the minting of coins and religious affairs flourished under the Ilkhans. The chief Mongol darughachi was thereafter stationed in the city.

References

- Amitai-Preiss, Reuven. 1998. *Mongols and Mamluks: The Mamluk-Ilkhanid War, 1260–1281* (first edition). Cambridge: Cambridge University Press. ISBN 0-521-46226-6.
- Demurger, Alain. 2005. *Les Templiers. Une chevalerie chrétienne au Moyen Âge*. Éditions du Seuil.
- ibid. 2006. *Croisades et Croisés au Moyen-Age*. Paris: Groupe Flammarion.
- Khanbaghi, Aptin. 2006. *The fire, the star, and the cross: minority religions in medieval and early modern Iran*. London: I. B. Tauris.
- Morgan, David. 1990. *The Mongols*. Boston: Blackwell. ISBN 0-631-17563-6.
- Nicolle, David, and Richard Hook (illustrator). 1998. *The Mongol Warlords: Genghis Khan, Kublai Khan, Hulegu, Tamerlane*. London: Brockhampton Press. ISBN 1-86019-407-9.
- Runciman, Steven. *A history of the Crusades*.
- Saunders, J.J. 2001. *The History of the Mongol Conquests*. Philadelphia: University of Pennsylvania Press. ISBN 0-8122-1766-7.
- Sicker, Martin. 2000. *The Islamic World in Ascendancy: From the Arab Conquests to the Siege of Vienna*. Westport, Connecticut: Praeger. ISBN 0-275-96892-8.
- Souček, Svat. 2000. *A History of Inner Asia*. Cambridge: Cambridge University Press, ISBN 0-521-65704-0.

External links

- article describing Hulagu's conquest of Baghdad[300], written by Ian Frazier, appeared in the April 25, 2005 issue of *The New Yorker*.

Coordinates: 33.3333°N 44.4333°E[301]

East Asia

Mongol invasions of Korea

Mongol invasions of Korea	
Date	1231, 1232, 1235–1239, 1251, 1254, 1255, 1257
Location	Korean Peninsula
Result	Mongol victory. Goryeo capitulates in 1259, and becomes a vassal between 1270 and 1356.

Belligerents	
Goryeo (Korea)	Mongol Empire

Commanders and leaders	
Choe Woo Pak Seo Kim Yun-hu	Ögedei Khan Möngke Khan Amuqan Danqu Saritai † Jalairtai

The **Mongol invasions of Korea** (1231–1259) comprised a series of campaigns between 1231 and 1270 by the Mongol Empire against the Kingdom of Goryeo (the proto-state of modern-day Korea). There were seven major campaigns at tremendous cost to civilian lives throughout the Korean peninsula, ultimately resulting in Korea becoming a vassal state of the Mongol Yuan Dynasty for approximately 80 years.

The initial campaigns

Fleeing from the Mongols, in 1216 the Khitans invaded Goryeo and defeated the Korean armies multiple times, even reaching the gates of the capital and raiding deep into the south, but were defeated by Korean General Kim Chwiryeo who pushed them back north to Pyongan, where the remaining Khitans were finished off by allied Mongol-Goryeo forces in 1219. These Khitans are possibly the origin of the Baekjeong.

Gojong of Goryeo (reigned 1213–1259) was the 23rd king of the Goryeo dynasty of Korea. In 1225, the Mongol Empire demanded tribute goods from Goryeo and the Mongol envoy Chu-ku-yu was killed. His death was used by the Mongols as a pretext to invade Goryeo.

In 1231, Ögedei Khan ordered the invasion of Korea. The experienced Mongol army was placed under the command of General Sartai (not to be confused with Sartaq, a later Mongol khan). The Mongol army crossed the Yalu river and quickly secured the surrender of the border town of Uiju. The Mongols were joined by Hong Bok-won, a traitor Goryeo general.[302] Choe Woo mobilized as many soldiers as possible into an army consisting largely of infantry, where it fought the Mongols at both Anju and Kuju (modern-day Kusong). The Mongols took Anju; however, they were forced to retreat after the Siege of Kuju. Frustrated by siege warfare, Sartai instead used his armies' superior mobility to bypass the Goryeo army and succeeded in taking the capital at Gaesong. Elements of the Mongol army reached as far as Chungju in the central Korean peninsula; however, their advance was halted by a slave army led by Ji Gwang-su where his army fought to the death. Realizing that with the fall of the capital Goryeo was unable to resist the Mongol invaders, Goryeo sued for peace. However, Mongols demanded 10,000 otter skins, 20,000 horses, 10,000 bolts of silk, clothing for 1,000,000 soldiers and a large number of children and craftsmen who would become slaves and servants of the Mongol empire. General Sartai began withdrawing his main force to the north in the spring of 1232, leaving seventy-two Mongol administrative officials stationed in various cities in northwestern Goryeo to ensure that Goryeo kept his peace terms.[303]

In 1232, Choe Woo, against the pleas of both King Gojong and many of his senior civil officials, ordered the Royal Court and most of Gaesong's population to be moved from Songdo to Ganghwa Island in the Bay of Gyeonggi, and started the construction of significant defenses to prepare for the Mongol threat. Choe Woo exploited the Mongols' primary weakness, fear of the sea. The government commandeered every available ship and barge to transport supplies and soldiers to Ganghwa Island. The evacuation was so sudden that King Kojong himself had to sleep in a local inn on the island. The government further ordered the common people to flee the countryside and take shelter in major cities, mountain citadels, or nearby offshore islands. Ganghwa Island itself was a strong defensive fortress. Smaller fortresses were built on the mainland side of the island and a double wall was also built across the ridges of Mt. Munsusan.

The Mongols protested the move and immediately launched a second attack. The Mongol army was led by a traitor from Pyongyang called Hong Bok-won and the Mongols occupied much of northern Korea. Although they reached parts of the southern peninsula as well, the Mongols failed to capture Ganghwa Island, which was only a few miles from shore, and were repelled in Gwangju. The Mongol general there, Sartai (撒禮塔), was killed by the monk Kim Yunhu (김윤후) amidst strong civilian resistance at the Battle of Cheoin near Yongin, forcing the Mongols to withdraw again.

Third campaign and treaty

In 1235, the Mongols began a campaign that ravaged parts of Gyeongsang and Jeolla Provinces. Civilian resistance was strong, and the Royal Court at Ganghwa attempted to strengthen its fortress. Goryeo won several victories but the Goryeo military and Righteous armies could not withstand the waves of invasions. In 1236, Gojong ordered the re-creation of the Tripitaka Koreana, destroyed during the 1232 invasion. This collection of Buddhist scriptures took 15 years to carve on some 81,000 wooden blocks and is preserved to this day. After the Mongols were unable to take either Ganghwa Island or Goryeo's mainland mountain castles, the Mongols began to burn Goryeo farmland in an attempt to starve the populace. When some fortresses finally surrendered, the Mongols executed everyone who resisted them.

In 1238, Goryeo relented and sued for peace. The Mongols withdrew, in exchange for Goryeo's agreement to send the Royal Family as hostages. However, Goryeo sent an unrelated member of the Royal line. Incensed, the Mongols demanded to clear the seas of Korean ships, relocate the court to the mainland, the hand-over of anti-Mongol bureaucrats, and, again, the Royal family as hostages. In response, Korea sent a distant princess and ten children of nobles.

Fourth and fifth campaigns

In 1247, the Mongols began the fourth campaign against Goryeo, again demanding the return of the capital to Songdo and the Royal Family as hostages. Güyük sent Amuqan to Korea and the Mongols camped near Yomju in July 1247. After the king Gojong of Goryeo refused to move his capital from Ganghwa island to Songdo, Amuqan's force pillaged the Korean Peninsula. With the death of Güyük Khan in 1248, however, the Mongols withdrew again. But the Mongol raids continued until 1250.

Upon the 1251 ascension of Möngke Khan, the Mongols again repeated their demands. Möngke Khan sent envoys to Goryeo, announcing his coronation in

October 1251. He also demanded the King Gojong be summoned before him in person and his headquarters be moved from Ganghwa Island to the Korean mainland. But the Goryeo court refused to send the king because the old king was unable to travel so far. Möngke again dispatched his envoys with specific tasks. The envoys were well received by the Goryeo officials but they also criticized them, saying their king did not follow his overlord Möngke's orders.[304] Möngke ordered the prince Yeku to command the army against Korea. However, a Korean in the court of Möngke convinced them to begin their campaign in July 1253. Yeku, along with Amuqan, demanded the Goryeo court to surrender. The court refused but did not resist the Mongols and gathered the peasantry into the mountain fortresses and islands. Working together with the Goryeo commanders who had joined the Mongols, Jalairtai Qorchi ravaged Korea. When one of Yeku's envoys arrived, Gojong personally met him at his new palace in Sin Chuan-bug. Gojong finally agreed to move the capital back to the mainland, and sent his stepson Angyeong as a hostage. The Mongols agreed to a cease fire in January 1254.

Sixth campaign and peace

The Mongols later learned that top Goryeo officials remained on Ganghwa Island, and had punished those who negotiated with the Mongols. Between 1253 and 1258, the Mongols under Jalairtai launched four devastating invasions in the final successful campaign against Korea.

Möngke realized that the hostage was not the blood prince of the Goryeo Dynasty. So Möngke blamed the Goryeo court for deceiving him and killing the family of Lee Hyeong, who was a pro-Mongol Korean general. Möngke' commander Jalairtai devastated much of Goryeo and took 206,800 captives in 1254.[305] Famine and despair forced peasants to surrender to the Mongols. They established a chiliarchy office at Yonghung with local officials. Ordering defectors to build ships, the Mongols began attacking the coastal islands from 1255 onward.[306] In the Liaodong Peninsula, the Mongols eventually massed Korean defectors into a colony of 5,000 households. In 1258, the king and the Choe clan retainer Kim Unjin staged a counter-coup, assassinated the head of the Choe family and sued for peace. When the Goryeo court sent the future king Wonjong as hostage to the Mongol court and promised to return to Kaegyong, the Mongols withdrew from Central Korea.

There were two parties within Goryeo: the literati party, which opposed the war with the Mongols, and the military junta — led by the Choe clan — which pressed for continuing the war. When the dictator Choe was murdered by the literati party, the peace treaty was concluded.[307] The treaty permitted the maintenance of the sovereign power and traditional culture of Goryeo, implying that the Mongols gave up incorporating Goryeo under direct Mongolian control and were content to give Goryeo autonomy, but the king of Goryeo must marry a Mongolian princess and be subordinate to the Mongolian Khans.[308]

Aftermath

Internal struggles within the royal court continued regarding the peace with the Mongols until 1270.

Since Choe Chung-heon, Goryeo had been a military dictatorship, ruled by the private army of the powerful Choe family. Some of these military officials formed the Sambyeolcho Rebellion (1270–1273) and resisted in the islands off the southern shore of the Korean peninsula.

Beginning with Wonjong, for approximately 80 years, Goryeo was a vassal state and compulsory ally of the Mongol Yuan Dynasty. The Mongols and Koreans rulers were also tied by marriages as some Mongol prince and aristocrats married Korean princesses and vice versa. During the reign of Kublai Khan, King Chungnyeol of Goryeo married one of Kublai's daughters. Later, a Korean princess called the Empress Gi became an empress through her marriage with Ukhaantu Khan, and her son, Biligtü Khan of Northern Yuan, became a Mongol Khan. The Kings of Goryeo held an important status like other important families of Mardin, Uyghurs and Mongols (Oirat, Hongirat, and Ikeres).[309] It is claimed that one of Goryeo monarchs was the most beloved grandson of Kublai Khan and had grown up at the Yuan court.[310]

The Mongol darughachis at the court of the Goryeo were offered provisions and sometimes were also willing to actively involved in the affairs of the Goryeo court. Part of Jeju Island converted to a grazing area for the Mongol cavalry stationed there. Even today, there are several Mongolian words used in the Jeju Island.[311] Furthermore, the Mongol domination of Eurasia encouraged cultural exchange, and this would include for example the transmission of some of the Korean ideas and technology to other areas under Mongol control.[312,313]

The Goryeo dynasty survived under influence of the Mongol Yuan Dynasty until it began to force Mongolian garrisons back starting in the 1350s, when the Yuan Dynasty was already beginning to crumble, suffering from massive rebellions in China. Taking advantage of the opportunity, the Goryeo king Gongmin also managed to regain some northern territories.

External links

- Korea Britannica article (in Korean)[314]
- Sanderson Beck[315]

Mongol conquest of China

Mongol conquest of China	
Part of Mongol conquests	
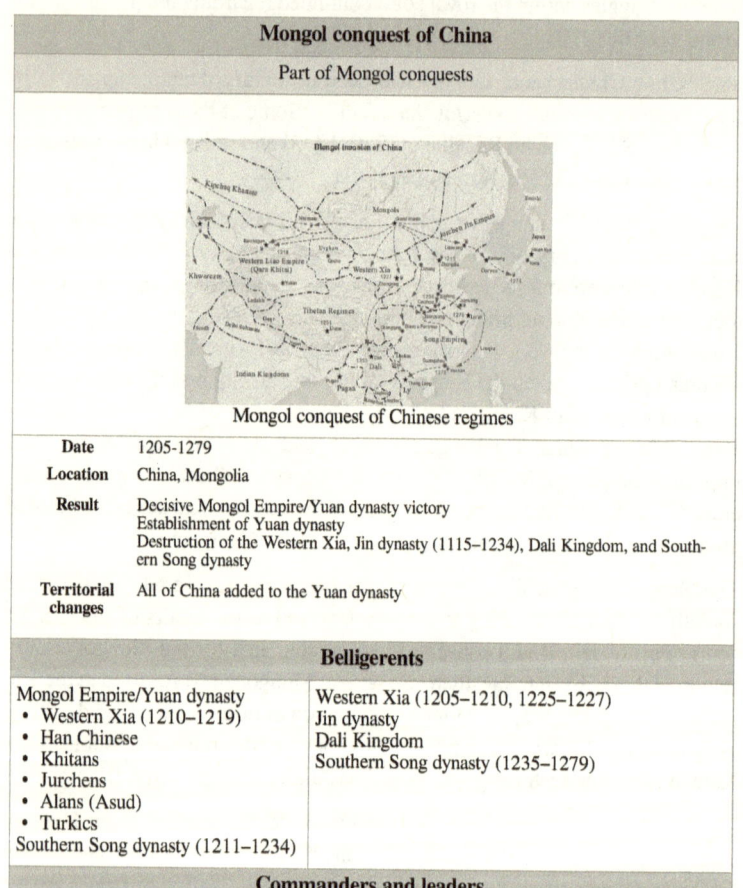 Mongol conquest of Chinese regimes	
Date	1205-1279
Location	China, Mongolia
Result	Decisive Mongol Empire/Yuan dynasty victory Establishment of Yuan dynasty Destruction of the Western Xia, Jin dynasty (1115–1234), Dali Kingdom, and Southern Song dynasty
Territorial changes	All of China added to the Yuan dynasty
Belligerents	
Mongol Empire/Yuan dynasty • Western Xia (1210–1219) • Han Chinese • Khitans • Jurchens • Alans (Asud) • Turkics Southern Song dynasty (1211–1234)	Western Xia (1205–1210, 1225–1227) Jin dynasty Dali Kingdom Southern Song dynasty (1235–1279)
Commanders and leaders	

Genghis Khan (possibly †) Jebe Muqali Boal (Bor) Doqolqu Tolui Ögedei Subutai Chagaan Kublai Khan Khochu Töregene Güyük Khan Möngke Khan (possibly †) Bayan Aju Arikhgiya Shi Tianze Zhang Hongfan Zhang Rou Yan Shi Liu Heima (Liu Ni) Xiao Zhala Uryankhadai Guo Kan Duan Xingzhi	Emperor Huanzong Emperor Li Anquan Kao Liang-Hui Wei-ming Ling-kung Wanyan Yongji † Emperor Xuanzong of Jin † Li Ying Moran Jinzhong Emperor Aizong of Jin † Wanyan Heda Puxian Wannu Pucha Guannu Ma Yong Emperor Mo of Jin † Emperor Xianzong Emperor Mozhu ☠ (1226–1227) Asha Duan Xingzhi (defected to Mongols) Emperor Lizong Emperor Duzong Emperor Gong of Song Emperor Duanzong Emperor Bing of Song † Jia Sidao Lü Wenhuan Li Tingzhi Zhang Shijie Wen Tianxiang

The **Mongol conquest of China** was a series of major military efforts by the Mongol Empire to invade China proper. It spanned six decades in the 13th century and involved the defeat of the Jin dynasty, Western Xia, the Dali Kingdom and the Southern Song. The Mongol Empire under Genghis Khan started the conquest with small-scale raids into Western Xia in 1205 and 1207.[316] By 1279, the Mongol leader Kublai Khan had established the Yuan dynasty in China and crushed the last Song resistance, which marked the onset of all of China under the Mongol Yuan rule. This was the first time in history that the whole of China was conquered and subsequently ruled by a foreign or non-native ruler.[317]

Conquest of Western Xia

In the early 1200s, Temujin, soon to be Genghis Khan, began consolidating his power in Mongolia. Following the death of the Kerait leader Ong Khan to Temujin's emerging Mongol Empire in 1203, Keriat leader Nilqa Senggum led a small band of followers into Western Xia, also known as Xi-Xia. However, after his adherents took to plundering the locals, Nilqa Senggum was expelled from Western Xia territory.

Using his rival Nilga Senggum's temporary refuge in Western Xia as a pretext, Temujin launched a raid against the state in 1205 in the Edsin region.[318]

Figure 48: *Battle between the Mongol and Jin Jurchen armies in north China in 1211 depicted in the Jami' al-tawarikh (Compendium of Chronicles) by Rashid-al-Din Hamadani.*

The Mongols plundered border settlements and one local Western Xia noble accepted Mongol supremacy.[319] The next year, 1206, Temujin was formally proclaimed Genghis Khan, ruler of all the Mongols, marking the official start of the Mongol Empire. In 1207, Genghis led another raid into Western Xia, invading the Ordo region and sacking Wuhai, the main garrison along the Yellow River, before withdrawing in 1208.

In 1209, the Genghis undertook a larger campaign to secure the submission of Western Xia. After defeating a force led by Kao Liang-Hui outside Wuhai, Genghis captured the city and pushed up along the Yellow River, defeated several cities, and besieged the capital, Yinchuan, which held a well-fortified garrison of 150,000.[320] The Mongols, at this point inexperienced at siege warfare, attempted to flood out the city by diverting the Yellow River, but the dike they built to accomplish this broke and flooded the Mongol camp. Nevertheless, Emperor Li Anquan, still threatened by the Mongols and receiving no relief from the Jin dynasty, agreed to submit to Mongol rule, and demonstrated his loyalty by giving a daughter, Chaka, in marriage to Genghis and paying a tribute of camels, falcons, and textiles.

After their defeat in 1210, Western Xia served as faithful vassals to the Mongol Empire for almost a decade, aiding the Mongols in their war against the Jin dynasty. In 1219, Genghis Khan launched his campaign against the Khwarazmian dynasty in Central Asia, and requested military aid from Western Xia. However, the emperor and his military commander Asha refused to take part in the campaign, stating that if Genghis had too few troops to attack Khwarazm, then he had no claim to supreme power. Infuriated, Genghis swore vengeance and left to invade Khwarazm, while Western Xia attempted alliances with the Jin and Song dynasties against the Mongols.

After defeating Khwarazm in 1221, Genghis prepared his armies to punish Western Xia for their betrayal, and in 1225 he attacked with a force of approximately 180,000. After taking Khara-Khoto, the Mongols began a steady advance southward. Asha, commander of the Western Xia troops, could not afford to meet the Mongols as it would involve an exhausting westward march from the capital Yinchuan through 500 kilometers of desert, and so the Mongols steadily advanced from city to city. Enraged by Western Xia's fierce resistance, Genghis engaged the countryside in annihilative warfare and ordered his generals to systematically destroy cities and garrisons as they went. Genghis divided his army and sent general Subutai to take care of the westernmost cities, while the main force under Genghis moved east into the heart of the Western Xia Empire and took Ganzhou, which was spared destruction upon its capture due to it being the hometown of Genghis's commander Chagaan.

In August 1226, Mongol troops approached Wuwei, the second-largest city of the Western Xia empire, which surrendered without resistance in order to escape destruction. In Autumn 1226, Genghis took Liangchow, crossed the Helan Shan desert, and in November lay siege to Lingwu, a mere 30 kilometers from Yinchuan.[321] Here, in the Battle of Yellow River, the Mongols destroyed a force of 300,000 Western Xia that launched a counter-attack against them.

Genghis reached Yinchuan in 1227, laid siege to the city, and launched several offensives into Jin to prevent them from sending reinforcements to Western Xia, with one force reaching as a far as Kaifeng, the Jin capital. Yinchuan lay besieged for about six months, after which Genghis opened up peace negotiations while secretly planning to kill the emperor. During the peace negotiations, Genghis continued his military operations around the Liupan mountains near Guyuan, rejected an offer of peace from the Jin, and prepared to invade them near their border with the Song. However, in August 1227, Genghis died of a historically uncertain cause, and, in order not to jeopardize the ongoing campaign, his death was kept a secret. In September 1227, Emperor Mozhu surrendered to the Mongols and was promptly executed. The Mongols then mercilessly pillaged Yinchuan, slaughtered the city's population, plundered the imperial tombs west of the city, and completed the effective annihilation of the Western Xia state.

Figure 49: *The siege of Zhongdu (modern Beijing) in 1213–14.*

Conquest of Jin dynasty

One of the major goals of Genghis Khan was the conquest of the Jin dynasty, allowing the Mongols to avenge the earlier death of a Mongol Khan, gain the riches of northern China and to establish the Mongols as a major power in the East-Asian world.

Genghis Khan declared war in 1211, and while Mongols were victorious in the field, they were frustrated in their efforts to take major cities. In his typically logical and determined fashion, Genghis and his highly developed staff studied the problems of the assault of fortifications. With the help of Chinese engineers, they gradually developed the techniques to take down fortifications. Islamic engineers joined later and especially contributed counterweight trebuchets, "Muslim phao", which had a maximum range of 300 meters compared to 150 meters of the ancient Chinese predecessor. It played a significant role in taking the Chinese strongholds and was as well used against infantry units on the battlefield. This eventually would make troops under the Mongols some of the most accomplished and most successful besiegers in the history of warfare.

As a result of a number of overwhelming victories in the field and a few successes in the capture of fortifications deep within China, Genghis had conquered and consolidated Jin territory as far south as the Great Wall by 1213.

He then advanced with three armies into the heart of Jin territory, between the Great Wall and the Yellow River. With the help of Chenyu Liu, one of the top officers who betrayed Jin, as well as the Southern Song, who wanted revenge on Jin, Genghis defeated the Jin forces, devastated northern China, captured numerous cities, and in 1215 besieged, captured and sacked the Jin capital of Yanjing (modern-day Beijing). However, the Jin emperor, Xuan Zong, did not surrender, but moved his capital to Kaifeng. The city fell in the siege of Kaifeng in 1232. Emperor Aizong fled to the town of Caizhou. The dynasty collapsed after the siege of Caizhou in 1234.

Han Defectors

Many Han Chinese and Khitan defected to the Mongols to fight against the Jin. Two Han Chinese leaders, Shi Tianze, Liu Heima (劉黑馬, Liu Ni),[322,323,324,325] and the Khitan Xiao Zhala (蕭札剌) defected and commanded the 3 Tumens in the Mongol army.[326,327,328,329] Liu Heima and Shi Tianze served Ogödei Khan.[330] Liu Heima and Shi Tianxiang led armies against Western Xia for the Mongols.[331] There were 4 Han Tumens and 3 Khitan Tumens, with each Tumen consisting of 10,000 troops. The three Khitan Generals Shimobeidier (石抹孛迭兒), Tabuyir (塔不已兒) and Xiaozhacizhizizhongxi (蕭札剌之子重喜) commanded the three Khitan Tumens and the four Han Generals Zhang Rou, Yan Shi, Shi Tianze, and Liu Heima commanded the four Han tumens under Ogödei Khan.[332,333,334,335] The Mongols received defections from Han Chinese and Khitans while the Jin were abandoned by their own Jurchen officers.

Shi Tianze was a Han Chinese who lived in the Jin dynasty (1115–1234). Interethnic marriage between Han and Jurchen became common at this time. His father was Shi Bingzhi (史秉直, Shih Ping-chih). Shi Bingzhi was married to a Jurchen woman (surname Na-ho) and a Han Chinese woman (surname Chang), it is unknown which of them was Shi Tianze's mother.[336]

The Yuan dynasty created a "Han Army" (漢軍) out of defected Jin troops and army of defected Song troops called the "Newly Submitted Army" (新附軍).[337]

Conquest of Dali Kingdom

Möngke Khan dispatched Kublai to the Dali Kingdom in 1253 to outflank the Song. The Gao family, dominated the court, resisted and murdered Mongol envoys. The Mongols divided their forces into three. One wing rode eastward into the Sichuan basin. The second column under Uryankhadai took a difficult way into the mountains of western Sichuan.[338] Kublai himself headed south over the grasslands, meeting up with the first column. While Uryankhadai galloping in along the lakeside from the north, Kublai took the capital city of Dali and spared the residents despite the slaying of his ambassadors. The Dali King Duan Xingzhi (段興智) himself defected to the Mongols, who used his troops to conquer the rest of Yunnan. The Mongols appointed King Duan Xingzhi as Maharajah and stationed a pacification commissioner there.[339] After Kublai's departure, unrest broke out among the Black Jang (one of the main ethnic groups of the Dali kingdom). By 1256, Uryankhadai, the son of Subutai had completely pacified Yunnan.

Use of Chinese soldiers in other campaigns

During their campaigns, the Mongol Empire recruited many nationalities in their warfare, such as those of Central and East Asia.[340,341,342,343,344] The Mongols employed Chinese troops, especially those who worked catapults and gunpowder to assist them in other conquests. In addition to Chinese troops, many scholars and doctors from China accompanied Mongol commanders to the west. The Mongols valued workers with specialized skills.

The ability to make cast iron which was tough enough for shooting objects with gunpowder was available to the Chinese in the Song dynasty and it was adopted by the Liao, Jin, and Yuan dynasties.

During the invasion of Transoxania in 1219, along with the main Mongol force, Genghis Khan used a Chinese specialist catapult unit in battle. They were used in Transoxania again in 1220. The Chinese may have used the catapults to hurl gunpowder bombs, since they already had them by this time (although there were other siege engineers and technologies used in the campaigns, too.[345]) While Genghis Khan was conquering Transoxania and Central Asia, several Chinese who were familiar with gunpowder were serving with Genghis's army. "Whole regiments" entirely made out of Chinese were used by the Mongols to command bomb hurling trebuchets during the invasion of Iran. Historians have suggested that the Mongol invasion had brought Chinese gunpowder weapons to Central Asia. One of these was the huochong, a Chinese mortar. Books written around the area afterward depicted the use of gunpowder weapons which resembled that of China.

One thousand northern Chinese engineer squads accompanied the Mongol Hulagu Khan during his conquest of the Middle East. 1,000 Chinese participated in the Siege of Baghdad (1258). The Chinese General Guo Kan was one of the commanders during the siege and appointed Governor of Baghdad after the city was taken.[346,347] But this is probably wrong since Hulagu's associate,

Nasir al-Din Tusi claims that the darugha was a certain Asuta Bahadur or according to Rashid and Bar Heabreus, Ali Bahadur who repulsed the Mamluk charge under the shadow Caliph in 1262.

While serving in the Mongol armies, Chinese generals were able to observe the invasion of West Asia.

According to Ata-Malik Juvayni during the assault on the Alamut Assassins fort, "Khitayan" built siege weapons resembling crossbows were used. "Khitayan" meant Chinese and it was a type of arcuballista, deployed in 1256 under Hulagu's command. Stones were knocked off the castle and the bolts "burnt" a great number of the Assassins. They could fire a distance around 2,500 paces. The device was described as an *ox's bow*.[348] Pitch which was lit on fire was applied to the bolts of the weapon before firing. Another historian thinks that instead gunpowder might have been strapped onto the bolts which caused the burns during the battle recorded by Juvayini.

Alans were recruited into the Mongol forces with one unit called "Right Alan Guard" which was combined with "recently surrendered" soldiers, Mongols, and Chinese soldiers stationed in the area of the former Kingdom of Qocho and in Besh Balikh the Mongols established a Chinese military colony led by Chinese general Qi Kongzhi (Ch'i Kung-chih).

Use of other conquered non-Mongol peoples

Against the Alans and the Cumans (Kipchaks), the Mongols used divide and conquer tactics: first the Mongols told the Cumans to stop allying with the Alans and then, after the Cumans followed their suggestion, the Mongols defeated the Alans[349] and then attacked the Cumans.[350] Alan and Kipchak guards were used by Kublai Khan. In 1368 at the end of the Yuan dynasty in China Toghan Temür was accompanied by his faithful Alan guards. "Mangu enlisted in his bodyguard half the troops of the Alan prince, Arslan, whose younger son Nicholas took a part in the expedition of the Mongols against Karajang (Yunnan). This Alan imperial guard was still in existence in 1272, 1286 and 1309, and it was divided into two corps with headquarters in the Ling pei province (Karakorúm)." Alans were converted to Roman Catholic Christianity as were Armenians in China by John of Montecorvino.

Conquest of Southern Song

At first, the Mongols allied with Song China as both had a common enemy in the form of Jin. However, this alliance broke down with the destruction of Jur'chen Jin in 1234. After Song forces captured the former Chinese capitals of Luoyang, Chang'an and Kaifeng from the Mongols and the Song had killed a Mongol ambassador, the Mongols declared war on the Song. Very quickly the Mongol armies forced the Song back to the Yangtze, although the two sides would be engaged in a four-decade war until the fall of the Song in 1276.

The Mongol force which invaded southern China was far greater than the force they sent to invade the Middle East in 1256.

While the Mongol forces had success against the non-Han Chinese ruled states of the Jin and Xia, conquering the Song took much more time. The Song forces were equipped with the best technology available at the time, such as an ample supply of gunpowder weapons like fire lances, rockets and flamethrowers. The fierce resistance of the Song forces resulted in the Mongols having to fight the most difficult war in all of their conquests, and the Mongols required every advantage they could gain and "every military artifice known at that time" in order to win. They looked to peoples they already conquered to acquire various military advantages. However, intrigues at the Song court would favour the Mongols.

After several indecisive wars, the Mongols unsuccessfully attacked the Song garrison at Diaoyu Fortress Hechuan when their Great Khan, Möngke, died of cholera or dysentery. However, the general responsible for this defence was not rewarded but instead was punished by the Song court. Discouraged, he defected to the Mongols and suggested to Möngke's successor, Kublai, that the key to the conquest of Song was the capture of Xiangyang, a vital Song stronghold.

The Mongols quickly enclosed Xiangyang and defeated any attempt to reinforce it by the Song. After a siege that lasted several years, and with the help of Muslim artillery created by Iraqi engineers, the Mongols finally forced the city of Xiangyang to surrender. The dying Song dynasty sent its armies against the Mongols at Yehue under the incompetent chancellor Jia Sidao. Predictably, the battle was a disaster. Running out of troops and supplies, the Song court surrendered to the Mongols in 1276.

Many Han Chinese were enslaved in the process of the Mongols invasion of China proper.[351] According to Japanese historian Sugiyama Masaaki (杉山正明) and Funada Yoshiyuki (舩田善之), there were also a certain number of Mongolian slaves owned by Han Chinese during the Yuan dynasty. However, there is no evidence that Han Chinese, who were considered people of the bottom of Yuan society according to some researchers, suffered particularly cruel abuse.[352,353]

With the desire to rule all of China, Kublai established the Yuan dynasty and became Emperor of China. However, despite the surrender of the Song court, resistance of Song remnants remained. Chinese resistance lasted for a few more years as Song loyalists organized themselves around a powerless boy

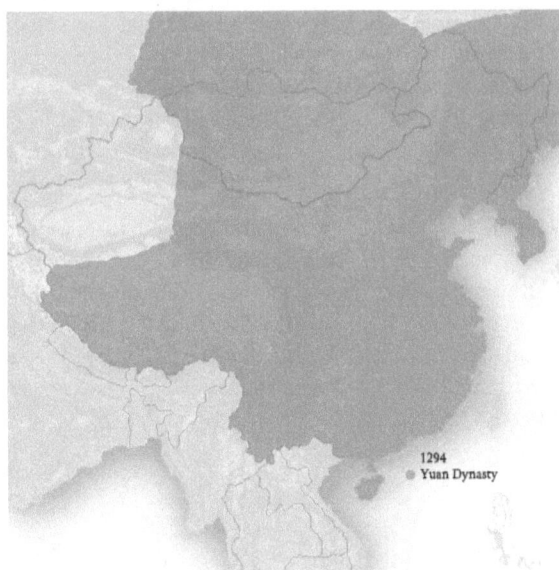

Figure 50: *The Yuan dynasty under Kublai Khan after the conquest of Southern Song dynasty.*

emperor, brother to the last formal Song emperor. In an attempt to restore the Song dynasty, several Song officials set up a government in Guangdong, aboard ships of the vast Song navy, which still maintained over a thousand ships (which then carried the Song army, which had been forced by the Mongol army off of the land onto these Song warships). Realizing this, in 1279 Kublai sent his fleet to engage the Song fleet at the battle of Yamen in the waters off of modern Hong Kong, winning a decisive victory in which the last Song Emperor Bing of Song and his loyal officials committed suicide. This was the final major military confrontation of the Mongol conquest of the Song in southern China.

However, members of the Song Imperial Family continued to live in the Yuan dynasty like Emperor Gong of Song, Zhao Mengfu, and Zhao Yong. Zhao Mengfu painted at the Yuan court and was personally interviewed by Kublai Khan. This practice was referred to as 二王三恪.

Chinese resistance in Vietnam against the Mongols

The ancestors of the Trần clan originated from the province of Fujian and later migrated to Đại Việt under Trần Kinh 陳京 (Chén Jīng), the ancestor of the Trần clan. Their descendants, the later rulers of Đại Việt who were of mixed-blooded descent later established the Tran dynasty, which ruled Vietnam (Đại

Việt). Despite many intermarriages between the Trần and several royal members of the Lý dynasty alongside members of their royal court as in the case of Trần Lý and Trần Thừa, some of the mixed-blooded descendants of the Trần dynasty and certain members of the clan were still capable of speaking Chinese such as when a Yuan dynasty envoy had a meeting with the Chinese-speaking Trần prince Trần Quốc Tuấn in 1282.[354]

Professor Liam Kelley noted that people from Song dynasty China like Zhao Zhong and Xu Zongdao fled to Tran dynasty ruled Vietnam after the Mongol invasion of the Song and they helped the Tran fight against the Mongol invasion. The ancestors of the Tran clan originated from the modern day province of Fujian as did the Daoist cleric Xu Zongdao who recorded the Mongol invasion and referred to them as "Northern bandits".[355,356] The Tran defeated the Mongol invasions of Vietnam.

References

Sources

- Li Bo, Zheng Yin. *5000 years of Chinese history*, Inner Mongolian People's publishing corp, 2001. ISBN 7-204-04420-7
- Smith, John Masson, Jr. (Jan–Mar 1998). "Review: Nomads on Ponies vs. Slaves on Horses". *Journal of the American Oriental Society*. American Oriental Society. **118** (1): 54–62. JSTOR 606298[357]. doi: 10.2307/606298[358].

Mongol invasions of Japan

Mongol invasions of Japan

Part of the Mongol invasion of East Asia and Kublai Khan's Campaigns

The samurai Suenaga facing Mongol and Korean arrows and bombs

Date	1274, 1281
Location	Northern Kyūshū, Japan
Result	Decisive Japanese victory

Belligerents

Japan
- Imperial Court
- Kamakura shogunate
- Hōjō clan
- Sō clan
- Shōni clan
- Sashi clan
- Taira clan
- Kikuchi clan
- Ōtomo clan
- Shimazu clan
- Matsura clan

Mongol Empire
- Yuan dynasty
- Goryeo (Korea)

Commanders and leaders

• Emperor Kameyama ▲ Hōjō Tokimune ❖ Shōni Sukeyoshi • Ōtomo Yoriyasu ❖ Shōni Tsuneyasu ❖ Shōni Kageyasu • Kikuchi Takefusa • Takezaki Suenaga Michiyasu Shiroishi • Fukuda Kaneshige • Tōgō Korechika Hida Nagamoto Mitsui Yasunaga ❖ Sō Sukekuni • Taira no Kagetaka Sashi Husashi Sashi Nao Sashi Tōdō Sashi Isamu Ishiji Kane Ishiji Jirō • Yamashiro Kai	**Mongol :** Kublai Khan Holdon **Korea :** King Wonjong Kim Bang-gyeong
Strength	
1274: 2,000-6,000[359] **1281**: 40,000 (?) Reinforcements by Rokuhara Tandai : 60,000 (not yet arrived)	**1274**: a force of Mongol, Chinese and Korean soldiers, numbering 23,000–39,700[360] with 600–800 ships (300 large vessels and 400–500 smaller craft) **1281**: two forces of Mongol, Chinese and Korean soldiers, numbering 100,000 and 40,000 with 3,500 and 900 ships (respectively)
Casualties and losses	
1274/1281: Minimal Wikipedia:Citation needed	**1274**: 13,500[361]–22,500 Wikipedia:Citation needed **1281**: 100,000[362]–130,500 Wikipedia:Citation needed 20,000–30,000 captured[363]

The **Mongol invasions of Japan** (元寇 *Genkō*), which took place in 1274 and 1281, were major military efforts undertaken by Kublai Khan to conquer the Japanese archipelago after the submission of Goryeo (Korea) to vassaldom. Ultimately a failure, the invasion attempts are of macro-historical importance because they set a limit on Mongol expansion and rank as nation-defining events in the history of Japan.

The Mongol invasions are considered a precursor to early modern warfare. One of the most notable technological innovations during the war was the use of explosive, hand-thrown bombs.

The invasions are referred to in many works of fiction, and are the earliest events for which the word *kamikaze* ("divine wind") is widely used, originating in reference to the two typhoons faced by the Mongol fleets.

Background

After a series of Mongol invasions of Korea between 1231 and 1281, Goryeo signed a treaty in favor of the Mongols and became a vassal state. Kublai was declared Khagan of the Mongol Empire in 1260 (although this was not widely recognized by the Mongols in the west) and established his capital at Khanbaliq (within modern Beijing) in 1264.

Japan at the time was ruled by the Shikken or Shogunate Regents of the Hōjō clan, who had intermarried with and wrested control from Minamoto no Yoriie, shogun of the Kamakura shogunate, after his death in 1203. The inner circle of the Hōjō clan had become so preeminent that they no longer consulted the council of the shogunate (*Hyōjō* (評定)), the Imperial Court of Kyoto, or their gokenin vassals, and made their decisions at private meetings in their residences (*yoriai* (寄合)).

The Mongols also made attempts to subjugate the native peoples of Sakhalin—the Ainu, Orok, and Nivkh peoples—from 1260 to 1308.[364]

Contact

In 1266, Kublai Khan dispatched emissaries to Japan with a letter saying:

> *Cherished by the Mandate of Heaven, the Great Mongol emperor sends this letter to the king of Japan. The sovereigns of small countries, sharing borders with each other, have for a long time been concerned to communicate with each other and become friendly. Especially since my ancestor governed at heaven's command, innumerable countries from afar disputed our power and slighted our virtue. Goryeo rendered thanks for my ceasefire and for restoring their land and people when I ascended the throne. Our relation is feudatory like a father and son. We think you already know this. Goryeo is my eastern tributary. Japan was allied with Goryeo and sometimes with China since the founding of your country; however, Japan has never dispatched ambassadors since my ascending the throne. We are afraid that the Kingdom is yet to know this. Hence we dispatched a mission with our letter particularly expressing our wishes. Enter into friendly relations with each other from now on. We think all countries belong to one family. How are we in the right, unless we comprehend this? Nobody would wish to resort to arms.*[365]

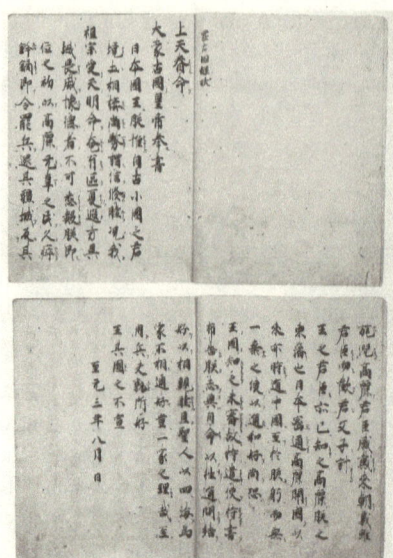

Figure 51: *Letter from Kublai Khan to the "King of Japan" (日本國王), written in Classical Chinese (the lingua franca in East Asia at the time), dated 8th Month, 1266. Now stored in Tōdai-ji, Nara, Japan.*

Kublai essentially demanded that Japan become a vassal and send tribute under a threat of conflict. However, the emissaries returned empty-handed. A second set of emissaries were sent in 1268, returning empty-handed like the first. Both sets of emissaries met with the Chinzei Bugyō, or Defense Commissioner for the West, who passed on the message to Shikken, Hōjō Tokimune, Japan's ruler in Kamakura and to the Emperor of Japan in Kyoto.

After discussing the letters with his inner circle, there was much debate, but the Shikken had his mind made up; he had the emissaries sent back with no answer. The Mongols continued to send demands, some through Korean emissaries and some through Mongol ambassadors on March 7, 1269; September 17, 1269; September 1271; and May 1272. However, each time, the bearers were not permitted to land in Kyushu.

The Imperial Court suggested compromise,[366] but really had little effect in the matter, due to political marginalization after the Jōkyū War. The uncompromising shogunate ordered all those who held fiefs in Kyūshū, the area closest to the Korean Peninsula and thus most likely to be attacked, to return to their lands and forces in Kyūshū moved west, further securing the most likely landing points.

Figure 52: *A stone defense wall, (Genko Borui), in Hakata, now Fukuoka*

After acknowledging its importance, the Imperial Court led great prayer services, and much government business was put off to deal with this crisis.

First invasion preparations

The Khan was willing to go to war as early as 1268 after having been rebuffed twice, but found that his empire did not have the resources to provide him with a sufficient navy at that time. With Mongol entry into the Korean court by marriage of the Korean crown prince to Kublai Khan's daughter, a mass construction of ships began on Korea's south-eastern shores, while the Mongols continued to demand Japan's surrender.

Kublai Khan founded the Yuan dynasty in 1271. In 1272, King Chungnyeol offered counsel to Kublai Khan. According to Goryeosa, *Japan is yet to know the world is hallowed. So dispatch emissaries and convey our military power to Japan. Battle ships and military rations are well prepared. If you appoint me, I encourage you to the extent of my power.*[367] According to the History of Yuan, *King of Goryeo ask Kublai Khan for conquering Japan. I am building 150 ships and encourage your conquest of Japan.*[368]

First invasion (1274)

According to the Yuanshi, the Yuan fleet set out with an estimated 15,000 Mongol and Chinese soldiers and 1,600-8000 Korean soldiers in 300 large vessels and 400-500 smaller craft along with several thousand sailors, although figures vary considerably depending on the source and many modern historians consider the numbers exaggerated.[369] The primary port for the operation was Quanzhou in Fujian, then the center of China's maritime trade. They landed on Komodahama beach on Tsushima Island on October 5, 1274. Sō Sukekuni, governor of Tsushima, led a cavalry unit of 80 to defend the island, but he and his outnumbered unit were killed in the engagement.

The Mongols and Koreans subsequently invaded Iki. Tairano Takakage, the Governor of Iki, fought the invaders with about 100 of his cavalrymen, but he killed himself after his unit was defeated.

The Mongol forces landed on November 19 in Hakata Bay, a short distance from Dazaifu, the ancient administrative capital of Kyūshū. The following day brought the Battle of Bun'ei (文永の役), also known as the "First Battle of Hakata Bay". The Japanese coalition force opposing them included 120 armed samurai each with a warband and likely numbered between 3,000 and 6,000 strong.[370] Later accounts have both sides believing themselves to be drastically outnumbered by the enemy; the Yuanshi provides an estimate of 102,000 for the Japanese force, while the Japanese *Hachiman Gudokun* describes the invaders as outnumbering the Japanese 10 to 1.[371] Conlan argues that the Yuanshi's account of the battle suggests that both the Japanese and Yuan forces were of similar size.[372]

The Japanese were inexperienced in managing such a large force (all of North Kyūshū had been mobilized), and the Mongols made significant initial progress. It had been approximately 50 years since the last major combat event in Japan (Go-Toba's adherents in 1221), leaving not a single Japanese general with adequate experience in moving large bodies of troops. In addition, the style of warfare that was customary within feudal Japan involved single combat, even on large battlefields.

The Mongols possessed foreign weapons which included superior long-range armaments (the short composite bows that the Mongols were famous for, with poisoned arrows, fire arrows, bow-launched arrows with small rocket engines attached and gunpowder-packed exploding arrows and grenades with ceramic shells thrown by slings to terrify the enemy's horses), and easily had the upper hand in open land combat. The Japanese force at Hakata Bay needed time to await the arrival of reinforcements, with which they would be able to overwhelm the Mongol invaders.

Figure 53: *The Mongol fleet destroyed in a typhoon, ink and water on paper, by Kikuchi Yōsai, 1847*

Around nightfall, a typhoon caused the Mongol ship captains to suggest that the land force reembark in order to avoid the risk of being marooned on Japanese soil. By daybreak, only a few ships had not set out to sea. Those that had were destroyed by the storm. Some accounts offer casualty reports that suggest 200 Mongol ships were lost. However, small Japanese boats were much more swift and maneuverable than Mongol ships, and the Japanese were able to board the remaining ships of the crippled Mongol army. The samurai approached and boarded the ships under cover of darkness and fell on the invaders ferociously. In the small confines of the ships, during the predawn darkness, the Mongols (trained as cavalrymen and horse archers) were unable to bring their bows to bear effectively. However, the long, thin Japanese swords got stuck and snapped off in the thick, boiled leather armor of the Mongols, causing Japanese blacksmiths to reevaluate their swords after the first invasion. This led to the beginning of the divergence of the katana from existing tachi swords in the 13th and 14th century.[373]

A story widely known in Japan is that back in Kamakura, Tokimune was overcome with fear when the invasion finally came, and wanting to overcome his cowardice, he asked Mugaku Sogen, his Zen master also known as Bukko, for advice. Bukko replied he had to sit in meditation to find the source of his cowardice in himself. Tokimune went to Bukko and said, "Finally there is the

Figure 54: *Kagesuke Shoni and his forces in Akasaka*

greatest happening of my life." Bukko asked, "How do you plan to face it?" Tokimune screamed, "*Katsu!*" ("Victory!") as if he wanted to scare all the enemies in front of him. Bukko responded with satisfaction, "It is true that the son of a lion roars as a lion!" Since that time, Tokimune was instrumental in spreading Zen and Bushido in Japan among the samurai.

Main battles of Battle of Bun'ei

Battle of Tsushima Island - Mongol victory

On October 5, About 1,000 soldiers of Mongolian Army landed at Komoda Beach.[374] Sukekuni So(宗助国), Shugodai of Tsushima Island was killed in action. The Mongolians slaughtered many dwellers of Tsushima island.[375]

Battle of Iki Island - Mongol victory

On October 14, Taira no Kagetaka(平景隆), Shugodai of Iki led about 100 soldiers. They were defeated by the Mongolian army and he committed suicide in Hidzume Castle(樋詰城).[376] About 1,000 Japanese soldiers were killed there.

Battle of Hirato Island , Taka Island and Nokono Island - Mongol victory

On October 16 to 17, the Mongolian army attacked the base of the Sashi Clan. Hundreds of Japanese soldiers and Husashi Sashi(佐志房), Tomaru Sashi(佐志留) and Isamu Sashi(佐志勇) were killed.[377]

Battle of Akasaka - Japanese victory

The Mongolian Army landed on Sawara District and encamped at Akasaka.[378] On seeing this situation, Takehusa Kikuchi(菊池武房) surprised the Mongolian army. The Mongolians escaped to Sohara, after losing about 100 soldiers.

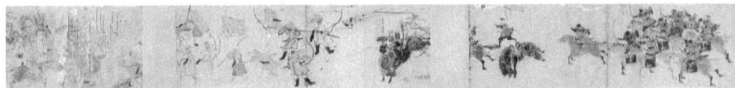

Figure 55: *Suenaga and escaping Mongolians*

Figure 56: *The defensive wall at Hakata*

Battle of Torikai-Gata - Japanese victory

Thousands of Mongolian soldiers were massed in Torikai-Gata. Suenaga Takezaki(竹崎季長), one of the Japanese commanders, attacked the Mongolian army and fought them. Soon, reinforcements led by Michiyasu Shiraisi(白石通泰) arrived and defeated the Mongolians soundly. The Mongolian casualties of this battle were about 3,500.[379]

Withdrawal of Mongol army

Due to the defeat in battle of Torikai-Gata, the Mongolian army was exhausted and withdrew to their ships. On seeing this situation, the Japanese army engaged in night attacks and killed many soldiers. Finally, Hong Dagu decided to withdraw to the Yuan-held continent. In the midst of withdrawal, they met a typhoon, most of their ships sank and many soldiers drowned.[380]

Developments leading to the second invasion

Starting in 1275, the Shogunate increased efforts to defend against the second invasion, which they thought was sure to come. In addition to better organizing the samurai of Kyūshū, they ordered the construction of forts and a large stone wall (石塁, Sekirui), and other defensive structures at many potential landing points, including Hakata Bay, where a two meter high wall was constructed in 1276.

Religious services increased and the Hakozaki Shrine, having been destroyed by the Yuan forces, was rebuilt. A coastal watch was instituted and rewards were given to some 120 valiant samurai. There was even a plan for a raid on Goryeo (modern-day Korea) to be carried out by Shōni Tsunesuke, a general from Kyūshū, though this was never executed.

Figure 57: *Japanese samurai boarding Yuan ships in 1281.*

After the failed invasion, Kublai Khan was tired of being ignored and not being allowed to land, so five Yuan emissaries were dispatched in September 1275 and sent to Kyūshū, refusing to leave without a reply. Tokimune responded by having them sent to Kamakura and then beheading them.[381] The graves of those five executed Yuan emissaries exist to this day at Jōryū Temple in Fujisawa, Kanagawa, near the Tatsunokuchi Execution Place in Kamakura.[382] Then again on July 29, 1279, five more Yuan emissaries were sent in the same manner, and again beheaded, this time in Hakata. Expecting another invasion, on Feb 21, 1280, the Imperial Court ordered all temples and shrines to pray for victory over the Yuan.

Second invasion (1281)

In the spring of 1281, the Mongols sent two separate forces. Per the Yuanshi, an impressive force of 900 ships containing 17,000 sailors, 10,000 Korean soldiers, and 15,000 Mongols and Chinese set out from Masan, Korea, while an even larger force of 100,000 sailed from southern China in 3,500 ships, for a combined force of 142,000 soldiers and sailors. Japanese sources also mention 150,000 men in the invading force.[383] Many modern historians believe these to be exaggerated figures, as were common in medieval chronicles. Professor Thomas Conlan states that they were likely exaggerated by an order of magnitude (implying 14,000 soldiers and sailors), expressing skepticism that a medieval kingdom managed an invasion on the scale of D-Day during World War II across over ten times the distance, and questions if even 10,000 soldiers attacked Japan in 1281.[384] Morris Rossabbi states that Conlan was correct in his assertion that the invasion force was much smaller than traditionally believed, but argues that the expenditures lavished on the mission confirm that the fighting force was sizable and much larger than 10,000 troops. He puts forward the alternative figure of 70,000 men, half of what is spoken of in the Yuanshi and later Japanese claims.[385] Turnbull thinks that 140,000+ is an exaggeration, but does not offer his own precise estimate for the size of the army. Rather, he only states that given the contributions of the Southern Song, the second invasion should've been around three times larger than the first. As he earlier listed the common figure of 23,000 for the first invasion uncritically, unlike the estimate of 140,000+ for the second, that would imply an invasion force of ~70,000, on par with Rossabbi's estimate.[386]

The Mongols' plan called for an overwhelming coordinated attack by the combined imperial Yuan fleets. The Chinese fleet of the Yuan was delayed by difficulties in provisioning and manning the large number of ships they had.[387] The Mongol fleet set sail, suffered heavy losses at Tsushima, and turned back. In the summer, the fleet took Iki-shima and moved on to Kyūshū, landing at several different locations. In a number of individual skirmishes, known collectively as the Kōan Campaign (弘安の役) or the "Second Battle of Hakata Bay", the Mongol forces were driven back to their ships. The Japanese army was heavily outnumbered, but had fortified the coastal line with two-meter high walls, and was easily able to repulse the auxiliaries that were launched against it. Beginning August 15, the now-famous *kamikaze*, a massive typhoon, assaulted the shores of Kyūshū for two days straight, and destroyed much of the Mongol fleet.

Furthermore, it is now believed that the destruction of the Mongol fleet was greatly facilitated by an additional factor. Most of the invasion force was composed of hastily acquired flat-bottomed Chinese riverboats and ships built in Goryeo and all of a similar type. According to Goryeosa, Southern Song-type ships were too costly and their construction was too slow, so the traditional types were constructed instead.[388] Such ships (unlike ocean-going ships, which have a curved keel to prevent capsizing) were difficult to use on high seas, let alone during a massive typhoon.

Main battles of the Kōan Campaign

Battle of Tsushima Island - Japanese victory

On May 21, the Mongolian Army landed on Tsushima island and invaded. They met fierce resistance there and later withdrew.[389]

Battle of Shikano Island - Japanese victory

On the morning of June 8, the Japanese army divided their force into two and attacked along Umi no Nakamichi.[390] The Japanese army lost 300 soldiers but defeated Hong Dagu, who nearly died in this battle, and Zhang Cheng.[391]

On June 9 Zhang Cheng solidified the defense of his army but the Mongolian army was again defeated by the fierce Japanese attacks.[392] After this defeat the Mongolian army escaped to Iki Island.

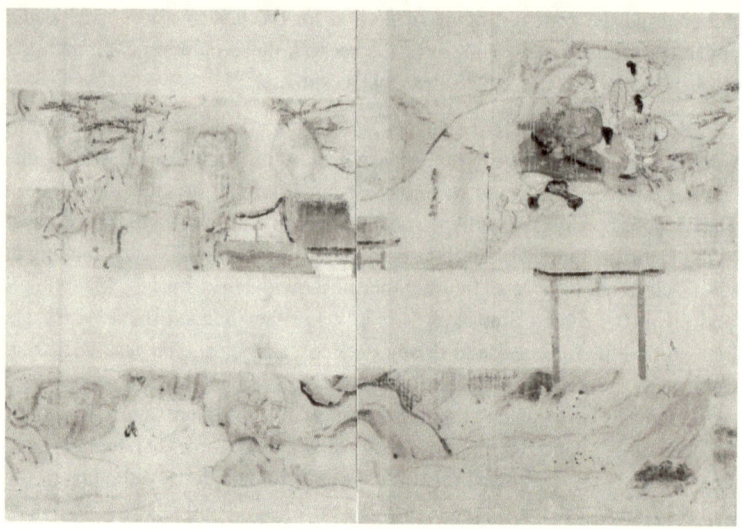

Figure 58: *Japanese soldiers in Shikano Island*

Battle of Iki Island - Japanese victory

On June 29, a Japanese army of approximately 10,000, led by the Matsura Clan, Ryuzoji Clan and Takagi Clan began an all-out attack on Iki Island.[393] On July 2, Iekiyo Ryuzoji landed on Setoura beach and defeated the Mongolian army. As a result, the Mongolian army decided to abandon Iki Island and withdrew to Hirato Island.[394]

Battle of Mikuriya - annihilation of Mongol navy

On July 5, Suenaga Takesaki attacked and annihilated the Mongolian Navy.[395] After this battle, most of the commanders of the Mongolian army escaped to their own country.[396,397]

Battle of Taka Island - annihilation of Mongol army

On July 7, there were about 100,000 soldiers of the Mongol army without commanders.[398,399,400] Upon realizing this situation, the Japanese army launched an attack. Korechika Togo, Koretoo Togo, Sukekado Hujiwara and Nagahisa Shimazu annihilated the remaining Mongolian army and took 20,000 to 30,000 prisoners in this battle. At the completion of this battle, Japan's victory was confirmed.

Figure 59: *Tsunesuke Shoni and Hisatsune Shimazu*

Figure 60: *Fierce battle in Taka Island*

Military significance

From a military perspective, the failed invasions of Kublai Khan were the first of only three instances when the samurai fought foreign troops rather than amongst themselves; the others being Japanese invasions of Korea (1592–98) and the Japanese invasion of Ryukyu (1609). It is also the first time samurai clans fought for the sake of Japan itself instead of for more narrowly defined clan interests. The invasions also exposed the Japanese to an alien fighting style which, lacking the single combat that characterized traditional samurai combat, they saw as inferior. This difference is noted in the *Hachiman Gudōkun*:

> *According to our manner of fighting we must first call out by name someone from the enemy ranks, and then attack in single combat. But the Mongols took no notice at all of such conventions. They rushed forward all together in a mass, grappling with any individuals they could catch and killing them.*[401]

The Mongol method of advances and withdrawals accompanied by bells, drums and war cries was also unknown in Japan, as was the technique of Mongolian archers, which involved shooting arrows *en masse* into the air rather than long-ranged one-on-one combat. The Zen Buddhism of Hojo Tokimune and his Zen master Bukko had gained credibility beyond national boundaries, and the first mass followings of Zen teachings among samurai began to flourish.

The Mongol invasions of Japan facilitated a change in the designs of Japanese swords. Thin tachi and chokuto style blades were often unable to cut through the boiled leather armor of the Mongols, with the blades often chipping or breaking off.[402] Tachi blades were shortened and thickened, with the katana eventually being introduced as a result.

The failed invasions also mark the first use of the word *kamikaze* ("Divine Wind"). The fact that the typhoon that helped Japan defeat the Mongol Navy in the first invasion occurred in late November, well after the normal Pacific typhoon season (May to October), perpetuated the Japanese belief that they would never be defeated or successfully invaded, which remained an important aspect of Japanese foreign policy until the very end of World War II. The failed invasions also demonstrated a weakness of the Mongols – the inability to mount naval invasions successfullyWikipedia:Citation needed (see also Mongol invasions of Vietnam.) After the death of Kublai, his successor, Temür Khan, unsuccessfully demanded the submission of Japan in 1295.

The Mongols and the Ashikaga shogunate of Japan made peace in the late 14th century during the reign of Toghon Temür, the last Yuan emperor in Khanbaliq. Long before the peace agreement, there was stable trade in East Asia under the dominance of the Mongols and Japan.

Figure 61: *Stoneware bombs, known in Japanese as Tetsuhau (iron bomb), or in Chinese as Zhentianlei (thunder crash bomb), excavated from Takashima shipwreck, October 2011.*

As a consequence of the destruction of the Mongol fleets, Japan's independence was guaranteed. Simultaneously, a power struggle within Japan led to the dominance of military governments and diminishing Imperial power.[403]

Technological significance

The Mongol invasions are an early example of gunpowder warfare. One of the most notable technological innovations during the war was the use of explosive bombs. The bombs are known in Chinese as "thunder crash bombs" and were fired from catapults, inflicting damage on enemy soldiers. An illustration of a bomb is depicted in a Japanese scroll, showing their use by the Mongols against mounted samurai. Archaeological evidence of the use of gunpowder was finally confirmed when multiple shells of the explosive bombs were discovered in an underwater shipwreck off the shore of Japan by the Kyushu Okinawa Society for Underwater Archaeology. X-rays by Japanese scientists of the excavated shells provided proof that they contained gunpowder.

Gallery

Figure 62: *Japanese attack ships*

Figure 63: *Mongol soldiers, second version*

Figure 64: *Mongol ships, second version*

References

- Satō, Kanzan (1983) *The Japanese Sword*. Kodansha International. ISBN 9780870115622
- Davis, Paul K. (1999). *100 Decisive Battles: From Ancient Times to the Present*.[404] Oxford: Oxford University Press. ISBN 978-0-19-514366-9; OCLC 0195143663[405]
- Reed, Edward J. (1880). *Japan: its History, Traditions, and Religions*. London: J. Murray. OCLC 1309476[406]
- Sansom, George. (1958). *A History of Japan to 1334*, Stanford University Press, 1958.
- Turnbull, Stephen R. (2003). *Genghis Khan and the Mongol Conquests, 1190–1400*.[407] London: Taylor & Francis. ISBN 978-0-415-96862-1
- Winters, Harold A.; Gerald E. Galloway Jr.; William J. Reynolds and David W. Rhyne. (2001). *Battling the Elements: Weather and Terrain in the Conduct of War*. Baltimore, Maryland: Johns Hopkins Press. ISBN 9780801866487; OCLC 492683854[408]

Further reading

- Conlan, Thomas. (2001). *In Little Need of Divine Intervention*[409], Cornell University Press, 2001 — includes a black-and-white reproduction of the *Moko Shurai Ekotoba*, as well as translations of relevant Kamakura-era documents and an essay by Prof. Conlan concerning the Invasions (in which he argues that the Japanese were better placed to withstand the Mongols than traditionally given credit for). The essay is available in pdf form at this link.[410]

External links

 Wikimedia Commons has media related to *Mongol invasions of Japan*.

- Mongol Invasion Scrolls Online[411] - an interactive viewer detailing the *Moko Shurai Ekotoba*, developed by Professor Thomas Conlan
- Mongol Invasions of Japan[412] - selection of photos by Louis Chor
- Mongol Invasions Painting Scrolls[413] - more illustrations from the *Moko Shurai Ekotoba*
- Goryeosa 高麗史 full text from the National Diet Library of Japan[414][415][416]
- Sasaki, Randall James (2008), *The origin of the lost fleet of the Mongol Empire*[417] (PDF) (An MA thesis discussing the construction of the invasion fleet, and the discovery of its remains by modern underwater archaeologists)
- Comprehensive Database of Archaeological Site Reports in Japan[418], Nara National Research Institute for Cultural Properties
- https//books.google.com

Mongol invasions of Tibet

Part of a series on the
History of Tibet
- Neolithic Tibet - Zhangzhung - Yarlung Dynasty - Tibetan Empire - Era of Fragmentation - Mongol Empire - Yuan rule - Phagmodrupa Dynasty - Rinpungpa Dynasty - Tsangpa Dynasty - Rise of Ganden Phodrang - Qing rule - Post-Qing to 1950 - Autonomous region of China
See also
- Timeline - Historical money - List of rulers - European exploration
Tibet portal
- v - t - e[419]

There were several **Mongol invasions of Tibet**. The earliest is the alleged plot to invade Tibet by Genghis Khan in 1206,[420] which is considered anachronistic; there is no evidence of Mongol-Tibetan encounters prior to the military campaign in 1240.[421] The first confirmed campaign is the invasion of Tibet by the Mongol general Doorda Darkhan in 1240,[422] a campaign of 30,000 troops[423,424] that resulted in 500 casualties.[425] The campaign was smaller than the full-scale invasions used by the Mongols against large empires. The purpose of this attack is unclear, and is still in debate among Tibetologists.[426] Then in the late 1240s Mongolian prince Godan invited Sakya lama Sakya Pandita, who urged other leading Tibetan figures to submit to Mongol authority.[427]

This is generally considered to have marked the beginning of Mongol rule over Tibet, as well as the establishment of patron and priest relationship between Mongols and Tibetans. These relations were continued by Kublai Khan, who founded the Mongol Yuan dynasty and granted authority over whole Tibet to Drogon Chogyal Phagpa, nephew of Sakya Pandita. The Sakya-Mongol administrative system and Yuan administrative rule over the region lasted until the mid-14th century, when the Yuan dynasty begans to crumble.

In the early 17th century, the Oirat Mongols again conquered the region and established the Khoshut Khanate. Since then the Mongols had intervened in Tibetan politics until the Qing conquest of Mongolia and Dzungaria.

Invasion

Prior to 1240

According to one traditional Tibetan account, the Mongol emperor Genghis Khan plotted to invade Tibet in 1206, but was dissuaded when the Tibetans promised to pay tribute to the Mongols.[428] Modern scholars consider the account to be anachronistic and factually wrong.[429] Genghis' campaign was targeted at the Tangut kingdom of Western Xia, not Tibet, and there was certainly no tribute being paid to the Mongols prior to 1240.[430] There are not evidences of interaction between the two nations prior to Doorda Darkhan's invasion in 1240.[431]

The earliest real Mongol contact with the ethnic Tibetan people came in 1236, when a Tibetan chief near Wenxian submitted to the Mongols campaigning against the Jin dynasty in Sichuan.

1240

Doorda Darkhan's Tibetan campaign	
Date	1240
Location	Tibet
Result	Mongols withdrew. All Mongol generals were called back to Mongolia to appoint a successor to Ogedai Khan.
Belligerents	
Mongol Empire	Tibet
Commanders and leaders	
Doorda Darkhan	Leaders of the Rwa-sgreng monastery
Strength	
30,000 soldiers	Unknown

Casualties and losses	
Minimal (or no loss)	500

In 1240, the Mongol Prince Godan, Ögedei's son and Güyük's younger brother, "delegated the command of the Tibetan invasion to the Tangut[432] general, Doorda Darqan (Dor-ta)".[433] The expedition was "the first instance of military conflict between the two nations". The attack consisted of 30,000 men (most possibly much smaller than that)[434,435] and resulted in 500 casualties, along with the burning of the Kadampa monasteries of Rwa-sgreṅ and Rgyal-lha-khang. The campaign was smaller than the full-scale invasions used by the Mongols against large empires. According to Turrell V. Wylie, that much is in agreement among Tibetologists. However, the purpose of invasion is disputed among Tibetan scholars, partly because of the abundance of anachronistic and factually erroneous sources.

However, modern studies find that the oldest sources credit the Mongol scouts with burning Rgyal-lha-khang only, while a large number of Rwa-sgreng monks were slain.[436] The bKa'-brgyud-pa monasteries of sTag-lung and 'Bri-gung, with their old link to the Western Xia dynasty, were spared because Doorda himself was a Tangut Buddhist.[437] The 'Bri-gung abbot or, according to Petech, the Rwa-sgreng abbot, suggested the Mongols had invited the Sakya hierarch, Sakya Pandita.[438] After he met Godan, Sakya Pandita died there leaving his two nephews. Sakya Pandita convinced other monasteries in Central Tibet to align with the Mongols. The Mongols kept them as hostages referring symbolic surrender of Tibet.[439]

One view, considered the most traditional, is that the attack was a retaliation on Tibet caused by the Tibetan refusal to pay tribute. Wylie points out that the Tibetans stopped paying tribute in 1227, while Doorda Darkhan's invasion was in 1240, suggesting that the Mongols, not known for their empathy, would not wait over a decade to respond. The text from which this claim is based on also makes other anachronistic mistakes, insisting that Genghis was planning to attack Tibet prior to Doorda Darkhan's invasion, when the real campaign was against the Tangut kingdom of Western Xia.

Another theory, supported by Wylie, is that the military action was a reconnaissance campaign meant to evaluate the political situation in Tibet.[440] The Mongols hoped to find a single monarch with whom they could threaten into submission, but instead found a Tibet that was religiously and politically divided, without a central government.

A third view is that the troops were sent as raids and "looting parties", and that the goal of the campaign was to pillage the "wealth amassed in the Tibetan monasteries".[441] This is disputed, as the Mongols deliberately avoided

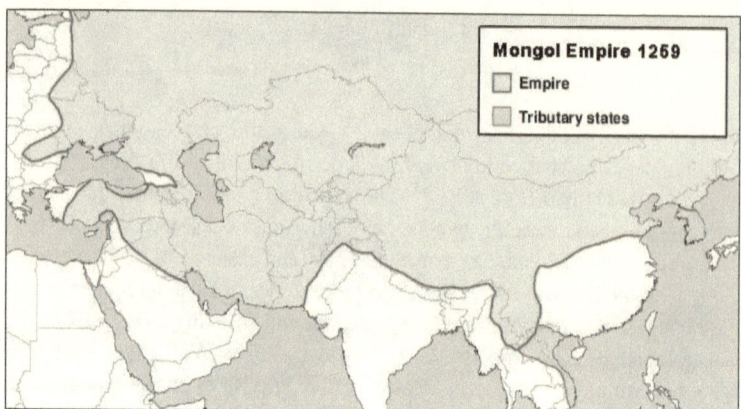

Figure 65: *The Mongol Empire in 1259*

attacking certain monasteries, a questionable decision if their only goal was profit.[442]

Whatever the purpose of the invasion, the Mongols withdrew in 1241, as all the Mongol princes were recalled back to Mongolia in preparation for the appointment of a successor to Ogedai Khan.[443] In 1244, the Mongols returned to Tibet. They invited Sakya Pandita to Godan's camp, where he agreed to capitulate Tibet, after the Mongols threatened a full-scale invasion of the region.

Putative invasion under Möngke Khan

Sa-skya Pandita died in 1251 and his master Köten possibly died at the same time (or, according to other sources, after 1253). Möngke Khan became Khagan in the same year. Some sources say there was a Mongolian invasion in 1251, in retribution for a failure to pay tribute, or in 1251-2 'to take formal possession of the country'. In order to strengthen his control over Tibet, Möngke made Qoridai commander of the Mongol and Han troops in Tufan in 1251. Two attacks are mentioned, one led by Dörbetei, the other by Qoridai, and the double campaign struck fear into the Tibetans.[444] Tibetan sources however only mention an attack on a place called *Bod kyi-mon-mkhar-mgpon-po-gdong*,. Wyle is sceptical however of all of these sources, arguing that the lack of substantive evidence for an invasion raises doubts about the extent of Mongol movements in Tibet proper.'[445] He concludes:-

> "Excluding the 1252 attack against the unidentified Mon-mkmar-mgon-po-gdong mentioned earlier, there seems to be no evidence to prove the presence of Mongol troops in central Tibet during the two

decades that 'Phags-pa Lama was away from Sa-skya (1244-65). During those years, external campaigns of conquest and internal feuds between scions of the sons of Chinggis Khan occupied the attention of the Mongols. Tibet, whose formidable terrain was politically fragmented by local lords and lamas, posed no military threat to the Mongols, and it was all but ignored by them.'[446]

In 1252-53 Qoridai invaded Tibet, reaching as far as Damxung. The Central Tibetan monasteries submitted to the Mongols. Möngke divided the lands of Tibet between his relatives as their appanages in accordance with Great Jasag of Genghis Khan. Many Mongol aristocrats including Khagan himself seem to have sought blessings of prominent Tibetan lamas. Möngke Khan patronized Karma Baqshi (1204–83) of the Karma-pa suborder and the 'Bri-gung Monastery, while Hulagu, khan of the Mongols in the Middle East, sent lavish gifts to both 'Bri-gung and the Phag-mo-gru-pa suborder's gDan-sa-thel monastery. Later William Rubruck reports that he saw Chinese, Tibetan, and Indian Buddhist monks at the capital city, Karakorum, of the Mongol Empire.

Although, Karmapa of the Karma Kagyu school politely refused to stay with him, preferring his brother the Khagan, in 1253 Prince Kubilai summoned to his court the Sa-skya-pa hierarch's two nephews, Blo-gros rGyal-mtshan, known as 'Phags-Pa lama (1235–80), and Phyag-na rDo-rje (1239-67) from the late Köten's ordo in Liangzhou. Khubilai Khan first met 'Phags-pa lama in 1253, presumably to bring the Sa-skya lama who resided in Köden's domain, and who was a symbol of Tibetan surrender, to his own camp.[447] At first Kublai remained shamanist, but his chief khatun, Chabui (Chabi), converted to Buddhism and influenced Kublai's religious view. During Kublai's expedition into Yunnan, his number two, Uriyangkhadai, had to station in Tibet in 1254-55 possibly to suppress war-like tribes in Tibet. Hulegu appointed his representative, Kokochu, in Tibet in mid-1250s while marching towards Iran.[448] Since then, the Ilkhans had had possessions in Tibet.

In 1265 Qongridar ravaged the Tufan/mDo-smad area, and from 1264 to 1275 several campaigns pacified the Tibetan and Yi peoples of Xifan around modern Xichang. By 1278 Mongol myriarchies: tumens and postroads reached through mDo-khams as far west as Litang.

Aftermath

Tibet was subdued to the Mongol Empire under Mongolian administrative rule,[449] but the region was granted with a degree of political autonomy. Kublai Khan would later include Tibet into his Yuan dynasty, and the region remained administratively separate from the conquered provinces of Song dynasty China.

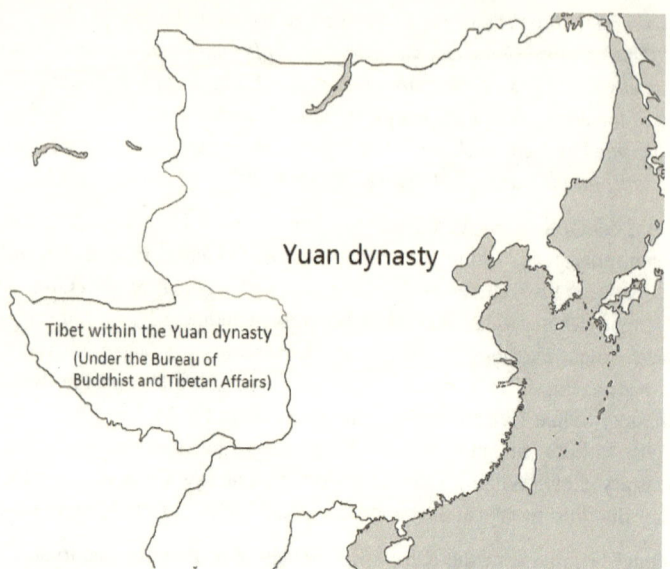

Figure 66: *Tibet within the Yuan dynasty under the top-level department known as the Bureau of Buddhist and Tibetan Affairs (Xuanzheng Yuan).*

According to the Tibetan traditional view, the khan and the lama established "priest-patron" relations. This meant administrative management and military assistance from the khan and assistance from the lama in spiritual issues. Tibet was conquered by the Mongols before the Mongol invasion of South China.[450] After the conquest of the Song dynasty, Kublai Khan consolidated Tibet into the new Yuan dynasty, but Tibet was ruled under the Bureau of Buddhist and Tibetan Affairs (Xuanzheng Yuan), separate from the Chinese provinces. The Mongols granted the Sakya lama a degree political authority, but retained control over the administration and military of the region.[451] As efforts to rule both territories while preserving Mongol identity, Kublai Khan prohibited Mongols from marrying Chinese, but left both the Chinese and Tibetan legal and administrative systems intact.[452] Though most government institutions established by Kublai Khan in his court resembled the ones in earlier Chinese dynasties,[453] Tibet never adopted the imperial examinations or Neo-Confucian policies.

Buddhist monks from Tibet were popular and well respected in Mongol-ruled Iran (the Ilkhanate), Mongolia, China (the Yuan) and Central Asia (the Chagatai Khanate).[454] Towards the end of the Yuan dynasty in the mid-14th century, Tibet regained its independence from the Mongols.

Post imperial expedition

The Ligdan Khan and prince Choghtu's campaign	
Date	1634-1637
Location	Tibet
Result	Victory of Oirat's Khoshut Khanate increased power of Gelug-Buddhism and fall Karma Kagyu and fall of the campaign prince Choghtu force.

Belligerents	
• Khoshut Khanate • Tibet by support • Khoshut Khanate	• Chahar Mongolian Khanate force • Northern khalkha's Khanate force
Commanders and leaders	
Güshi Khan	• Ligdan Khan • Prince Choghtu • Prince Arslang Tayji
Strength	
unknown	50 000
Casualties and losses	
minimally	heavy

The Oirats converted to Tibetan Buddhism around 1615, and it was not long before they became involved in the conflict between the Gelug and Karma Kagyu schools. At the request of the Gelug school, in 1637, Güshi Khan, the leader of the Khoshuts in Koko Nor, defeated Choghtu Khong Tayiji (1581-1637), the Khalkha prince who supported the Karma Kagyu school.

Tsogtu Khuntaiji had established a base on the Tuul river. Known as an intellectual, he embraced the Karma sect and built monasteries and castles. He submitted himself to Ligdan Khan, last grand khan of the Mongols. He took part in Ligdan's campaign to Tibet to help the Karma sect although Ligdan Khan died in 1634 before they joined together. But Tsogtu pursued the campaign. In the same year he conquered the Tümed around Kokonor (Qinghai Lake) and moved his base there. By request from Shamar Rabjampa he sent an army under his son Arslan to central Tibet in 1635. However, Arslan attacked his ally, the Tsang army. He met the fifth Dalai Lama and paid homage to Gelukpa monasteries instead of destroying them. Arslan was eventually assassinated by Choghtu's order.

The Geluk sect asked for help Törü Bayikhu (Güshi Khan), the leader of the Khoshut tribe of the Oirat confederation. In 1636 Törö Bayikhu led the Khoshuts and the Dzungars to Tibet. In the next year a decisive war between Tsogtu Khuntaiji and Törü Bayikhu ended in the latter's victory and Tsoghtu was killed.

He has traditionally been portrayed as evil by the Geluk sect. On the other hand, the Mongolian movie "Tsogt taij" (1945) treated him as a national hero. It reflected the communist regime's attitude toward Tibetan Buddhism.Wikipedia:Please clarify

With his crushing victory over Tsogtu, Güshi Khan conquered Amdo (present-day Qinghai). The unification of Tibet followed in 1641-42, when Güshi Khan invaded Central Tibet and defeated the indigenous Tsangpa Dynasty. After his victory he was proclaimed (chogyal), i.e. the King of Dharma, or Teaching, by the Fifth Dalai Lama. With these events the establishment of a Khoshut Khanate was confirmed. Gushi khan granted to the Dalai Lama authority over Tibet from Dartsedo to Ladakh. The title "Dalai Lama" itself had previously been bestowed upon the third lama of the Gelug tulku lineage by Altan Khan (not to be confused with the Altan Khans of the Khalkha), and means, in Mongolian, "Ocean of Wisdom."

Resurfacing of the struggle between Dzungar Khanate and Qing dynasty

Mongol invasions of Tibet	
Date	1688-1755
Location	Tibet
Result	Victory of the Qing empire.
Belligerents	
• Dzungar Khanate • Kokonur rebels	Qing empire
Commanders and leaders	
• Galdan Boshugtu Khan • prince Tsewang Arabtan • Galdan Tseren Khan • Tsering Dhondup • Loupsang Danzan	• Kangxi • Yongzheng • Qianlong • Lha-bzang Khan

Intervention in Tibet

Amdo, meanwhile, became home to the Khoshuts. The descendants of Güshi Khan continued to rule as Dharma kings (chogyals) of Tibet, although they were eclipsed by the Dalai Lama and his regent for long periods. In 1717, however, the Dzungars, led by Tsewang Rabtan's brother Tsering Dondup, invaded Tibet. The invaders defeated and killed Lha-bzang Khan (the last khan of the Khoshut Khanate), a great-grandson of Güshi Khan and the fifth Dharma king of Tibet. The Dzungars deposed a pretender to the position of the Dalai Lama who had previously been promoted by Lha-bzang Khan. The 5th

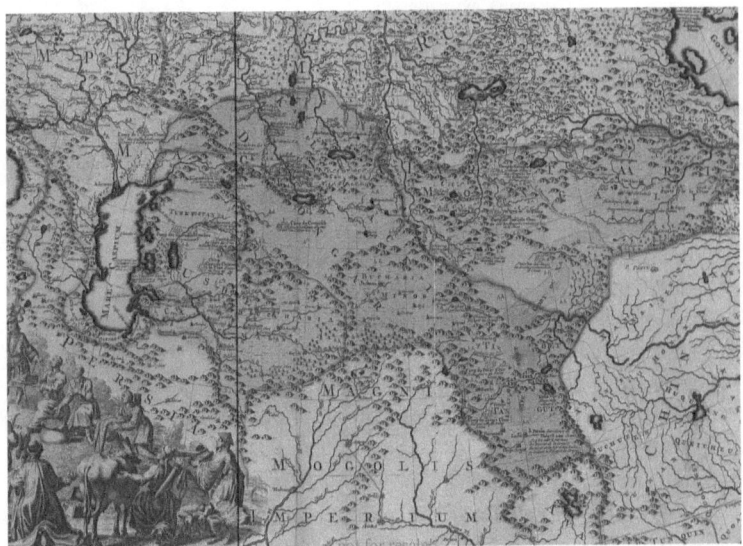

Figure 67: *The Dzungar and Kalmyk states (a fragment of the map of the Russian Empire of Peter the Great, created by a Swedish soldier in c. 1725).*

Dalai Lama had encouraged Mongolian lamas to prevent any non-dGe-lugs-pa teaching among the Mongols. The Dzungars soon began to loot Lhasa, thus losing initial Tibetan goodwill towards them. Many Nyingmapa and Bonpos were executed and Tibetans visiting Dzungar officials were forced to stick their tongues out so the Dzungars could tell if the person recited constant mantras (which was said to make the tongue black or brown). This allowed them to pick the Nyingmapa and Bonpos, who recited many magic-mantras.[455] This habit of sticking one's tongue out as a mark of respect on greeting someone has remained a Tibetan custom until recent times.

The Dzungar invasion was a challenge to the imperial policy of the Kangxi Emperor, since Lha-bzang Khan had been allied to the Qing dynasty. The Emperor retaliated in 1718, but his military expedition suffered inadequate logistics and was annihilated by the Dzungars at the Battle of the Salween River not far from Lhasa.[456] A second and larger expedition was dispatched by the Emperor and met with rapid success. The Manchus expelled Tsewang Rabtan's force from Tibet in 1720 and the troops were hailed as liberators. They brought Kälzang Gyatso with them from Kumbum to Lhasa and he was installed as the 7th Dalai Lama in 1721.[457] In 1723 Lobzang Danjin, another descendant of Güshi Khan, defended Amdo against Qing dynasty's attempts to extend its rule into Tibet, but was crushed in the following year. Thus, Amdo fell under Chinese domination.

References

Sources

- Laird, Thomas. *The Story of Tibet: Conversations with the Dalai Lama* (2006) Grove Press. ISBN 0-8021-1827-5
- Rossabi, Morris. *China Among Equals: The Middle Kingdom and Its Neighbors, 10th-14th Centuries* (1983) Univ. of California Press. ISBN 0-520-04383-9
- Sanders, Alan J. K. *Historical dictionary of Mongolia* (2003) Scarecrow Press. ISBN 0-8108-4434-6
- Saunders, John Joseph. *The history of the Mongol conquests.* (2001) University of Pennsylvania Press. ISBN 0-8122-1766-7
- Shakabpa, W.D. *Tibet: A Political History.* (1967) Yale University Press. ISBN 0-9611474-1-5
- Smith, Warren W., Jr. *Tibetan Nation: A History Of Tibetan Nationalism And Sino-tibetan Relations* (1997) Westview Press. ISBN 978-0-8133-3280-2

Europe

Mongol invasion of Europe

Mongol invasion of Europe
Part of Mongol invasions and conquests
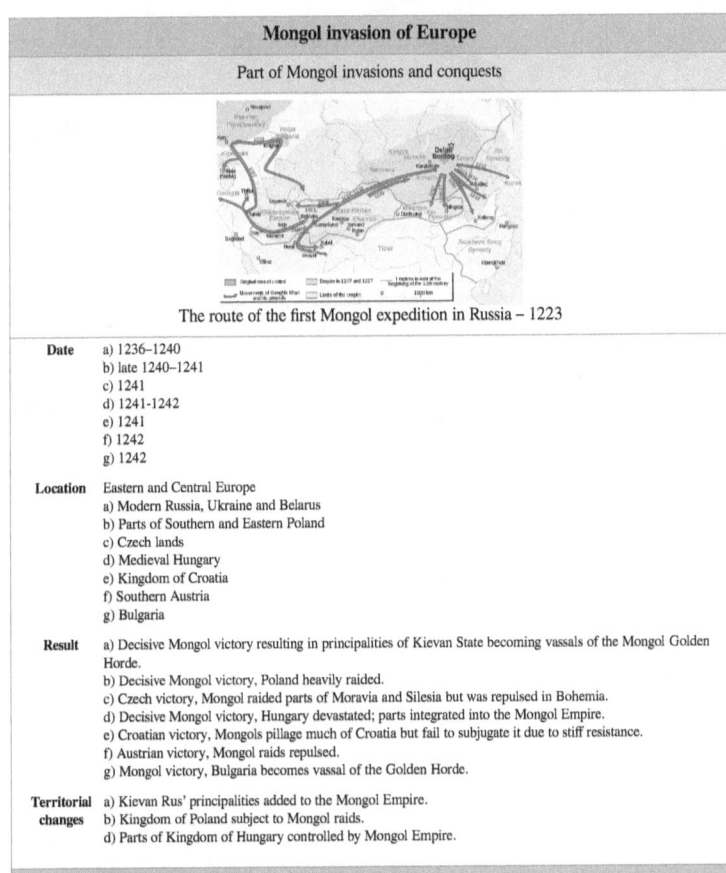 The route of the first Mongol expedition in Russia – 1223

Date	a) 1236–1240 b) late 1240–1241 c) 1241 d) 1241-1242 e) 1241 f) 1242 g) 1242
Location	Eastern and Central Europe a) Modern Russia, Ukraine and Belarus b) Parts of Southern and Eastern Poland c) Czech lands d) Medieval Hungary e) Kingdom of Croatia f) Southern Austria g) Bulgaria
Result	a) Decisive Mongol victory resulting in principalities of Kievan State becoming vassals of the Mongol Golden Horde. b) Decisive Mongol victory, Poland heavily raided. c) Czech victory, Mongol raided parts of Moravia and Silesia but was repulsed in Bohemia. d) Decisive Mongol victory, Hungary devastated; parts integrated into the Mongol Empire. e) Croatian victory, Mongols pillage much of Croatia but fail to subjugate it due to stiff resistance. f) Austrian victory, Mongol raids repulsed. g) Mongol victory, Bulgaria becomes vassal of the Golden Horde.
Territorial changes	a) Kievan Rus' principalities added to the Mongol Empire. b) Kingdom of Poland subject to Mongol raids. d) Parts of Kingdom of Hungary controlled by Mongol Empire.
Belligerents	

Golden Horde (Mongol Empire)	a) Kievan Rus' principalities: Kiev, Chernigov, Vladimir-Suzdal, Galicia-Volhynia, Novgorod Republic, Principality of Ryazan, Volga Bulgaria, Alans, Cuman-Kipchak confederation, Circassians, North Caucasian peoples
	b) Polish duchies: Silesia, Masovia, Lesser Poland, Greater Poland, Opole
	c) Kingdom of Bohemia, Moravian Magraviate
	d) Kingdom of Hungary, Knights Templar
	e) Kingdom of Croatia
	f) Duchy of Austria
	g) Bulgarian Empire
Commanders and leaders	

Mongol invasion of Europe

a) Batu Khan Möngke Khan Subutai Jebe Burundai Berke Orda Güyük Khan	a) Prince Mstislav Mstislavich Prince Yuri II of Vladimir † Prince Mstislav III (POW) Prince Mstislav II Khan Köten Prince Daniel of Galicia
b) Baidar (possibly †) Kadan Orda Khan	b) Duke Henry II † Mieszko II the Fat Voivode Włodzimierz † Sulisław † Voivode Pakosław †
c) Batu Khan Subutai Shiban Berke Burundai	c) King Wenceslaus I Margrave Děpolt III
	d) King Béla IV Archbishop Ugrin Csák † Archbishop Matthias Rátót † Palatine Denis Tomaj †
d) Batu Khan Kadan	
	e) King Béla IV Duke Coloman (DOW)
	f) Duke Frederick II
	g) Tsar Ivan Asen II
Strength	
a) 75,000+ cavalry including Turkic auxiliaries	a) 25,000-50,000 including garrisons and Cumans[461]
b) 10,000 cavalry (one tumen)[458]	b) ~10,000 soldiers (2,000-8,000 at Legnica)[462]
d) 30,000 cavalry (contemporary sources)[459] other estimates: 70,000[460] 25,000	d) 10,000-15,000 soldiers (contemporary sources)[463] other estimates: 80,000[464] 25,000
Casualties and losses	
a) More than 7,000	a) 500,000 civilians[465] thousands of soldiers
b) Minimal	b) Heavy
d) Few thousand soldiers killed	d) 10,000-20,000 soldiers killed[466] 300,000-500,000 civilians
f) 300-700 soldiers killed	f) 100 soldiers killed

The **Mongol invasion of Europe** in the 13th century was the conquest of Europe by the Mongol Empire, by way of the destruction of East Slavic principalities, such as Kiev and Vladimir. The Mongol invasions also occurred in Central Europe, which led to warfare among fragmented Poland, such as the

Figure 68: *Returning to Vladimir by Yaroslav II of Vladimir after Mongol destruction. From the medieval Russian annals*

Battle of Legnica (9 April 1241) and in the Battle of Mohi (11 April 1241) in the Kingdom of Hungary.

The operations were planned by General Subutai (1175–1248) and commanded by Batu Khan (c. 1207–1255) and Kadan (d. c. 1261). Both men were grandsons of Genghis Khan; their conquests integrated much European territory to the empire of the Golden Horde. Warring European princes realized they had to cooperate in the face of a Mongol invasion, so local wars and conflicts were suspended in parts of central Europe, only to be resumed after the Mongols had withdrawn.

Invasions and conquest of Rus' lands

Ögedei Khan ordered Batu Khan to conquer Rus' in 1235. The main force, headed by Jochi's sons, and their cousins, Möngke Khan and Güyük Khan, arrived at Ryazan in December 1237. Ryazan refused to surrender, and the Mongols sacked it and then stormed Suzdalia. Many Rus' armies were defeated; Grand Prince Yuri was killed on the Sit River (March 4, 1238). Major cities such as Vladimir, Torzhok, and Kozelsk were captured.

Afterward, the Mongols turned their attention to the steppe, crushing the Kypchaks and the Alans and sacking Crimea. Batu appeared in Ukraine in

Mongol invasion of Europe

Figure 69: *The Mongol army captures a Rus' city*

1239, sacking Pereiaslav and Chernihiv. Most of the Rus' princes fled when it became clear resistance was futile. The Mongols sacked Kiev on December 6, 1240 and conquered Galich and Volodymyr-Volynskyi. Batu sent a small detachment to probe the Poles before passing on to Central Europe. One column was routed by the Poles while the other defeated the Polish army and returned.

The Mongols had acquired Chinese gunpowder, which they deployed in battle during the invasion of Europe to great success.

Invasion into Central Europe

The attack on Europe was planned and executed by Subutai, who achieved perhaps his most lasting fame with his victories there. Having devastated the various Rus' principalities, he sent spies into Poland and Hungary, and as far as eastern Austria, in preparation for an attack into the heartland of Europe.[467] Having a clear picture of the European kingdoms, he prepared an attack nominally commanded by Batu Khan and two other familial-related princes. Batu Khan, son of Jochi, was the overall leader, but Subutai was the strategist and commander in the field, and as such, was present in both the northern and southern campaigns against Rus' principalities.[468] He also commanded the central column that moved against Hungary. While Kadan's northern force

Figure 70: *Henry II the Pious who lost his life at the battle of Legnica, 19th-century painting by Jan Matejko.*

won the Battle of Legnica and Güyük's army triumphed in Transylvania, Subutai was waiting for them on the Hungarian plain. The newly reunited army then withdrew to the Sajo River where they inflicted a decisive defeat on King Béla IV of Hungary at the Battle of Mohi. Again, Subutai masterminded the operation, and it would prove one of his greatest victories.

Invasion of fragmented Poland

The Mongols invaded Central Europe with three armies. One army defeated an alliance which included forces from fragmented Poland and their allies, led by Henry II the Pious, Duke of Silesia in the Battle of Legnica. A second army crossed the Carpathian mountains and a third followed the Danube. The armies re-grouped and crushed Hungary in 1241, defeating the Hungarian army at the Battle of Mohi on April 11, 1241. The devastating Mongol invasion killed half of Hungary's population.[469] The armies swept the plains of Hungary over the summer, and in the spring of 1242, regained impetus and extended their control into Dalmatia and Moravia. The Great Khan had, however, died in December 1241, and on hearing the news, all the "Princes of the Blood," against Subotai's recommendation, went back to Mongolia to elect the new Khan.[470]

Mongol invasion of Europe

Figure 71: *The Mongols at Liegnitz display the head of King Henry II of the Duchy of Silesia.*

After sacking Kiev,[471] Batu Khan sent a smaller group of troops to Poland, destroying Lublin and defeating an inferior Polish army. Other elements—not part of the main Mongol force—saw difficulty near the Polish-Galich border.

The Mongols then reached Polaniec on the Czarna Hańcza, where they set up camp.[472] There, the Voivode attacked them with the remaining Cracovian knights, which were few in number, but determined to vanquish the invader or die. Surprise gave the Poles an initial advantage and they managed to kill many Mongol soldiers. When the invaders realized the actual numerical weakness of the Poles, they regrouped, broke through the Polish ranks and defeated them. During the fighting, many Polish prisoners of war found ways to escape and hide in the nearby woods. The Polish defeat was partly influenced by the initially successful Polish knights having been distracted by looting.

Invasion of Czech lands

After the defeat of the European forces at Legnica, the Mongols then continued pillaging throughout Poland's neighboring kingdoms, particularly Silesia and Moravia. King Wenceslaus I of Bohemia fled back to protect his kingdom after arriving late and discovering the devastation the Mongols caused in those places; gathering reinforcements from Thuringia and Saxony as he retreated. He stationed his troops in the mountainous regions of Bohemia where the Mongols wouldn't be able to utilize their cavalry effectively.[473]

By that time, the Mongolian forces had divided into two, one led by Batu and Subutai who were planning to invade Hungary, and another led by Baidar and Kadan who were ravaging their way through Silesia and Moravia. When they arrived to attack Bohemia, the kingdom's defenses discouraged them from attacking and they withdrew to the town of Othmachau.[474] A small force of Mongolians did attack Kłodzko but the Bohemian cavalry under Wenceslaus managed to fend them off.[475,476] The Mongols then tried to take the town of Olomouc, but Wenceslaus managed to get the aid of the Duke of Austria and they repulsed the raid.[477,478] A Mongol commander was captured in a sortie near Olomouc.[479] Under Wenceslaus' leadership during the Mongol invasion, Bohemia remained one of a few European kingdoms that was never conquered and molested by the Mongols even though most kingdoms around it such as Poland and Moravia were ravaged. Such was his success that chroniclers sent messages to Emperor Frederick II of his "victorious defense".[480] After these failed attempts, Baidar and Kadan continued raiding Moravia before finally going southward to reunite with Batu and Subutai in Hungary.

Invasion of the Kingdom of Hungary

The Hungarians had first learned about the Mongol threat in 1229, when King Andrew II granted asylum to some fleeing Russian boyars. Some Magyars (Hungarians), left behind during the main migration to the Pannonian basin, still lived on the banks of the upper Volga (it is believed by some that the descendants of this group are the modern-day Bashkirs, although this people now speaks a Turkic language, not Magyar). In 1237 a Dominican friar, Julianus, set off on an expedition to lead them back, and was sent back to King Béla with a letter from Batu Khan. In this letter, Batu called upon the Hungarian king to surrender his kingdom unconditionally to the Tatar forces or face complete destruction. Béla did not reply, and two more messages were later delivered to Hungary. The first, in 1239, was sent by the defeated Cuman tribes, who asked for and received asylum in Hungary. The second was sent in February 1241 by the defeated Polish princes.

Only then did King Béla call upon his magnates to join his army in defense of the country. He also asked the papacy and the Western European rulers for help. Foreign help came in the form of a small knight-detachment under the leadership of Frederick II, Duke of Austria, but it was too small to change the outcome of the campaign. The majority of the Hungarian magnates also did not realize the urgency of the matter. Some may have hoped that a defeat of

Figure 72: *Battle of Mohi in a Medieval-era depiction*

the royal army would force Béla to discontinue his centralization efforts and thus strengthen their own power.

Although the Mongol danger was real and imminent, Hungary was not prepared to deal with it; in the minds of a people who had lived free from nomadic invasions for the last few hundred years, an invasion seemed impossible, and Hungary was no longer a predominantly soldier population. Only rich nobles were trained as heavy-armored cavalry. The Hungarians had long since forgotten the light-cavalry strategy and tactics of their ancestors, which were similar to those now used by the Mongols. The Hungarian army (some 60,000 on the eve of the Battle of Mohi) was made up of individual knights with tactical knowledge, discipline, and talented commanders. Because his army was not experienced in nomadic warfare, King Béla welcomed the Cuman King Kuthen (also known as Kotony) and his fighters. However, the Cuman invitation proved detrimental to the Hungarians because Batu Khan considered this acceptance of a group he considered rebels as justifications for his invasion of Hungary. After rumors began to circulate in Hungary that the Cumans were agents of the Mongols, some hot-headed Hungarians attacked the Cuman camp and killed Kotony. This led the enraged Cumans to ride south, looting, ravaging the countryside, and slaughtering the unsuspecting Magyar population. The Austrian troops retreated to Austria shortly thereafter to gain more western aid. The Hungarians now stood alone in the defense of their country.

The 1241 Mongol invasion first affected Moldavia and Wallachia (situated east and south of the Carpathians). Tens of thousands of Wallachians and Moldavians lost their lives defending their territories from the Golden Horde. Crops and goods plundered from Wallachian settlements seem to have been a primary supply source for the Golden Horde. The invaders killed up to half of the population and burned down most of their settlements, thus destroying much of the cultural and economic records from that period. Neither Wallachians nor the army of Hungary offered much resistance against the Mongols. The swiftness of the invasion took many by surprise and forced them to retreat and hide in forests and the enclosed valleys of the Carpathians. In the end, however, the main target of the invasion was the Kingdom of Hungary.

The Hungarian army arrived and encamped at the Sajó River on April 10, 1241, without having been directly challenged by the Mongols. The Mongols, having largely concealed their positions, began their attack the next night; after heavier-than-expected losses inflicted by Hungarian crossbowmen, the Mongols adjusted their strategy and routed the Hungarian forces rapidly. A major Hungarian loss was imminent, and the Mongols intentionally left a gap in their formation to permit the wavering Hungarian forces to flee and spread out in doing so, leaving them unable to effectively resist the Mongols as they picked off the retreating Hungarian remnants. While the king escaped with the help of his bodyguard, the remaining Hungarian army was mercilessly killed by the Mongols or drowned in the river as they attempted escape. Following their decisive victory, the Mongols now systematically occupied the Great Hungarian Plains, the slopes of the northern Carpathian Mountains, and Transylvania. Where they found local resistance, they ruthlessly killed the population. Where the locale offered no resistance, they forced the men into servitude in the Mongol army. Still, tens of thousands avoided Mongol domination by taking refuge behind the walls of the few existing fortresses or by hiding in the forests or large marshes along the rivers. The Mongols, instead of leaving the defenseless and helpless people and continuing their campaign through Pannonia to Western Europe, spent the entire summer and fall securing and pacifying the occupied territories. On Christmas day 1241, the costly siege of Esztergom destroyed the capital and economic center of the Kingdom of Hungary, forcing the capital to be moved to Budapest.[481]

During the winter, contrary to the traditional strategy of nomadic armies which started campaigns only in spring-time, they crossed the Danube and continued their systematic occupation, including Pannonia. They eventually reached the Austrian borders and the Adriatic shores in Dalmatia. The Mongols appointed a *darughachi* in Hungary and minted coins in the name of Khagan.[482] According to Michael Prawdin, the country of Béla was assigned to Orda by Batu as an appanage. At least 20%-40% of the population died, by slaughter or epidemic. Rogerius of Apulia, an Italian monk and chronicler who witnessed and survived the invasion, pointed out not only the genocidal element of the occupation, but also that the Mongols especially "found pleasure" in humiliating local women. But while the Mongols claimed control of Hungary, they could not occupy fortified cities such as Fehérvár, Veszprém, Tihany, Győr, Pannonhalma, Moson, Sopron, Vasvár, Újhely, Zala, Léka, Pozsony, Nyitra, Komárom, Fülek and Abaújvár. Learning from this lesson, fortresses came to play a significant role in Hungary. King Béla IV rebuilt the country and invested in fortifications. Facing a shortage of money, he welcomed the settlement of Jewish families, investors, and tradesmen, granting them citizenship rights. The King also welcomed tens of thousands of Kun (Cumans) who had fled the country before the invasion. Chinese fire arrows were deployed by Mongols against the city of Buda on December 25, 1241, which they overran.

The Mongolian invasion taught the Magyars a simple lesson: although the Mongols had destroyed the countryside, the forts and fortified cities had survived. To improve their defense capabilities for the future, they had to build forts, not only on the borders but also inside the country. In the siege of Esztergom, the Spanish defenses manage to hold off the Mongolians despite having overwhelming numerical superiority and 30 siege machines which they had just used to reduce the wooden towers of the city.[483,484] During the remaining decades of the 13th century and throughout the 14th century, the kings donated more and more royal land to the magnates with the condition that they build forts and ensure their defenses.

Invasion of the Kingdom of Croatia

During the Middle Ages, the Kingdom of Croatia was in a personal union with the Kingdom of Hungary, with Béla IV as a king.[485]

When routed on the banks of the Sajo River in 1241 by the Mongols, Béla IV fled to today's Zagreb in Croatia. Batu sent a few tumens (roughly 20,000 men at arms) under Khadan in pursuit of Bela. The major objective was not the conquest but the capture of the Arpad king. The poorly fortified Zagreb was unable to resist the invasion and was destroyed, its cathedral burned by Mongols.[486] In preparation for a second invasion, Gradec was granted a royal charter or Golden Bull of 1242 by King Béla IV, after which citizens of Zagreb engaged in building defensive walls and towers around their settlement.[487]

The Mongols' pursuit of Béla IV continued from Zagreb through Pannonia to Dalmatia. While in pursuit, the Mongols under the leadership of Kadan (Qadan) suffered a major defeat at Klis Fortress in Croatia in March 1242.[488] The Mongols pursued Béla IV from town to town in Dalmatia, while Croatian nobility and Dalmatian towns such as Trogir and Rab helped Béla IV to escape. After their defeat against the Croatian soldiers, the Mongols retreated and Béla

Figure 73: *At Klis Fortress the Mongols experienced defeat in 1242.*

IV was awarded Croatian towns and nobility. Only the city of Split did not aid Béla IV in his escape from the Mongols. Some historians claim that the mountainous terrain of Croatian Dalmatia was fatal for the Mongols because of the great losses they suffered from Croat ambushes set up in mountain passes. In any case, though much of Croatia was plundered and destroyed, long-term occupation was unsuccessful.

Saint Margaret (January 27, 1242 – January 18, 1271), a daughter of Béla IV and Maria Laskarina, was born in Klis Fortress during the Mongol invasion of Hungary-Croatia in 1242.[489]

Invasion of Austria

The subjugation of Hungary opened a pathway for the Mongol Horde to invade Vienna. Using similar tactics during their campaigns in previous Eastern and Central European countries, the Mongols first launched small squadrons to attack isolated settlements in the outskirts of Vienna in an attempt to instill fear and panic among the populace. In 1241 the Mongols raided Wiener Neustadt and its neighboring districts, located south of Vienna. Wiener Neustadt took the brunt of the attack and like previous invasions the Mongols committed horrible atrocities on the relatively unarmed populace. The Duke of Austria, Frederick II, had previously engaged the Mongols in Olomouc and in the initial stages of the Battle of Mohi. Unlike in Hungary however, Vienna under the leadership of Duke Frederick and his knights, together with their foreign allies, managed to rally quicker and annihilate the small Mongolian squadron.[490,491] After the battle, the Duke estimated that the Mongols lost over 300 to 700 men while the Europeans only lost 100. Austrian knights also subsequently defeated the Mongols at the borders of the River March in the district of Theben.[492] After the failed initial raids, the rest of the Mongols retired back into Russia after learning of the Great Khan Ögedei's death.

Invasion of Bulgaria

During his withdrawal from Hungary back into Russia, part of Batu Khan's army invaded Bulgaria. A Mongolian force was defeated by the Bulgarian army under Tsar Ivan Asen II.[493] A larger force returned to raid Bulgaria again the same year, though little is known of what happened. According to the Persian historian Rashid-al-Din Hamadani, the Buglarian capital of Tarnovo was sacked. This is unlikely, but rumor of it spread widely, being repeated in Palestine by Bar Hebraeus.[494] The invasion of Bulgaria is mentioned in other contemporary sources, such as Philippe Mouskès, Thomas of Cantimpré and Ricoldo of Montecroce.[495] Contemporary documents indicate that by 1253, Kaliman I was a tribute-paying vassal of the Mongols, a status he had probably been forced to accept during the invasion of 1242.[496]

European tactics against Mongols

The traditional European method of warfare of melee combat between knights ended in catastrophe when it was deployed against the Mongol forces as the Mongols were able to keep a distance and advance with superior numbers. The *New Encyclopædia Britannica*, Volume 29 says that "Employed against the Mongol invaders of Europe, knightly warfare failed even more disastrously for the Poles at the Battle of Legnica and the Hungarians at the Battle of Mohi in 1241. Feudal Europe was saved from sharing the fate of China and Muscovy not by its tactical prowess but by the unexpected death of the Mongols' supreme ruler, Ögedei, and the subsequent eastward retreat of his armies."

However, during the initial Mongol invasion and the subsequent raids afterwards, heavily armored knights and cavalry proved more effective at fighting the Mongols than their light-armored counterparts. During the Battle of Mohi for example, while the Hungarian light cavalry and infantry were decimated by Mongol forces, the heavily armored knights in their employ (such as the Knights Templar) fought significantly better.[497] During the Battle of Legnica, the Knights Templar that numbered between 65-88 during the battle lost only three knights and 2 sergeants.[498] Austrian knights under Duke Frederick also fared better in fighting the Mongol invasion in Vienna.

King Béla IV hired the help of the Knights of St. John, as well as training his own better-armed local knights, in preparation for the Second Mongol invasion of Hungary.[499] In the decades following the Mongolian raids on European settlements, Western armies (particularly Hungary) have started to adapt to the Mongol tactics by building better fortifications against siege weapons and improving their heavy cavalry.[500] During the next invasion of Hungary by the Mongols, Hungary had increased their proportion of knights (led by Ladislaus IV of Hungary) and they quickly defeated the main Mongolian Army in the hills of western Transylvania.[501]

By this time as well, many Eastern and Central European countries had ended their hostilities with one another and united to finally drive out the Mongols.[502] Guerrilla warfare and stiff resistance also helped many Europeans, particularly those in Croatia and Dzurdzuketia, in preventing the Mongols from setting a permanent hold and driving them off.[503,504]

Mongol diffusion of Chinese gunpowder to Europe

Several sources mention Chinese firearms and gunpowder weapons being deployed by the Mongols against European forces at the Battle of Mohi in various forms, including bombs hurled via catapult. Professor Kenneth Warren Chase credits the Mongols for introducing gunpowder and its associated weaponry into Europe.

A later legend arose in Europe about a mysterious Berthold Schwarz who is credited with the invention of gunpowder by 15th- through 19th-century European literature.[505] However, it is known that William of Rubruck, a Flemish missionary who visited the Mongol court of Mongke Khan at Karakorum and returned to Europe in 1257, was a friend of English philosopher Roger Bacon, who recorded the earliest known European recipe for gunpowder in his *Opus Majus* of 1267.[506,507] This came more than two centuries after the first known Chinese description of the formula for gunpowder in 1044.[508,509]

End of the Mongol advance

In *A History of the English-Speaking Peoples*, Winston Churchill wrote:

> But Asia too was marching against the West. At one moment it had seemed as if all Europe would succumb to a terrible menace looming up from the East. Heathen Mongol hordes from the heart of Asia, formidable horsemen armed with bows, had rapidly swept over Russia, Poland, Hungary, and

in 1241 inflicted simultaneous crushing defeats upon the Germans near Breslau and upon European cavalry near Buda. Germany and Austria at least lay at their mercy. Providentially in this year the Great Khan died in Mongolia; the Mongol leaders hastened back the thousands of miles to Karakorum, their capital, to elect his successor, and Western Europe escaped.

During the summer and autumn of 1241, most of the Mongol forces were resting on the Hungarian Plain. In late March, 1242, they began to withdraw. The most common reason given for this withdrawal is the Great Khan Ögedei's death on December 11, 1241. Ögedei Khan died at the age of fifty-six after a binge of drinking during a hunting trip, which forced most of the Mongolian army to retreat back to Mongolia so that the princes of the blood could be present for the election of a new great khan. This is attested to by one primary source: the chronicle of Giovanni da Pian del Carpine, who after visiting the Mongol court, stated that the Mongols withdrew for this reason; he further stated that God had caused the Great Khan's death to protect Latin Christendom.[510] By Carpini's account, a messenger would have to be able to make the journey from Mongolia to Central Europe in a little over 3 months at a minimum; according to Carpini, the messenger actually arrived in January, meaning he took about 1 month in the middle of winter. Carpini himself accompanied a Mongol party in a much shorter journey (from Kiev to Mongolia) during the summer and fall of 1246, where the party "made great speed" in order to reach the election ceremony in time, and made use of several horses per person while riding nearly all day and night. It took five months.[511]

Rashid Al-Din, a historian of the Mongol Ilkhanate, explicitly states in the Ilkhanate's official histories that the Mongols were not even aware of Ogedei's death when they began their withdrawal.[512] Rashid Al-Din, writing under the auspices of the Mongol Empire, had access to the official Mongol chronicle when compiling his history (Altan Debter). John Andrew Boyle asserts, based on the orthography, that Rashid Al-Din's account of the withdrawal from central Europe was taken verbatim from Mongolian records.[513]

Another theory is that weather data preserved in tree rings points to a series of warm, dry summers in the region until 1242. When temperatures dropped and rainfall increased, the local climate shifted to a wetter and colder environment. That, in turn, caused flooding of the formerly dry grasslands and created a marshy terrain. Those conditions would have been less than ideal for the nomadic Mongol cavalry and their encampments, reducing their mobility and pastureland, curtailing their invasion into Europe west of the Hungarian plain, and hastening their retreat.

The true reasons for the Mongol withdrawal are not fully known, but numerous plausible explanations exist. The Mongol invasion had bogged down into a series of costly and frustrating sieges, where they gained little loot and ran into stiff resistance. They had lost a large number of men despite their victories (see above). Finally, they were stretched thin in the European theater, and were experiencing a rebellion by the Cumans in what is now southern Russia, and the Caucasus (Batu returned to put it down, and spent roughly a year doing so).[514] Other argue Europe's bad weather had an effect: Hungary has a high water table so it floods easily. An analysis of tree rings there found that Hungary had a cold wet winter in early 1242, which likely turned Hungary's central plain into a huge swamp; so, lacking pastures for their horses, the Mongols would have had to fall back to Russia in search of better grasslands.[515]

Regardless of their reasons, the Mongols had completely withdrawn from Central Europe by mid-1242, though they still launched military operations in the west at this time, most notably the 1241–1243 Mongol invasion of Anatolia. In fact, Batu specifically decided against attending the kurultai in favor of staying in Europe, which delayed the ceremony for several years.[516]

The historian Jack Weatherford claims that European survival was due to Mongol unwillingness to fight in the more densely populated German principalities, where the weather affected the glue and sinew of the Mongol bows. However, a counter to this assertion is that the Mongols were willing to fight in the densely populated areas of Song China and India. Furthermore, the Mongols were able to conquer Southern China which is located in a tropical climate zone and would have received far more rainfall and humidity than anywhere in Europe.[517,518] The territory of Western Europe had more forests and castles than the Mongols were accustomed, and there were opportunities for the European heavy cavalry to counter-attack. Also, despite the steppe tactics of the Avars and early Hungarians, both were defeated by Western states in the 9th and 10th centuries. A significant number of important castles and towns in Hungary had also resisted the formidable and infamous Mongol siege tactics.

Sir John Keegan claimed the Mongols failed against the geographical and weather conditions of Europe:

> [The Mongol armies], ferocious though they were, ultimately failed to translate their light cavalry power from the semi-temperate and desert regions where it flourished in to the high-rainfall zone of Western Europe. Whenever [they] encountered ... peoples living by intensive agriculture, accumulating thereby food surpluses which enabled them to sustain campaigns longer than the foraging nomads ever could, and breeding on their rich grasslands horses which outmatched the nomad pony in battle, [they] had to admit defeat. Light cavalry conquerors were in time either forced back into the arid environment where nomadism flourished, as on the borders of Western Europe, or, as in China, corrupted by the softness of agricultural civilization and absorbed by it.[519]

Some historians believe that the reason for Batu's stopping at the Mohi River was that he never intended to advance further. He had made the Russian conquest safe for the years to come, and when the Great Khan died and Batu rushed back to Mongolia to put in his claim for power, it ended his westward expansion. Subutai's recall at the same time left the Mongol armies without their spiritual head and primary strategist. Batu Khan was not able to resume his plans for conquest to the "Great Sea" (the Atlantic Ocean) until 1255, after the turmoil after Ögedei's death had finally subsided with the election of Möngke Khan as Great Khan. Though he was capable of invading Western Europe, he was no longer interested.

Mongol infighting

From 1241 to 1248 a state of almost open warfare existed between Batu, son of Jochi, and Güyük, son of Ögedei. The Mongol Empire was ruled by a regency under Ögedei's widow Töregene Khatun, whose only goal was to secure the Great Khanate for her son, Güyük. There was so much bitterness between the two branches of the family that Güyük died in 1248 on his way to confront Batu to force him to accept his authority. He also had problems in his last years with the Principality of Halych-Volhynia, whose ruler, Danylo of Halych, adopted a policy of confronting the Golden Horde and defeated some Mongol assaults in 1254. He was only defeated in 1259, under the Berke's rule. Batu Khan was unable to turn his army west until 1255, after Möngke had become Great Khan in 1251, and he had repaired his relations with the Great Khanate. However, as he prepared to finish the invasion of Europe, he died. His son did not live long enough to implement his father and Subutai's plan to invade Europe, and with his death, Batu's younger brother Berke became Khan of the Kipchak Khanate. Berke was not interested in invading Europe as much as halting his cousin Hulagu Khan from destroying the Holy Land. Berke had converted to Islam and watched with horror as his cousin destroyed the Abbasid Caliph, the spiritual head of Islam as far as Berke was concerned. The Mamluks of Egypt, learning through spies that Berke was both a Muslim and not fond of his cousin, appealed to him for help and were careful to nourish their ties to him and his Khanate.

Both entities were Turkic in origin.[520] Many of the Mamluks were of Turkic descent and Berke's Khanate was almost totally Turkic also. Jochi, Genghis Khan's oldest son, was of disputed parentage and only received 4,000 Mongol warriors to start his Khanate. His nearly 500,000 warriors were virtually all Turkic people who had submitted to the Mongols. Thus, the Khanate was Turkic in culture and had more in common with their Muslim Turkic Mamluks brothers than with the Mongol shamanist Hulagu and his horde. Thus, when Hulagu Khan began to mass his army for war against the Mamluk-controlled

Holy Land, they swiftly appealed to Berke Khan who sent armies against his cousin and forced him to defend his domains in the north.

Hulagu returned to his lands by 1262, but instead of being able to avenge his defeats, had to turn north to face Berke Khan, suffering severe defeat in an attempted invasion north of the Caucasus in 1263, after Berke Khan had lured him north and away from the Holy Land. Thus, the Kipchak Khanate never invaded Europe; keeping watch to the south and east instead. Berke only sent troops into Europe twice, in two relatively light raids in 1259 and 1265, simply to collect booty he needed to pay for his wars against Hulagu from 1262-65.

European Disunity at the time of the Mongol Invasion

The Mongol army did not face a unified Europe in the years during the Mongol invasions. The Papacy had rejected the pleas of Georgia in favor of launching crusades in Spain and the Middle East, as well as preaching a Crusade against Kievan Rus in 1238 for refusing to join his earlier Balkan Crusade. Meanwhile Emperor Frederick II, a well-educated ruler who disliked organized religion, wanted to annex Italy to unite his separated kingdoms of Germany and Sicily. In addition to calling a council to depose the Holy Roman Emperor, Pope Gregory IX and his successor Innocent IV excommunicated Frederick four times and labeled him the Antichrist.[521]

In the 1240's the efforts of Christendom were already divided between five Crusades, only one of which was aimed against the Mongols. Initially when Bela sent messengers to the Pope to request a Crusade against the Mongols, the Pope tried to convince them to instead join his Crusade against the Holy Roman Emperor. Eventually Pope Gregory did promise a Crusade and the Church finally helped sanction a small Crusade against the Mongols in mid-1241, but it was diverted when he died in August 1241. Instead of fighting the Mongols, the resources gathered by the Crusade was used to fight a Crusade against the Hohenstaufen Dynasty after the German barons revolted against the Holy Roman Emperor's son Conrad in September 1241.[522]

Later raids

The Golden Horde raids in the 1280s (those in Bulgaria, Hungary, and Poland), were much greater in scale than any raid since the 1241–1242 invasion, due to the lack of civil war in the Mongol Empire at the time. They have sometimes been collectively referred to as "the second Mongol invasion of Europe", "the second Tatar-Mongol invasion of central and south-eastern Europe",[523] or "the second Mongol invasion of central Europe."[524]

Figure 74: *Martyrdom of Sadok and 48 Dominican martyrs of Sandomierz during the Second Mongol invasion of Poland.*

Against Poland (1259 and 1287)

In 1259, eighteen years after the first attack, two tumens (20,000 men) from the Golden Horde, under the leadership of Berke, attacked Poland after raiding Lithuania.[525] This attack was commanded by general Burundai with young princes Nogai and Talabuga. Lublin, Sieradz, Sandomierz, Zawichost, Kraków, and Bytom were ravaged and plundered. Berke had no intention of occupying or conquering Poland. After this raid the Pope Alexander IV tried without success to organize a crusade against the Tatars.

An unsuccessful raid followed in 1287, led by Talabuga and Nogai Khan. 30,000 men (three tumens) in two columns under Nogai (10,000 Mongol cavalry) and Talabuga (20,000 Mongols and Ruthenians) respectively invaded Lesser Poland to plunder the area and meet up north of Kraków. Lublin, Mazovia, and Sieradz were successfully raided, but the Mongols failed to capture Sandomierz and Kraków and were repulsed with heavy casualties when they attempted to assault the cities, although the cities were devastated. Talabuga's main army (the rest of his column having dissolved across the countryside for raiding) was defeated by Duke Leszek II at the Battle of Łagów. After this severe setback, Talabuga linked back up with the raiding parties and fled Poland with the loot that was already taken. Nogai's column, after suffering losses during the assault on Kraków, split up to raid the lands both north and south of the city. One detachment headed towards the town of Stary Sącz, another to Podolínec, and others to the Duchy of Sieradz. The first detachment was surprised and defeated by the Poles and their Hungarian allies in the Battle of Stary Sącz, while the second devastated the area of Podhale while skirmishing with the locals. After the defeat at Stary Sącz, Nogai's whole column retreated into Ruthenia.[526]

Against Byzantine Thrace (1265, 1324 and 1337)

During the reign of Berke there was also a raid against Thrace. In the winter of 1265, the Bulgarian czar, Constantine Tych, requested Mongol intervention against the Byzantines in the Balkans. Nogai Khan led a Mongol raid of 20,000 cavalry (two *tumens*) against the territories of Byzantine eastern Thrace. In the spring of 1265, Michael VIII Palaeologus confronted the Mongols, but his smaller squadron apparently had very low morale and was quickly routed. Most of them were cut down as they fled. Michael was forced to retreat to Constantinople on a Genoese ship while Nogai's army plundered all of Thrace. Following this defeat, the Byzantine emperor made an alliance with the Golden Horde (which was massively beneficial for the latter), giving his daughter Euphrosyne in marriage to Nogai. Michael also sent much valuable fabric to Golden Horde as tribute.[527]

Also during Uzbeg Khan reign Thrace suffered raids in 1324 and 1337.[528]

Against Bulgaria (1271, 1274, 1280 and 1285)

The successors of Tsar Ivan Asen II – the regency of Kaliman Asen I decided to pay tax to the Golden Horde. In 1271 Nogai Khan led a successful raid against the country, which was a vassal of the Golden Horde until the early 14th century. Bulgaria was again raided by the Tatars in 1274, 1280 and 1285. In 1278 and 1279 Tsar Ivailo lead the Bulgarian army and crushed the Mongol raids before being surrounded at Silistra.[529] After a three-month siege, he managed to once again break through the elite Mongol forces, forcing them to retreat north of the Danube. In 1280 a rebellion inspired by Byzantium left Ivailo without much support, and so he fled to Nogai's camp, asking him for help before being killed by the Mongols. Tsar George I, however, became a Mongol vassal before the Mongol threat was finally ended with the reign of Theodore Svetoslav.

Figure 75: *Mongol invasion of Hungary in 1285*

Against Hungary (1285)

In 1285 Nogai Khan led a raid of Hungary alongside Talabuga. Nogai lead an army that ravaged Transylvania with success: Cities like Reghin, Braşov and Bistriţa were plundered and ravaged. However Talabuga, who led the main army in Northern Hungary, was stopped by the heavy snow of the Carpathians and the invading force was defeated[530] near Pest by the royal army of Ladislaus IV and ambushed by the Székely in the return. Nogai's own column suffered serious casualties at the hands of the local troops (Saxons and Vlachs), and was harried on his withdrawal by the royal army, fresh from their victory over Talabuga. As with later invasions, it was repelled handily, the Mongols losing much of their invading force. The outcome could not have contrasted more sharply with the 1241 invasion, mostly due to the reforms of Béla IV, which included advances in military tactics and, most importantly, the widespread building of stone castles, both responses to the defeat of the Hungarian Kingdom in 1241. The failed Mongol attack on Hungary greatly reduced the Golden Horde's military power caused them to stop disputing Hungarian borders.[531,532]

Against Serbia (1291)

In 1291 a large Mongol-Bulgarian alliance raided into Serbia, where Serbian king Stefan Uroš II Milutin defeated them. However, the Serbian king acknowledged Nogai's supremacy and sent his son as hostage to prevent further hostility when Nogai threatened to lead a punitive expedition himself.[533]

Figure 76: *Serbian king Uroš II Milutin after victory over Mongols.*

Counter-Invasions of Europe

By the mid-14th century the grip of the Golden Horde over Central and Eastern Europe has started to weaken. Several European kingdoms started various incursions into Mongol-controlled lands with the aim of reclaiming captured territories as well as add new ones from the Empire itself. The Kingdom of Georgia, under the leadership of King George V the Brilliant, restored Georgian dominance in their own lands and even took the Empire of Trebizond from Mongol hands.[534] Lithuania, taking advantage with the internal strifes in the Golden Horde, started an invasion of their own, defeating the Mongols at the Battle at Blue Waters, as well as conquering territories of the Golden Horde such as the Principality of Kiev all the way to the Dnieper River, before being halted after their defeat at the Battle of the Vorskla River.[535] Russia has also started to reclaim many Rus lands. In 1345, the Kingdom of Hungary, took the initiative and launched their own invasion force into Mongolian territory, capturing what would become Moldavia.[536]

By this point, some Western European armies have also started to meet the Mongols in their conquered territories. In Caffa for example, when the Mongols under Janibeg besieged it after a large fight between Christians and Muslims began, a relief force of an Italian army came and defeated the Mongols, killing 15,000 of their troops and destroying their siege engines. A year later, the Italians blockaded Mongol ports in the region, forcing Janibeg to negotiate, and in 1347 the Italians were allowed to reestablish their colony in Tana.[537]

Maps

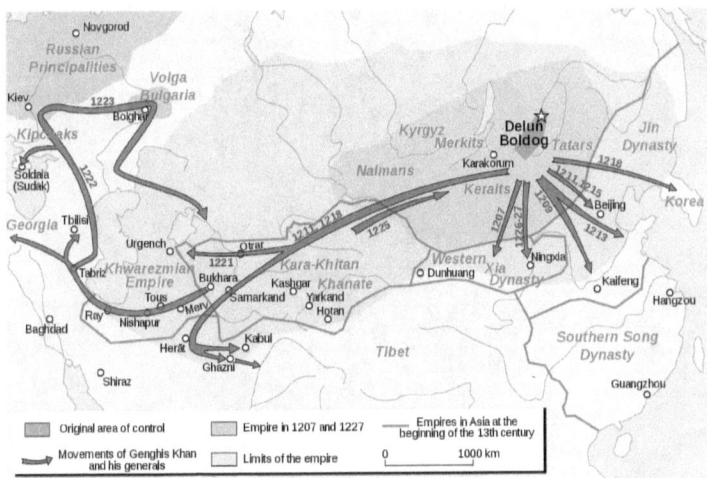

File:Genghis Khan empire-en.svg

Mongol expansion

Gallery

Figure 77: *Golden Horde raid at Ryazan*

Figure 78: *Golden Horde raid at Kiev*

Figure 79: *Golden Horde raid at Kozelsk*

Figure 80: *Golden Horde raid Vladimir*

Figure 81: *Golden Horde raid Suzdal*

Figure 82: *The Hungarian King Béla IV on the flight from the Mongols under general Kadan of the Golden Horde.*

References

- Sverdrup, Carl (2010). "Numbers in Mongol Warfare". Journal of Medieval Military History. Boydell Press. 8: 109–17 [p. 115]. ISBN 978-1-84383-596-7.

Further reading

- Allsen, Thomas T. *Culture and Conquest in Mongol Eurasia*[538]. Cambridge UP.
- Atwood, Christopher P. *Encyclopedia of Mongolia and the Mongol Empire* (2004)
- Chambers, James. *The Devil's Horsemen: The Mongol Invasion of Europe* (London: Weidenfeld and Nicolson, 1979)
- Christian, David. *A History of Russia, Central Asia and Mongolia Vol. 1: Inner Eurasia from Prehistory to the Mongol Empire* (Blackwell, 1998)
- Cook, David, "Apocalyptic Incidents during the Mongol Invasions", in Brandes, Wolfram / Schmieder, Felicitas (hg), *Endzeiten. Eschatologie in den monotheistischen Weltreligionen* (Berlin, de Gruyter, 2008) (Millennium-Studien / Millennium Studies / Studien zu Kultur und Geschichte des ersten Jahrtausends n. Chr. / Studies in the Culture and History of the First Millennium C.E., 16), 293-312.

- Halperin, Charles J. *Russia and the golden horde: the Mongol impact on medieval Russian history* (Indiana University Press, 1985)
- May, Timothy. *The Mongol conquests in world history* (Reaktion Books, 2013)
- Morgan, David. *The Mongols*, ISBN 0-631-17563-6
- Nicolle, David. *The Mongol Warlords*, Brockhampton Press, 1998
- Reagan, Geoffry. *The Guinness Book of Decisive Battles*, Canopy Books, New York (1992)
- Saunders, J.J. *The History of the Mongol Conquests*, Routledge & Kegan Paul Ltd, 1971, ISBN 0-8122-1766-7
- Sinor, Denis (1999). "The Mongols in the West"[539]. *Journal of Asian History*. **33** (1).; also in JSTOR[540]
- Vernadsky, George. *The Mongols and Russia* (Yale University Press, 1953)
  - Halperin, Charles J. "George Vernadsky, Eurasianism, the Mongols, and Russia." *Slavic Review* (1982): 477-493. in JSTOR[541]
- Craughwell, Thomas J. *The Rise and Fall of the Second Largest Empire in History: How Genghis Khan almost conquered the world*[542]. Fair Winds. ISBN 9781616738518.
- Kauffman, JE. *The medieval Fortress:Castles, Forts and Walled Cities of the medieval ages*. Da Capo Press. ISBN 0-306-81358-0.\
- Fagan, Brian. *The Great Warming:Climate Change and the Rise and Fall of Civilization*. Bloomsbury Press. ISBN 978-1-59691-780-4.
- Penn, Imma. *Dogma Evolution & Papal Fallacies:An Unveiled History of Catholicism*. AuthorHouse. ISBN 978-1-4343-0874-0.

External links

- The Islamic World to 1600: The Golden Horde[543]

South Asia

Mongol invasions of India

Invasions of India	
Part of the Mongol conquests, Mongol invasion of Central Asia	
Date	1222–1225, 1235–1241, 1254–1255, 1257–1258, 1293–1298, 1299–1306, 1320, 1327
Location	North-Western Indian subcontinent and parts of Central Asia
Result	Mongol Empire conquers Indian borderlands but repelled from interior. Mongols continue raids throughout the 14th century.
Territorial changes	Mongol Empire gains control of Central Asia, Kashmir, and exterior portions of Indian subcontinent. Delhi Sultanate retains hold of Indian interior.

Belligerents		
Mongol Empire	Punjab Sindh	Khwarazmian dynasty
Mongol Empire Khokhar	Kerman	Ghor Peshawar
	Kashmir	Salt Range
Mongol Empire Ilkhanate Qara'unas Sindh	Delhi Sultanate	Ghori Turkmen
	Delhi Sultanate	
Chagatai Khanate Qara'unas	Delhi Sultanate	
Chagatai Khanate Qara'unas	Delhi Sultanate	
Qara'unas		

Commanders and leaders

Genghis Khan Dorbei the Fierce Bala Turtai	Unknown	Jalal ad-Din Ming-burnu
	Unknown	Kalich Khan Uzbek Pai
	Unknown	Hassan Qarlugh
Ögedei Khan Dayir Möngke Khan Sali Sham al-Din Muhammad Kart	Zafar Khan	
	Alauddin Khalji Zafar Khan Ghazi Malik	
Hulagu Khan Sali Bahadur Sali Noyan	Malik Kafur Ulugh Khan Muhammad bin Tughluq	
▪ Abdullah ▪ Ulugh ▪ Saldi	Suhadeva Ramacandra	
Qutlugh Khwaja ▪ Kopek ▪ Ali Beg ▪ Tartaq ▪ Abachi ▪ Tarmashirin		
Zulju		

The Mongol Empire launched several invasions into the Indian subcontinent from 1221 to 1327, with many of the later raids made by the unruly Qaraunas of Mongol origin. The Mongols occupied parts of modern Pakistan and other parts of Punjab for decades. As the Mongols progressed into the Indian hinterland and reached the outskirts of Delhi, the Delhi Sultanate led a campaign against them in which the Mongol army inflicted huge losses on the rival army, but were beaten back nonetheless.

The Mughal Empire founded by Babur, however, successfully conquered most of the Indian subcontinent in the 16th and the 17th centuries.

Background

After pursuing Jalal ad-Din into India from Samarkand and defeating him at the battle of Indus in 1221, Genghis Khan sent two tumens (20,000 soldiers) under commanders Dorbei the Fierce and Bala to continue the chase. The Mongol commander Bala chased Jalal ad-Din throughout the Punjab region and attacked outlying towns like Bhera and Multan and had even sacked the outskirts of Lahore. Jalal ad-Din regrouped, forming a small army from survivors of the battle and sought an alliance, or even an asylum, with the Turkic rulers of Delhi Sultanate, but was turned down.

Jalal ad-Din fought against the local rulers in the Punjab, and usually defeated them in the open and occupied their lands. Local tribes of Punjab came in

Figure 83: *Genghis Khan*

his service, like the khokhar tribe of the Salt Range. The Khokhar Rai's son joined Jalal ad-Din's army along with his clansmen. Jalal ad-Din's soldiers were under his officers Uzbek Pai and Hassan Qarlugh.

While fighting against the local governor of Sindh, Jalal ad-Din heard of an uprising in the Kirman province of southern Iran and he immediately set out for that place, passing through southern Baluchistan on the way. Jalal ad-Din was also joined by forces from Ghor and Peshawar, including members of the Khalji, Turkoman, and Ghori tribes. With his new allies he marched on Ghazni and defeated a Mongol division under Turtai, which had been assigned the task of hunting him down. The victorious allies quarreled over the division of the captured booty; subsequently the Khalji, Turkoman, and Ghori tribesmen deserted Jalal ad-Din and returned to Peshawar. By this time Ögedei Khan, third son of Genghis Khan, had become Great Khan of the Mongol Empire. A Mongol general named Chormaqan sent by the Khan attacked and defeated him, thus ending the Khwārazm-Shāh dynasty.[544]

Mongol conquest of Kashmir and conflicts with the Delhi Sultanate

Some time after 1235 another Mongol force invaded Kashmir, stationing a darughachi (administrative governor) there for several years, and Kashmir became a Mongolian dependency.[545] Around the same time, a Kashmiri Buddhist master, Otochi, and his brother Namo arrived at the court of Ögedei. Another Mongol general named Pakchak attacked Peshawar and defeated the army of tribes who had deserted Jalal ad-Din but were still a threat to the Mongols. These men, mostly Khaljis, escaped to Multan and were recruited into the army of the Delhi Sultanate. In winter 1241 the Mongol force invaded the Indus valley and besieged Lahore. However, on December 30, 1241, the Mongols under Munggetu butchered the town before withdrawing from the Delhi Sultanate.[546] At the same time the Great Khan Ögedei died (1241).

The Kashmiris revolted in 1254–1255, and Möngke Khan, who became Great Khan in 1251, appointed his generals, Sali and Takudar, to replace the court and appointed the Buddhist master, Otochi, as darugachi of Kashmir. However, the Kashmiri king killed Otochi at Srinagar. Sali invaded Kashmir, killing the king, and put down the rebellion, after which the country remained subject to the Mongol Empire for many years.[547]

The Delhi prince, Jalal al-Din Masud, traveled to the Mongol capital at Karakorum to seek the assistance of Möngke Khan in seizing the throne from his elder brother in 1248. When Möngke was crowned as Great Khan, Jalal al-Din Masud attended the ceremony and asked for help from Möngke. Möngke ordered Sali to assist him to recover his ancestral realm. Sali made successive attacks on Multan and Lahore. Sham al-Din Muhammad Kart, the client malik (ruling prince) of Herat, accompanied the Mongols. Jalal al-Din was installed as client ruler of Lahore, Kujah and Sodra. In 1257 the governor of Sindh offered his entire province to Hulagu Khan, Möngke's brother, and sought Mongol protection from his overlord in Delhi. Hulagu led a strong force under Sali Bahadur into Sindh. In the winter of 1257 - beginning of 1258, Sali Noyan entered Sind in strength and dismantled the fortifications of Multan; his forces may also have invested the island fortress of Bakhkar on the Indus.

But Hulagu refused to sanction a grand invasion of the Delhi Sultanate and a few years later diplomatic correspondence between the two rulers confirmed the growing desire for peace. Hulagu had many other areas of conquests to take care of in Syria and southwestern Asia. Large-scale Mongol invasions of India ceased and the Delhi Sultans used the respite to recover the frontier towns like Multan, Uch, and Lahore, and to punish the local Ranas and Rais who had joined hands with either the Khwarazim or the Mongol invaders.

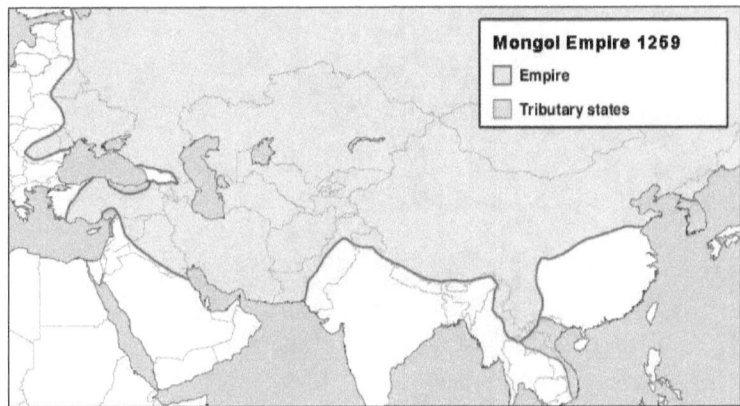

Figure 84: *The Mongol Empire during the reign of Mongke Khan (r.1251-59)*

Large numbers of tribes that took shelter in the Delhi Sultanate as a result of the Mongol invasions changed the balance of power in North India. The Khalji tribe usurped power from the older Delhi Sultans and began to rapidly project their power into other parts of India. At about this time the Mongol raids into India were also renewed (1300).

Chagatai Khanate vs. the Khaljis

The medieval sources claim invasions by hundreds of thousands of Mongols, numbers approximating (and probably based on) the size of the entire cavalry armies of the Mongol realms of Central Asia or the Middle East: about 150,000 men. A count of the Mongol commanders named in the sources as participating in the various invasions might give a better indication of the numbers involved, as these commanders probably led tumens, units nominally of 10,000 men.[548] These invasions were led by either various descendants of Genghis Khan or by Mongol divisional commanders; the size of such armies was always between 10,000-30,000 cavalry although the chroniclers of Delhi exaggerated the number to 100,000-200,000 cavalry.[549]

After civil war broke out in the Mongol Empire in the 1260s, the Chagatai Khanate controlled Central Asia and its leader since the 1280s was Duwa Khan who was second in command of Kaidu Khan. Duwa was active in Afghanistan, and attempted to extend Mongol rule into India. Negudari governor Abdullah, who was a son of Chagatai Khan's great grandson,[550] invaded Punjab with his force in 1292, but their advance guard under Ulghu was defeated and taken prisoner by the Khalji Sultan Jalaluddin. The 4000 Mongol captives of the advance guard converted to Islam and came to live in Delhi as "new Muslims".

Sultan Aala-Ouddine Khildji (1295)

Figure 85: *A 20th century artist's imagination of Alauddin Khalji (d. 1316), the Turkic ruler of Delhi.*

The suburb they lived in was appropriately named Mughalpura.[551] Chagatai tumens were beaten by the Delhi Sultanate several times in 1296–1297.[552]

Subsequently, the Mongols thereafter repeatedly invaded northern India during the reign of Jalaluddin's successor Alauddin; on at least two occasions, they came in strength. In the winter of 1297, the Chagatai noyan Kadar led an army that ravaged the Punjab region, and advanced as far as Kasur.[553] Alauddin's army, led by Ulugh Khan (and probably Zafar Khan), defeated the invaders on 6 February 1298.[553]

Later in 1298-99, a Mongol army (possibly Neguderi fugitives) invaded Sindh, and occupied the fort of Sivistan.[554] These Mongols were defeated by Zafar Khan: a number of them were arrested and brought to Delhi as captives.[555] At this time, the main branch of Alauddin's army, led by Ulugh Khan and Nusrat Khan was busy raiding Gujarat. When this army was returning from Gujarat to Delhi, some of its Mongol soldiers staged a mutiny over payment of *khums* (one-fifth of the share of loot).[556] The mutiny was crushed, and the mutineers families in Delhi were severely punished.[557]

In late 1299, Duwa dispatched his son Qutlugh Khwaja to conquer Delhi.[558] Alauddin led his army to Kili near Delhi, and tried to delay the battle, hoping that the Mongols would retreat amid a scarcity of provisions and that he would receive reinforcements from his provinces. However, his general Zafar Khan attacked the Mongol army without his permission.[559] The Mongols feigned a retreat, and tricked Zafar Khan's contingent into following them. Zafar Khan and his men were killed after inflicting heavy casualties on the invaders.[560] The Mongols retreated a couple of days later: their leader Qutlugh Khwaja was seriously wounded, and died during the return journey.[561]

In the winter of 1302-1303, Alauddin dispatched an army to ransack the Kakatiya capital Warangal, and himself marched to Chittor. Finding Delhi unprotected, the Mongols launched another invasion around August 1303.[562] Alauddin managed to reach Delhi before the invaders, but did not have enough time to prepare for a strong defence. He took shelter in a heavily-guarded camp at the under-construction Siri Fort. The Mongols ransacked Delhi and its neighbourhoods, but ultimately retreated after being unable to breach Siri.[563] This close encounter with the Mongols prompted Alauddin to strengthen the forts and the military presence along their routes to India.[564] He also implemented a series of economic reforms to ensure sufficient revenue inflows for maintaining a strong army.[565]

Shortly afterward, Duwa Khan sought to end the ongoing conflict with the Yuan Khagan Temür Öljeytü, and around 1304 a general peace among the Mongol khanates was declared, bringing an end to the conflict between the Yuan Dynasty and western khanates that had lasted for the better part of a half century. Soon after, he proposed a joint Mongol attack on India, but the campaign did not materialize.

In December 1305, Duwa sent another army that bypassed the heavily guarded city of Delhi, and proceeded south-east to the Gangetic plains along the Himalayan foothills. Alauddin's 30,000-strong cavalry, led by Malik Nayak, defeated the Mongols at the Battle of Amroha.[566,567] A large number of Mongols were taken captive and killed.[568]

In 1306, another Mongol army sent by Duwa advanced up to the Ravi River, ransacking the territories along the way. This army included three contingents, led by Kopek, Iqbalmand, and Tai-Bu. Alauddin's forces, led by Malik Kafur, decisively defeated the invaders.[569]

In that same year the Mongol Khan, Duwa, died and in the dispute over his succession this spate of Mongol raids into India ended. Taking advantage of this situation, Alauddin's general Malik Tughluq regularly raided the Mongol territories located in present-day Afghanistan.[570,571]

Late Mongol invasions

In 1320 the Qaraunas under Zulju (Dulucha) entered Kashmir by the Jehlam Valley without meeting any serious resistance. The Kashmiri king, Suhadeva, tried to persuade Zulju to withdraw by paying a large ransom.[572] After he failed to organize resistance, Suhadeva fled to Kishtwar, leaving the people of Kashmir to the mercy of Zulju. The Mongols burned the dwellings, massacred the men and made women and children slaves. Only refugees under Ramacandra, commander in chief of the king, in the fort of Lar remained safe. The invaders continued to pillage for eight months until the commencement of winter. When Zulju was departing via Brinal, he lost most of his men and prisoners due to a severe snowfall in Divasar district.

The next major Mongol invasion took place after the Khaljis had been replaced by the Tughlaq dynasty in the Sultanate. In 1327 the Chagatai Mongols under Tarmashirin, who had sent envoys to Delhi to negotiate peace the previous year, sacked the frontier towns of Lamghan and Multan and besieged Delhi. The Tughlaq ruler paid a large ransom to spare his Sultanate from further ravages. Muhammad bin Tughluq asked the Ilkhan Abu Sa'id to form an alliance against Tarmashirin, who had invaded Khorasan, but an attack didn't materialize.[573] Tarmashirin was a Buddhist who later converted to Islam. Religious tensions in the Chagatai Khanate were a divisive factor among the Mongols.

No more large-scale invasions or raids into India were launched after Tamashirin's siege of Delhi. However, small groups of Mongol adventurers hired out their swords to the many local powers in the northwest. Amir Qazaghan raided northern India with his Qara'unas. He also sent several thousand troops to aid the Delhi Sultan Muhammad bin Tughluq in suppressing the rebellion in his country in 1350.

Timur and Babur

The Delhi sultans had developed cordial relations with the Yuan dynasty in Mongolia and China and the Ilkhanate in Persia and the Middle East. Around 1338, Sultan Muhammad bin Tughluq of the Delhi Sultanate appointed Moroccan traveler Ibn Battuta an ambassador to the Yuan court under Toghon Temür (Emperor Huizong). The gifts he was to take included 200 slaves.

The Chagatai Khanate had split up by this time and an ambitious Mongol Turk chieftain named Timur had brought Central Asia and the regions beyond under his control. He followed the twin policies of Imperialism and Islamization, shifting various Mongol tribes to different parts of his empire and giving primacy to the Turkic people in his own army. Timur also reinforced the Islamic faith over the Chagatai Khanate and gave primacy to the laws of the Quran

Mongol invasions of India

Figure 86: *Timur*

Figure 87: *Timur defeats the Sultan of Delhi, Nasir Al-Din Mahmum Tughluq, in the winter of 1397–1398*

Figure 88: *Babur, the Turco-Mongol descendant of Timur, who later invaded India in the 16th century.*

over Genghis Khan's shamanist laws. He invaded India in 1398 to make war and plunder the wealth of the country.

Timur's empire broke up and his descendants failed to hold on to Central Asia, which split up into numerous principalities. The descendants of the Mongol Chagtais and the descendants of Timur empire lived side by side, occasionally fighting and occasionally inter-marrying.

One of the products of such a marriage was Babur, founder of the Mughal Empire. His mother belonged to the family of the Mongol Khans of Tashkent. Babur was a true descendant of Timur and shared his beliefs: he believed that rules and regulations of Genghis Khan were deficient as he remarked, "they had no divine authority."

Even though his own mother was a Mongol, Babur was not very fond of the Mongol race and wrote a stinging verse in his autobiography:

"Were the Mughals an angel race, it would be bad,

Even write in gold, the Mughal name would be bad."

When Babur occupied Kabul and began invading the Indian subcontinent, he was called a Mughal like all the earlier invaders from the Chagatai Khanate. Even the invasion of Timur had been considered a Mongol invasion since the

Mongols had ruled over Central Asia for so long and had given their name to its people.

Both Timur and Babur continued the military system of Genghis Khan. One part of this system was the name Ordu - used for the collective of tents that formed the military camp — it was now pronounced Urdu. In all their campaigns in India the Mughal camp was called the Urdu and this word became current in the languages of the various soldiers that formed the body of this camp.

In time these Indian and foreign languages mingled together in the Urdu and a new language of that name was born. This language of the military camp survived in some of the North Indian cities after the fall of the Mughal Empire. The Urdu that passed through all these centuries of political changes ultimately became the language of poetry, of music, and of other forms of cultural expression—today it is recognized as one of languages in modern India and national language of Pakistan .

References

Bibliography

- Banarsi Prasad Saksena (1992). "The Khaljis: Alauddin Khalji". In Mohammad Habib and Khaliq Ahmad Nizami. *A Comprehensive History of India: The Delhi Sultanat (A.D. 1206-1526)*[574]. **5** (Second ed.). The Indian History Congress / People's Publishing House. OCLC 31870180[575].
- *Chormaqan Noyan: The First Mongol Military Governor in the Middle East* by Timothy May[576]
- Harold Lamb, *Genghis Khan: Emperor of All Men*. ISBN 0-88411-798-7
- J.A. Boyle, "The Mongol Commanders in Afghanistan and India According to the Tabaqat-i-Nasiri of Juzjani." *Central Asiatic Journal* 9 (1964): 235-247. Reprinted in *The Mongol World Empire, 1206–1370*, edited by John A. Boyle, Variorum Reprints, 1977.
- John Masson Smith, Jr. - *MONGOL ARMIES AND INDIAN CAMPAIGNS*, University of California, Berkeley[577]
- Kishori Saran Lal (1950). *History of the Khaljis (1290-1320)*[578]. Allahabad: The Indian Press. OCLC 685167335[579].
- Peter Jackson (2003). *The Delhi Sultanate: A Political and Military History*[580]. Cambridge University Press. ISBN 978-0-521-54329-3.
- René Grousset (1970). *The Empire of the Steppes: A History of Central Asia*[581]. Rutgers University Press. ISBN 978-0-8135-1304-1.

Southeast Asia

First Mongol invasion of Burma

<indicator name="good-star"> ⊕ </indicator>

First Mongol invasions of Burma
Part of the Mongol invasions and Kublai Khan's Campaigns
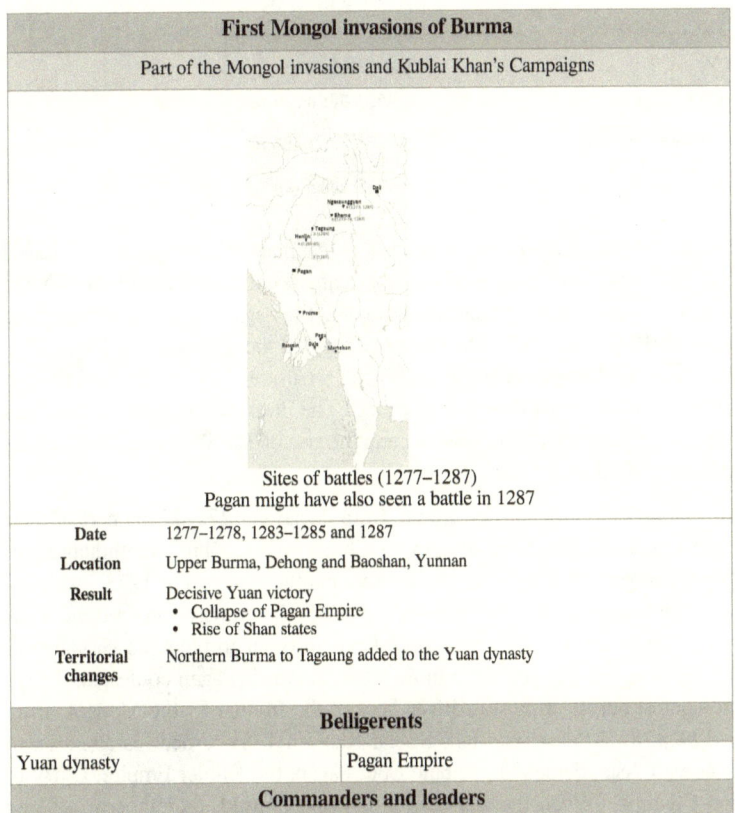 Sites of battles (1277–1287) Pagan might have also seen a battle in 1287

Date	1277–1278, 1283–1285 and 1287
Location	Upper Burma, Dehong and Baoshan, Yunnan
Result	Decisive Yuan victory • Collapse of Pagan Empire • Rise of Shan states
Territorial changes	Northern Burma to Tagaung added to the Yuan dynasty

Belligerents	
Yuan dynasty	Pagan Empire
Commanders and leaders	

• Kublai Khan • Huthukh (1277) • Nasr al-Din (1277–1278) • Sangudar (1283–1285) • Ye-sin Timour (1287)	• Narathihapate • Ananda Pyissi (1277–1285) • Yanda Pyissi † (1277–1284?) • Maha Bo (1283–1285) • Athinkhaya (1287) • Yazathingyan (1287) • Thihathu (1287)
Units involved	
Imperial Mongol Army • Turkic regiments • Central Asian regiments • Persian regiments • Mongol regiments	Royal Burmese Army
Strength	
1277–78: 12,000	1277–78: unknown
1283–85: 24,000+[582] • 10,000 Sichuan troops • 14,000 Persian troops • Other regiments	1283–85: 10,000+
	1287: unknown
1287: 20,000+[583]	
Casualties and losses	
1277–78: unknown	1277–78: unknown
1283–85: unknown	1283–85: 10,000+
1287: 7000	1287: unknown

The **first Mongol invasions of Burma** (Myanmar) (Burmese: ▯▯▯▯▯▯–▯▯▯▯▯ ▯▯▯ (▯▯▯▯–▯▯▯▯)) were a series of military conflicts between Kublai Khan's Yuan dynasty, division of the Mongol Empire, and the Pagan Empire that took place between 1277 and 1287. The invasions toppled the 250-year-old Pagan Empire, and the Mongol army seized Pagan territories in present-day Dehong, Yunnan and northern Burma to Tagaung. The invasions ushered in 250 years of political fragmentation in Burma and the rise of Tai-Shan states throughout mainland Southeast Asia.

The Mongols first demanded tribute from Pagan in 1271–72, as part of their drive to encircle the Song dynasty of China. When King Narathihapate refused, Emperor Kublai Khan himself sent another mission in 1273, again demanding tribute. It too was rejected. In 1275, the emperor ordered the Yunnan government to secure the borderlands in order to block an escape path for the Song, and permitted a limited border war if Pagan contested. Pagan did contest but its army was driven back at the frontier by the Mongol Army in 1277–78. After a brief lull, Kublai Khan in 1281 turned his attention to Southeast Asia, demanding tribute from Pagan, the Khmer Empire, Đại Việt and Champa. When the Burmese king again refused, the emperor ordered an invasion of northern Burma. Two dry season campaigns (1283–85) later, the Mongols had occupied down to Tagaung and Hanlin, forcing the Burmese king to flee to Lower Burma. The Mongols organized northern Burma as the province of Zhengmian.

Ceasefire negotiations began in 1285, and ended with Narathihapate finally agreeing to submit in June 1286. The Burmese embassy, received by the emperor in Beijing in January 1287, agreed to a treaty that acknowledged the suzerainty of the Yuan dynasty or the Mongol Empire over the Pagan Empire and annual payments in taxes to the Yunnan government in exchange for the evacuation of Mongol troops from northern Burma. But the treaty never really took effect as Narathihapate was assassinated in July 1287, and no authority who could honor the treaty emerged. The Mongol command at Yunnan now deemed the imperial order to withdraw void, and ordered an invasion of central Burma. They may not have reached Pagan, and even if they did, after having suffered heavy casualties, they returned to Tagaung.

The Pagan Empire disintegrated and anarchy ensued. The Mongols, who probably preferred the situation, did nothing to restore order in the next ten years. In March 1297, they accepted the voluntary submission of King Kyawswa of Pagan although he controlled little beyond the capital city of Pagan (Bagan). But Kyawswa was overthrown nine months later, and the Mongols were forced to intervene, leading to their second invasion in 1300–01.

Marco Polo reported the first invasions (1277–87) in his travelogue, *Il Milione*. The Burmese referred to the invaders as the *Taruk* (after the central Asian Turkic troops that largely made up the Mongol invasion army); today, the term *Taruk* (□□□□) refers to the Han Chinese instead. King Narathihapate is unkindly remembered in Burmese history as Taruk-Pye Min, ("the King who Fled from the *Taruk*").[584]

Background

Pagan and Dali

In the 13th century, the Pagan Empire, along with the Khmer Empire, was one of the two main empires in mainland Southeast Asia.[585] For much of its history, Pagan's neighbor to the northeast was not China but the independent Dali Kingdom and its predecessor Nanzhao, both with Dali as their capital city. Dali-based kingdoms were a power in their own right, at times allying themselves with the Tibetan Empire to their west and at other times with China's Tang and Song dynasties. Indeed, Nanzhao's mounted armies ventured deep into what is today Burma and may have been behind the founding of the medieval city of Pagan and the Pagan Dynasty itself.[586]

Figure 89: *Pagan Empire during Sithu II's reign. Burmese chronicles also claim Kengtung and Chiang Mai. Core areas shown in darker yellow. Peripheral areas in light yellow.*

Figure 90: *Dali Kingdom c. mid-12th century*

Between the newly conquered Mongol territory and Pagan were a wide swath of borderlands stretching from present-day Dehong, Baoshan and Lincang prefectures in Yunnan as well as the Wa and Palaung regions (presumably in present-day northern Shan State),[587] which Pagan and Dali had both claimed and exercised overlapping spheres of influence.[588] Then as now, the borderlands mostly consist of forbidding terrains of high mountain ranges.[586]

Mongol conquest of Dali

The Mongol Empire first arrived at the doorstep of the Pagan Empire in 1252 by invading the Dali Kingdom in its attempt to outflank Song China. The Mongol armies captured the capital, Dali, on 7 January 1253, and went on to pacify much of the kingdom by 1257.[589]

The arrival of the Mongols did not initially upset the existing order at the borderlands as the Mongols were intent on finishing off the Song. For the next dozen years, they consolidated their hold over the newly conquered land, which not only provided them with a base from which to attack the Song from the rear but also was strategically located on the trade routes from China to Burma and India. The Mongols set up military garrisons, manned mostly by Turkic-speaking Muslims from Central Asia, in 37 circuits of the former Dali Kingdom.[590]

Decline of Pagan

By then, the Pagan Empire, despite outward appearances of calmness, had been in long and slow decline since the early 13th century. The continuous growth of tax-free religious wealth had greatly reduced the tax base of the kingdom. The crown had lost resources needed to retain the loyalty of courtiers and military servicemen, inviting a vicious circle of internal disorders and external challenges.[585] Although it was able to put down the first batch of serious rebellions in 1258–60 in South Arakan and Martaban (Mottama), the decline continued. On the eve of the Mongol invasions, between one and two-thirds of Upper Burma's cultivable land had been donated to religion. The crown's ability to mobilize defenses was in serious jeopardy.

Figure 91: *Pagan plains today*

Prelude to war

First Mongol mission (1271–72)

The period of calm for Pagan ended in the early 1270s. By then, the Song were on the ropes, and Emperor Kublai Khan, who officially founded the Yuan dynasty on 18 December 1271, sought to cut off the retreat of Song refugees in all directions.[591] In Pagan's case, he had ordered the Mongol governor of Dali to tighten control of the borderlands, and in January 1271[583] to send a mission to Pagan to demand tribute.[592] The tribute he demanded was nominal. Given his higher priority preoccupations elsewhere, the emperor was not looking to replace the regime at Pagan. At the border, the ruler of the Wa and Palaung regions submitted to the Mongols.

When the Mongol envoys led by Qidai Tuoyin showed up, the Pagan court led by Chief Minister Ananda Pyissi was well aware of the military power of the Mongols and advised King Narathihapate to use diplomacy. The king was furious at the demand and kept the Mongol envoys waiting for weeks. The court finally devised a compromise: the envoys were sent back without ever seeing the king. Accompanying them was a Burmese envoy who carried a letter expressing friendly sentiments and the Burmese king's wish to one day worship a Buddha tooth at Beijing. The king then promptly ordered an expedition, which retook the rebellious borderland regions in April 1272. The rebel leader A-Pi (☐☐☐) was brought back to Pagan. Dali relayed the news to Beijing but did not carry out any military action.

Second Mongol mission (1273)

At Beijing, Kublai Khan, who was preparing an invasion of Japan, decided against a war with Pagan—for the time being. On 3 March 1273, he sent a 4-member delegation led by an imperial ambassador, the First Secretary to the Board Rites, to Pagan. The delegation carried a letter from the emperor. The letter says:

> "If you have finally decided to fulfill your duties towards the All-Highest, send one of your brothers or senior ministers, to show men that all the world is linked with Us, and enter into a perpetual alliance. This will add to your reputation, and be in your own interests; for if it comes to war, who will be the victor? Ponder well, O king, Our words."

This time, the Burmese king received the imperial envoys but still refused to submit. The Burmese chronicles say that the king was so insulted that he had the envoys executed.[593] But both Burmese inscriptional evidence and Yuan records indicate that the envoys were not executed. At any rate, the imperial envoys did not get back to Yunnan in due time. The newly formed Yunnan government sent another delegation to investigate the whereabouts of the delegation, but the delegation could not reach Pagan because of an ongoing rebellion en route.[589]

Mongol consolidation of borderlands (1275–76)

Meanwhile, in 1274, the former Dali Kingdom was officially reorganized as the Province of Yunnan, with Sayyid Ajjal Shams al-Din Omar as governor.[594] In May 1275, the governor sent a report to the emperor stating that the embassy had not returned;[595] that the Burmese evidently had no intention of submitting; and that war was the only way forward.[592]

But the emperor rejected an outright invasion. Just coming off a disastrous Japanese campaign, the emperor was unwilling to commit the central government troops to what he considered a low priority affair. He was now focused on delivering the final blow against the Song; the emperor ordered the Yunnan provincial army to secure the borderlands in order to block the escape path of the Song refugees. He also sanctioned a limited border war if Pagan contested the takeover. As planned, the Yunnan army proceeded to consolidate the borderlands in 1275–76. Elsewhere, the main Mongol armies had captured most of the Song territory by 1276.

By 1277, at least one Burmese vassal state named "Gold Teeth" (modern Yingjiang) had submitted to the Mongols.[596] Like in 1272, the Burmese government responded by sending an army to reclaim the rebellious state; but unlike in 1272, the Mongols had posted a sizable garrison there. Though it was

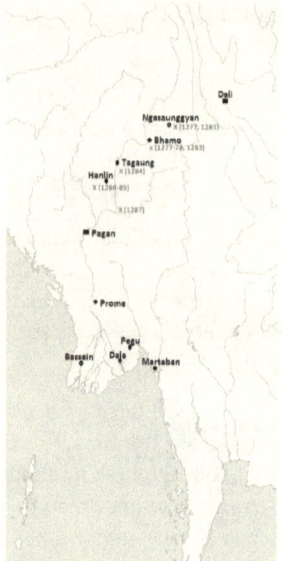

Figure 92: *Mongol invasions 1277–87*

ultimately under Mongol command, many of the officers and most of the soldiers of the garrison were Turkic-speaking peoples or people from the further west: Turks from Samarkand, Bukhara, Merv and Nishapur, but also captive soldiers from the Persian Khwarazmid empire, the Kipchaks, and even Bulgars from the lower Volga.[586]

Border war (1277–78)

What followed was a border war in 1277–78. It was reported mainly in the Yuan dynasty chronicle and the travelogue of Marco Polo.[597] Although the Burmese chronicles have no record of the border war, a 1278 Burmese inscription mentions the army's defeat at Ngasaunggyan. The Mongol accounts of the border war contain certain errors of location and numbers although the overall narrative is probably accurate.[598]

Battle of Ngasaunggyan

According to the Yuan dynasty chronicle and Marco Polo's accounts, a Burmese army "invaded" the Mongol territory of Gold Teeth, and was defeated by the Mongol army in April 1277. The battle took place either at the Vochang valley (in present-day Baoshan Prefecture) or 110 km southwest

Figure 93: *Mongol mounted archer*

at Kanngai (present-day Yingjiang, Dehong Prefecture), which the Burmese called *Ngasaunggyan*.[599]

The Yuan Chronicle reports that only 700 men defeated a Burmese army of 40,000 to 50,000 with 10,000 horses and 800 elephants. It also reports only one Mongol was killed, in trying to catch an elephant.[600,592] According to Marco Polo, the Mongol army consisted of 12,000 mounted archers, and the Burmese army numbered 60,000 men with 2000 elephants, "on each of which was set a tower of timber, well-framed and strong, and carrying from 12 to 16 well-armed fighting men."[586] Even then, the 40,000 to 60,000 figures of the Burmese army strength were likely eye estimates and may still be too high; the Mongols may have erred "on the side of generosity" not to "diminish their glory in defeating superior numbers."[592]

According to Marco Polo's account, in the early stages of the battle, the Turkish and Mongol horsemen "took such fright at the sight of the elephants that they would not be got to face the foe, but always swerved and turned back," while the Burmese forces pressed on. But the Mongol commander Huthukh[601] did not panic; he ordered his troops to dismount, and from the cover of the nearby treeline, aim their bows directly at the advancing elephants. The Mongol archers' arrows threw the animals into such pain that they fled.

Raid of Kaungsin

The Mongol army pressed on after the monsoon season. In the following dry season of 1277–78, c. December 1277, a Mongol army of 3800 led by Nasr al-Din, son of Gov. Sayyid Ajjal, advanced to Kaungsin, which defended the Bhamo Pass.[593] They occupied the fort and destroyed a large number of abandoned stockades. But they found the heat excessive and returned.[592]

Interlude (1278–83)

Despite the Mongol military success, the control of the borderlands remained contested. Pagan did not relinquish its claim to the frontier regions, and the Burmese, apparently taking advantage of Mongol preoccupations elsewhere, rebuilt their forts at Kaungsin and Ngasaunggyan later in 1278, posting permanent garrisons commanded by Einda Pyissi.[588] But their control was short-lived. The Great Khan's attention turned to Southeast Asia once more in 1281.[589] He had had mixed success: his vaunted forces had finished off the last of the Song in 1279 but had again failed to take Japan in 1281. That year, the Mongol emperor sent another mission to Pagan, demanding tribute yet again. The Burmese king was to send his ten senior ministers accompanied by one thousand cavalry officers to the emperor's court.[593] (With Champa, the emperor summoned the king of Champa himself to Beijing.[589])

At Pagan, Narathihapate deliberated with his court for an appropriate response but ultimately refused to submit. The Burmese court may have been counting on another limited border war but the emperor now ordered an invasion of northern Burma. (He also ordered an invasion of Champa, whose king too had refused to submit.) The Burmese king's troubles did not go unnoticed elsewhere in the kingdom. In the same year, a usurper named Wareru seized the southern port city of Martaban (Mottama) by killing its Pagan-appointed governor. Although the king's three sons were viceroys of the nearby Lower Burma cities (in Bassein (Pathein), Prome (Pyay), and Dala), the king, preoccupied with much more serious threat in the north, did not (or could not) take any action on Martaban.

Throughout 1282, the Mongol command made preparations for the upcoming invasions of Champa and northern Burma. The objective of the Burma campaign was to take over northern Burma but no further; the emperor did not sanction an attack on Pagan itself.[592] At least one army consisted of 14,000 men of the erstwhile Persian Khwarezmid Empire under the command of Yalu Beg was sent to Yunnan to reinforce the Burma invasion force, which again was made up of Turks and other central Asians. On the Burmese side, the king managed to raise an army although given his low standing with his vassals, he probably could not have raised a large one. By mid-1283, a Burmese

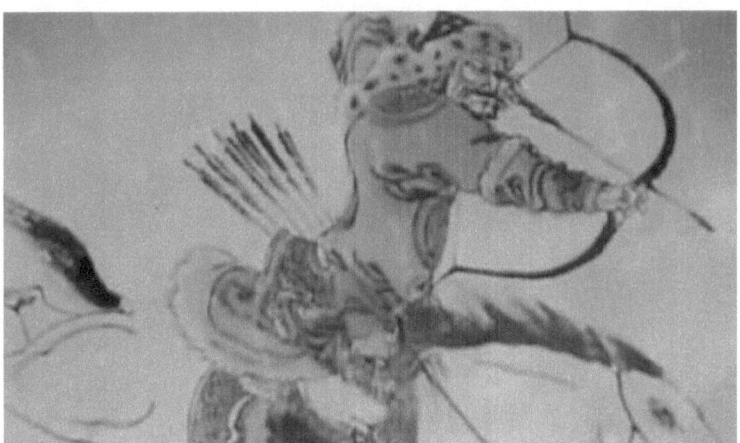

Figure 94: *Mongol warrior on horseback, preparing a mounted archery shot.*

army led by generals Ananda Pyissi and Yanda Pyissi was deployed at a fort at Ngasaunggyan.

Invasion (1283–85)

Battle of Ngasaunggyan (1283)

The invasion began on 22 September 1283. Prince Sangqudar was the commander-in-chief of the invasion force; his deputies were Vice Governor Taipn, and commander Yagan Tegin.[602] The Mongol armies marched to the border in two columns. One column advanced along the Taping River using over 200 boats; the other proceeded by land and joined the first column at the Burmese fort at Ngasaunggyan.[603] The Burmese chronicles report an overwhelming number of Mongol forces laying siege to the fort although their numbers are greatly exaggerated. (The chronicles say that the Burmese army numbered 400,000 men while the Mongol army numbered 20 million men and 6 million horses.) The Burmese withstood the siege for over two months but the fort fell on 3 December 1283.

Invasion of northern Burma

The defeat at Ngasaunggyan broke the back of Burmese defenses. The Burmese army lost several thousand men as well as senior commanders. Kaungsin, the next fort inline, fell just six days later on 9 December 1283.[589] The Mongol sources say that the Burmese lost 10,000 men at Kaungsin. The Mongol armies pushed farther south into the Irrawaddy valley. They took the

Figure 95: *Kublai Khan, founder and first emperor of the Yuan dynasty*

ancient Burmese capital of Tagaung, about 380 km north of Pagan on 5 February 1284.[604] There, the invaders paused their advance. They found the heat of the searing Irrawaddy valley excessive, and evacuated Tagaung, allowing the Burmese to return to Tagaung on 10 May 1284.[605] But the Mongol army renewed their offensive in the following dry season. They retook Tagaung, and defeated another Burmese stand south of Tagaung, probably near Hanlin, on 26 January 1285, opening the way to Pagan, about 270 km south.[602,588] After the defeat, the king panicked, and fled to Lower Burma. The evacuation proved premature. The Mongol forces did not advance on Pagan as it was not part of their invasion plan.

The country fell into chaos. In Lower Burma, the king found himself isolated, let alone plan a counterattack. Although his sons ruled the key Lower Burma ports (Prome, Dala and Bassein), the king did not trust any of them, and he and his court settled at Hlegya, west of Prome.[602] Without the full support of his sons, the presence of the king and his small army impressed no one. The governor of Pegu revolted that same year. The king managed to send two small expeditions to Pegu but they both failed. Now, the entire eastern half of Lower Burma (Pegu and Martaban) was in open revolt.[606]

Peace negotiations (1285–87)

Ceasefire

Given his precarious position, Narathihapate decided to buy time, and sue for peace with the Mongols.[607] In November/December 1285, the king ordered his generals Ananda Pyissi and Maha Bo to enter into ceasefire negotiations.[608] The Mongol commanders at Hanlin, who had organized northern Burma as a protectorate named Zhengmian (Chinese: 征緬 ; Wade–Giles: *Cheng-Mien*),[609] agreed to a ceasefire but insisted on a full submission. They repeated their 1281 demand that the Burmese king send a formal delegation to the emperor. The two sides had reached a tentative agreement by 3 March 1286,[610] which calls for a full submission of the Pagan Empire, and central Burma to be organized as the province of Mianzhong (Chinese: 緬中 ; Wade–Giles: *Mien-Chung*). After a long deliberation, the king agreed to submit but wanted the Mongol troops to withdraw. In June 1286, he sent an embassy led by Shin Ditha Pamauk, a learned monk, to the emperor's court.

Treaty of Beijing

In January 1287, the embassy arrived at Beijing, and was received by the Yuan emperor. The Burmese delegation formally acknowledged Mongol suzerainty of their kingdom, and agreed to pay annual tribute tied to the agricultural output of the country. (Indeed, the tribute was no longer nominal.) In exchange, the emperor agreed to withdraw his troops. For the emperor, the Burma campaign was the only bright spot; his other Southeast Asian expeditions had gone badly. He did not want to invest more troops pacify the rest of the kingdom. He preferred a vassal ruler. The Burmese embassy arrived back at Hlegya in May 1287, and reported the terms to the king.

Breakdown

But the agreement broke down a month later. In late June, the defeated king and his small retinue left their temporary capital for Pagan. But on 1 July 1287, the king was captured en route and assassinated by his second son Thihathu, the Viceroy of Prome.[602] Anarchy ensued. Each region in the country which had not revolted broke away. No successor to Narathihapate, who could honor and enforce the terms of the treaty of Beijing, emerged. Indeed, a king would not emerge until May 1289.[588]

Mongol intervention (1287)

Given the chaos, the governor of Yunnan ignored the imperial orders of evacuation. The Mongol army commanded by Prince Ye-sin Timour, a grandson of the emperor, marched south toward Pagan. According to mainstream traditional (British colonial era) scholarship, the Mongol army ignored the imperial orders to evacuate; fought its way down to Pagan with the loss of 7000 men; occupied the city; and sent out detachments to receive homage, one of which reached south of Prome.[592] But not all colonial period scholars agreed with the assessment as none of the contemporary Mongol/Chinese records specifically mentioned the conquest of Pagan or the temporary completeness of the conquest.[593]

Recent research shows that the Mongol forces most probably never reached Pagan.[611,585] They were held at bay by the Burmese defenses led by commanders Athinkhaya, Yazathingyan and Thihathu, and probably never got closer than 160 km north of Pagan. (An inscription dated 16 February 1293 by the three brothers claimed that they defeated the Mongol army.[612,588]) Even if the Mongols did reach Pagan, the damage they inflicted was probably minimal.[585] At any rate, the Mongol army suffered heavy casualties, and retreated north to Tagaung. They remained there as the treaty was now void.

Aftermath

The disintegration of the Pagan Empire was now complete. But the Mongols refused to fill in the power vacuum they had created. They would send no more expeditions to restore order. The emperor apparently had no interest in committing troops that would be required to pacify the fragmented country. Indeed, his real aim all along may have been "to keep the entire region of Southeast Asia broken and fragmented."[612] It would be another two years until one of Narathihapate's sons, Kyawswa, emerged as king of Pagan in May 1289. But the new "king" controlled just a small area around the capital, and had no real army. The real power in central Burma now rested with the three commander brothers.

The uneasy arrangement would persist until 1297. The Mongols continued to occupy northern Burma to Tagaung as the province of Zhengmian (Cheng-Mien) but ended the fictional central Burma province of Mianzhong on 18 August 1290. Meanwhile, the power struggle in central Burma continued with the three brothers blatantly consolidating support. To check their rising power, Kyawswa submitted to the Mongols in January 1297, and was recognized by the Yuan emperor Temür Khan as King of Pagan on 20 March 1297. The emperor also gave Chinese titles to the brothers as subordinates of Kyawswa.

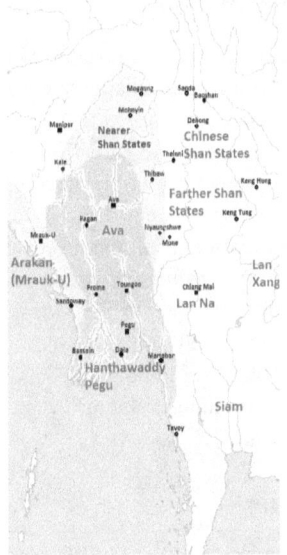

Figure 96: *Burma c. 1450 with Ava at its peak, nearer Shan states paid tribute to Ava*

The brothers resented the new arrangement as it directly reduced their power. On 17 December 1297, the three brothers overthrew Kyawswa, and founded the Myinsaing Kingdom.[588,612] The dethronement forced the Mongol government to intervene again, leading to the second Mongol invasion of Burma (1300–01). The invasion failed. Two years later, on 4 April 1303, the Mongols abolished the province of Zhengmian (Cheng-Mien), evacuated Tagaung, and returned to Yunnan.

Legacy

The war was one of several near simultaneous wars waged by the Mongol Empire and the Yuan dynasty in the late 13th century. Though it was never more than a minor frontier war to the Mongols, the war set off a series of enduring developments in Burma. The invasions ushered in a period of political fragmentation, and the rise of Tai-Shan states throughout mainland Southeast Asia.

Age of political fragmentation

The immediate result of the war was the collapse of the Pagan Empire. However, the war merely accelerated the collapse but did not cause it.[613] Pagan's disintegration was "in fact more prolonged and agonized." The kingdom had been in long gradual decline since the early 13th century. Had Pagan possessed a stronger central government, the collapse could have been temporary, and the country "could have risen again".[592] But the dynasty could not recover, and because the Mongols refused to fill the power vacuum, no viable center emerged in the immediate aftermath. As a result, several minor states fought it out for supremacy for the better part of the 14th century. It was only in the late 14th century that two relatively strong powers emerged in the Irrawaddy basin, restoring some semblance of normalcy.[614] The vast region surrounding the Irrawaddy valley would continue to be made up of several small Tai-Shan states well into the 16th century.[613]

Rise of Tai-Shan states

Perhaps the most enduring legacy of the Mongol invasions was the emergence of Tai-Shan states in mainland Southeast Asia. The Tai-Shan people who came down with the Mongol invasions stayed. By the early 14th century, several Tai-Shan states had come to dominate a vast region from present-day Assam to northern and eastern Myanmar to northern and central Thailand and Laos. Their rise was encouraged by the Mongols, who viewed the states as a useful buffer between Yunnan and the rest of Southeast Asia. The Mongols, who were still trying to incorporate Yunnan into the central administration, were unwilling or unable to make necessary sustained investments to bring the vast regions south of Yunnan into the fold. (The integration of Yunnan itself into "China Proper" was to take several more centuries, and continues to today.) As such, from the newly formed Tai-Shan states in western and central Southeast Asia to Dai Viet and Champa in eastern Southeast Asia, the Mongols elected to receive nominal tribute.[615] Though the rulers of these states were technically governors of the Yuan government, they were the native chieftains, "who would have ruled there in any case, and they did as they pleased."[592]

Arrival of China on the Burmese border

The war also marked the arrival of China at the doorstep of Burma. The old Dali Kingdom, known to the Burmese as Gandalarit (□□□□□□□□, after Gandhara Raj)[586] was now a Mongol Chinese province. (The Burmese now called the new powers at Yunnan "Taruk" after the Turkic-speaking soldiers of Yunnan. Over the years, the term Taruk came to be used to refer to the Han Chinese. Today, King Narathihapate is remembered as Taruk-Pye Min, ("the

King who fled from the Taruk [Chinese]).[593,616]) From a geopolitical standpoint, the Mongol–Chinese presence in Yunnan pushed the Shan migrations in the direction of Burma (and parts of the Khmer Empire).[585] The raids by various Shan states into Upper Burma would continue until the mid-16th century.[585]

Mongolia–Myanmar relations

During the official visit by the President Tsakhiagiin Elbegdorj to Myanmar in November 2013, Aung San Suu Kyi, the chairperson of National League for Democracy, said this was the first ever Mongol mission since the Mongols came 730 years earlier.

Bibliography

- Aung-Thwin, Michael (1985). *Pagan: The Origins of Modern Burma*. Honolulu: University of Hawai'i Press. ISBN 0-8248-0960-2.
- Aung-Thwin, Michael Arthur; Hall, Kenneth R. (2011). *New Perspectives on the History and Historiography of Southeast Asia*. Routledge. ISBN 9781136819643.
- Aung-Thwin, Michael A.; Maitrii Aung-Thwin (2012). *A History of Myanmar Since Ancient Times* (illustrated ed.). Honolulu: University of Hawai'i Press. ISBN 978-1-86189-901-9.
- Coedès, George (1968). *The Indianized States of South-East Asia*. University of Hawaii Press. ISBN 9780824803681.
- Cocks, Samuel W. (1919). *A Short History of Burma* (2 ed.). London: Macmillan and Co.
- Hall, Kenneth R. (2010). *A History of Early Southeast Asia: Maritime Trade and Societal Development, 100–1500* (illustrated ed.). Lanham: Rowman & Littlefield. ISBN 9780742567627.
- Harvey, G. E. (1925). *History of Burma: From the Earliest Times to 10 March 1824*. London: Frank Cass & Co. Ltd.
- Haw, Stephen G. (2006). *Marco Polo's China: A Venetian in the Realm of Khubilai Khan*. New York: Routledge. ISBN 9781134275427.
- Htin Aung, Maung (1967). *A History of Burma*. New York and London: Cambridge University Press.
- Kala, U (1724). *Maha Yazawin* (in Burmese). **1–3** (2006, 4th printing ed.). Yangon: Ya-Pyei Publishing.
- Lieberman, Victor B. (2003). *Strange Parallels: Southeast Asia in Global Context, c. 800–1830, volume 1, Integration on the Mainland*. Cambridge University Press. ISBN 978-0-521-80496-7.

- Maha Sithu (1798). Myint Swe (1st ed.); Kyaw Win, Ph.D. and Thein Hlaing (2nd ed.), eds. *Yazawin Thit* (in Burmese). **1–3** (2012, 2nd printing ed.). Yangon: Ya-Pyei Publishing.
- Marco Polo (1874). Henry Yule, ed. *The book of Ser Marco Polo, the Venetian, concerning the kingdoms and marvels of the East*. **2**. Location: John Murray.
- Myint-U, Thant (2006). *The River of Lost Footsteps—Histories of Burma*. Farrar, Straus and Giroux. ISBN 978-0-374-16342-6.
- Myint-U, Thant (2011). *Where China Meets India: Burma and the New Crossroads of Asia*. New York: Farrar, Straus and Giroux. ISBN 978-0-374-16342-6.
- Pan Hla, Nai (1968). *Razadarit Ayedawbon* (in Burmese) (8th printing, 2005 ed.). Yangon: Armanthit Sarpay.
- Phayre, Lt. Gen. Sir Arthur P. (1883). *History of Burma* (1967 ed.). London: Susil Gupta.
- Rossabi, Morris (1981). "The Muslims in the Early Yuan Dynasty". In John D. Langlois, Jr. *China Under Mongol Rule* (2014 ed.). Princeton University Press. ISBN 9781400854097.
- Royal Historical Commission of Burma (1832). *Hmannan Yazawin* (in Burmese). **1–3** (2003 ed.). Yangon: Ministry of Information, Myanmar.
- Sarpay Beikman, ed. (1961). *Myanma Swezon Kyan* (in Burmese). **5** (1 ed.). Heartford, Heartfordshire: Stephen Austin & Sons, Ltd.
- Stuart-Fox, Martin (2001). "Review of "Myth and History in the Historiography of Early Burma" by Michael A. Aung-Thwin". *Journal of the Economic and Social History of the Orient*. Brill. **44** (1): 88–90. JSTOR 3632565[617].
- Than Tun (December 1959). "History of Burma: A.D. 1300–1400". *Journal of Burma Research Society*. **XLII** (II).
- Than Tun (1964). *Studies in Burmese History* (in Burmese). **1**. Yangon: Maha Dagon.
- Wade, Geoff (2009). Eugene Perry Link, ed. *The Scholar's Mind: Essays in Honor of Frederick W. Mote*. Chinese University Press. ISBN 9789629964030.

Second Mongol invasion of Burma

Second Mongol invasion of Burma	
Part of the Mongol conquests	
Date	January 1300 – 6 April 1301
Location	Burma
Result	Burmese victory
Belligerents	
Yuan dynasty	Myinsaing Kingdom
Commanders and leaders	
Temür Khan Mangu Turumish Kumara Kassapa	Athinkhaya Yazathingyan Thihathu
Strength	
12,000	Unknown
Casualties and losses	
Unknown	Unknown

The **second Mongol invasion of Burma** by the Yuan dynasty under Temür Khan was repulsed by the Burmese Myinsaing Kingdom in 1301.

Background

After the first Mongol invasion by the Yuan dynasty, Narathihapate fled Pagan, which subsequently was sacked by the invading Mongol forces. Already experienced commanders, the brothers strengthened their garrison at Myinsaing. After the Mongols left, Kyawswa succeeded his father Narathihapate. But he was just a nominal king of Pagan for he controlled no more than a few miles outside Pagan. Indeed, the Pagan Empire had ceased to exist. Instead, the real power in central Burma rested with the brothers who through their small but well-disciplined army controlled the Kyaukse district, the most important granary of Pagan. Kyawswa had no choice but to recognize them as lords of Kyaukse. On 19 February 1293 (12th waxing of Tabaung 654 ME), the king appointed the eldest brother as viceroy of Myinsaing, the second brother as viceroy of Mekkara, and the third brother as viceroy of Pinle.

The brothers already behaved like sovereign kings nonetheless. When King Wareru of Hanthawaddy received recognition as a tributary of the Sukhothai Kingdom in 1294, it was the brothers, not Kyawswa, who sent a force to reclaim the former Pagan territory of Hanthawaddy (Lower Burma). While their attempt to reconquer Hanthawaddy was unsuccessful, it left no doubt as to who held the real power in central Burma.

With the Three Shan Brothers increasingly acting as sovereign kings, Kyawswa sent his son to the Mongols army base in Tagaung and asked for recognition as their vassal king in January 1297. He received the official recognition and a Chinese title on 20 March 1297. In December, the brothers invited the now puppet king to Myinsaing, their stronghold, to take part in the dedication ceremony of a monastery built by them. The king, with the backing of the Mongols, felt secure and went to Myinsaing. But as soon as the ceremony was over, he was arrested, dethroned, and forced to become a monk in the very monastery he had just dedicated.[618]

Mongol invasion (1300–1301)

On 17 December 1297, the three brothers overthrew Kyawswa, and founded the Myinsaing Kingdom. At Pagan, Kyawswa's son Sawhnit was elected king by the dowager Queen Saw but soon became a governor under the authority of Myinsaing. Another of Kyawswa's sons, Kumara Kassapa, escaped to China. The Mongols did not know about the dethronement until June–July 1298.[588] In 1300, the Myinsaing forces led by Athinkhaya attacked the Mongol garrisons north of Mandalay named Nga Singu and Male. On 22 June 1300, the Mongol Emperor declared that Kumara Kassapa was the rightful king of Burma, and sent in an army from Yunnan. The invasion force reached Myinsaing on 25 January 1301 but could not break through. The besiegers took the bribes by the three brothers, and withdrew on 6 April 1301.[588] The Mongol government at Yunnan executed their commanders[588,588] but sent no more invasions. They withdrew entirely from Upper Burma starting on 4 April 1303.[588]

By then, the city of Pagan, once home to 200,000 people,[619] had been reduced to a small town, never to regain its preeminence. (It survived into the 15th century as a human settlement.) The brothers placed one of Kyawswa's sons as the governor of Pagan. Anawrahta's line continued to rule Pagan as governors under Myinsaing, Pinya and Ava kingdoms until 1369. The male side of Pagan ended there although the female side passed into Pinya and Ava royalty.[620] But the Pagan line continued to be claimed by successive Burmese dynasties down to the last Burmese dynasty Konbaung.[621]

Further reading

- Bor, J. *History of diplomatic relations of Mongol-Eurasia*. **II**.
- Grousset, Rene (2000). *The Empire of the Steppes: A History of Central Asia*. New Brunswick: Rutgers University Press. ISBN 0-8135-1304-9.
- Than Tun (December 1959). "History of Burma: A.D. 1300–1400". *Journal of Burma Research Society*. **XLII** (II).

Mongol invasions of Vietnam

Mongol invasions of Đại Việt and Champa	
Part of the Mongol invasions	

The Battle of Bạch Đằng (1288) during the Third Mongol invasion	
Date	1258, 1285 and 1287–88
Location	Đại Việt and Champa
Result	Decisive Đại Việt/Champa Victory • To avoid further conflict, Đại Việt and Champa agreed to a tributary relationship with the Yuan dynasty • The capital city of the Tran was sacked by the Mongols three times • Huge fiscal loss suffered by all parties
Belligerents	
▶ Mongol Empire (1258) ▶ Yuan dynasty (1285 and 1287–88)	Đại Việt under the Trần dynasty Champa
Commanders and leaders	
▶ Möngke Khan ▶ Kublai Khan ▶ Uriyangkhadai ▶ Aju ▶ Sodu ▶ Toghan ▶ Umar bin Nasr al-Din (Yunnan) ▶ Abachi ▶ Fanji ▶ Aqatai ▶ Arikhgiya	Trần Thái Tông Trần Thánh Tông Trần Nhân Tông Trần Hưng Đạo Trần Quang Khải Jaya Indravarman VI
Strength	

3,000 Mongols and 10,000 Yi tribesmen in 1257[622] Less than 100,000 in 1285 70,000 Yuan troops, 21,000 tribal auxiliaries, 500 ships in 1287–88[623]	Đại Việt more than 200,000–300,000 people in 1285 Champa about 60,000 people Wikipedia:Citation needed
Casualties and losses	
Unknown but minimal in 1257 heavy in 1285 and heavy in 1288	unknown

The **Mongol invasions of Vietnam** or **Mongol-Vietnamese War** refer to the three times that the Mongol Empire and its chief khanate the Yuan dynasty invaded Đại Việt during the time of the Trần dynasty, along with Champa: in 1258, 1285, and 1287–88.[624] Although the invasions resulted in disastrous military defeats for the Mongols, both the Trần dynasty and Champa decided to accept the nominal supremacy of the Yuan dynasty in order to avoid further conflicts.

Background

By the 1250s, the Mongol Empire controlled large amounts of Eurasia including much of Eastern Europe, Anatolia, North China, Mongolia, Manchuria, Central Asia, Tibet and Southwest Asia. Möngke Khan (r. 1251–59) planned to attack the Song dynasty in South China from three directions in 1259. Therefore, he ordered the prince Kublai to pacify the Dali Kingdom. After subjugating Dali, Kublai sent one column under Uriyangkhadai to the southeast. Uriyangkhadai sent envoys to demand the submission of Đại Việt, but the Trần rulers imprisoned the Mongol envoys.[625] This action led Uriyangkhadai and his son Aju to invade Đại Việt with 40,000 Mongols and 10,000 Yi people.

The ancestors of the Trần clan originated from the province of Fujian and later migrated to Đại Việt under Trần Kinh 陳京 (Chén Jīng), the ancestor of the Trần clan. Their descendants, the later rulers of Đại Việt who were of mixed-blooded descent later established the Tran dynasty, which ruled Vietnam (Đại Việt); despite many intermarriages between the Trần and several royal members of the Lý dynasty alongside members of their royal court as in the case of Trần Lý and Trần Thừa, some of the mixed-blooded descendants of the Trần dynasty and certain members of the clan could still speak Chinese such as when a Yuan dynasty envoy had a meeting with the Chinese-speaking Trần prince Trần Quốc Tuấn in 1282.[626]

Professor Liam Kelley noted that people from Song dynasty China like Zhao Zhong and Xu Zongdao fled to Tran dynasty ruled Vietnam after the Mongol invasion of the Song and they helped the Tran fight against the Mongol invasion. The ancestors of the Tran clan originated from the area now

Figure 97: *Kublai Khan, the fifth Great Khan of the Mongol Empire, and the founder of the Yuan dynasty*

known as Fujian region of modern China as did the Daoist cleric Xu Zongdao who recorded the Mongol invasion and referred to them as "Northern bandits".[627,628]

First Mongol invasion in 1258

In 1258, a Mongol column under Uriyangkhadai, the son of Subutai, invaded Đại Việt. A battle was fought in which the Vietnamese used war elephants. Aju ordered his troops to fire arrows at the elephants' feet. The animals turned in panic and caused disorder in the Đại Việt army, which was routed. The King of Đại Việt fled to an offshore island, and the Mongols occupied the capital city Thăng Long (now Hanoi). When they found their envoys in prison, one of whom died, they responded by massacring the population of the capital. Though the Mongols retained supremacy on land, their forces were unable to withstand the tropical heat, mosquitoes, and malaria, and after securing a submission and promise of tribute from the Dai Viet King, Uriyangkhadai ordered a retreat.[629]

The following year (1259), Uriyangkhadai returned to Đại Việt with an army of three thousand Mongols and ten thousand local troops from the conquered Kingdom of Dali, now the Yuan province of Yunnan. He led this army into

Song China, and fought his way to the Yangtze River, joining with an army led by Kublai which had invaded from the north and was besieging Ezhou (modern Wuhan).[630]

The Vietnamese had submitted unwillingly, and were reluctant vassals. The Vietnamese emperor repeatedly ignored demands to attend the Yuan court and offer his personal submission to the Great Khan. Nevertheless, according to the history of the Yuan dynasty, the Trần court sent tribute every three years and received a darughachi. By 1266, however, a standoff developed, as the Emperor Thánh Tông sought a loose tributary relationship, while Kublai demanded full submission. Trần Thánh Tông sent an official letter requiring Kublai to take his darughachi back. Because of civil war in the Mongol Empire, and the Yuan conquest of Song China, armed conflict was delayed. Instead, Kublai reminded him of the peace treaty signed by the Mongols and Đại Việt.

As a result of the Mongol conquest of the Song Empire, by 1278–79, Mongol troops reached Đại Việt's northern borders. Some former Song officials fled to Đại Việt and Champa, former vassals of Song China, during the final stage of Mongolian conquest of China.[631] The Trầns' new ruler Nhân Tông resisted renewed Mongol demands for personal attendance at Kublai's court, but dispatched his uncle Tran Di Ai as envoy. Kublai tried to enthrone Di Ai as prince in 1281 but Di Ai and his small army were ambushed by Đại Việt forces.

Champa

Sogetu of the Jalairs, the governor of Guangzhou, was dispatched to demand the submission of Champa. Although the king of Champa accepted the status of a Mongol protectorate,[632] his submission was unwilling. In 1282, Sogetu led a maritime invasion of Champa with 5,000 men, but could only muster 100 ships because most of the Yuan ships had been lost in the invasions of Japan.[633]

However, Sogetu was successful in capturing Vijaya, the Champa capital later that year. The aged Champa king Indravarman V retreated out of the capital, avoiding Mongol attempts to capture him in the hills. His son would wage guerrilla warfare against the Mongols for the next few years, eventually wearing down the invaders.[634] Stymied by the withdrawal of the Champa king, Sogetu asked reinforcements from Kublai but sailed home in 1284 just as another Mongol fleet with more than 15,000 troops under Ataqai and Arigh Khaiya reembarked on a fruitless mission to reinforce him. Sogetu presented his plan to have more troops invade Champa through Đại Việt. Kublai accepted his plan and put his son Toghan in command, with Sogetu as second in command.

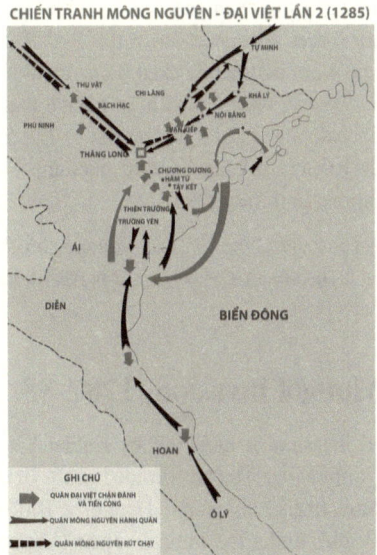

Figure 98: *Map depicting Mongol campaign in Đại Việt in the north and Champa in the south*

Second Mongol invasion in 1285

This was the first invasion of Đại Việt by Kublai Khan's Yuan dynasty. In 1284 Kublai appointed his son Toghan (Vietnamese: *Thoát Hoan*) to conquer Champa. Toghan demanded from the Trần a route to Champa, which would trap the Champan army from both north and south. While Nhân Tông accept the demand reluctantly, General Hưng Đạo rallied 15,000 troops and help the Champan.

Planning to weaken the enemies first, the Đại Việt royal family abandoned the capital, letting the Mongols capture it and retreated south while enacting a scorched earth campaign by burning villages and crops. At the same time, Sogetu moved his army up north in an attempt to envelop the royal family in a pincer movement, which the Vietnamese managed to escape.

Sogetu's army was weakened by the summer heat and the lack of food, so they stopped chasing the royal family and move north to join with Toghan. Seeing the Mongol's movement, Trần Hưng Đạo concluded that the Mongol was weakened and decided to take the opportunity to strike, selecting battlefields where the Mongol cavalry could not be fully employed.

The Cham were in pursuit of Sogetu as he was heading north, and killed him and defeated his army.[635] However, according to Vietnamese history, Sogetu was defeated in Hàm Tử, Hưng Yên and was killed by the Vietnamese in his retreat. As the Yuan forces advanced down the Red River, dispersing their power, General Quang Khải counterattacked them at Chương Dương, forcing Toghan to withdraw. Toghan returned without a huge loss of the army under him thanks to the Kipchak officer Sidor and his navy. The Yuan army retreated north, but few made it back to China due to pursuing Đại Việt troops and warriors from the Hmong and Yao tribes.

The next year, Kublai installed Nhân Tông's younger brother Trần Ích Tắc, a defector to the Yuan, as prince of Đại Việt, but hardship in the Yuan's Hunan supply base aborted his plan.

Third/Final Mongol invasion, 1287-88

This was the second invasion of Đại Việt by Kublai Khan's Yuan dynasty. In 1287 the Yuan commander Toghan invaded with 70,000 regular troops, 21,000 tribal auxiliaries from Yunnan and Hainan, a 1000-man vanguard under Abachi, and 500 ships under the Muslim Omar (Vietnamese: Ô Mã Nhi) (who was the son of Nasr al-Din (Yunnan)) and Chinese Fanji (according to some sources, the Mongol force was composed of 300,000–500,000 men). Kublai sent veterans such as Arigh Khaiya, Nasir al-Din and his grandson Esen-Temür. The strategy of this invasion was different: a huge base was to be established just inland from Hải Phòng, and a large-scale naval assault mounted as well as a land attack. Despite the Mongol large-scaled invasion, Trần Quốc Tuấn confidently told the king that the invaders can be defeated easily this time. Trần Hưng Đạo withdrew from inhabited areas, leaving the Mongols with nothing to conquer. The whole fleet bringing food provisions to Toghan's army by maritime route was ambushed and destroyed by Trần Khánh Dư. Facing the lack of food again, Toghan retreated to China through the Bạch Đằng River.

Borrowing a tactic used by general Ngô Quyền in 938 to defeat an invading Chinese fleet, the Đại Việt forces drove iron-tipped stakes into the bed of the Bạch Đằng River, and then, with a small flotilla, lured the Mongol fleet into the river just as the tide was starting to ebb, while their route to the sea had been blockaded by large warships. Unable to return or escape to the sea, the entire Mongol fleet of 400 craft was caught in a bloody boarding and missile battle, sunk, captured, or burned by fire arrows. This would later become known as the Battle of Bạch Đằng (1288). The invading Mongol army of the Yuan retreated to China, harassed en route by Trần Hưng Đạo's troops. The Yuan officers such as Abachi and Fanji died in the bloody retreat and Omar was captured and executed.

Aftermath

In Đại Việt

Kublai angrily banished Toghan to Yangzhou for life. The Mongols and the Tran Vietnamese agreed to exchange their war prisoners. While Nhan Tong was willing to pay tribute to the Yuan, relations again foundered on the question of attendance at the Yuan court and hostile relations continued.

The Trần Dynasty decided to accept the supremacy of the Yuan dynasty in order to avoid further conflicts. Because he refused to come in person, Kublai detained his envoy, Dao-tu Ki, in 1293. Kublai's successor Temür Khan (r. 1294-1307), finally released all detained envoys, settling for a tributary relationship, which continued to the end of the Yuan.

In Champa

The Champa Kingdom decided to accept the supremacy of the Yuan dynasty as well. A tributary relationship continued for some time, but Champa disappears from Yuan records before 1300. The king of Champa made the act of vassalage to the Mongols.

Legacy

The incredible victories against the Mongols, three times, despite having been debated for many years by many historians, could not deny the fact that the Vietnamese had done more incredible thing against the Mongols than other people. Some historians[636] have considered the Vietnamese victories over the Mongols had successfully prevented the Mongol conquest of Southeast Asia, and further more, saving all other Southeast Asian kingdoms from being ruled by the Mongols.

It is regarded as one of the greatest military victories of Vietnam, a country with typical militaristic history in the region.

References

- Atwood, Christopher Pratt. (2004). *Encyclopedia of Mongolia and the Mongol Empire*. New York: Facts of File. ISBN 978-0-8160-4671-3.
- Connolly, Peter. (1998). *The Hutchinson Dictionary of Ancient & Medieval Warfare*. Routledge. ISBN 978-1-57958-116-9.
- Delgado, James P. (2008). *Khubilai Khan's Lost Fleet: In Search of a Legendary Armada*. Vancouver: Douglas & McIntyre. ISBN 978-0-520-25976-8.

- Grousset, René. (1970). *The Empire of the Steppes*. Rutgers University Press. ISBN 978-0-8135-1304-1.
- Haw, S. G. (2013) "The Deaths of Two Khaghans", *Bulletin of the School of Oriental and African Studies*.

Mongol invasion of Java

Mongol invasion of Java	
Part of the Mongol invasions and Kublai Khan's Campaigns	
Date	1293
Location	Java, Majapahit
Result	Majapahit victory
Belligerents	
Yuan dynasty	Kingdom of Singhasari Kediri Kingdom Majapahit Empire
Commanders and leaders	
Kublai Khan (supreme commander) Gaoxing (generals) Shi-bi Ike Mese	Jayakatwang (supreme commander) Raden Wijaya (general, later ruler - allied to Yuan invaders in earlier phases of the war)
Strength	
20,000–30,000 soldiers 1,000 ships	More than 100,000 soldiers
Casualties and losses	
More than 3,000 killed	More than 2,000 killed and drowned

The **Mongol invasion of Java** was a military effort made by Kublai Khan, founder of the Yuan dynasty (one of the fragments of the Mongol Empire), to invade Java, an island in modern Indonesia. In 1293, he sent a large invasion fleet to Java with 20,000 to 30,000 soldiers. This was a punitive expedition against King Kertanegara of Singhasari, who had refused to pay tribute to the Yuan and maimed one of its ministers. However, it ended with failure for the Mongols.

Background

Kublai Khan, founder of the Yuan dynasty, the principal khanate of the Mongol Empire, had sent envoys to many states to ask them to put themselves under his protection and pay tribute. Men Shi or Meng-qi (孟琪), one of his ministers who was sent to Java, was not well received there. The king of Singhasari,

Kertanagara, was offended by his proposal and branded his face with a hot iron as was done to common thieves, cut his ears, and scornfully sent him on his way.

Kublai Khan was shocked and ordered a punitive expedition against Kertanagara, whom he labeled a barbarian, in 1292. According to the *Yuan shi*, the history of the Yuan dynasty, 20,000-30,000 men were collected from Fujian, Jiangxi and Huguang in Southern China, along with 1,000 ships and enough provisions for a year.[637] The officers were the Mongol Shi-bi, the Uyghur Ike Mese, and the Chinese Gaoxing. What kind of ships they used for the campaign is not mentioned in the Yuan shi, but they were apparently large since smaller boats had to be constructed for entering the rivers of Java.

Meanwhile, after defeating Malayu Dharmasraya in Sumatra in 1290, Singhasari became the most powerful kingdom in the region. Kertanegara sent a massive army to Sumatra in this Pamalayu campaign. However, seizing the opportunity of the lack of army guarding the capital, in 1292 Jayakatwang, the duke of Kediri (Gelang-gelang), a vassal state of Singhasari, revolted against Kertanegara. Jayakatwang revolt was assisted by Arya Wiraraja,:[199] a regent from Sumenep on the island of Madura, whom secretly despised Kertanegara.

The Kediri (Gelang-gelang) army attacked Singhasari simultaneously from both north and south flanks. The king only realised the invasion from the north and sent his son-in-law, Nararya Sanggramawijaya (Raden Wijaya) northward to vanquish the rebellion. The northern attack was quashed, but the southern attack successfully remained undetected until they reached and sacked the unprepared capital city of Kutaraja. Jayakatwang usurped and killed Kertanagara during the Tantra sacred ceremony, thus bring an end to the Singhasari kingdom.

Having learned of the fall of the Singhasari capital of Kutaraja to Kadiri rebellion, Raden Wijaya tried to return and defend Singhasari but failed. He and his three colleagues, Ranggalawe, Sora and Nambi, went to exile to Madura under the protection of the regent Arya Wiraraj, Nambi's father, who then turned to Jayakatwang's side. Kertanegara's son-in-law, Raden Wijaya, submitted to Kediri, brokered by Arya Wiraraja and was pardoned by Jayakatwang. Wijaya was then given the permision to establish a new settlement in Tarik timberland. The new settlement was named Majapahit, which was taken from *maja* fruit that had a bitter taste in that timberland (*maja* is the fruit name and *pahit* means bitter).

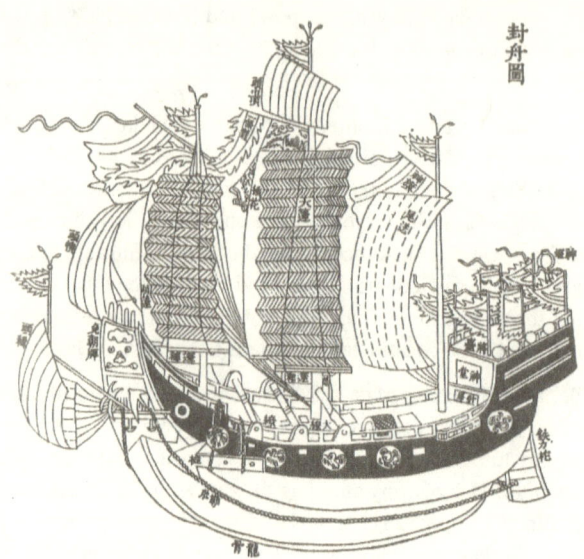

Figure 99: *Painting of a 14th-century Yuan junk. Yuan naval armada consisted of this kind of ships.*

Invasion

The Yuan forces departed from southern port of Quanzhou, traveled along the coast of Dai Viet and Champa along the way to their primary target. The small states of Malay and Sumatra submitted and sent envoys to them, and Yuan commanders left darughachis there. It is known that the Yuan forces stopped at Ko-lan (Biliton). After arriving in Java, Shi-bi split their forces, sending one group ashore and another to proceed by boat. As noted in Kidung Panji-Wijayakrama, they probably looted the coastal village of Tuban.

When the Yuan army arrived in Java, Wijaya allied himself with the army to fight against Jayakatwang and gave the Mongols a map of the country Kalang (Gelang-gelang, another name for Kediri). According to the Yuan-shi, Wijaya attacked Jayakatwang without success when he heard of the arrival of the Yuan navy. Then he requested their aid. In return, Yuan generals demanded his submission to their emperor, and he gave it.

The account of the war which appears in the Yuan-shi (Books 210) is brief:

> ...The soldiers from Dahanese came to attack Wijaya on the seventh day of the month, Ike Mese and Gaoxing came on the eighth, some Dahanese were defeated, the rest of them fled to the mountains. On the nineteenth

day, the Mongols and their allies arrived in Daha, fought more than 100,000 soldiers, attacking 3 times, killing 2,000 outright while forcing many thousands into the river where they drowned. Jayakatwang retreated into his palace ...

Once Jayakatwang was captured by the Mongols, Raden Wijaya returned to Majapahit, ostensibly to prepare his tribute settlement, leaving his allies to celebrate their victory. Shi-bi and Ike Mese allowed Raden Wijaya to go back to his country to prepare his tribute and a new letter of submission, but Gaoxing disliked the idea and he warned other two. Wijaya asked the Yuan forces to come to his country unarmed.

Two hundred unarmed Yuan soldiers led by two officers were sent to Raden Wijaya's country, but Raden Wijaya quickly mobilized his forces again and ambushed the Yuan convoy. After that Raden Wijaya marched his forces to the main Yuan camp and launched a surprise attack, killing many and sending the rest running back to their ships. The Yuan forces had to withdraw in confusion, as the monsoon winds to carry them home would soon end, leaving them to wait on a hostile island for six months. The Yuan army lost more than 3,000 of its elite soldiers.[638]

Aftermath

The three generals, demoralized by the considerable loss of their elite soldiers due to the ambush, went back to their empire with the surviving soldiers. Upon their arrival, Shi-bi was condemned to receive 70 lashes and have a third of his property confiscated for allowing the catastrophe. Ike Mese also was reprimanded and a third of his property taken away. But Gaoxing was awarded 50 taels of gold for protecting the soldiers from a total disaster. Later, Shi-bi and Ike Mese were shown mercy, and the emperor restored their reputation and property.

This failure was the last expedition in Kublai Khan's reign. Majapahit, in contrast, became the most powerful state of its era in the region which is now Indonesia.

Further reading

- Bade, David W. (2002), *Khubilai Khan and the Beautiful Princess of Tumapel: the Mongols Between History and Literature in Java*, Ulaanbaatar: A. Chuluunbat
- Man, John (2007), *Kublai Khan: The Mongol king who remade China*, London: Bantam Books, ISBN 0-553-81718-3

- Levathes, Louise (1994), *When China Ruled the Seas*, New York: Simon & Schuster, p. 54, ISBN 0-671-70158-4, <q>The ambitious khan [Kublai Khan] also sent fleets into the South China Seas to attack Annam and Java, whose leaders both briefly acknowledged the suzerainty of the dragon throne</q>
- d'Ohsson, Constantin Mouradgea (2002), "Chapitre 3 Kublai Khan, Tome III", *Histoire des Mongols, depuis Tchinguiz-Khan jusqu'à Timour Bey ou Tamerlan*, Boston: Adamant Media, ISBN 978-0-543-94729-1

Mongol military tactics and organization

Mongol military tactics and organization

The **Mongol military tactics and organization** enabled the Mongol Empire to conquer nearly all of continental Asia, the Middle East and parts of eastern Europe.

The original foundation of that system was an extension of the nomadic lifestyle of the Mongols. Other elements were invented by Genghis Khan, his generals, and his successors. Technologies useful to attack fortifications were adapted from other cultures, and foreign technical experts integrated into the command structures. Always returned to turn the result around in their favor. In many cases, they won against significantly larger opposing armies.

Their first defeat in the West came in 1223 at the Battle of Samara Bend by the hands of the Volga Bulgars. The second one was at the Battle of Ain Jalut in 1260, against the first army, which was specifically trained to use their own tactics against them.[639,640,641] But again they would return over 40 years later and defeat the Egyptian Mamluks at the Battle of Wadi al-Khazandar in 1299 and annex Syria, Palestine as well as Gaza. The Mongols suffered defeats in attempted invasions of Vietnam empire became divided around the same time, its combined size and influence remained largely int In accordance with Mongol civil and social structure, outstanline provided the backbone for their military. According to Italian explorer Giovanni da Pian del Caprine, *"The Tatars—that is, the Mong 1190–1400] Hardback ed New York: Routledge, 2004 p.17</ref>* Army delegates were chosen either by their blood association of the Khan family or by military-related meritocracy. Each delegate received responsibility and their respective titles:[642]

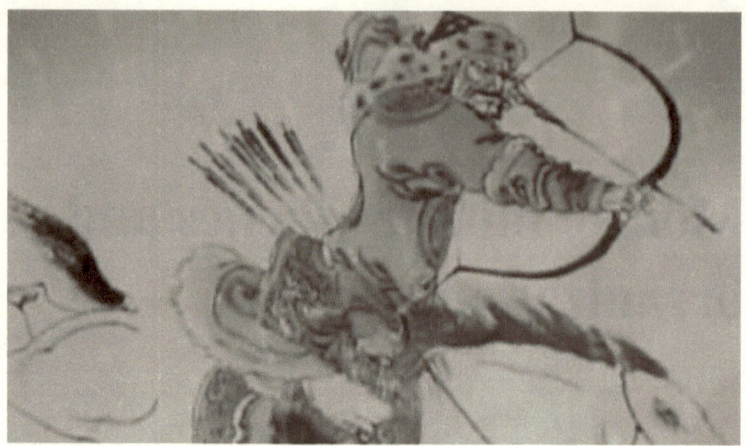

Figure 100: *Mongol warrior on horseback, preparing a mounted archery shot.*

Military Title	Number of Men
Arban	Ten(s)
Zuun	Hundreds
Mingghan	Thousands
Tumen	Tens of Thousands

Mongol military tactics and organization

Figure 101: *Drawing of a mobile Mongol soldier with bow and arrow wearing deel. The right arm is semi-naked because of the hot weather.*

Transfers between units were forbidden. The leaders on each level had significant license to execute their orders in the way they considered best. This command structure proved to be highly flexible and allowed the Mongol army to attack *en masse*, divide into somewhat smaller groups to encircle and lead enemies into an ambush, or divide into small groups of 10 to mop up a fleeing and broken army. Individual soldiers were responsible for their equipment, weapons, and up to five mounts, although they fought as part of a unit. Their families and herds would accompany them on foreign expeditions.

Above all units, there existed an elite force called Kheshig. They functioned as imperial guard of the Mongol Empire as well as a training ground for potential young officers, the great Subutai having started his career there.

Mobility

Each Mongol soldier typically maintained 3 or 4 horses. Changing horses often allowed them to travel at high speed for days without stopping or wearing out the animals. Their ability to live off the land, and in extreme situations off their animals (mare's milk especially), made their armies far less dependent on the traditional logistical apparatus of agrarian armies. In some cases, as during the invasion of Hungary in early 1241, they covered up to 100 miles (160 km) per day, which was unheard of by other armies of the time.

The mobility of individual soldiers made it possible to send them on successful scouting missions, gathering intelligence about routes and searching for terrain suited to the preferred combat tactics of the Mongols.

During the invasion of Kievan Rus, the Mongols used frozen rivers as highways, and winter, the time of year usually off-limits for any major activity due to the intense cold, became the Mongols' preferred time to strike.

To avoid the deadly hail of missiles, enemies would frequently spread out, or seek cover, breaking up their formations and making them more vulnerable to the lancers' charges. Likewise, when they packed themselves together, into dense square or phalanx style formations, they would become more vulnerable to the arrows.

Once the enemy was deemed sufficiently weakened, the noyans would give the order. The drums would beat and the signal flags wave, telling the lancers to begin their charge. Often, the devastation of the arrows was enough to rout an enemy, so the lancers were only needed to help pursue and mop up the remnants. At the Battle of Mohi, the Mongols left open a gap in their ranks, luring the Hungarians into retreating through it. This resulted in the Hungarians being strung out over all the countryside and easy pickings for mounted archers who simply galloped along and picked them off, while the lancers skewered them as they fled.

Training and discipline

Mongol armies practiced horsemanship, archery, and unit tactics, formations and rotations over and over again. This training was maintained by a hard, but not overly harsh or unreasonable, discipline.

Officers and troopers alike were usually given a wide leeway by their superiors in carrying out their orders, so long as the larger objectives of the plan were well served and the orders promptly obeyed. The Mongols thus avoided the pitfalls of overly rigid discipline and micromanagement, which have impeded armed forces throughout history. However, all members had to be unconditionally loyal to each other and to their superiors, and especially to the Khan. If one soldier ran from danger in battle, he and his nine comrades from the same arban would face the death penalty together.

Figure 102: *Mongol cavalry archery from Rashid-al-Din Hamadani's Universal History using the Mongol bow.*

Cavalry

Six of every ten Mongol troopers were light cavalry horse archers; the remaining four were more heavily armored and armed lancers. Mongol light cavalry were extremely light troops compared to contemporary standards, allowing them to execute tactics and maneuvers that would have been impractical for a heavier enemy (such as European knights). Most of the remaining troops were heavier cavalry with lances for close combat after the archers had brought the enemy into disarray. Soldiers usually carried scimitars or halberds as well.

The Mongols protected their horses in the same way as did they themselves, covering them with lamellar armor. Horse armor was divided into five parts and designed to protect every part of the horse, including the forehead, which had a specially crafted plate, which was tied on each side of the neck.[643]

Mongolian horses are relatively small, but extremely hardy, self-sufficient and longwinded. These horses could survive in climates that would have killed other breeds, enabling the Mongols to launch successful winter attacks on Russia. Mongol horses typically do not require a daily supply of grain. Their ability to forage grass and twigs on their own—and to survive on such fodder—helped free the Khan's army from the need for supply lines. The Mongol horse has excellent stamina. In 30 km traditional races between Mongol horses and breeds like the Arabian or Thoroughbred, it has been found that the latter are faster, but that Mongol horses are better able to run at length. The tireless nature of the Mongol horse meant that it would have stayed fresh longer in battle, granted Genghis Khan's armies an endurance advantage.

Seen as a "machine of war," the Mongol horse is an all-terrain, all-weather vehicle requiring little gas or maintenance and providing excellent mileage. A warrior relied on his herd to provide him with staple foods of milk and meat; hide for bowstrings, shoes, and armor; dried dung to be used as fuel for his fire; hair for rope, battle standards, musical instruments and helmet decorations; milk also used for shamanistic ceremonies to ensure victory; and for hunting and entertainment that often served as military training. If he died in battle, a horse would sometimes be sacrificed with him to provide a mount for the afterlife.

The main drawback to Mongol horses was their lack of speed. They would lose short-distance races under equal conditions with larger horses from other regions. However, since most other armies carried much heavier armor, the Mongols could still outrun most enemy horsemen in battle. In addition, Mongolian horses were extremely durable and sturdy, allowing the Mongols to move over large distances quickly, often surprising enemies that had expected them to arrive days or even weeks later.

All horses were equipped with stirrups. This technical advantage made it easier for the Mongol archers to turn their upper body, and shoot in all directions, including backwards. Mongol warriors would time the loosing of an arrow to the moment when a galloping horse would have all four feet off the ground, thus ensuring a steady, well-aimed shot.

Each soldier had two to four horses—so when a horse tired they could change to one of the others. This made them one of the fastest armies in the world, but also made the Mongol army vulnerable to shortages of fodder. Campaigning in arid regions such as Central Asia or forested regions of Southern China were thus difficult and even in ideal steppe terrain, a Mongol force had to keep moving to ensure sufficient grazing for its massive horse herd.

Figure 103: *A Mongol warrior with a cheetah*

Logistics

Supply

Mongol armies traveled light, and were able to live largely off the land. Their equipment included fish hooks and other tools meant to make each warrior independent of any fixed supply source. The most common travel food of the Mongols was dried and ground meat *borts*, which remains common in Mongolian cuisine today. Borts is light and easy to transport, and can be cooked with water similarly to a modern "instant soup".

To ensure they would always have fresh horses, each trooper usually had 3 or 4 mounts. The horse is viewed much like a cow in Mongolia, and is milked and slaughtered for meat as such. Since most of the Mongols' mounts were mares, they were able to live off their horses' milk or milk products as they moved through enemy territory. In dire straits, the Mongol warrior could drink some of the blood from his string of remounts. They could survive a whole month only by drinking mare's milk combined with mare's blood.Wikipedia:Citation needed

Heavier equipment was brought up by well organized supply trains. Wagons and carts carried, amongst other things, large stockpiles of arrows. The main logistical factor limiting their advance was finding enough food and water for

Figure 104: *A Mongol melee in the 13th century.*

their animals. This would lead to serious difficulties during some of the Mongol campaigns, such as their conflicts with the Mamluks, the arid terrain of Syria and the Levant making it difficult for large Mongol armies to penetrate the region, especially given the Mamluk's scorched earth policy of burning grazing lands throughout the region. It also limited the Mongol ability to exploit their success following the Battle of Mohi, as even the Great Hungarian Plain was not large enough to provide grazing for all the flocks and herds following Subutai's army permanently.Wikipedia:Citation needed

Communications

The Mongols established a system of postal-relay horse stations, similar to the system employed in ancient Persia for fast transfer of written messages. The Mongol mail system was the first such empire-wide service since the Roman Empire. Additionally, Mongol battlefield communication utilized signal flags and horns and to a lesser extent, signal arrows to communicate movement orders during combat.

Costume

The basic costume of the Mongol fighting man consisted of a heavy coat fastened at the waist by a leather belt. From the belt would hang his sword, dagger, and possibly an axe. This long robe-like coat would double over, left breast over right, and be secured with a button a few inches below the right armpit. The coat was lined with fur. Underneath the coat, a shirt-like undergarment with long, wide sleeves was commonly worn. Silk and metallic thread were increasingly used. The Mongols wore protective heavy silk undershirts. Even if an arrow pierced their mail or leather outer garment, the silk from the undershirt would stretch to wrap itself around the arrow as it entered the body, reducing damage caused by the arrow shaft, and making removal of the arrow easier.

The boots were made from felt and leather and though heavy would be comfortable and wide enough to accommodate the trousers tucked in before lacing tightly. They were heelless, though the soles were thick and lined with fur. Worn with felt socks, the feet were unlikely to get cold.

Lamellar armor was worn over the thick coat. The armor was composed of small scales of iron, chain mail, or hard leather sewn together with leather tongs and could weigh 10 kilograms (22 lb) if made of leather alone and more if the cuirass was made of metal scales. The leather was first softened by boiling and then coated in a crude lacquer made from pitch, which rendered it waterproof.[644] Sometimes the soldier's heavy coat was simply reinforced with metal plates.

Helmets were cone shaped and composed of iron or steel plates of different sizes and included iron-plated neck guards. The Mongol cap was conical in shape and made of quilted material with a large turned-up brim, reversible in winter, and earmuffs. Whether a soldier's helmet was leather or metal depended on his rank and wealth.

Weapons

Mounted archers were a major part of the armies of the Mongol Empire, for instance at the 13th-century Battle of Liegnitz, where an army including 20,000 horse archers defeated a force of 30,000 troops led by Henry II, duke of Silesia, via demoralization and continued harassment.

Mongol bow

The primary weapon of the Mongol forces was their composite bows made from laminated horn, wood, and sinew. The layer of horn is on the inner face as it resists compression, while the layer of sinew is on the outer face as it resists tension. Such bows, with minor variations, had been the main weapon of steppe herdsmen and steppe warriors for over two millennia; Mongols (and many of their subject peoples) were extremely skilled with them. Some were said to be able to hit a bird on the wing. Composite construction allows a

Figure 105: *Mongol soldiers using bow, in Jami al-Tawarikh by Rashid al-Din, 1305–1306.*

powerful and relatively efficient bow to be made small enough that it can be used easily from horseback.

Quivers containing sixty arrows were strapped to the backs of the cavalrymen and to their horses. Mongol archers typically carried 2 to 3 bows (one heavier and intended for dismounted use, the other lighter and used from horseback) that were accompanied by multiple quivers and files for sharpening their arrowheads. These arrowheads were hardened by plunging them in brine after first heating them red hot.[645]

The Mongols could shoot an arrow over 200 metres (660 ft). Targeted shots were possible at a range of 150 or 175 metres (492 or 574 ft), which determined the optimal tactical approach distance for light cavalry units. Ballistic shots could hit enemy units (without targeting individual soldiers) at distances of up to 400 metres (1,300 ft), useful for surprising and scaring troops and horses before beginning the actual attack. Shooting from the back of a moving horse may be more accurate if the arrow is loosed in the phase of the gallop when all four of the horse's feet are off the ground.[646]

The Mongols may have also used crossbows (possibly acquired from the Chinese), also both for infantry and cavalry, but these were scarcely ever seen or used in battle And small cannons were established will can use in war upon horses The Manchus forbade archery by their Mongol subjects, and the Mongolian bowmaking tradition was lost during the Qing Dynasty. The present bowmaking tradition emerged after independence in 1921 and is based on Manchu types of bow, somewhat different to the bows known to have been used by the Mongol empire. Mounted archery had fallen into disuse and has been revived only in the 21st century.

Sword

Mongol swords were a slightly curved scimitar, which they used for slashing attacks but could also use to cut and thrust, due to its shape and construction. This made it easier to use from horseback. Warriors could use the sword with a one-handed or two-handed grip. Its blade was usually around 2.5 feet (0.76 m) in length, with an overall length of approximately 1 metre (3 ft 3 in).

Fire weapons and gunpowder

Several modern scholars speculate that Chinese firearms and gunpowder weapons were deployed by the Mongols at the Battle of Mohi.[647] Reliable sources mention weapons like "flaming arrows" and "naphtha bombs" being used against not just the Hungarian army but also against the Persians.[648,649] It is well documented that the Mongols used cannons and bombs during the invasions of Japan, which were an early example of gunpowder warfare in action. One of the most notable weapons the Mongols used during the invasions was explosive bombs. A mounted samurai being attacked with these bombs is depicted on a Japanese scroll.

Catapults and machines

Technology was one of the important facets of Mongolian warfare. For instance, siege machines were an important part of Genghis Khan's warfare, especially in attacking fortified cities. The siege engines were not disassembled and carried by horses to be rebuilt at the site of the battle, as was the usual practice with European armies. Instead the Mongol horde would travel with skilled engineers who would build siege engines from materials on site.

The engineers building the machines were recruited among captives, mostly from China and Persia led by a Han general Guo Kan. When Mongols slaughtered the whole population from settlements that resisted or didn't opt to surrender, they often spared the engineers and other units, swiftly assimilating them into the Mongol armies.

Engineers in Mongol service displayed a considerable degree of ingenuity and planning; during a siege of a fortified Chinese city the defenders had taken

Figure 106: *Mongols besieging Baghdad in 1258*

care to remove all large rocks from the region to deny the Mongols an ammunition supply for their trebuchets, but the Mongol engineers resorted to cutting up logs which they soaked in water to make suitably heavy spheres. During the siege of the Assassins' fortress of Alamut the Mongols gathered large rocks from far and wide, piling them up in depots a day's journey from one another all the way to their siege lines so that a huge supply was available for the breaching batteries operating against the mighty citadel. The Mongols also scouted the hills around the city to find suitable higher ground on which to mount ballistas manned by northern Chinese engineers, allowing these to snipe into the interior of the fortress. The Mongols made effective use of the siege technologies developed by their subject peoples; Genghis Khan utilized the Chinese engineers and traction trebuchets he had gained from his victories over the Jurchens and Tanguts during his Khwarezmian campaign, while Kublai Khan later called upon Muslim engineers from his Ilkhanate cousins to build counterweight trebuchets that finally concluded the six year siege of Fancheng and Xiangyang.

Figure 107: *Helmet and costume of the Mongol Yuan warrior during the Mongol invasion of Japan*

Kharash

A commonly used tactic was the use of what was called the "kharash". During a siege the Mongols would gather prisoners captured in previous battles, and would drive them forward in sieges and battles. These "shields" would often take the brunt of enemy arrows and crossbow bolts, thus leaving the Mongol warriors safer.[650] The kharash were also used as assault units to breach walls.

Strategy

The Mongol battlefield tactics were a combination of masterful training with excellent communication and discipline in the chaos of combat. They trained for virtually every possibility, so when it occurred, they could react accordingly. Unlike many of their foes, the Mongols also protected their ranking officers well. Their training and discipline allowed them to fight without the need for constant supervision or rallying, which often placed commanders in dangerous positions.

Whenever possible, Mongol commanders found the highest ground available, from which they could make tactical decisions based on the best view of the battlefield as events unfolded. Furthermore, being on high ground allowed their forces to observe commands conveyed by flags more easily than if the ground were level. In addition, keeping the high command on high ground made them easier to defend. Unlike the European armies, which placed enormous emphasis on personal valor, and thus exposed their leaders to death from anyone bold enough to kill them, the Mongols regarded their leaders as a vital asset.Wikipedia:Disputed statement A general such as Subutai, unable to ride a horse in the later part of his career due to age and obesity, would have been ridiculed out of most any European army of the time.[651] Wikipedia:Verifiability But the Mongols recognized and respected his still-powerful military mind, who had been one of the Genghis' most able subordinates, so he was transported around in a cart.

Intelligence and planning

The Mongols carefully scouted out and spied on their enemies in advance of any invasion. Prior to the invasion of Europe, Batu and Subutai sent spies for almost ten years into the heart of Europe, making maps of the old Roman roads, establishing trade routes, and determining the level of ability of each principality to resist invasion. They made well-educated guesses as to the willingness of each principality to aid the others, and their ability to resist alone or together. Also, when invading an area, the Mongols would do all that was necessary to completely conquer the town or cities. Some tactics involved diverting rivers from the city/town Wikipedia:Citation needed, closing supplies to the city and waiting for its inhabitants to surrender, gathering civilians from the nearby areas to fill the front line for the city/town attack before scaling the wall, and pillaging the surrounding area and killing some of the people, then letting some survivors flee to the main city to report their losses to the main populace to weaken resistance, simultaneously draining the resources of the city with the sudden influx of refugees.

Psychological warfare and deception

The Mongols used psychological warfare successfully in many of their battles, especially in terms of spreading terror and fear to towns and cities. They often offered an opportunity for the enemy to surrender and pay tribute, instead of having their city ransacked and destroyed. They knew that sedentary populations were not free to flee danger as were nomad populations, and that the destruction of their cities was the worst loss a sedentary population could experience. When cities accepted the offer, they were spared, but were required to support the conquering Mongol army with manpower, supplies, and other services.

If the offer was refused, however, the Mongols would invade and destroy the city or town, but allow a few civilians to flee and spread terror by reporting their

Figure 108: *Drawing of Mongols outside Vladimir presumably demanding submission before its sacking.*

loss. These reports were an essential tool to incite fear in others. However, both sides often had a similar if differently motivated interest in overstating the enormity of the reported events: the Mongols' reputation would increase and the townspeople could use their reports of terror to raise an army. For that reason, specific data (e.g. casualty figures) given in contemporary sources needs to be evaluated carefully.

The Mongols also used deception very well in their wars. For instance, when approaching a mobile army the units would be split into three or more army groups, each trying to outflank and surprise their opponents. This created many battlefield scenarios for the opponents where the Mongols would seem to appear out of nowhere and there were seemingly more of them than in actuality. Flanking and/or feigned retreat if the enemy could not be handled easily was one of the most practiced techniques. Other techniques used commonly by the Mongols were completely psychological and were used to entice/lure enemies into vulnerable positions by showing themselves from a hill or some other predetermined locations, then disappearing into the woods or behind hills while the Mongols' flank troops already strategically positioned would appear as if out of nowhere from the left, right and/or from their rear. During the initial states of battlefield contact, while camping in close proximity of their enemies at night, they would feign numerical superiority by ordering each soldier to light at least five fires, which would appear to the enemy scouts and spies that their force was almost five times larger than it actually was.

Another way the Mongols used deception and terror was by tying tree branches or leaves behind their horses. They dragged the foliage drag behind them in a systematic fashion to create dust storms behind hills to appear to the enemy as a much larger army, thereby forcing the enemy to surrender. Because each Mongol soldier had more than one horse, they would let prisoners and civilians ride their horses for a while before the conflict, also to fake numerical superiority.

Inclusion

As Mongols started conquering other people, they recruited the men into their ranks if they only surrendered, willingly or under a threat to be destroyed otherwise. Therefore, as they expanded into other areas, their troop numbers increased as other people were included in their conquests, such as during the Battle of Baghdad, which included many diverse people fighting under Mongol lordship.

However, the Mongols were never able to gain long-term loyalty from the settled peoples that they conquered.[652]

Ground tactics

The tumens would typically advance on a broad front, five lines deep. The first three lines would be composed of horse archers, the last two of lancers. Once an enemy force was located, the Mongols would try to avoid risky or reckless frontal assaults (in sharp contrast to their European and Middle-Eastern opponents). Instead they would use diversionary attacks to fix the enemy in place, while their main forces sought to outflank or surround the foe. First the horse archers would lay down a withering barrage of arrow fire. Additional arrows were carried by camels who followed close by, ensuring a plentiful supply of ammunition.

Flanking

In all battlefield situations, the troops would be divided into separate formations of 10, 100, 1,000 or 10,000 depending on the requirements. If the number of troops split from the main force was significant, for instance 10,000 or more, these would be handed over to a significant or second-in-command leader, while the main leader concentrated on the front line. The leader of the Mongols would generally issue the tactics used to attack the enemy. For instance the leader might order, upon seeing a city or town, "500 to the left and 500 to the

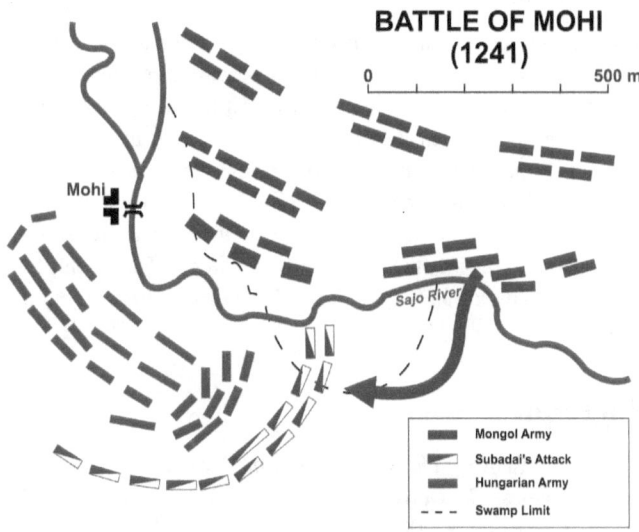

Figure 109: *Mongols in Battle of Mohi split into more than three separate formations and one formation under Subutai flanking the opponent from the right*

right" of the city; those instructions would then be relayed to the relevant 5 units of 100 soldiers, and these would attempt to flank or encircle the town to the left and right.

Encirclement and opening

The main reason for these manoeuvers was to encircle the city to cut off escape and overwhelm from both sides. If the situation deteriorated on one of the fronts or flanks, the leader from the hill directed one part of the army to support the other. If it appeared that there was going to be significant loss, the Mongols would retreat to save their troops and would engage the next day, or the next month, after having studied the enemies' tactics and defences in the first battle, or again send a demand to surrender after inflicting some form of damage. There was no fixture on when or where units should be deployed: it was dependent on battle circumstances, and the flanks and groups had full authority on what to do in the course of battle - such as supporting other flanks or performing an individual feigned retreat as conditions seemed appropriate, in small groups of 100 to 1000 - so long as the battle unfolded according to the general directive and the opponents were defeated.

Feigned retreat

The Mongols very commonly practiced the feigned retreat, perhaps the most difficult battlefield tactic to execute. This is because a feigned rout amongst untrained troops can often turn into a real rout if an enemy presses into it.[653] Pretending disarray and defeat in the heat of the battle, the Mongols would suddenly appear panicked and turn and run, only to pivot when the enemy was drawn out, destroying them at their leisure. As this tactic became better known to the enemy, the Mongols would extend their feigned retreats for days or weeks, to falsely convince the chasers that they were defeated, only to charge back once the enemy again had its guard down or withdrew to join its main formation.

Bibliography

- Amitai-Preiss, Reuven. *The Mamluk-Ilkhanid War*, 1998
- Chambers, James, *The Devil's Horsemen: The Mongol Invasion of Europe*. Book Sales Press, 2003.
- R.E. Dupuy and T.N. Dupuy – *The Encyclopedia Of Military History: From 3500 B.C. To The Present. (2nd Revised Edition 1986)*
- Hildinger, Erik – *Warriors of the Steppe: A Military History of Central Asia, 500 B.C. to A.D. 1700*. Da Capo Press, 2001.
- Morgan, David – *The Mongols*. Wiley-Blackwell, ISBN 0-631-17563-6
- Jones Archer – *Art of War in the Western World* [1]
- May, Timothy "The Mongol Art of War."[654] Westholme Publishing, Yardley. 2007.
- Nicolle, David – *The Mongol Warlords* Brockhampton Press, 1998
- Charles Oman – *The History of the Art of War in the Middle Ages* (1898, rev. ed. 1953)
- Saunders, J.J. – *The History of the Mongol Conquests,* Routledge & Kegan Paul Ltd, 1971, ISBN 0-8122-1766-7
- Sicker, Martin – *The Islamic World in Ascendancy: From the Arab Conquests to the Siege of Vienna*, Praeger Publishers, 2000
- Soucek, Svatopluk – *A History of Inner Asia*, Cambridge, 2000
- Verbruggen, J.F. – *The Art of Warfare in Western Europe during the Middle Ages*, Boydell Press, Second English translation 1997, ISBN 0-85115-570-7
- Iggulden, Conn – *Genghis, Birth of an Empire*, Bantham Dell.

External links

Medieval History: Mongol Invasion of Europe at http://historymedren.about.com/library/prm/bl1mongolinvasion.htm

 Wikimedia Commons has media related to *Military of Mongolia*.

Appendix

References

[1] Mote 2003, p. 403.
[2] Mote 2003, p. 415-416.
[3] Mote 2003, p. 419.
[4] Atwood 2004, p. 259.
[5] Twitchett 1994, p. 246.
[6] Twitchett 1994, p. 251.
[7] Sinor 1990, p. 29.
[8] Mote 2003, p. 421.
[9] Atwood 2004, p. 425.
[10] Mote 2003, p. 422.
[11] Mote 2003, p. 424.
[12] Twitchett 1994, p. 206.
[13] Twitchett 1994, p. 343.
[14] Mote 2003, p. 254.
[15] Sinor 1990, p. 30.
[16] Twitchett 1994, p. 208.
[17] Atwood 2004, p. 445.
[18] Atwood 2004, p. 531.
[19] Atwood 2004, p. 81.
[20] Atwood 2004, p. 265.
[21] Atwood 2004, p. 224.
[22] Biran 2005, p. 75.
[23] Atwood 2004, p. 281.
[24] Atwood 2004, p. 416.
[25] Atwood 2004, p. 277.
[26] Atwood 2004, p. 620.
[27] Twitchett 1994, p. 415.
[28] Biran 2005, p. 83.
[29] Atwood 2004, p. 455.
[30] Atwood 2004, p. 393.
[31] Atwood 2004, p. 431.
[32] Atwood 2004, p. 591.
[33] Atwood 2004, p. 446.
[34] Atwood 2004, p. 319.
[35] Atwood 2004, p. 307.
[36] Twitchett 1994, p. 210.
[37] Atwood 2004, p. 308.
[38] Atwood 2004, p. 283.
[39] Atwood 2004, p. 121.
[40] Atwood 2004, p. 53.
[41] Twitchett 1994, p. 213.
[42] Atwood 2004, p. 100.
[43] Twitchett 1994, p. 367.
[44] Andrade 2016, p. 46.
[45] Atwood 2004, p. 32).
[46] Atwood 2004, p. 196.
[47] Twitchett 1994, p. 372.
[48] Twitchett 1994, p. 264.
[49] Atwood 2004, p. 418.
[50] Atwood 2004, p. 51.

[51] Atwood 2004, p. 479.
[52] Andrade 2016, p. 47.
[53] Atwod 2004, p. 479.
[54] Atwood 2004, p. 36.
[55] Atwood 2004, p. 538.
[56] Atwood 2004, p. 79.
[57] Twitchett 1994, p. 382.
[58] Atwood 2004, p. 73.
[59] Atwood 2004, p. 82.
[60] Atwood 2004, p. 331.
[61] Atwood 2004, p. 323.
[62] Atwood 2004, p. 363.
[63] Twitchett 1994, p. 385.
[64] Atwood 2004, p. 83.
[65] Twitchett 1994, p. 389.
[66] Twitchett 1994, p. 392.
[67] Twitchett 1994, p. 394.
[68] Twitchett 1994, p. 405.
[69] Twitchett 1994, p. 463.
[70] Atwood 2004, p. 539.
[71] Twitchett 1994, p. 410.
[72] Twitchett 1994, p. 461.
[73] Twitchett 1994, p. 407.
[74] Twitchett 1994, p. 408.
[75] Twitchett 1994, p. 409.
[76] Atwood 2004, p. 37.
[77] Atwood 2004, p. 225.
[78] Twitchett 1994, p. 418.
[79] Atwood 2004, p. 202.
[80] Atwood 2004, p. 28.
[81] Atwood 2004, p. 29.
[82] Twitchett 2009, p. 869.
[83] Atwood 2004, p. 320.
[84] Twitchett 2009, p. 870.
[85] Twitchett 2009, p. 410.
[86] Twitchett 1994, p. 411.
[87] Twitchett 1994, p. 422-423.
[88] Twitchett 1994, p. 423.
[89] Atwood 2004, p. 6.
[90] Twitchett 1994, p. 412.
[91] Twitchett 1994, p. 431.
[92] Twitchett 1994, p. 460.
[93] Twitchett 1994, p. 449.
[94] Twitchett 1994, p. 426.
[95] Twitchett 1994, p. 257.
[96] Atwood 2004, p. 226.
[97] Twitchett 1994, p. 447.
[98] Twitchett 1994, p. 474.
[99] Twitchett 1994, p. 452.
[100] Twitchett 1994, p. 462.
[101] Atwood 2004, p. 234.
[102] Twitchett 1994, p. 443.
[103] Twitchett 1994, p. 454.
[104] Twitchett 1994, p. 458.
[105] Twitchett 1994, p. 459.
[106] Atwood 2004, p. 122.

[107] Twitchett 2009, p. 922.
[108] Twitchett 1994, p. 437.
[109] Twitchett 1994, p. 466.
[110] Atwood 2004, p. 231.
[111] Twitchett 1994, p. 451.
[112] Twitchett 1994, p. 457.
[113] https//www.amazon.ca
[114] https://books.google.com/books?id=1_03AAAAIAAJ
[115] http//www.amazon.ca
[116] /tə'mu:dʒɪn/;
Mongolian: Тэмүжин *Temüjin* [tʰemutʃiŋ] (About this soundlisten);
Middle Mongol: *Temüjin*;<ref>
[117] Chinese: 成吉思汗 ; pinyin: *Chéngjísī Hán*; Wade–Giles: *Ch'eng^2-chi^2-szu^1 Han^4*
[118] While his name is most commonly rendered as "Genghis" in English, historians of the Mongol empire generally prefer the spelling "Chinggis", which more closely approximates the name's correct pronunciation.<ref>
[119] Ian Jeffries (2007). *Mongolia: a guide to economic and political developments* https://books.google.com/books?id=fcgQ9nX0H3gC&pg=PA5&dq&hl=en#v=onepage&q=&f=false. Taylor & Francis. pp. 5–7.
[120] "Genghis Khan" https://www.ahdictionary.com/word/search.html?q=Genghis+Khan at *American Heritage Dictionary of the English Language* online.
[121]
[122] Guida Myrl Jackson-Laufer, Guida M. Jackson, *Encyclopedia of traditional epics*, p. 527
[123] "Genghis Khan: A Biography", Zofia Stone
[124] "The Leadership Secrets of Genghis Khan", John Man, Random House, 31 Oct 2010
[125] Hildinger 1997, pg. 113.
[126] Hildinger 1997, pg. 114
[127] Lane 2004, pg. xxvii
[128] Lane 2004, pg. 23
[129] " Central Asian world cities https://faculty.washington.edu/modelski/CAWC.htm ", University of Washington.
[130] John Chambers, *The Devil's Horsemen: The Mongol Invasion of Europe*, Atheneum, 1979. p. 31
[131] http://dispenser.info.tm/~dispenser/cgi-bin/dab_solver.py?page=Genghis_Khan&editintro=Template:Disambiguation_needed/editintro&client=Template:Dn
[132] Man (2004), pp. 329–333.
[133] Man (2004), p. 338.
[134] Jack Weatherford, Genghis Khan: War of the Khans (New York: Random House, Inc., 2004), 58
[135] Clive Foss, *The Tyrants*, page 57, Quercus, London, 2007.
[136] Christopher Kaplonski: *The case of the disappearing Chinggis Khaan* http://www.chriskaplonski.com/downloads/Disappearing.pdf.
[137] Once Shunned, Genghis Khan Conquers Mongolia Again http://www.foxnews.com/story/0,2933,202695,00.html
[138] //en.wikipedia.org/w/index.php?title=Genghis_Khan&action=edit
[139] MIYAWAKI-OKADA, JUNKO. "The Japanese Origin of the Chinggis Khan Legends." Inner Asia 8, no. 1 (2006): 123–34.
[140] William Bonner, Addison Wiggin (2006). " *Empire of debt: the rise of an epic financial crisis* https://books.google.com/books?id=C1BL5UCTFOgC&pg=PA43&dq&hl=en#v=onepage&q=&f=false". John Wiley and Sons. pp.43–44.
[141] Graziella Caselli, Gillaume Wunsch, Jacques Vallin (2005). " *Demography: Analysis and Synthesis, Four Volume Set: A Treatise in Population* https://books.google.com/books?id=nmgNXoiAiU4C&pg=RA2-PA34&dq&hl=en#v=onepage&q=&f=false". Academic Press. p.34.
[142] "The Legacy of Genghis Khan" at Los Angeles County Museum of Art—again http://www.payvand.com/news/03/jun/1074.html.

[143] *Genetics: Analysis Of Genes And Genomes* by Daniel L. Hartl, Elizabeth W. Jones, p. 309.
[144] Lucas, F. L., *From Many Times and Lands* (London, 1953), pp. 148–155
[145] https://web.archive.org/web/20060113174030/http://www.historychannel.com/thcsearch/thc_resourcedetail.do?encyc_id=210250
[146] http://www.historychannel.com/thcsearch/thc_resourcedetail.do?encyc_id=210250
[147] http://www.fsmitha.com/h3/h11mon.htm
[148] https://archive.org/details/genghiskhantheem035122mbp
[149] https://web.archive.org/web/20080518020854/http://www.accd.edu/sac/history/keller/Mongols/empsub2.html
[150] http://www.accd.edu/sac/history/keller/Mongols/empsub2.html
[151] //web.archive.org/web/20080625210646/http://ideas.union.edu/articles/files/22_Stevens_Heirs_to_Discord.pdf
[152] https://archive.org/details/historyoftheworl011691mbp
[153] https://www.questia.com/PM.qst?a=o&d=109217551
[154] http://www.bbc.co.uk/programmes/b00773mr
[155] http://www.coldsiberia.org/
[156] http://lcweb2.loc.gov/frd/cs/mntoc.html
[157] http://necrometrics.com/pre1700a.htm#Mongol
[158] https://web.archive.org/web/20040813232348/http://www.isidore-of-seville.com/genghis/
[159] http://nobsnews.blogspot.com/1994/01/inspirations-of-historians.html#rashid-ad-din-juwayni
[160] http://www.wdl.org/en/item/2378
[161] http://news.nationalgeographic.com/news/2014/03/140310-genghis-khan-mongols-mongolia-climate-change
[162] http://www.imdb.com/character/ch27804/
[163] Ratchnevsky, Paul. *Genghis Khan: His Life and Legacy*, p. 120.
[164] D. S. Benson *The Mongol campaigns in Asia*, p.179
[165] Jeremiah Curtin *The Mongols: A history*, p.178
[166] *The Cambridge History of Egypt: Islamic Egypt, 640-1517*, p.255
[167] Ryley-Smith in *Atlas of the Crusades*, p.112 (French Edition): "When the Golden Horde allied with the Mamluks, the Ilkhanate looked towards an alliance with the Christians"
[168] "The alliance which Berke had created between the Mongols and the Mamluks against the Ilkhanate remained constant", Morgan, p.144
[169] "The Mongols of Iran were all but encircled by a chain of alliances linking the Mamluks to the Golden Horde, and this power to Kaidu", Setton, p.529
[170] "The friendship between Egypt and the Golden Horde, which would last until the conclusion of peace between the Mamluks and the Il-Khan in 1320" *The New Cambridge Medieval History*, page 710, by David Abulafia - 1999
[171] "In order to fight their common enemy [the Ilkhanate], the Kipchack Mongols and the Mamluks entered into an alliance." Luisetto, p.157
[172] Mantran, Robert (Fossier, Robert, ed.) "A Turkish or Mongolian Islam" in *The Cambridge Illustrated History of the Middle Ages: 1250-1520*, p. 298
[173] Morgan, *Mongols and the West*
[174] Luisetto, p.155
[175] *The Mongols*, David Morgan, p.144
[176] "It is a fact of crucial importance that the Mamluks of Egypt and the Mongols of the Golden Horde were natural allies (...) simply because the ruling class of Egypt and an important and influential segment of the Golden Horde belonged in fact to the same ethnic group." A History of the Crusades, Kenneth Meyer Setton, p.427
[177] Setton, p.527
[178] By ultimately becoming Muslims, the Mongols of the Golden Horde conspicuously identified themselves with their Turkish subjects and with the people to the south, rather than with the Christian Russians to the North" Morgan, p.128
[179] "On the contrary, Hulagu, accompanied by Dokuz Khatun greatly favoured Christianity", Luisetto, p.155-156
[180] "In order to fight their common enemy [the Ilkhanate], the Kipchack Mongols and the Mamluks entered into an alliance. This was based on a defensive rather than an offensive policy: if one

of their territories was attacked, the second would fight for the other, on his own front, in order to create a diversion or weaken enough Persian troops so that their action would be stopped." Luisetto, p.157

[181] "Before invading Syria in 1299, Ghazan was forced to send troops in the Caucasus, in order to reinforce his Christian-Mongol troops. These were so many soldiers who could not fight in Palestine.", Luisetto, p.156

[182] Luisetto, p.158

[183] Demurger, p.143

[184] Demurger, p.142 (French edition) "He was soon joined by King Hethum, whose forces seem to have included Hospitallers and Templars from the kingdom of Armenia, who participate to the rest of the campaign."

[185] Demurger, p.142 "The Mongols pursued the retreating troops towards the south, but stopped at the level of Gaza"

[186] Demurger 142-143

[187] Runciman, p.439

[188] Demurger, p.146

[189] Demurger (p.146, French edition): "After the Mamluk forces retreated south to Egypt, the main Mongol forces retreated north in February, Ghazan leaving his general Mulay to rule in Syria".

[190] "Meanwhile the Mongol and Armenian troops raided the country as far south as Gaza." Schein, 1979, p. 810

[191] Amitai, "Mongol Raids into Palestine (AD 1260 and 1300)"

[192] "Arab historians however, like Moufazzal Ibn Abil Fazzail, an-Nuwairi and Makrizi, report that the Mongols raided the country as far as Jerusalem and Gaza"— Sylvia Schein, p.810

[193] The Arab historian Yahia Michaud, in the 2002 book *Ibn Taymiyya, Textes Spirituels I-XVI*, Chap XI, describes that there were some firsthand accounts at the time, of forays of the Mongols into Palestine, and quotes two ancient Arab sources stating that Jerusalem was one of the cities that was invaded by the Mongols

[194] Demurger, p.144

[195] "After Ghazan had left, some Christians from Cyprus arrived in Gibelet and Nefin, led by Guy, Count of Jaffa, and Jean d'Antioche with their knights, and from there proceeded to go to Armenia where the camp of the Tatars was. But Ghazan was gone, so they had to return."|Le Templier de Tyr, 614. *Le Templier de Tyr*, 614: "Et apres que Cazan fu partis aucuns crestiens de Chipre estoient ales a Giblet et a Nefin et en seles terres de seles marines les quels vous nomeray: Guy conte de Jaffe et messire Johan dantioche et lor chevaliers; et de la cuyderent aler en Ermenie quy estoit a lost des Tatars. Cazan sen estoit retornes: il se mist a revenir"

[196] Jean Richard, p.481

[197] J.J. Saunders, "History of the Mongol Conquests," page 144

[198] Josef W. Meri, "Medieval Islamic Civilization," page 573

[199] Meri, p.541

[200] http://www.muslimphilosophy.com/it/works/ITA%20Texspi.pdf

[201] //www.worldcat.org/issn/0013-8266

[202] //www.jstor.org/stable/565554

[203] //doi.org/10.1093%2Fehr%2FXCIV.CCCLXXIII.805

[204] Josef W. Meri, Jere L. Bacharach *Medieval Islamic Civilization: A-K, index*, p.442

[205] H. M. Balyuzi *Muḥammad and the course of Islám*, p.342

[206] John Freely *Storm on Horseback: The Seljuk Warriors of Turkey*, p.83

[207] Mehmet Fuat Köprülü, Gary Leiser *The origins of the Ottoman empire*, p.33

[208] Peter Partner *God of battles: holy wars of Christianity and Islam*, p.122

[209] *Osman's Dream: The History of the Ottoman Empire*, p.13

[210] Artuk-Osmanli Beyliginin Kurucusu, 27f

[211] Pamuk *A Monetary history*, p.30-31

[212] D. S. Benson, *The Mongol Campaigns in Asia*, p. 177

[213] C. P. Atwood, *Encyclopedia of Mongolia and the Mongol Empire*, p. 555

[214] //en.wikipedia.org/w/index.php?title=Template:History_of_Turkey&action=edit

[215] Claude Cahen, *Pre-Ottoman Turkey: a general survey of the material and spiritual culture and history*, trans. J. Jones-Williams, (New York: Taplinger, 1968) p.137.

[216] Shepherd, William R. *Historical Atlas*, 1911.
[217] Peter Jackson *The Mongols and the West*, p.103
[218] John Man, "Genghis Khan: Life, Death, and Resurrection", Feb. 6 2007. Page 180.
[219] The Islamic World to 1600: The Mongol Invasions (The Il-Khanate) https://www.ucalgary.ca/applied_history/tutor/islam/mongols/ilkhanate.html
[220] Ratchnevsky, Paul. *Genghis Khan: His Life and Legacy*, p. 120.
[221] Saunders, J. J. *The History of the Mongol Conquests*
[222] Hildinger, Eric. *Warriors of the Steppe: A Military History of Central Asia, 500 B.C. to A.D. 1700*
[223] Soucek, Svatopluk *A History of Inner Asia*
[224] Prawdin, Michael. *The Mongol Empire.*
[225] Ratchnevsky 1994, p. 129.
[226] See "Mongol military tactics and organization" for overall coverage.
[227] Chambers, James. *The Devil's Horsemen*
[228] France, p. 113
[229] Rashid Al-Din, "Compendium of Chronicles," 2:346.
[230] John Mason Smith, "Mongol Manpower and Persian Population," p. 276, p. 272
[231] France, p. 109-113
[232] France, p. 113-114
[233] McLynn, F. (2015). Genghis Khan: His Conquests, His Empire, His Legacy. Da Capo Press. Page 263.
[234] Ibid, p. 268
[235] Juyaini, p. 511, 518. Cited in John Mason Smith, "Mongol Manpower and Persian Population," Journal of the Economics and Social History of the Orient, Vol XVIII, Part III, page 278.
[236] France p. 113, citing David Morgan
[237] M.S. Asimov and C.E. Bosworth, "History of Civilizations of Central Asia: The Age of Achievement", Part 1, Volume 4, p. 181
[238] David Morgan, "The Mongols," p. 61.
[239] John Andrew Boyle, ed., "The Cambridge History of Iran, Volume 5: The Saljuq and Mongol Periods." (Cambridge: Cambridge University Press, 1968), p. 307.
[240] Ibn al-Athir, The Chronicle, 207
[241] Ibn al-Athir, The Chronicle, 207.
[242] Ata-Malik Juvayni, "History of The World Conqueror," p. 160-161 (Boyle's translation)
[243] Juvayni, World Conqueror, 83-85.
[244] Ibn al-Athir, The Chronicle, 229
[245] Ibn al-Athir, The Chronicle, 229.
[246] Paul Ratchnevsky, "Genghis Khan," p. 173
[247] Morgan, p. 67
[248] Minhaj Siraj Juzjani, Tabakat-i-Nasiri: A General History of the Muhammadan Dynasties of Asia, trans. H. G. Raverty (London: Gilbert & Rivington, 1881), 1068-1071
[249] John Man, "Genghis Khan: Life, Death, and Resurrection", Feb. 6 2007. Page 180.
[250] Additionally, the population of roughly the same area (Persia and Central Asia) plus some others (Caucasia and northeast Anatolia) is estimated at 5-6 million nearly 400 hundreds later, under the rule of the Safavid dynasty. Page 19.
[251] Tertius Chandler & Gerald Fox, "3000 Years of Urban Growth," p. 232-236
[252] Chandler & Fox, p. 232: Merv, Samarkand, and Nipashur are referred to as "vying for the [title of] largest" among the "Cities of Persia and Turkestan in 1200", implying populations of less than 70,000 for the other cities (Otrar and others don't have precise estimates given). "Turkestan" seems to refer to Central Asian Turkic countries in general in this passage, as Samarkand, Merv, and Nishapur are located in modern Uzbekistan, Turkmenistan, and northeastern Iran respectively.
[253] Sverdrup 2017, p. 148, 150
[254] Juvayni, Rashid al-Din.
[255] Frank McLynn, Genghis Khan (2015).
[256] Sverdrup 2017, p. 148. Citing Rashid Al-Din, 107, 356-362.
[257] Frank Mclynn, Genghis Khan (2015)

[258] Juvayni, p. 83-84
[259] Juvayni, p. 85
[260] Greene, Robert "The 33 Strategies of War"
[261] Sverdrup, Carl. "The Mongols Conquests: The Military Operations of Genghis Khan and Sube'etei." Helion and Company, 2017. Page 148.
[262] Morgan, David *The Mongols*
[263] Frank McLynn.
[264] Sverdrup 2017, p. 148.
[265] Ibid, p. 151
[266] McLynn, p. 280
[267] Central Asian world cities https://faculty.washington.edu/modelski/CAWC.htm
[268] Nicolle, David. *The Mongol Warlords*
[269] Stubbs, Kim. *Facing the Wrath of Khan.*
[270] Mongol Conquests http://users.erols.com/mwhite28/warstat0.htm#Mongol
[271] http://www.timespacemap.com/search/eventsearch.htm?_what=%22Mongolian%20Invasion%20of%20Central%20Asia%22&_maptype=2
[272] John Masson Smith, Jr. *Mongol Manpower and Persian Population*, pp. 276
[273] John Masson Smith, Jr. - Mongol Manpower and Persian Population, pp.271-299
[274]
[275] *National Geographic*, v. 191 (1997)
[276] Andre Wink, *Al-Hind: The Making of the Indo-Islamic World*, Vol.2, (Brill, 2002), 13.
[277] *The different aspects of Islamic culture: Science and technology in Islam*, Vol.4, Ed. A. Y. Al-Hassan, (Dergham sarl, 2001), 655.
[278] Matthew E. Falagas, Effie A. Zarkadoulia, George Samonis (2006). "Arab science in the golden age (750–1258 C.E.) and today", *The FASEB Journal* **20**, pp. 1581–1586.
[279] Jack Weatherford *Genghis Khan and the making of the modern world*, p.135
[280] Jack Weatherford *Genghis Khan and the making of the modern world*, p.136
[281] Sh.Gaadamba *Mongoliin nuuts tovchoo (1990)*, p.233
[282] Timothy May *Chormaqan Noyan*, p.62
[283] Al-Sa'idi,., op. cit., pp. 83, 84, from Ibn al-Fuwati
[284] C. P. Atwood *Encyclopedia of Mongolia and the Mongol Empire*, p.2
[285] Spuler, op. cit., from Ibn al-'Athir, vol. 12, p. 272.
[286] Giovanni, da Pian del Carpine (translated by Erik Hildinger) *The story of the Mongols whom we call the Tartars (1996)*, p. 108
[287] http://depts.washington.edu/silkroad/lectures/wulec3.html
[288] Rashiddudin, *Histoire des Mongols de la Perse*, E. Quatrieme ed. and trans. (Paris, 1836), p. 352.
[289] Demurger, 80-81; Demurger 284
[290] Khanbaghi, 60
[291] Nicolle
[292] James Chambers, "The Devil's Horsemen," p. 144.
[293] (Sicker 2000, p. 111)
[294] "In Threatening Baghdad, Militants Seek to Undo 800 Years of History" http://www.thedailybeast.com/articles/2014/08/16/in-threatening-baghdad-militants-seek-to-undo-800-years-of-history.html
[295] *The Mongols* http://www.uwgb.edu/dutchs/WestTech/xmongol.htm Steven Dutch
[296] Alltel.net http://home.alltel.net/bsundquist1/ir5.html
[297] Maalouf, 243
[298] Runciman, 306
[299] Foltz, 123
[300] http://www.newyorker.com/archive/2005/04/25/050425fa_fact4
[301] //tools.wmflabs.org/geohack/geohack.php?pagename=Siege_of_Baghdad_(1258)&params=33.3333_N_44.4333_E_source:wikidata-and-enwiki-cat-tree_region:IQ
[302] Oleg Pirozhenko, 'Political Trends of Hong Bog Won Clan in the Period of Mongol Domination', International Journal of Korean History, Vol. 9 (2005); available at http://ijkh.khistory.

org/journal/view.php?number=469; English translation here: http://ijkh.khistory.org/upload/pdf/9-08_oleg%20pirozhenko.pdf
[303] http://www.koreanhistoryproject.org/Ket/C06/E0602.htm
[304] J. Bor *Mongol hiigeed Eurasiin diplomat shashtir, boyi II*, p.254
[305] John Man *Kublai Khan*, p.208
[306] C. P. Atwood *Encyclopedia of Mongolia and the Mongol Empire*, p.319
[307] 국방부 군사편찬연구소, 고려시대 군사 전략 (2006) (The Ministry of National Defense, Military Strategies in Goryeo)
[308] 국사편찬위원회, 고등학교국사교과서 p63(National Institute of Korean History, History for High School Students, p64)http://www.e-history.go.kr/book/index.htm
[309] Ed. Morris Rossabi *China among equals: the Middle Kingdom and its neighbors, 10th-14th centuries*, p.244
[310] Baasanjavyin Lkhagvaa *Solongos, Mongol-Solongosyin harilstaanii ulamjlalaas*, p.172
[311] Examples of such words include colors of horses, Agibato-a hero boy and Songgol-falcon, see Baasanjavyin Lkhagvaa-Solongos, Mongol-Solongosyin harilstaanii ulamjlalaas, *p.173 for more information*.
[312] Thomas T. Allsen *Culture and Conquest in Mongol Eurasia*, p.53
[313] Namjil *Solongos-Mongolyin haritsaa: Ert, edugee*, p.64
[314] http://enc.daum.net/dic100/viewContents.do?&m=all&articleID=b07m4328a
[315] http://www.san.beck.org/3-10-Koreato1875.html
[316] http://www.imperialchina.org/Xi-Xia.html
[317] Hugh D. Walker "Traditional Sino-Korean Diplomatic Relations : A Realistic Historical Appraisal", *Monumenta Serica*, Vol. 24 (1965), pp. 155–16, (p.159)
[318] C. P. Atwood *Encyclopedia of Mongolia and the Mongol Empire*, p.590
[319] J. Bor *Mongol hiigeed Eurasiin diplomat shashtir*, vol.II, p.204
[320] Jack Weatherford *Genghis Khan and the Making of the Modern World*, p.85
[321] Hartog 2004, pg. 134
[322] Collectif 2002 https://books.google.com/books?ei=oj8sVYfZEYb4yASM8oCADQ&id=1yMnAQAAIAAJ&dq=liu+heima+mongols&focus=searchwithinvolume&q=liu+heima+, p. 147.
[323] http://big5.xjass.com/ls/content/2013-02/27/content_267592.htm
[324] http://www.wenxue100.com/book_LiShi/138_190.thtml
[325] http://www.iqh.net.cn/info.asp?column_id=7794
[326] May 2004 https//books.google.com, p. 50.
[327] http://123.125.114.20/view/ca3dae260722192e4536f629.html?re=view
[328] http://121.199.12.114:99/main/wz_xs.tom?c_name=%CF%F4%D7%D3%CF%D4&d_id=wzadd20120314102439zw&searh_text=
[329] http://www.docin.org/p-716638698.html
[330] Schram 1987 https//books.google.com, p. 130.
[331] eds. Seaman, Marks 1991 https://books.google.com/books?id=MztuAAAAMAAJ&q=liu+heima+mongols&dq=liu+heima+mongols&hl=en&sa=X&ei=oj8sVYfZEYb4yASM8oCADQ&ved=0CCYQ6AEwAg, p. 175.
[332] http://d.wanfangdata.com.cn/periodical/xbsdxb-shkxb200106008
[333] http://www.nssd.org/articles/article_detail.aspx?id=5638208
[334] https://zh.wikisource.org/zh-hant/□□□/□146
[335] http://www.klxsw.com/files/article/html/87/87953/23237374.html
[336] ed. de Rachewiltz 1993 https://books.google.com/books?id=kG45gi7E3hsC&pg=PA41#v=onepage&q&f=false, p. 41.
[337] Hucker 1985 https//books.google.com, p.66.
[338] John Man *Kublai Khan*, p.79
[339] C. P. Atwood *Encyclopedia of Mongolia and the Mongols*, p.613
[340] Reuven Amitai-Preiss *Mongols and Mamluks: The Mamluk-Ilkhanid War, 1260–1281* p. 189
[341] Angus Donal Stewart *The Armenian kingdom and the Mamluks*, p. 54
[342] Michael Biran *The empire of the Qara Khitai in Eurasian history: between China and the Islam*, p.143
[343] Stepehen Turnball *The Mongol Invasions of Japan 1274 and 1281*, p.72

³⁴⁴ Peter Jackson *The Mongols and the West*, p.86
³⁴⁵ *The Devil's Horsemen: The Mongol Invasion of Europe* by James Chambers, p.71
³⁴⁶ Original from the University of Michigan
³⁴⁷ (Original from the University of Michigan)
³⁴⁸ Wright, David C. "The Sung-Kitan War of A.D. 1004–1005 and the Treaty of Shan-Yüan." Journal of Asian History, vol. 32, no. 1, 1998, p. 20.
³⁴⁹ Halperin, Charles J.. 2000. "The Kipchak Connection: The Ilkhans, the Mamluks and Ayn Jalut". *Bulletin of the School of Oriental and African Studies*, University of London **63** (2). Cambridge University Press: 235.
³⁵⁰ Sinor, Denis. 1999. "The Mingols in the West". *Journal of Asian History*, **33** (1). Harrassowitz Verlag: 1–44.
³⁵¹ Junius P. Rodriguez, "The Historical Encyclopedia of World Slavery", ABC-CLIO, 1997, pp146
³⁵² 杉山正明《忽必烈的挑战》，社会科学文献出版社，2013年，第44–46頁
³⁵³ 船田善之《色目人与元代制度、社会－－重新探讨蒙古、色目、汉人、南人划分的位置》，〈蒙古学信息〉2003年第2期
³⁵⁴ p. 190. https//books.google.com
³⁵⁵ https://leminhkhai.wordpress.com/2015/12/04/giac-bac-den-xam-luoc-translations-and-exclamation-points/
³⁵⁶ proof that he runs the blog https://web.archive.org/web/20141014090118/http://manoa.hawaii.edu/history/node/44
³⁵⁷ //www.jstor.org/stable/606298
³⁵⁸ //doi.org/10.2307%2F606298
³⁵⁹ Thomas, p. 261-263; cites a variety of estimate from various Japanese historians as well as the author's own.
³⁶⁰ 『高麗史』一百四 列伝十七 金方慶「以蒙漢軍二萬五千、我軍（高麗軍）八千、梢工引海水手六千七百、口艦九百餘艘、留合浦、以待女眞軍、女眞後期、乃發船。」
³⁶¹ 『高麗史』二十八 世家二十八 忠烈王一 元宗十五年（十一月）己亥（二十七日）「己亥、東征師還合浦、遣同知樞密院事張鎰勞之。軍不還者無慮萬三千五百餘人。」
³⁶² 『高麗史』二十九 世家二十九 忠烈王二 忠烈王七年閏（八）月条「是月、忻都茶丘范文虎等還元、官軍不返者、無慮十萬有幾。」
³⁶³ 『元史』二百八 列傳第九十五 外夷一 日本國「（至元十八年）官軍六月入海、七月至平口島（平戸島）、移五龍山（鷹島？）、八月一日、風破舟、五日、文虎等諸帥各自擇堅好船乘之、棄士卒十餘萬于山下、衆議推張百戸者口主帥、號之曰張總管、聽其約束、方伐木作舟欲還、七日日本人來戰、盡死、餘二三萬口其虜去、九日、至八角島、盡殺蒙古、高麗、漢人、謂新附軍口唐人、不殺而奴之、閻輩是也、蓋行省官議事不相下、故皆棄軍歸、久之、莫青與吳萬五者亦逃遇、十萬之衆得還者三人耳。」
³⁶⁴ The conquest of Ainu lands: ecology and culture in Japanese expansion, 1590–1800 By Brett L. Walker, p.133
³⁶⁵ Original text in Chinese: 上天眷命大蒙古國皇帝奉書日本國王朕惟自古小國之君境土相接尚務講信修睦況我祖宗受天明命奄有區夏遐方異域畏威懷德者不可悉數朕即位之初以高麗無辜之民久瘁鋒鏑即令罷兵還其疆域反其旄倪高麗君臣感戴來朝義雖君臣歡若父子計王之君臣亦已知之高麗朕之東藩也日本密邇高麗開國以來亦時通中國至於朕躬而無一乘之使以通和好尚恐王國知之未審故特遣使持書布告朕志冀自今以往通問結好以相親睦且聖人以四海為家不相通好豈一家之理哉以至用兵夫孰所好王其圖之不宜至元三年八月日
³⁶⁶ Smith, Bradley *Japan: A History in Art* 1979 p.107
³⁶⁷ Goryeosa『高麗史』世家第二十七 元宗十三年 三月己亥（March 11, 1272）「惟彼日本 未蒙聖化。 故發詔使 繼縱軍容 戰艦兵糧 方在所須。儻以此事委臣 庶幾勉盡心力 小助王師」 http://kindai.ndl.go.jp/BIImgFrame.php?JP_NUM=50001638&VOL_NUM=00001&KOMA=217&ITYPE=0
³⁶⁸ History of Yuan『元史』卷十二 本紀第十二 世祖九 至元十九年七月壬戌（August 9, 1282）「高麗国王請、自造船百五十艘、助征日本。」
³⁶⁹ Turnbull, p. 41
³⁷⁰ Turnbull 2013: "About 120 armed samurai received rewards for their participation in 1275... If the average warband was 50-strong then the Japanese defenders may have been about 6,000. Other non-rewarded samurai took part, some with as few as one follower, so perhaps a figure between 3,000 and 6,000 is most likely for 1274."

[371] Turnbull 2013, p. 42: "For partial justification of their defeat in 1274, the number of Japanese warriors ranged against the invaders is given in the Yuan Shi as the very unlikely figure of 102,000... Hachiman Gudokun, by contrast, sees the brave Japanese as being outnumbered by the Mongols by a factor of ten to one."

[372] Conlan, p. 264

[373] Sato 105

[374] 『八幡ノ蒙古記』「同十一年十月五日卯時に、對馬國府八幡宮假御殿の内より、火焔おひたゝしく、もえいつ、國府在家の人々、焼亡出来しよと見るに、もゆへき物もなきを、怪しみけるほとに、同日申時に、對馬の西おもて、佐須浦に、異國船見ゆ、」（１ウ）其数四五百艘はかりに、凡三四萬人もやあらんと、見るはかり寄来る、同日酉時、國府の地頭につく、即地頭宗馬允資國、八十餘騎、同日丑時、彼浦にゆきつく、翌日卯時、通人宗□男を使者として、蒙古人に、事のしさいを尋る処に、散々に舟よりいる、大船七八艘より、あさち原へ、おりたつ勢、一千人もあらんと見ゆ、其時、宗馬允、陣をとりて□ふ、いはなつ矢に異國人、数しらす、いとる、此中に大将軍と、おほし」（２オ）き者四人、あし毛なる馬にのりて、一はんに、かけむかふ者、宗馬弥二郎に右の乳の上を、いられて、馬よりおつ、此時、馬允に射倒さるゝ者、四人、宗馬允かく□ふといへとも、終にうたれぬ、同子息宗馬次郎、養子弥二郎、同八郎親頼、刑部丞郎等に三郎、庄太郎、入道源八、で左近馬允手人、肥後國御家人、口井藤三、源三郎、已上十二人、同時に討死す、蒙古、佐須浦に火をつけて、焼拂ふよし、宗馬允か郎等、小太郎、兵衛次郎」（２ウ）博多にわたりて告しらす、」

[375] 『高麗史』□一百四 列伝十七 金方慶「入對馬島、□殺甚衆」

[376] 『八幡ノ蒙古記』「同十四日申時に壹岐嶋の西おもてに蒙古の兵船つく、其中に二艘より四百人はかりおりて、赤旗をさして東の方を三度、敵の方を三度拜す、其時、守護代平内左衛門尉景隆并御家人百餘騎、庄三郎か城の前にて矢合す、蒙古人か矢は、二時はかりいる間に守護代か方にも二人手負、異敵は大勢なり、終に叶ふへくもなかりければ、城のうちへ引退て合□す、同十五日に、攻めおとされ」（３オ）て城の内にて自害す、」

[377] 『八幡ノ蒙古記』「同十六□（日カ）、十七日の間、平戸、能古、鷹嶋の男女多く捕らる、松浦黨敗す。」

[378] 『蒙古襲来□詞』詞四「たけふさ（武房）にけうと（凶徒）あかさか（赤坂）のちん（陣）をか（□）けお（落）とされて、ふたて（二手）になりて、おほせい（大勢）はすそはら（麁原）にむ（向）きてひ（退）く。こせい（小勢）はへふ（別府）のつかハら（塚原）へひ（退）く、」

[379] 『高麗史』□八十七　表□第二「十月、金方慶與元元帥忽敦洪茶丘等征日本、至壹岐戰敗、軍不還者萬三千五百餘人」

[380] 『高麗史』□一百四 列伝十七 金方慶「諸軍與戰、及暮乃解、方慶謂忽敦茶丘曰、『兵法千里縣軍、其鋒不可當、我師雖少、已入敵境、人自□戰、即孟明焚船淮陰背水也、請復戰』、忽敦曰、『兵法小敵之堅、大敵之擒、策疲乏之兵、敵日滋之衆、非完計也、不若回軍』復亨中流矢、先登舟、遂引兵還、會夜大風雨、戰艦觸岩多敗、？墜水死、到合浦、」

[381] Reed, Edward J. (1881).

[382] http://www.kamakura-burabura.com/meisyoenosimajyourituji.htm

[383] Conlan, p. 264

[384] Conlan, p. 264

[385] Rossabi, Morris. "Khubilai Khan: His Life and Times." 1988. Page xiii.

[386] Turbull 2013, p. 57

[387] Winters, Harold et al. (2001).

[388] Goryeosa 『高麗史』 列伝□十七　「若依蛮□則工費多将不及期」「用本國船□督造」 http://kindai.ndl.go.jp/BIImgFrame.php?JP_NUM=50001638&VOL_NUM=00003&KOMA=125&ITYPE=0

[389] 『高麗史』□一百四 列伝十七 金方慶「方慶與忻都茶丘朴球金周鼎等發、至日本世界村大明浦」

[390] 『高麗史節要』□二十 十四葉 忠烈王七年六月壬申（八日）「六月壬申（八日）、金方慶金周鼎朴球朴之亮荊萬戶等、與日本兵力戰、斬首三百餘級、官軍潰、茶丘乘馬走、王萬戶復橫□之、斬五十餘級、日本兵之退、茶丘僅免、翼日復戰敗績、」

[391] 『高麗史』□一百四 列伝十七 金方慶「六月、方慶周鼎球之亮荊萬戶等、與日本兵合戰、斬三百餘級、日本兵突進、官軍潰、茶丘棄馬走、王萬戶復橫□之、斬五十餘級、日本兵之退、茶丘僅免、翼日復戰敗績、」

256

392 『元敦武校尉管軍上百戸張成墓碑銘』「（至元）十八年、樞密院檄君、仍管新附□□（軍百？）率所統、?千戸岳公琇、往征倭、四月□（發？）合浦登海州、以六月六日至倭之志賀島、夜將半、賊兵□□來襲、君與所部據艦□、至□、賊船廻退、八日、賊遵陸復來、君率繼弓弩、先登岸迎敵、奪占其□要、賊弗能前、日？、賊軍復集、又返殺之、明日、倭大會兵來□、君統所部、入陣奮□、賊不能□（支？）殺傷過□（當？）賊敗去。」

393 『歷代鎮西要略』

394 『元史』□一百五十四 列傳第四十一 洪福源.附洪俊奇「十七年、授龍虎衞上將軍、征東行省右丞、十八年、與右丞欣都、將舟師四萬、由高麗金州合浦以進、時右丞范文虎等、將兵十萬、由慶元、定海等処渡海、期至日本一岐、平戸等島合兵登岸、兵未交、秋八月、風壞舟而還。」

395 『肥前武雄神社文書』□尾社大宮司藤原□門申状「肥前国御家人□尾社大宮司藤原資門謹言上欲早且依合□忠節、且任傍例、預勳功賞去弘安四年遺賊合□事、　右、遺賊襲來之時、於千崎息登移於賊船、資門乍致疵、生擒一人分取一人了、將又攻上鷹嶋棟門、致合□忠之刻、生慮二人了、此等子細、於鎮西談議所、被□其沙汰、相尋証人等、被注進之処、相漏平均恩賞之条、愁吟之至、何事如之哉、且如傍例者、到越訴之輩、面々蒙其賞了、且資門自身被疵之条、宰府注進分明也、争可相漏平均軍賞哉、如承及者、防□警固之輩、皆以蒙軍賞了、何自身手負資門不預忠賞、空送年月之条、尤可有御哀憐哉、所詮於所々□場、或自身被疵、或分取生慮之条、証人等状？宰府注進分明之上者、依合□忠節、任傍例欲預平均軍賞、仍恐々言上如件、　永仁四年八月　日」

396 『高麗史』□二十九　世家二十九　忠烈王二　忠烈王八年六月己丑（一日）の条「蠻軍？把沈聰等六人、自日本逃來言、本明州人、至元十八年六月十八日、從葛剌歹萬戸上船至日本、值□風船敗、衆軍十三四萬、同栖一山、十月初八日、日本軍至、我軍飢不能戰、皆降日本、擇留工匠及知田者、餘皆殺之、王遣上將軍印侯郎將柳庇、押聰等送干元。／（八月）甲午（九月）、蠻軍五人、自日本逃來」

397 『元史』□二百八　列傳第九十五　外夷一　日本國「（至元十八年）官軍六月入海、七月至平□島（平戸島）、移五龍山（鷹島か）、八月一日、風破舟、五月、文虎等諸將各自擇堅好船乘之、棄士卒十餘萬于山下、衆議推張百戸者□主帥、號之曰張總管、聽其約束、方伐木作舟欲還、七日日本人來戰、盡死、餘二三萬□其虜去、九日、至八角島、盡殺蒙古、高麗、漢人、謂新附軍□唐人、不殺而奴之、?輩也是、蓋行省官議事不相下、故皆棄軍歸、久之、莫青與吳萬五者亦逃還、十萬之衆得還者三人耳。」

398 『薩摩比志島文書』比志島時範軍忠状案「次月七月七日鷹嶋合□之時、自陸地馳向事、爰時範依合□之忠勤、仍御裁許、粗言上如件、　弘安五年二月　日」

399 『薩摩比志島文書』島津長久證状「同閏七月七日鷹嶋合□之時、五郎次郎自陸地馳向候之条、令見知候了、若此條僞申候者、日本國中大少神爵可罷蒙長久之身候、恐惶謹言、　弘安五年四月十五日　大炊助長久」

400 『江上系図』「西牟田彌次郎永家。弘安四年。大元大將督六万艘十万人。寇鎮西。此時永家戰于松浦之鷹島抽功。於是□之賞。肥前國神崎郡中數箇。」

401 Turnbull, Stephen R. (2003).
402 Satō, Kanzan. Kodansha International. 1983. Page 104
403 Davis, Paul K. (2001).
404 https://books.google.com/books?id=nv73QlQs9ocC&client=firefox-a
405 https://www.worldcat.org/oclc/0195143663
406 https://www.worldcat.org/oclc/1309476
407 https://books.google.com/books?id=wURfQ0y7JP8C&client=firefox-a
408 https://www.worldcat.org/oclc/492683854
409 http://www.einaudi.cornell.edu/eastasia/publications/item.asp?id=44
410 http://www.deremilitari.org/resources/pdfs/conlan.pdf
411 http://www.bowdoin.edu/mongol-scrolls/
412 http://www.louis-chor.ca/mongolin.htm
413 http://www.louis-chor.ca/emaki3.htm
414 http://kindai.ndl.go.jp/BIImgFrame.php?JP_NUM=50001638&VOL_NUM=00001&KOMA=1&ITYPE=0
415 http://kindai.ndl.go.jp/BIImgFrame.php?JP_NUM=50001638&VOL_NUM=00002&KOMA=1&ITYPE=0
416 http://kindai.ndl.go.jp/BIImgFrame.php?JP_NUM=50001638&VOL_NUM=00003&KOMA=1&ITYPE=0

[417] http://repository.tamu.edu/bitstream/handle/1969.1/ETD-TAMU-3100/SASAKI-THESIS.pdf
[418] http://sitereports.nabunken.go.jp/en
[419] //en.wikipedia.org/w/index.php?title=Template:History_of_Tibet&action=edit
[420] Wylie. p.105
[421] Wylie. p.106
[422] Wylie. p.110, 'delegated the command of the Tibetan invasion to an otherwise unknown general, Doorda Darkhan'.
[423] Shakabpa. p.61: 'thirty thousand troops, under the command of Leje and Dorta, reached Phanpo, north of Lhasa.'
[424] Sanders. p. 309, *his grandson Godan Khan invaded Tibet with 30000 men and destroyed several Buddhist monasteries north of Lhasa*
[425] Wylie. p.104
[426] Wylie. p.103
[427] *Authenticating Tibet: Answers to China's 100 Questions*, by Anne-Marie Blondeau and Katia Buffetrille, p13
[428] Wylie. p.105: 'Why would Chinggis plan an invasion of Tibet as soon as he became Khan of the Mongols in 1206.'
[429] Wylie. p.107, 'the statement that the 1240 expedition was a punitive raid for failure to pay tribute is without foundation.'
[430] Wylie. p.106, '...erred in identifying Tibet as the country against Chinggis launched that early campaign. His military objective was the Tangut kingdom of Hsi-hsia.'
[431] Wylie. p.106, 'the first instance of military conflict between the two nations'
[432] C. P. Atwood *Encyclopedia of Mongolia and Mongol Empire*, p.538
[433] Wylie. p.110.
[434] Shakabpa. p.61: 'thirty thousand troops, under the command of Leje and Dorta, reached Phanpo, north of Lhasa.'
[435] Sanders. p. 309, *his grandson Godan Khan invaded Tibet with 30,000 men and destroyed several Buddhist monasteries north of Lhasa*
[436] Turrel J. Wylie *The First Mongol Conquest of Tibet Reinterpreted*, pp.110; Tucci, Giuseppe (1949) *Tibetan Painted Scrolls*, 2 Volumes, Rome: La Libreria dello Stato, Vol. II, p. 652.
[437] C. P. Atwood *Encyclopedia of Mongolia and the Mongol Empire*, p.538
[438] Petech, Luciano (1990) *Central Tibet and the Mongols*. Rome: IsIMEO, p. 8.
[439] Wylie. p.112
[440] Wylie. p.110
[441] Kwanten, Luc, *Imperial Nomads: A History of Central Asia, 500–1500* (University of Pennsylvania Press, 1979) p.74.
[442] Wylie. p.107
[443] Wylie. p.111
[444] Petech 2003 p.342.
[445] Wylie, ibid.p.323: 'it is suggested here that references in Chinese sources pertain to campaigns in peripheral areas and that there was no Mongol invasion of central Tibet at that time.'
[446] Wylie, ibid. p.326.
[447] Wylie p.323-324.
[448] http://www.ashgate.com/pdf/SamplePages/Islam_and_Tibet_Interactions_along_the_Musk_Routes_Intro.pdf
[449] Wylie. p.104: 'To counterbalance the political power of the lama, Khubilai appointed civil administrators at the Sa-skya to supervise the Mongol regency.'
[450] Laird 2006, pp. 114-117
[451] Dawa Norbu. *China's Tibet Policy* https//books.google.com, pp. 139. Psychology Press.
[452] Schirokauer, Conrad. *A Brief History of Chinese Civilization*. Thomson Wadsworth, (c)2006, p 174
[453] Rossabi, M. *Khubilai Khan: His Life and Times*, p56
[454] Dai Matsui - A Mongolian Decree from the Chaghataid Khanate
[455] Norbu, Namkhai. (1980). "Bon and Bonpos". *Tibetan Review*, December, 1980, p. 8.
[456] Richardson, Hugh E. (1984). *Tibet and its History*. Second Edition, Revised and Updated, pp. 48-9. Shambhala. Boston & London. (pbk)

[457] Richardson, Hugh E. (1984). *Tibet and its History*. Second Edition, Revised and Updated, pp. 48-9. Shambhala. Boston & London. (pbk)

[458] Sverdrup, p.114-115. Mongol sources state one tumen (standard tumens consisted of 10,000 men) was sent to Poland, while historians' estimates vary, with estimates of Mongol forces from 3,000 to 50,000.

[459] Sverdrup, p. 114-115, citing Rashid al-Din's chronicles, 1:198, 2:152. Rashid Al-Din's figures give Batu and Subutai about 40,000 horsemen total when they invaded Central Europe in 1241 (including Turkic auxiliaries recruited since the conquest of Rus), divided into five columns (three in Hungary, one in Transylvania, and one in Poland).

[460] Carey states on p. 128 that Batu had 40,000 in the main body and ordered Subutai to take 30,000 troops in an encircling maneuver. Batu commanded the central prong of the Mongols' three-pronged assault on Europe. This number seems correct when compared with the numbers reported at the Battles of Leignitz to the north and Hermannstadt (Sibiu) to the south. All three victories occurred in the same week.

[461] Fennell, John. "The Crisis of Medieval Russia: 1200-1304." London, 1983. Page 85. Excerpt: "If we assume that each of the larger cities could field, say, between 3,000 and 5,000 men, we can arrive at a total of about 60,000 fighting troops. If we add to this another 40,000 from smaller towns and from the various Turkic allies in the Principality of Kiev, then the total coincides with the 100,000 estimated by S.M. Solov'ev in his *History o Russia*. But then this is only a rough estimate of the *potential* number. We have no idea how many, towns and districts actually mustered troops- for instance, it seems highly unlikely that Novgorod sent any at all. Certainly none came to help their outpost at Torzhok. Perhaps then half or a quarter - or even a smaller fraction- of the total was the most the Russians could muster."

[462] Numbers disputed, vary from as low as 2,000 to above 10,000; see Battle of Legnica for further details.

[463] Sverdrup, p. 114-115, p. 109-110, contains lists of cited estimates provided by various sources and historians as well as the author's own estimates. The estimates for the Hungarian army at the time of the first Mongol invasion vary from not far above 10,000 (Grassman), to 25,000 (Jackson), to 50,000 (Kosztolnyik), to 65,000 (Sinor), to 80,000 (Todd). For his part, Sverdrup finds 10,000 to be the most likely estimate of those listed, based on other army sizes of the time and the fact that the 10,000 figure is attested to in two primary sources.

[464] Carey, Brian Todd, p. 124

[465] Colin McEvedy, Atlas of World Population History (1978) http://users.erols.com/mwhite28/warstat0.htm#Mongol

[466] Sverdrup, p. 115. Citing: Gustav Strakoschd-Grassmann. Der Einfall Der Mongolen In Mitteleuropa In Den Jahren 1241 und 1242 (Innsbruck, 1893), p.183: 10,000 killed at Mohi.

[467] Bitwa pod Legnicą Chwała Oręża Polskiego Nr 3. Rzeczpospolita and Mówią Wieki. Primary author Rafał Jaworski. 12 August 2006 (in Polish) p. 8

[468] Bitwa pod Legnicą Chwała Oręża Polskiego Nr 3. Rzeczpospolita and Mówią Wieki. Primary author Rafał Jaworski. 12 August 2006 (in Polish) p. 4

[469] The Mongol invasion: the last Arpad kings http://www.britannica.com/eb/article-34789/Hungary

[470] Hildinger, Erik. Mongol Invasions: Battle of Liegnitz http://www.historynet.com/mongol-invasions-battle-of-liegnitz.htm/2. First published as: "The Mongol Invasion of Europe" in *Military History*, (June, 1997).

[471] The Destruction of Kiev https://tspace.library.utoronto.ca/citd/RussianHeritage/4.PEAS/4.L/12.III.5.html

[472] Trawinski, Allan. *The Clash of Civilizations*. Page Publishing, Inc. (March 20, 2017). Section 15.

[473] de Hartog, Leo. *Genghis Khan: Conqueror of the World*. Tauris Parke Paperbacks (January 17, 2004). p. 173.

[474] Hildinger, Eric. *Warriors Of The Steppe: Military History Of Central Asia, 500 Bc To 1700 Ad*. Da Capo Press; 3rd printing edition (July 21, 1997). p. 144.

[475] August 29, 2016

[476] Zimmermann, Wilhelm. *A Popular History of Germany from the Earliest Period to the Present Day*. Nabu Press (February 24, 2010). p. 1109.

[477] Maurice, Charles Edmund. *The Story of Bohemia from the Earliest Times to the Fall of National Independence in 1620: With a Short Summary of Later Events - Primary Source Edition*. Nabu Press (March 18, 2014). p. 75.
[478] Berend, Nora, *Central Europe in the High Middle Ages: Bohemia, Hungary and Poland, c. 900-c.1300*. Cambridge University Press (February 17, 2014). p. 447.
[479] Długosz, The Annals, 181.
[480] Christianity, Europe, and (Utraquist) Bohemia http://www.brrp.org/proceedings/brrp7/hlavacek.pdf
[481] "Genghis Khan: his conquest, his empire, his legacy"by Frank Lynn
[482] Michael Prawdin, Gerard (INT) Chaliand *The Mongol Empire*, p.268
[483] Stephen Pow, Lindsay – Deep Ditches and Well-built walls. pp. 72, 132
[484] Z. J. Kosztolnyik – Hungary in the 13th Century, East European Monographs, 1996. p. 174
[485] Font, Marta: Hungarian Kingdom and Croatia in the Middle Age http://www.ceeol.com/aspx/issuedetails.aspx?issueid=58576a72-3bb3-47bf-b159-23daa7dc1cd2&articleId=07451a0b-fbed-4269-a7cb-3883dfa477b5
[486] 750th Anniversary of the Golden Bull Granted by Bela IV http://mirror.veus.hr/stamps/1992/bula.html
[487] Klaić V., Povijest Hrvata, Knjiga Prva, Druga, Treća, Četvrta i Peta Zagreb 1982
[488] Prošlost Klisa http://portal.klis.com.hr/povijest-klisa/
[489] Klis - A gateway to Dalmatia http://www.casopis-gradjevinar.hr/dokumenti/200109/6.pdf
[490] Jackson, Peter. *The Mongols and the West: 1221-1410*. Routledge; 1 edition (April 9, 2005). p. 67.
[491] Howorth, Henry Hoyle. *History of the Mongols from the 9th to the 19th Century: Part 1 the Mongols Proper and the Kalmyks*. Cosimo Classics (January 1, 2013). p. 152.
[492] Howorth, Sir Henry Hoyle. *History of the Mongols: From the 9th to the 19th Century, Volume 1*. Forgotten Books (June 15, 2012). p. 152. ASIN B008HHQ8ZY
[493] Андреев (Andreev), Йордан (Jordan); Лалков (Lalkov), Милчо (Milcho) (1996). Българските ханове и царе (The Bulgarian Khans and Tsars) (in Bulgarian). Велико Търново (Veliko Tarnovo): Абагар (Abagar). pp. 192–193
[494] Peter Jackson. The Mongols and the West: 1221-1410. 2005. p.65
[495] Jackson, p.79
[496] Jackson, p.105
[497] Peter F. Sugar, Péter Hanák, Tibor Frank – *A History of Hungary*. p.27: "The majority of the Hungarian forces consisted of light cavalry, who appeared 'oriental' to the Western observers. Yet this army had given up nomadic battle tactics and proved useless when facing the masters of this style of warfare. Hungarian tactics were a mix of eastern and western military traditions, as were the ineffective walls of clay bricks and palisades. Two elements of the Hungarian defense had proved effective, however: close combat with mass armored knights and stone fortifications".
[498] Jackson, Peter (2005). *The Mongols and the West*, 1221–1410. Longman. p. 205.
[499] Peter F. Sugar, Péter Hanák, Tibor Frank – *A History of Hungary* pp. 28-29
[500] Stephen Pow, Lindsay – *Deep Ditches and Well-built walls* pp. 59, 76
[501] Z. J. Kosztolnyik – *Hungary in the 13th Century, East European Monographs*, 1996, p. 286
[502] Peter Jackson. *The Mongols and the West: 1221-1410*. 2005. p.205
[503] Anchalabze, George. *The Vainakhs*. Page 24
[504] Klaić V., Povijest Hrvata, Knjiga Prva, Druga, Treća, Četvrta i Peta Zagreb 1982. (Croatian)
[505] Kelly (2005), p.23
[506] Needham, Joseph; et al. (1987), *Science and Civilisation in China, Vol. V, Pt. 7*, Cambridge: Cambridge University Press, pp 48-50, .
[507] Pacey, Arnold (1991), *Technology in World Civilization: A Thousand-year History*, Boston: MIT Press, p. 45, .
[508] Ebrey, Patricia Buckley (2010) [1996]. *The Cambridge Illustrated History of China* (2nd ed.). New York: Cambridge University Press, p. 138, .
[509] Needham, Joseph (1987). *Science and Civilisation in China: Military technology: The Gunpowder Epic, Volume 5, Part 7*. New York: Cambridge University Press, pp 118-124.

[510] John of Plano Carpini, "History of the Mongols," in *The Mission to Asia*, ed. Christopher Dawson (London: Sheed and Ward, 1955), 44
[511] Carpini, "History of the Mongols", 60.
[512] Rashid al-Din, Successors, 70-71.
[513] Rashid al-Din, Successors, 10-11. Translated by John Andrew Boyle. Boyle's preamble notes: "There are not infrequent interpolations from the Mongolian chronicle, and he even adopts its faulty chronology, in accordance with which the events of the European campaign take place a year later than in reality. In the present volume, Juvaini is down to the reign of Mongke (1251-1259) Rashid al-Din's main authority, but with considerable additional material from other sources. Thus the earlier historian's account of the invasion of eastern Europe (1241-1242) is repeated almost verbatim and is then followed, in a later chapter, by a much more detailed version of the same events, based, like the preceding description of the campaigns in Russia (1237-1240), on Mongol records, as is evident from the orthography of the proper names."
[514] Rashid al-Din, Successors, 71-72.
[515] http://www.nature.com/articles/srep25606
[516] J. J. Saunders, *The History of the Mongol Conquests* (London: Routledge & Kegan Paul, 1971), 79.
[517] Climate
[518] Rain#Wettest known locations
[519] Sir John Keegan (1987) [i]The Mask of Command[/i], Viking: London, page 118
[520] Amitai-Preiss, Reuven. *The Mamluk-Ilkhanid War*
[521] Frank McLynn, Genghis Khan (2015); Chris Peers, the Mongol War Machine (2015); Timothy May, the Mongol Art of War (2016). pp. 448-51
[522] Frank McLynn, Genghis Khan (2015); Chris Peers, the Mongol War Machine (2015); Timothy May, the Mongol Art of War (2016). pp. 450-1.
[523] Peter Jackson, "The Mongols and the West", 2005. Page 199
[524] Victor Spinei. "Moldavia in the 11th-14th centuries." Editura Academiei Republicii Socialiste România. Bucharest, 1986. Pages 121-122.
[525] Stanisław Krakowski, *Polska w walce z najazdami tatarskimi w XIII wieku*, MON, 1956, pp. 181-201
[526] Stanisław Krakowski, *Polska w walce z najazdami tatarskimi w XIII wieku*, MON, 1956.
[527] René Grousset The Empire of Steppes, page 399-400
[528] Denis Sinor, "The Mongols in the West". *Journal of Asian History* (1999) pp: 1-44.
[529] Андреев (Andreev), Йордан (Jordan); Лалков (Lalkov), Милчо (Milcho) (1996). Българските ханове и царе (The Bulgarian Khans and Tsars) (in Bulgarian). Велико Търново (Veliko Tarnovo): Абагар (Abagar). pp. 222
[530] Pál Engel, Tamás Pálosfalvi, Andrew Ayton: *The Realm of St. Stephen: A History of Medieval Hungary, 895-1526*, I.B.Tauris & Co Ltd, London, pp. 109 https//books.google.com
[531] The Roots of Balkanization: Eastern Europe C.E. 500-1500 - By Ion Grumeza https://books.google.com/books?id=DTxu6RxdecUC&pg=PA37&dq=cumans+fierce&hl=en&sa=X&ei=ThHdU_jQE4OJ7AbqkYGAAg&redir_esc=y#v=onepage&q=cumans&f=false Google Books.
[532] Victor Spinei. "Moldavia in the 11th-14th centuries." Editura Academiei Republicii Socialiste România. Bucharest, 1986. Pages 121-122.
[533] István Vásáry *Cumans and Tatars: Oriental military in the pre-Ottoman Balkans, 1185–1365*, p.89
[534] D. Kldiashvili, *History of the Georgian Heraldry*, Parlamentis utskebani, 1997, p. 35.
[535] Sedlar, Jean W. (1994). *East Central Europe in the Middle Ages, 1000–1500*. University of Washington Press. p. 380.
[536] Kortüm, Hans-Henning. *Transcultural Wars: from the Middle Ages to the 21st Century* Akademie Verlag (March 22, 2006). p. 227
[537] Biological Warfare at the 1346 Siege of Caffa https://wwwnc.cdc.gov/eid/article/8/9/01-0536_article
[538] https://books.google.com/books?id=0StLNcKQNUoC&pg=PA4
[539] http://www.deremilitari.org/resources/articles/sinor1.htm
[540] http://www.jstor.org/stable/41933117

[541] http://www.jstor.org/stable/2497020
[542] https://books.google.com/books?isbn=1616738510
[543] http://www.ucalgary.ca/applied_history/tutor/islam/mongols/goldenHorde.html
[544] Chormaqan Noyan: The First Mongol Military Governor in the Middle East by Timothy May
[545] Thomas T. Allsen-Culture and Conquest in Mongol Eurasia, p.84
[546] Islamic Culture Board-Islamic culture, p.256
[547] André Wink-Al-Hind, the Making of the Indo-Islamic World, p.208
[548] John Masson Smith, Jr. *Mongol Armies and Indian Campaigns.*
[549] John Masson Smith, Jr. *Mongol Armies and Indian Campaigns* and J.A. Boyle, *The Mongol Commanders in Afghanistan and India.*
[550] Rashid ad-Din - The history of World
[551] J.A. Boyle, "The Mongol Commanders in Afghanistan and India According to the Tabaqat-I-Nasiri of Juzjani," Islamic Studies, II (1963); reprinted in idem, The Mongol World Empire (London: Variorum, 1977), see ch. IX, p. 239
[552] Although Muslim historians claimed Mongols were outnumbered and their army ranged from 100,000 to 200,000, their force was not enough to cow down Delhi mamluks in reality. See John Masson Smith, Jr. *Mongol Armies and Indian Campaigns.*
[553] Banarsi Prasad Saksena 1992, p. 332.
[554] Peter Jackson 2003, pp. 219-220.
[555] Banarsi Prasad Saksena 1992, p. 336.
[556] Kishori Saran Lal 1950, p. 87.
[557] Kishori Saran Lal 1950, p. 88.
[558] Banarsi Prasad Saksena 1992, p. 338.
[559] Banarsi Prasad Saksena 1992, p. 340.
[560] Banarsi Prasad Saksena 1992, p. 341.
[561] Peter Jackson 2003, pp. 221-222.
[562] Banarsi Prasad Saksena 1992, p. 368.
[563] Banarsi Prasad Saksena 1992, pp. 369-370.
[564] Banarsi Prasad Saksena 1992, p. 372.
[565] Banarsi Prasad Saksena 1992, p. 373.
[566] Banarsi Prasad Saksena 1992, pp. 392-393.
[567] Peter Jackson 2003, pp. 227-228.
[568] Banarsi Prasad Saksena 1992, p. 393.
[569] Kishori Saran Lal 1950, pp. 171-172.
[570] Kishori Saran Lal 1950, p. 175.
[571] Peter Jackson 2003, p. 229.
[572] Mohibbul Hasan-Kashmir Under the Sultans, p.36
[573] The Chaghadaids and Islam: the conversion of Tarmashirin Khan (1331-34). The Journal of the American Oriental Society, October 1, 2002. Biran
[574] https://books.google.com/books?id=_9cmAQAAMAAJ
[575] //www.worldcat.org/oclc/31870180
[576] http://radar.ngcsu.edu/~tmmay/Chormaqan_thesis.pdf
[577] http://www.mongolianculture.com/MONGOL-ARMIES.htm
[578] https://books.google.com/books?id=2XXqAQAACAAJ
[579] //www.worldcat.org/oclc/685167335
[580] https://books.google.com/books?id=lt2tqOpVRKgC&pg=PA221
[581] https://books.google.com/books?id=CHzGvqRbV_IC
[582] (Wade 2009: 36–37): The exact strength of the 1283 invasion force is not known. The Yunnan command initially requested 10,000 men from the high command, which determined that the invasion required 60,000 men. The high command sent troops from Sichaun, Helazhang, Sizhou, Bozhou and Xuzhou. It is not clear if the number of troops totaled 60,000.
[583] Wade 2009: 27
[584] Yian, Goh Geok. 2010. "The Question of 'china' in Burmese Chronicles". Journal of Southeast Asian Studies 41 (1). [Cambridge University Press, Department of History, National University of Singapore]: 125. http://www.jstor.org/stable/27751506.
[585] Lieberman 2003: 24

[586] Myint-U 2011: 165

[587] Burmese sources per (Than Tun 1964: 136) simply refer to Wa and Palaung regions. It is unclear if the regions in the 13th century were located in the same Wa and Palaung regions of the present day. According to Marco Polo (Yule 1874: 81) (Haw 2006: 104), Pagan attacked Zardandan or the Gold Teeth state in 1272; if it is true, the Wa and Palaung regions may have been the same as the Gold Teeth region in present-day Dehong and Baoshan prefectures.

[588] Than Tun 1964: 136

[589] Coedes 1968: 190

[590] Rossabi 2014: 289

[591] Hall 255

[592] Harvey 1925: 64

[593] Hmannan Vol. 1 2003: 352

[594] (Myint-U 2011: 172): Ajjall's official title was "Director of Political Affairs of the Regional Secretariat of Yunnan."

[595] (Wade 2009: 20): The envoys were located in November/December 1275.

[596] (Haw 2006: 104): Marco Polo called the state as Zardandan, Persian for Gold Teeth. According to the Burmese records, it seems to be the same Wa and Palaung states where the Army had put down a rebellion in 1272.

[597] (Harvey 1925: 65): Marco Polo, who served a Privy Councillor on the Emperor's staff, claimed to have witnessed the war but he "doubtless heard the tale from the officers who took part in the action."

[598] (Haw 2006: 104): The Yuan account of the war seems "far-fetched". (Turnbull 2003: 84): Marco Polo's description of the battle in 1277 "actually compresses a decade of history into one episode, and contains certain errors of location and numbers, but the overall impression of what happened is probably quite accurate." (Harvey 1925: 336): Regarding the battle of Ngasaunggyan, "Marco Polo catches the spirit of it all but his details need modification."

[599] Some historians such as Stephen Haw (Haw 2006: 104) accept Marco Polo's account. But others such as G.E. Harvey (Harvey 1925: 336–337) believe the Burmese army never made it to Vochang, and was stopped en route at Ngasaunggyan, which according to Harvey was about 110 km southwest of Vochang.

[600] Haw 2006: 104

[601] (Harvey 1925: 336): Marco Polo's account that Nasr al-Din commanded the Mongol army at the battle of Ngasaunggyan is incorrect. Nasr al-Din led the raid on Kaungsin in the following dry-season. According to (Yule 1874: 87), the initial 1277 expedition was led by the Commandant of Dali-fu, Huthukh, which may refer to Kutuka.

[602] Yazawin Thit Vol. 1 2012: 147, footnote 3

[603] Cocks 1919: 24–25

[604] Luce in MSK 1961: 263

[605] Aung-Thwin 1985: 195

[606] Pan Hla 2005: 28–29

[607] Stuart-Fox 2001: 88–90

[608] Burmese chronicles (Hmannan Vol. 1 2003: 354) say that Ananda Pyissi died in action during the 1283–84 campaign. Per (Than Tun 1964: 136), Ananda Pyissi was still alive in 1285 according to a contemporary inscription. The general who died may have been Ananda Pyissi's brother Yanda Pyissi since Gen. Maha Bo presumably had become the second in command in 1285.

[609] Wade-Giles transcription per (Than Tun 1959: 121); (Htin Aung 1967: 70) gives it as Chiang-Mien, "the Burmese province".

[610] *jiachen* day of the 2nd month of the 23rd year of the Zhiyuan reign = 3 March 1286

[611] Aung-Thwin and Hall 2011: 34–35

[612] Htin Aung 1967: 72

[613] Aung-Thwin and Aung-Thwin 2012: 105

[614] King Thado Minbya of Ava reunified central Burma in 1364–67. King Razadarit of Pegu unified Lower Burma's three Mon-speaking provinces in 1388–89.

[615] Aung-Thwin 2011: 34–35

[616] Phayre 1967: 8–9

[617] //www.jstor.org/stable/3632565
[618] Htin Aung 1967: 74
[619] Köllner, Bruns 1998: 115
[620] Harvey 1925: 365
[621] Aung-Thwin 1985: 196–197
[622] Christopher Atwood, Encyclopedia of Mongol Empire and Mongolia, p. 579
[623] Christopher Atwood, Encyclopedia of Mongol Empire and Mongolia, p. 579-80
[624] Tansen Sen - The Yuan Khanate and India: Cross-Cultural Diplomacy in the Thirteenth and Fourteenth Centuries http://www.ihp.sinica.edu.tw/~asiamajor/pdf/2006ab/13%20AM%20vol19%20Sen.pdf, pp. 305
[625] Atwood, C. (2004) p. 579
[626] p. 190. https//books.google.com
[627] https://leminhkhai.wordpress.com/2015/12/04/giac-bac-den-xam-luoc-translations-and-exclamation-points/
[628] proof that he runs the blog https://web.archive.org/web/20141014090118/http://manoa.hawaii.edu/history/node/44
[629] The deaths of two Khaghans, Stephen G. Haw; Descending Dragon, Rising Tiger: A History of Vietnam By Vu Hong Lien, Peter Sharrock
[630] Haw, S. G. (2013)
[631] Hok-Lam Chan - Chinese Refugees in Annam and Champa at the End of the Sung Dynasty, Journal of Southeast Asian History, Vol. 7, No. 2 (Sep., 1966), pp. 1-10
[632] Grousset, R. (1970) p. 290
[633] Delgado, J. (2008) p. 158
[634] Delgado, J. (2008) p. 159
[635]
[636] citation needed
[637] Weatherford (2004), and also Man (2007).
[638] Yuan shi History of Yuan.
[639] Oliver,Roland Anthony/Atmore, Anthony. *Medieval Africa, 1250-1800* https://books.google.com/books?id=SqKR_xbRU5MC&pg=PA17&dq=mamluk+mongol+tactics&lr=#v=onepage&q=mamluk%20mongol%20tactics&f=false Cambridge University Press, 2001, pg. 17 ,
[640] Amitai-Preiss, Reuven. *Mongols and Mamluks: the Mamluk-Īlkhānid War, 1260-1281* https//books.google.com, Cambridge University Press, 1995, pg. 222. ,
[641] Amitai-Preiss, Reuven. [https://books.google.com/books?id=dIaFbxD64nUC&pg=PA217&dq=some+of+the+halqa+was+actually+quite+similar&lr=#v=onepage&q=some%20of%20the%20halqa%20was%20actually%20quite%20similar&f=false *Mongols and Mamluks: the Mamluk-Īlkhānid War*, rsity Press, 1995, pg. 217. ,
[642] Turnbull, Stephen R. Essential Histories: Genghis Khan & the Mongol Conquests 1190–1400 http://0-lib.myilibrary.com.mercury.concordia.ca/Open.aspx?id=10264 Hardback ed New York: Routledge, 2004 p.17
[643] George Lane. *Genghis Khan and Mongol Rule.* Westport, CT: Greenwood, 2004. Print. p.31
[644] George Lane - Ibid, p.99
[645] "Daily Life in the Mongol Empire", George Lane, (page 102)
[646] Saunders, John Joseph. The History of The Mongol Conquests https//books.google.co.uk Univ of Pennsylvania Press, 2001.
[647] (the University of Michigan)
[648] (the University of Michigan)
[649] (the University of Michigan)
[650] "Genghis Khan: A Biography", Zofia Stone
[651] *Genghis Khan and the Making of the Modern World* - Jack Weatherford
[652] Lane, G. (2006). Propaganda. In Daily Life in the Mongol Empire. Westport, Connecticut: Greenwood Publishing Group.
[653] *A History of Warfare* - John Keegan
[654] http://www.westholmepublishing.com/mongolartofwar.html

Article Sources and Contributors

The sources listed for each article provide more detailed licensing information including the copyright status, the copyright owner, and the license conditions.

Timeline of the Mongol Empire *Source:* https://en.wikipedia.org/w/index.php?oldid=807559511 *License:* Creative Commons Attribution-Share Alike 3.0 *Contributors:* Altamel, AntiCompositeNumber, Bollyjeff, CAPTAIN RAJU, Cabe6403, CanisRufus, Cartakes, Choulin, ClueBot NG, Colonies Chris, Cromage, Dcirovic, Docu, Dragonpyramid, ERobson, Elonka, Enchyin, Enerelt, Evecurid, Favonian, Flamarial, Flyer22 Reborn, Fratrep, Hamza725, Haranoh, Historywithjames, Hollomis, Iohannes Animosus, Jim1138, Kafka Liz, Kavas, Khanate General, LilHelpa, Lord British, Marianna251, Mblumber, Mediran, Mowsbury, Mukadderat, Onel5969, Phatom87, PhnomPencil, Plantdrew, QuiteUnusual, R'n'B, R0uge, Serendipodous, StaticGull, Swammeyjoe, Taketa, Thaeolon, Tim!, Titodutta, Tommy2010, Tony Tan, Topbanana, Ulric1313, Vanished user vjhsduheuiui4t5hjri, Vyom25, Widr, Wikipelli, Winner 42, Yaan, Yprpyqp, 102 anonymous edits 1

Genghis Khan *Source:* https://en.wikipedia.org/w/index.php?oldid=807845515 *License:* Creative Commons Attribution-Share Alike 3.0 *Contributors:* 0leckh, 0x5849857, 23h112e, 3family6, 86WikiEditor, AManWithNoPlan, Alex Bakharev, Alexandre8, Andrew Gunner, AndrewOne, ArisMethymna, Arjayay, Arosa, AtheismAnarchist887, BabelStone, Barefact, Beaumain, Bender235, Bobby.Han22, Boing! said Zebedee, Boneyard90, BooCookie, Brachney, Brandmeister, BulgariaSources, Cartakes, Ceithe, Chamboz, Charmii, Chewings72, Cirolchou, ClueBot NG, Contact '97, Cuchullain, DadaNeem, David rex, David.moreno72, Diabedia, Diannaa, Dinkytown, Dirkbb, District101, Dkapetansky, Doc James, Double sharp, Doug Weller, Download, Dr.suaro, DrKay, DragoniteLeopard, EatePurple, Enredados, Eric Kvaalen, Eric WVGG, Ermahgerd9, Esb, Florian Blaschke, Floyd M. Bunsen, FrantzFanon2000, Gadget850, Gaugec, George Ho, Gob Lofa, Great Brightstar, Guettarda, Hairy Dude, Heimstern, Hibernian, Hillbillyholiday, HoboMcJoe, Howcheng, Ian.thomson, Ifny, Incrassate, Insertcleverphrasehere, Iridescent, J 1982, JCSantos, Jagiello, Jaguar BKN, JamesBWatson, Jasonanaggie, JesseW900, John of Reading, JorisvS, Julymath321, Jungshi, KAMiKAZOW, Kaitymh, Kaldari, Karenlhall, Keith D, Keivan.f, Khiruge, Laszlo Panaflex, Latebird, Lavateraguy, Lds, Le Gâteau Blanc, LeoRomero, Library Guy, Linguist111, Lizard the Wizard, Lordtobi, MB298, MER-C, MRD2014, Magioladitis, Mailmindlin, Mansour001, Maproom, Markeer, Master of Time, Md.altaf.rahman, Mezafo, Mezigue, Mmm333k, Mogism, Mojoworker, Monticores, Mr Stephen, NapoleonX, Nczempin, NeilN, Niceguyedc, No such user, No1lovesu, Norm mit, Omnipaedista, Orange U-turn, Oshwah, Owain Knight, P. S. Burton, PMathew42, Paine Ellsworth, Pat power11, Pavan santhosh.s, Payppp, Pgan002, Philg88, Piamz, Polar Mermaid, Prinsgezinde, Prisencolin, Red Director, Regulov, RenRen070193, Retrieverlove, Robert4565, Rosa Lichtenstein, Royal Bishop 123, SA 13 Bro, Samuelpla7z, Sarah Layton, Shrikanthv, Simnos, Smart Nomad, Sogomonyan, Spa4499, Srnec, Steve03Mills, Sunnya343, Super48paul, Thnidu, Thắng L.Đ.Q., Timmyshin, Tobby72, Toghuchar, Tom.Reding, Topbanana, TopologyonWings, Umairastro, Uniquark9, UpstreamPaddler, Vikram maingi, Waldo12, Wikimedes, WindWalk55555, WorldCreaterFighter, Yaan, Ye eunuch, Yprpyqp, YuHuw, ZacBro7682, Zanhe, Zenedits, Zzuuzz, Шкурба Андрій Вікторович 17

Mongol invasion of Central Asia *Source:* https://en.wikipedia.org/w/index.php?oldid=800963605 *License:* Creative Commons Attribution-Share Alike 3.0 *Contributors:* 3family6, Abu Shawka, Anthony Appleyard, BD2412, Bachrach44, Bebljallo, Bender235, Benlisquare, Boneyard90, CanisRufus, Cartakes, ChrisGualtieri, Cowlibob, DPdH, DaltonCastle, Dcirovic, Enerelt, Forbes72, Hugo999, Hzh, Intothefire, J-Scythian, J04n, JahlilMA, Jonesey95, Kintetsubuffalo, Lieutenant of Melkor, Lugia2453, Michaeldsuarez, Myasuda, Nick-D, Odinsothereye, RekishiEJ, Ricky81682, SchreiberBike, Selrahcmattmonde, Snori, Spindoctor13, Squids and Chips, Taketa, Thermokarst, Tilk Tem, Tim!, Toghuchar, Topbanana, Woohookitty, 10 anonymous edits 63

Mongol invasions of the Levant *Source:* https://en.wikipedia.org/w/index.php?oldid=807484501 *License:* Creative Commons Attribution-Share Alike 3.0 *Contributors:* 3family6, Adam Bishop, Adûnâi, Aemilius 04, Altzinn, Andrewman327, Arado, BD2412, Bender235, Benramm, Bgwhite, Catlemur, Chewings72, Citation bot 1, Colonies Chris, Cplakidas, Darwinek, Dbachmann, Dennis Kercher, Dimadick, Drilnoth, Egsan Bacon, Elonka, Enerelt, Franco aq, Ghirlandajo, GoingBatty, Good Olfactory, Greyshark09, Hairy Dude, Hmainsbot1, Isa Alcala, JaGa, Jaraalbe, Jazz19, John K, Kafka Liz, Kansas Bear, Khan Khanate, Khanate General, Kober, Lauren68, MapMaster, Muhends, Neddyseagoon, Nihlus1, Nik Sage, Nogai Khan, R'n'B, RBK613, Rjwilmsi, Robotman1974, SamEV, ShelfSkewed, Srnec, The Rambling Man, Ulric1313, Ville Lehtonen, Yendor1958, YinchuanKiev, ZYjacklin, Zoeperkoe, Zozo2kx, Кардам, 44 anonymous edits 67

Mongol invasions of Anatolia *Source:* https://en.wikipedia.org/w/index.php?oldid=801703263 *License:* Creative Commons Attribution-Share Alike 3.0 *Contributors:* Aldux, BD2412, Colonies Chris, Cplakidas, Dallyripple, Enerelt, Flyer22 Reborn, Hanberke, Jbribeiro1, JesseRafe, John of Reading, Kalem, Karamanli86, Kharadea, LilHelpa, Llywrch, Marcocapelle, Nimetapoeg, Protector of Wiki, R'n'B, Rrostrom, Sardanaphalus, Takabeg, TimBentley, WereSpielChequers, 6 anonymous edits 79

Mongol conquest of Khwarezmia *Source:* https://en.wikipedia.org/w/index.php?oldid=808087217 *License:* Creative Commons Attribution-Share Alike 3.0 *Contributors:* 0nlyth3truth, 3family6, 4nn1l2, A. Parrot, Abu Shawka, Agthies, Alborzagros, AllGloryToTheHypnotoad, Analytikone, Anthony Appleyard, Arab Hafez, Arvand, Banedon, Bender235, Benlisquare, Bobyrr, Cartakes, Charlik, ClueBot NG, Cwsavage78, DPdH, Dcirovic, Deelith, Delirium, Dimadick, DocWatson42, DrRC, Dsp13, Dvavasour, ERcheck, Edgar181, Enerelt, Ewlyahoocom, Faceless Enemy, Findan, Flyte35, Foobaz, Gavia immer, Geoffg, Ghirlandajo, Giraffedata, H1nkles, Haida19, Hairy Dude, Hans yulun lai, Hmains, Hmainsbot1, Hospitallier, Howard61313, Hugo999, ILBobby, IchLiebeKasachstan, Ira Leviton, Iridescent, Ithoughtitwasapig, Jagged 85, Jalwikip, Jimmyeatskids, Jinnai, Jonesey95, JorisvS, KLBot2, KNewman, KTo288, Katharineamy, Kesal, Khoikhoi, Kirill Lokshin, Kukini, Lao Wai, Laserbeamcrossfire, Latebird, Lauren68, Louiebb, Lrguy, Mais oui!, Marcocapelle, Mboverload, Michael Devore, Mister India, Mmm333k, Monkeydoesbetter, Mr d logan, Mukadderat, MusikAnimal, Myasuda, Nightscream, Nihlus1, Nimetapoeg, Noah Salzman, Nogai Khan, Nogburt, Novinar～enwiki, Oldwindybear, Omnipaedista, PhnomPencil, Poetaris, Pol098, Porsenna1, Prinsgezinde, Prolog, R'n'B, Ramanujanredux, Riana, Ricky81682, Rjwilmsi, Robth, Rrostrom, Rui Gabriel Correia, Sammers23, Shadowjams, Shizhao, Shticksnshtuff, Smjg, SummerPhD, Supersume, Tarret, Tasmn, ThreeBlindMice, Tigeroo, Tigga, Tilk Tem, Tim!, Toghuchar, Trolleymusic, Underbar dk, Viator313, Wandalstouring, Wetman, Whatthree16, WolfmanSF, Wotsrovert, XXxJediKnightxXx, Yamaguchi先生 , 115 anonymous edits 84

Siege of Baghdad (1258) *Source:* https://en.wikipedia.org/w/index.php?oldid=803393647 *License:* Creative Commons Attribution-Share Alike 3.0 *Contributors:* 3family6, 90 Auto, Alotaibi43, AndreaFox, Anthon.Eff, Aramgar, Attilios, Ayazid, Ben Ben, Bender235, Benlisquare, Bensin, BiggestSataniaFanboy89, Bill Conn, BjKa, Bobrayner, Boneyard90, BrianBoru10, Bribroder, BrokenMirror2, Buistr, Caesarus III, CharacterZero, Chendjer, Chenopodiaceous, Chewings72, Chinyin, Chris the speller, ChrisGualtieri, ClueBot NG, Colonies Chris, Corymchapman, Cplakidas, Damián A. Fernández Beanato, Dat Boi Ibrahim, DavidMann, Davidcannon, Demiurge1000, Dissident93, Dj777cool, Doug Weller, Dr B2, Elonka, Enerelt, Epbr123, Escravoes, Eugene-elgato, Evenrød, Fauzan, Favonian, Fayenatic london, Gary, Ghaly, Gilliam, Giorgi Mechurchle, Gob Lofa, Got Milked, GregoryBowerman, Gun Powder Ma, Gundu1000, Halagu khan, Hamath-Zobah 17, Harlandski, Hinio, Hmains, Hocimi, Howcheng, Hugo999, Hurmata, Hyrudagon, IP 213, Illegitimate Barrister, Ithinkicahn, Jagged 85, Jamez42, Jauerback, JayEsJay, Jeff5102, Jfmantis, Jojuko, Kafka Liz, Kansas Bear, Kendrick7, Kgansen, Kharadea, Klemen Kocjancic, Kober, KureCewlik81, Lauren68, Levellend, Lilac Soul, Lotje, Manul, Manxruler, Marcocapelle, Materialscientist, Mbarbier, Meowy, Millelacs, MohammedBinAbdullah, Mominzed, Moonraker, Mr.Z-man, Muhammad Umair Mirza, Mumbo-jumbophobe, Nick Number, Nick-D, Nihlus1, Nimetapoeg, Nishkid64, Nukkri, Nukrizuxba, Omar-toons, Pavel Vozenilek, Pmsyyz, Prari, Prickett45, R'n'B, RScheiber, Rashti, RayAYang, Ricky81682, Rjwilmsi, Robyvecchio, Rosiestep, Sam Medany, SchreiberBike, Scythian1, Selrahcmattmonde, Super48paul, Tabletop, Tech77, The Anomebot2, Thusz, Tilk Tem, Tim!, TimBentley, Tpbradbury, Tty29a, Twas Now, Underbar dk, Underpants, Urban cowboy, Utcursch, Vmenkov, Whaleyland, WolfmanSF, Woohookitty, YellowMonkey, ZxxZxxZ, Zzztriple2000, 179 anonymous edits 101

Mongol invasions of Korea *Source:* https://en.wikipedia.org/w/index.php?oldid=786173258 *License:* Creative Commons Attribution-Share Alike 3.0 *Contributors:* 3family6, 4Jays1034, ALEXF971, Againme, Aldis90, Allenwlee, Andres rojas22, Andrewcarbonneau, Ante Aikio, Aocduio, Appleby, Argiecon, BUjjsp, Bamnamu, Banedon, Becks7, Bender235, Benlisquare, Bkell, Carcharoth, Cartakes, Caspian blue, Ceph'Ji'Wu, Character.assassin, Cherry Blossom OK, Chinyin, Choulin, ClueBot NG, Colonies Chris, CommonsDelinker, Confuzion, Cplakidas, Crispy park, Cypoet, Dangerous-Boy, Diablonhn, Dimadick, Dragonpyramid, Durova, Easternknight, Ecthelion83, Eiimsine, Enerelt, Flamarial, Genghiskhanviet, Giraldusfaber, Goguryeo, H27kim, Hairwizard91, HammerFilmFan, Historiographer, Hojuhanguk, Hugo999, Iktus, Illegitimate Barrister, Imbonwwwww, Incrassate, Iohannes Animosus, J.delanoy, Jhaidri, John of Reading, Kor Ph, Krusader6, Ksyrie, Kuebie, Kusunose, Lauren68, Lbydmn, Little green rosetta, Luke Kern Choi 5, Magioladitis, Nimetapoeg, Only2sea, OpieNn, Phoenix7777, Qstacy, RScheiber, Ri hwa won, Ricky81682, Rjwilmsi, Robotman1974, Siafu, Sjl0523, Sun Creator, Super-Magician, Supersaiyen312, Tahmasp, Tascha96, Teemeah, Timmyshin, Travelbybus, Vachims, Whlee, William Avery, 92 anonymous edits 111

Mongol conquest of China *Source:* https://en.wikipedia.org/w/index.php?oldid=807181701 *License:* Creative Commons Attribution-Share Alike 3.0 *Contributors:* 3family6, A D Monroe III, Aeti, Aknanaka, Alicia Florrick, Amortias, Anbu121, AnnaFrance, BD2412, BUjjsp, Benlisquare, Boson, CLCStudent, Cartakes, Cattus, Chinyin, Chris the speller, ChrisGualtieri, ClueBot NG, Cold Season, Colonies Chris, CommonsDelinker, ContinentalAve, DPdH, Davidcannon, Dcirovic, Denisarona, Drewmutt, Edward321, Enerelt, Faradayplank, Flyer22 Reborn, Fratrep, Frietjes, GeneralizationsAreBad, Gilliam, Glrx, GregorB, Hans yulun lai, Hemlock Martinis, I dream of horses, Im the nerdiest, Incrassate, Iridescent, Jackfork, Jagged 85, Jaredtb2, JimVC3, Jjnoodles1, John of Reading, Jonesey95, Joseph2302, Jpop100, Khanate General, Kintetsubuffalo, Klemdog, KylieTastic, Lauren68, Lds, Little green rosetta, M-le-mot-dit, Materialscientist, MaxPrem, NebY, Nev1, Nihiltres, Nitpicking polish, No1lovesu, Pevernagie, Pinethicket, R'n'B, Radphilosophe, RekishiEJ, Ricky81682, Rincewind42, SchreiberBike, Seasonsinthesun, Shore3, SilkTork, Slb nsk, Squids and Chips, TTTAssasinator, Teeninvestor, Tilk Tem, Tim!, Toghuchar, Tongolss, Ulric1313, Unbuttered Parsnip, Uniquark9, VS6507, VexorAbVikipædia, Vmenkov, WereSpielChequers, Woohookitty, Zanhe, Île flottante, 174 anonymous edits 116

Mongol invasions of Japan *Source:* https://en.wikipedia.org/w/index.php?oldid=807601601 *License:* Creative Commons Attribution-Share Alike 3.0 *Contributors:* .marc., 3family6, A Japanologist, Achowat, Alcmaeonid, AndrewOne, Antiqueight, BUjisp, Bahramm 2, Bans51, Bender235, Benlisquare, Boneyard90, Bosley John Bosley, CardinalDan, Cartakes, Cattus, Chealer, Chris the speller, ClueBot NG, Coolfacemcgee, Cwkmail, DPdH, DadaNeem, Denisarona, DrHacky, EDAMAMEMAST, Ecthelion83, El C, Elassint, Enchyin, Enerelt, Enkyo2, Esemono, FlieGerFaUstMe262, Flyer22 Reborn, Gamaliel, Glane23, GunnnBadshhahhh99999, GünniX, Hairy Dude, Hebrides, Hibernian, Historiographer, Hocimi, Howcheng, IAC-62, Ichiro Kikuchi, JaGa, JimRenge, Jmgwr12, John of Reading, Johnanth, JoshuSasori, JueLinLi, Kanon und wikipedia, Kiahuna, Kilmer-san, Kintetsubuffalo, Kiwifist, Kor Ph, Kuppper, Kusunose, Lauren68, LlywelynII, MWAK, Madalibi, Magioladitis, Marchjuly, Marek69, Materialscientist, Melonkelon, Miyashita, Momotarou2012, Mr Bucket, Nanacuty73, Niceguyedc, Nihlus1, Oda Mari, Ogress, Onel5969, Oshi niko, Owain Knight, P. S. Burton, Pax85, Pepesia, Peter Erwin, Phillipa21, Phoenix7777, Piermd, Pol098, Prisencolin, Remotelysensed, Ricky81682, Rurik the Varangian, Rushkente, SamHolt6, ScorchingPheonix, Sinoxin, Skyxxzc, Sligocki, Spock of Vulcan, Squids and Chips, Sturmgewehr88, Taeguk, Thane, Theinstantmatrix, Thomas Veil, Tim!, Toghuchar, Treepeonies2011, Ttwaring, Tzaquiel, Uncle G, Underbar dk, Vmenkov, WNYY98, Wiae, Woohookitty, Xania, Ymblanter, Yoshi Canopus, Yoyi ling, Ypacaraf, Yprpyqp, Yulun5566, Zanhe, 七戦功成, 正親町三条, 武士道, 鑢 2016, 169 anonymous edits 127

Mongol invasions of Tibet *Source:* https://en.wikipedia.org/w/index.php?oldid=802181783 *License:* Creative Commons Attribution-Share Alike 3.0 *Contributors:* 10Guillot, 3family6, A ri gi bod, Aisteco, Andres rojas22, BD2412, BabelStone, Bender235, Benlisquare, Bertport, Boneyard90, Cartakes, Chinyin, ChrisGualtieri, Colonies Chris, CommonsDelinker, Dragão Guerreiro, Enchyin, Enerelt, Eraserhead1, Esobocinski, Evecurid, Everyking, Goustien, HHEHUM, Hmains, Hugo999, Iampython, Jloost-gamer, John of Reading, Lauren68, LilHelpa, Look2See1, Lourdes, Myasuda, Nick Number, NikStg, Nishidani, Ricky81682, SakyaTrizin, Srnec, Tibetologist, Tim!, Toghuchar, Topbanana, Tr56tr, Woohookitty, Zanhe, ⵙ, 23 anonymous edits 145

Mongol invasion of Europe *Source:* https://en.wikipedia.org/w/index.php?oldid=807851773 *License:* Creative Commons Attribution-Share Alike 3.0 *Contributors:* 01racman, 3family6, AllGloryToTheHypnotoad, Andrei Stroe, Asteriset, Audaciter, Azgar, BernardZ, Bgwhite, Bulls123, CalebZamora, Chas. Caltrop, ClueBot NG, Colonies Chris, DPdH, Dan Koehl, Donner60, Dschslava, Ecthelion83, Gd051203, Godzilladude123, HistorianVictory, Incrassate, Inops, Insertcleverphrasehere, Jandalhandier, Jhenderson8, Jim1138, Jodosma, John of Reading, Kintetsubuffalo, Koertefa, Mancocapelle, Marek69, Natg 19, Nihlus1, Norden1990, OnWikiNo, Oshwah, PainMan, Palindromedairy, PericlesofAthens, Pinethicket, Rich Farmbrough, Rrostrom, Rui Gabriel Correia, Samhanin, Topbanana, Ulric1313, User178198273998166172, Williamteoh97, WorldlyVoice, Zyksnowy, 七战功成, 308 anonymous edits 155

Mongol invasion of India *Source:* https://en.wikipedia.org/w/index.php?oldid=806671619 *License:* Creative Commons Attribution-Share Alike 3.0 *Contributors:* 3family6, Abductive, Ahendra, Alx bio, Anastomoses, Andres rojas22, Anwarlnsaan, Arcandam, Audunum, BD2412, Benlisquare, Benzband, Betterthanbond, Beypeople, Cartakes, Choulin, Chris the speller, ClueBot NG, Colonies Chris, CommonsDelinker, DPdH, Darklilac, Denisarona, Desibhagera, Diannaa, Dimadick, Dude1224, Enchyin, Enerelt, Ericmachmer, Eyesnore, Fahadrana123, Hebrides, Hemlock Martinis, Hmains, J04n, JaGa, Jagged 85, John of Reading, Johnpacklambert, Johnuniq, Julliedon, Julnap, Ka Faraq Gatri, Kautilya3, Keo110, Lauren68, LilHelpa, Ljosi, MANGOSEEDSDATES, Mar4d, Mdmday, Moon2908, Niceguyedc, Nick Number, Nizil Shah, Nogai Khan, Outrun, Petrb, R'n'B, Rao Ravindra, Ravichandar84, Ricky81682, Rigley, Ronbarak, SchreiberBike, Serols, Sonic99, Sro23, Tabletop, Toghuchar, Ugog Nizdast, Underbar dk, Uniquark9, Utcursch, Woohookitty, ⵙ, 93 anonymous edits 183

First Mongol invasion of Burma *Source:* https://en.wikipedia.org/w/index.php?oldid=806833853 *License:* Creative Commons Attribution-Share Alike 3.0 *Contributors:* Asifneok, Benlisquare, Cartakes, Chris the speller, DPdH, Dcirovic, Hocimi, Hugo999, Hybernator, Incrassate, Niceguyedc, Ogress, Phyo WP, Ricky81682, Rigaduno, Shoshui, Spinningspark, Stonnefrety7777, Taeguk, Unbuttered Parsnip, Wiki-uk, Zanhe, 烤麵包機, 5 anonymous edits 195

Second Mongol invasion of Burma *Source:* https://en.wikipedia.org/w/index.php?oldid=799142303 *License:* Creative Commons Attribution-Share Alike 3.0 *Contributors:* Cartakes, Catlemur, DimensionQualm, Hybernator, Mmm333k, Ricky81682, Shoshui, Srnec, 烤麵包機 213

Mongol invasions of Vietnam *Source:* https://en.wikipedia.org/w/index.php?oldid=807561819 *License:* Creative Commons Attribution-Share Alike 3.0 *Contributors:* AKS.9955, AMorozov, Aisteco, Amore Mio, Andy261, AsceticRose, BUjisp, Banedon, Boneyard90, Bqn1996, Brisim, Cartakes, Catlemur, Chymicus, Classicalmania, Colonies Chris, CommonsDelinker, Crazynyancat, DHN, Delusion23, Dewritech, Dper, Dimadick, DnDkB2, EagleFan, Elizium23, Elonka, Enerelt, Ertly, Esperant, GSS-1987, Gene Nygaard, Gho2t993, Gia Thế tiên sinh 2, Godzilladude123, Hocimi, Howcheng, Hugo999, Incrassate, Indymanyr, Jeremy112233, John of Reading, Johnanth, Jspeed1310, Lauren68, LilHelpa, LuckyTran, Luong the Viet, Madalibi, Magioladitis, Meoau, Mimihitam, Narky Blert, Nick Number, Nimetapoeg, No way in hell, Ogress, Pdtch, Rajnnaam, Remitonova, Ricky81682, TRMC, TTTAssasinator, Taeguk, Taw, Tl2008, Tim!, Toghuchar, Toilahoanglong, Tom3605, Tran Ai Quoc Vietnam, Tvn3ki, Tsai8x, Twinsday, Uniquark9, VanTQ12, Wandalstouring, Wavelength, Woohookitty, Wortonedge, Zackbao1011, Ziggymister, 七战功成, 99 anonymous edits 215

Mongol invasion of Java *Source:* https://en.wikipedia.org/w/index.php?oldid=807755101 *License:* Creative Commons Attribution-Share Alike 3.0 *Contributors:* A. Parrot, ALEXF971, Andreas Kaganov, Awewe, Bender235, Benlisquare, Bennylin, Boneyard90, Cartakes, Chongkian, Choulin, Citation bot 1, DatGuy, Davehi1, Diannaa, Dre.comandante, Edward321, Enerelt, Fratrep, Gisling, Gunkarta, Hibernian, Hmains, Hocimi, Hugo999, Ibrahmin, IceKarma, Incrassate, Jaraalbe, JarrahTree, Jonesey95, Julian permata, Kevlar67, Kinh Duong Vuong, Madalibi, Marqueed, Masrudin, Merbabu, Mimihitam, NewEnglandYankee, Nimetapoeg, Peyre, Rich Farmbrough, Ricky81682, SSJGokuPower, Sib nsk, Taeguk, Tim!, Trappist the monk, Underlying lk, Verosaurus, Ymblanter, ⵙ, 61 anonymous edits 222

Mongol military tactics and organization *Source:* https://en.wikipedia.org/w/index.php?oldid=807815190 *License:* Creative Commons Attribution-Share Alike 3.0 *Contributors:* *Treker, Adam9007, Alexandre8, Altamel, Alyb2, Ancientsteppe, Anirudh Emani, Arthur Rubin, Awesomenessdoctor, BD2412, Babitaarora, Backendgaming, Bekamancer, Bgwhite, Bilsonius, BrettAllen, CAPTAIN RAJU, Cabalamat, Cwwncewn, Chinneeb, Christian75, ClueBot NG, Cujodog69, DPdH, Dannycho182, DivineAlpha, Donner60, Dthomsen8, Elassint, Enerelt, EoGuy, EuroCarGT, Excirial, FatShip, Fluffernutter, Flyer22 Reborn, Fraggle81, Frosty, Gilliam, Giraffedata, GorillaWarfare, HistoryTimP, Hmainsbot1, Hmrox, Ian Page, Insertcleverphrasehere, IronGargoyle, JaconaFrere, KConWiki, Kharadea, Khorichar, Kirsion, Lauren68, Littledman, Materialscientist, Mediran, Michael Keenan, Mikebrand, Moe Epsilon, Mogism, Muhandes, NewEnglandYankee, Ngebendi, Nick Number, Nishelperqm, Ocaasi, Og of Bashan, Oscarg, Oshwah, P.Sridhar Babu, Palindromedairy, Petrb, Pjoona11, Pleiotrop3, Potatoesarenice, Pqnelson, PraetorianFury, Pratyya Ghosh, ProffessorDano, Qwerty 9012, Rich Farmbrough, Richard Keatinge, Rigley, Rjwilmsi, Rocketrod1960, SQGibbon, Samdacruel, Siafu, Simplexity22, Smd75jr, Snori, Sriharsh1234, Stesmo, Stonnefrety7777, Student7, Tacoman12345687, Teles, Tentinator, Theonlytruemathnerd, Thirdright, Twerges, Uhlan, Ujjain, Undefined51, Vigyani, Vikroy, Vranak, Wikih101, Wpf pokefan, Yintan, Zanderzed, Zundark, 270 anonymous edits 227

Image Sources, Licenses and Contributors

The sources listed for each image provide more detailed licensing information including the copyright status, the copyright owner, and the license conditions.

Image *Source:* https://en.wikipedia.org/w/index.php?title=File:East-Hem_1200ad.jpg *License:* Creative Commons Attribution-Sharealike 3.0 *Contributors:* Thomas Lessman (Contact!) ... 13

Image *Source:* https://en.wikipedia.org/w/index.php?title=File:Genghis_khan_empire_at_his_death.png *License:* Public Domain *Contributors:* Hardcore-Mike, Karlfk, Koavf, Latebird, Look2See1, MapMaster, Nik Sage, Vercingetorix～commonswiki, Verdy p ... 13

Image *Source:* https://en.wikipedia.org/w/index.php?title=File:Mongol_dominions1.jpg *License:* Public Domain *Contributors:* Briangotts, Latebird, Leyo, Maksim, McPot, Nik Sage, RNLion, Shyam, 1 anonymous edits ... 13

Image *Source:* https://en.wikipedia.org/w/index.php?title=File:Padlock-olive.svg *License:* Public Domain *Contributors:* Anomie, Mr. Stradivarius 17

Image *Source:* https://en.wikipedia.org/w/index.php?title=File:Padlock-silver.svg *Contributors:* This image file was created by AJ Ashton. Uploaded from English WP by User:Eleassar. Converted by User:AzaToth to a silv ... 17

Image *Source:* https://en.wikipedia.org/w/index.php?title=File:YuanEmperorAlbumGenghisPortrait.jpg *Contributors:* Choufanging, Ecummenic, KirmiziAdam, Mattbuck, Newone, Poyekhali, Sevilledade, Soerfm, Turkmenhazara, Yaan, Yann, 圓周率 , 5 anonymous edits ... 17

Image *Source:* https://en.wikipedia.org/w/index.php?title=File:Cinggis_qagan.svg *License:* Public Domain *Contributors:* Yaan ... 18

Image *Source:* https://en.wikipedia.org/w/index.php?title=File:Loudspeaker.svg *License:* Public Domain *Contributors:* User:Dbenbenn, User:Optimager, User:Tsca, User:Dbenbenn, User:Optimager, User:Tsca, User:Dbenbenn, User:Optimager, User:Tsca ... 19

Figure 1 *Source:* https://en.wikipedia.org/w/index.php?title=File:Onon.jpg *License:* GNU Free Documentation License *Contributors:* Arria Belli, BotMultichillT, Latebird, Look2See1, Mircea, Nk ... 20

Figure 2 *Source:* https://en.wikipedia.org/w/index.php?title=File:Mongolia_XI.jpg *Contributors:* User:Khiruge ... 23

Figure 3 *Source:* https://en.wikipedia.org/w/index.php?title=File:Serven_Khaalga_Jurchen_inscription.jpg *License:* Creative Commons Attribution-Sharealike 3.0 *Contributors:* User:Yastanovog ... 24

Figure 4 *Source:* https://en.wikipedia.org/w/index.php?title=File:Djengiz_Khân_et_Toghril_Ong_Khan.jpeg *License:* Public Domain *Contributors:* Sayf al-Vâhidî. Hérât. Afghanistan ... 25

Figure 5 *Source:* https://en.wikipedia.org/w/index.php?title=File:Genghis_Khan's_enthronement_in_1206.jpg *License:* Public Domain *Contributors:* Sayf al-vâhidî et al. ... 26

Figure 6 *Source:* https://en.wikipedia.org/w/index.php?title=File:Mongol_Empire_c.1207.png *Contributors:* User:Khiruge ... 27

Figure 7 *Source:* https://en.wikipedia.org/w/index.php?title=File:Bataille_entre_mongols_&_chinois_(1211).jpeg *License:* Public Domain *Contributors:* Sayf al-Vâhidî. Hérât. Afghanistan ... 29

Figure 8 *Source:* https://en.wikipedia.org/w/index.php?title=File:Siège_de_Beijing_(1213-1214).jpeg *License:* Public Domain *Contributors:* Sayf al-Vâhidî. Hérât. Afghanistan ... 29

Figure 9 *Source:* https://en.wikipedia.org/w/index.php?title=File:During_the_battle_of_Indus.jpg *License:* Public Domain *Contributors:* Mas'ud b. Osmani Kuhistani ... 31

Figure 10 *Source:* https://en.wikipedia.org/w/index.php?title=File:Genghis_Khan_empire-en.svg *License:* Creative Commons Attribution-Sharealike 2.5 *Contributors:* derivative work: Bkkbrad (talk) Gengis_Khan_empire-fr.svg: historicair 17:01, 8 October 2007 (UTC) ... 32

Figure 11 *Source:* https://en.wikipedia.org/w/index.php?title=File:Mongol_Great_Khans_coin_minted_at_Balk_Afghanistan_AH_618_AD_1221.jpg *License:* Public Domain *Contributors:* PHGCOM ... 34

Figure 12 *Source:* https://en.wikipedia.org/w/index.php?title=File:China_11b.jpg *License:* GNU Free Documentation License *Contributors:* User:LiDaobing ... 35

Figure 13 *Source:* https://en.wikipedia.org/w/index.php?title=File:Genghis_Khan_and_three_of_his_four_sons.jpg *License:* Public Domain *Contributors:* Sayf al-vâhidî et al. ... 36

Figure 14 *Source:* https://en.wikipedia.org/w/index.php?title=File:Genghis_khan_empire_at_his_death.png *License:* Public Domain *Contributors:* Hardcore-Mike, Karlfk, Koavf, Latebird, Look2See1, MapMaster, Nik Sage, Vercingetorix～commonswiki, Verdy p ... 38

Figure 15 *Source:* https://en.wikipedia.org/w/index.php?title=File:GhinggisKhanMausoleum.jpg *License:* Creative Commons Attribution-Sharealike 3.0 *Contributors:* Fanghong ... 39

Figure 16 *Source:* https://en.wikipedia.org/w/index.php?title=File:Mongol_Empire_map.gif *License:* Creative Commons Attribution-ShareAlike 3.0 Unported *Contributors:* User:Astrokey44 ... 40

Figure 17 *Source:* https://en.wikipedia.org/w/index.php?title=File:Mock_Mongolian_battle_at_Khaan_Quest_07.jpg *License:* Public Domain *Contributors:* BabelStone, Reguyla, Sanandros, Slick, 1 anonymous edits ... 42

Figure 18 *Source:* https://en.wikipedia.org/w/index.php?title=File:Harhorin.jpg *License:* Creative Commons Attribution-Sharealike 2.5 *Contributors:* Frithjof Spangenberg ... 43

Figure 19 *Source:* https://en.wikipedia.org/w/index.php?title=File:Ogadai_Khan.jpg *License:* Public Domain *Contributors:* Bahatur, GDK, Kürschner, Nik Sage, Patronanejo, Saperaud～commonswiki, Yaan, 刻意 , 1 anonymous edits ... 44

Figure 20 *Source:* https://en.wikipedia.org/w/index.php?title=File:GhingisHan-rev.jpg *License:* Public Domain *Contributors:* based on painting by A Dzelkjanov ... 45

Figure 21 *Source:* https://en.wikipedia.org/w/index.php?title=File:Chinggis_Khan_hillside_portrait.JPG *License:* Public domain *Contributors:* Latebird, OgreBot 2, Underwaterbuffalo, 1 anonymous edits ... 46

Figure 22 *Source:* https://en.wikipedia.org/w/index.php?title=File:Tsakhiagiin_Elbegdorj_takes_oath_on_10_July_2013.jpg *License:* Creative Commons Attribution-Sharealike 3.0 *Contributors:* User:Mongolkhun ... 47

Figure 23 *Source:* https://en.wikipedia.org/w/index.php?title=File:GenghisKhanMonument.jpg *License:* Creative Commons Attribution-Sharealike 3.0 *Contributors:* Fanghong ... 48

Figure 24 *Source:* https://en.wikipedia.org/w/index.php?title=File:DiezAlbumsFallOfBaghdad.jpg *License:* Public Domain *Contributors:* unknown / (of the reproduction) Staatsbibliothek Berlin/Schacht ... 49

Figure 25 *Source:* https://en.wikipedia.org/w/index.php?title=File:MongolsInHungary1285.jpg *License:* Public Domain *Contributors:* unknown / (of the reproduction) Széchényi National Library, Budapest ... 51

Figure 26 *Source:* https://en.wikipedia.org/w/index.php?title=File:1000_Tugriks_-_Recto.jpg *License:* GNU Free Documentation License *Contributors:* User Methos31 on fr.wikipedia ... 51

Figure 27 *Source:* https://en.wikipedia.org/w/index.php?title=File:GhinggisKhanStatue.jpg *License:* Creative Commons Attribution-Sharealike 3.0 *Contributors:* Fanghong ... 52

Figure 28 *Source:* https://en.wikipedia.org/w/index.php?title=File:Mural_of_siege_warfare,_Genghis_Khan_Exhibit,_Tech_Museum_San_Jose,_2010.jpg *License:* Creative Commons Attribution 2.0 *Contributors:* Bill Taroli ... 53

Figure 29 *Source:* https://en.wikipedia.org/w/index.php?title=File:GhinggisKhanMausoleumGate.jpg *License:* Creative Commons Attribution-Sharealike 3.0 *Contributors:* Fanghong ... 55

Figure 30 *Source:* https://en.wikipedia.org/w/index.php?title=File:GenghisKhanMonumentInHulunbuir.jpg *License:* Creative Commons Attribution-Sharealike 3.0 *Contributors:* Fanghong ... 56

Image *Source:* https://en.wikipedia.org/w/index.php?title=File:Skull_and_crossbones.svg *Contributors:* Andux, Andy0101, AnselmiJuan, Bayo, BotMultichill, BotMultichillT, Coyau, D0ktorz, Derbeth, Eugenio Hansen, OFS, Franzenshof, Ies, J.delanoy, JMCC1, Jahoe, Juliancolton, Karelj, MarianSigler, Natr, Sarang, Shuhazmir, Sidpatil, Silsor, Stas1995, Stepshep, Str4nd, Sven Manguard, SweetCanadianMullet, The Evil IP address, Tiptoety, Túrelio, W!B:, Wknight94, 22 anonymous edits ... 63

Image *Source:* https://en.wikipedia.org/w/index.php?title=File:Mongol_raids_in_Syria_and_Palestine_1260.svg *License:* Creative Commons Attribution 3.0 *Contributors:* Map Master ... 67

Image *Source:* https://en.wikipedia.org/w/index.php?title=File:Flag_of_Ilkhanate.gif *License:* Public Domain *Contributors:* image created by Tomislav Todorovic ... 67

Image *Source:* https://en.wikipedia.org/w/index.php?title=File:Rubenid_Flag.svg *License:* Creative Commons Attribution-Sharealike 3.0 *Contributors:* Orange Tuesday (talk) Richardprins. Andrew Andersen for source image. S@m and Min's for lion. Fleur de lis on the cro ... 67

Image *Source:* https://en.wikipedia.org/w/index.php?title=File:Sakartvelo_-_drosha.svg *License:* Creative Commons Attribution 3.0 *Contributors:* Ec.Domnowall ... 67

Image *Source:* https://en.wikipedia.org/w/index.php?title=File:Armoiries_Bohémond_VI_d'Antioche.svg *License:* Creative Commons Attribution-Sharealike 3.0,2.5,2.0,1.0 *Contributors:* user:Odejea, user:Odejea ... 67

Image *Source:* https://en.wikipedia.org/w/index.php?title=File:Armoiries_Tripoli.svg *License:* Creative Commons Attribution-Sharealike 3.0,2.5,2.0,1.0 *Contributors:* user:Odejea, user:Odejea ... 67

Image *Source:* https://en.wikipedia.org/w/index.php?title=File:Golden_Horde_flag_1339.svg *License:* Creative Commons Zero *Contributors:* AnonMoos, Dbachmann, File Upload Bot (Magnus Manske), Frhdkazan, Michele-sama, OgreBot 2, Sarang, Stewi101015 67
Image *Source:* https://en.wikipedia.org/w/index.php?title=File:Cross_of_the_Knights_Templar.svg *License:* Public domain *Contributors:* User:Kbolino 67
Image *Source:* https://en.wikipedia.org/w/index.php?title=File:Mameluke_Flag.svg *License:* Public Domain *Contributors:* Anime Addict AA, AnonMoos, Ashashyou, Bobrayner, CommonsDelinker, Cycn, Dbachmann, Homo lupus, JMCC1, Latebird, Lliura, Ryucloud∼commonswiki, Sarang, SiBr4, TRAJAN 117, Takabeg, Tom-L, 1 anonymous edits 77
Image *Source:* https://en.wikipedia.org/w/index.php?title=File:Flag_of_Ayyubid_Dynasty.svg *License:* Public Domain *Contributors:* Ch1902 . 67
Image *Source:* https://en.wikipedia.org/w/index.php?title=File:Karamanid_Dynasty_flag.svg *License:* Public Domain *Contributors:* Jecowa ... 67
Image *Source:* https://en.wikipedia.org/w/index.php?title=File:Black_flag.svg *License:* Public Domain *Contributors:* PavelD 67
Image *Source:* https://en.wikipedia.org/w/index.php?title=File:Armoiries_Héthoumides.svg *License:* Creative Commons Attribution-Sharealike 3.0 *Contributors:* user:Bruno Vallette, user:Odejea, user:Rinaldum, user:Yorick, user:Odejea, user:Odejea 68
Figure 31 *Source:* https://en.wikipedia.org/w/index.php?title=File:EdwardICrusadeMap.jpg *License:* Creative Commons Attribution-Share Alike *Contributors:* PHGCOM 70
Figure 32 *Source:* https://en.wikipedia.org/w/index.php?title=File:Siege_of_Tripoli_Painting_(1289).jpg *License:* Public Domain *Contributors:* Not listed 72
Figure 33 *Source:* https://en.wikipedia.org/w/index.php?title=File:DisasterOfMari1266.JPG *License:* Public Domain *Contributors:* Bohème, JMCC1, Jimmy44, Kilom691, Mattes, Mel22, Taron Saharyan, World Imaging, Wst, 2 anonymous edits 73
Figure 34 *Source:* https://en.wikipedia.org/w/index.php?title=File:1281BattleOfHoms.JPG *License:* Public Domain *Contributors:* Hayton of Coricos 74
Figure 35 *Source:* https://en.wikipedia.org/w/index.php?title=File:BattleOfHoms1299.JPG *License:* Public Domain *Contributors:* Ashashyou, Bahatur, Dbachmann, Franco aq, JMCC1, Thib Phil, World Imaging, Иван Дулин, 3 anonymous edits 75
Figure 36 *Source:* https://en.wikipedia.org/w/index.php?title=File:1301FrancoMongolOffensiveLevant.jpg *License:* Creative Commons Attribution-Sharealike 3.0,2.5,2.0,1.0 *Contributors:* PHGCOM 76
Figure 37 *Source:* https://en.wikipedia.org/w/index.php?title=File:Bahri_Dynasty_1250_-_1382_(AD).PNG *License:* Creative Commons Attribution-Sharealike 2.5 *Contributors:* BotMultichill, Dcoetzee, Diannaa, File Upload Bot (Magnus Manske), Ghazan, JMCC1, Kopiersperre, MGA73bot2, Quadell, VernoWhitney, Wst, Zykasaa 77
Figure 38 *Source:* https://en.wikipedia.org/w/index.php?title=File:Mongol_dominions1.jpg *License:* Public Domain *Contributors:* Briangotts, Latebird, Leyo, Maksim, McPot, Nik Sage, RNLion, Shyam, 1 anonymous edits 78
Figure 39 *Source:* https://en.wikipedia.org/w/index.php?title=File:LatinEmpire2.png *License:* Creative Commons Attribution-ShareAlike 3.0 Unported *Contributors:* LatinEmpire 80
Image *Source:* https://en.wikipedia.org/w/index.php?title=File:Turkey_topo.jpg *License:* GNU Free Documentation License *Contributors:* Atilim-GunesBaydin, Gryffindor, Juetho, MGA73bot2, Qualc1, Rapsar, Saperaud∼commonswiki, Taragui, Tarih, 2 anonymous edits 81
Image *Source:* https://en.wikipedia.org/w/index.php?title=File:Flag_of_Turkey.svg *License:* Public Domain *Contributors:* User:Dbenbenn 81
Image *Source:* https://en.wikipedia.org/w/index.php?title=File:Bataille_de_Kōzā_Dagh_(1243).jpeg *License:* Public Domain *Contributors:* Unknown. Catalonia. ....
Figure 40 *Source:* https://en.wikipedia.org/w/index.php?title=File:Khwarezmian_Empire_1190_-_1220_(AD).PNG *License:* Public Domain *Contributors:* Alex:D, BokicaK, Briangotts, Codrinb, Cplakidas, Flamarande∼commonswiki, Hailey C. Shannon∼commonswiki, Julieta39, Karlfk, Kilom691, Martin H., Mschlindwein, Neuceu, Nihad Hamzic, OgreBot 2, PANONIAN, Parsecboy, Rupert Clayton, Shakko, Taron Saharyan, باسم, 1 anonymous edits 83
Image *Source:* https://en.wikipedia.org/w/index.php?title=File:ShepherdByzempire1265.jpg *License:* Public Domain *Contributors:* Dcoetzee, File Upload Bot (Magnus Manske), HistoryofIran, MGA73bot2, MaxxL, Quadell, Teratornis, VernoWhitney, Zykasaa, باسم, 1 anonymous edits 84
Figure 42 *Source:* https://en.wikipedia.org/w/index.php?title=File:Bataille_de_vāliyān_(1221).jpeg *License:* Public Domain *Contributors:* Sayf al-Vāhidī. Hérât. Afghanistan. ....
Figure 43 *Source:* https://en.wikipedia.org/w/index.php?title=File:Madrasah_Kukaldash_(Tashkent)_11-44.JPG *License:* Public Domain *Contributors:* User:Bobyrr .. 90
Figure 44 *Source:* https://en.wikipedia.org/w/index.php?title=File:Urgench.jpg *License:* GNU Free Documentation License *Contributors:* Lohen11, MBxd1, MGA73bot2, OgreBot 2, Olivier ....
Figure 45 *Source:* https://en.wikipedia.org/w/index.php?title=File:Terken-Khatun-Captive-Initi.gif *License:* Public Domain *Contributors:* Retrieverlove 96
Image *Source:* https://en.wikipedia.org/w/index.php?title=File:Bagdad1258.jpg *License:* Public Domain *Contributors:* Sayf al-vāhidī et al. 101
Image *Source:* https://en.wikipedia.org/w/index.php?title=File:Il-Khanate_Flag.svg *License:* Public domain *Contributors:* Orange Tuesday (talk) 101
Figure 46 *Source:* https://en.wikipedia.org/w/index.php?title=File:Persian_painting_of_Hülegü's_army_attacking_city_with_siege_engine.jpg *License:* Public Domain *Contributors:* Bahatur, Filo cz, INeverCry, Michele-sama, Nick Number, Sridhar1000, Sémhur, Иван Дулин 105
Figure 47 *Source:* https://en.wikipedia.org/w/index.php?title=File:HulaguInBagdad.JPG *License:* Public Domain *Contributors:* Maître de la Mazarine 106
Image *Source:* https://en.wikipedia.org/w/index.php?title=File:Mongol_Invasion_of_China.png *License:* Public Domain *Contributors:* User:Seasonsinthesun 116
Figure 48 *Source:* https://en.wikipedia.org/w/index.php?title=File:Bataille_entre_mongols_&_chinois_(1211).jpeg *License:* Public Domain *Contributors:* Sayf al-Vāhidī. Hérât. Afghanistan. 118
Figure 49 *Source:* https://en.wikipedia.org/w/index.php?title=File:Siège_de_Beijing_(1213-1214).jpeg *License:* Public Domain *Contributors:* Sayf al-Vāhidī. Hérât. Afghanistan. 120
Figure 50 *Source:* https://en.wikipedia.org/w/index.php?title=File:Yuan_Dynasty_1294.png *License:* Creative Commons Attribution 3.0 *Contributors:* Ian Kiu 125
Image *Source:* https://en.wikipedia.org/w/index.php?title=File:Moko_Shūrai_Ekotoba.jpg *License:* Allforrous, Ao-take, MathieuMD, Phoenix7777, Usiwakamaru, Worldantiques, 1 anonymous edits 127
Image *Source:* https://en.wikipedia.org/w/index.php?title=File:Imperial_Seal_of_Japan.svg *License:* Public Domain *Contributors:* User:Philip Nilsson 127
Image *Source:* https://en.wikipedia.org/w/index.php?title=File:Sasa_Rindo.svg *License:* Creative Commons Attribution-Sharealike 3.0 *Contributors:* 百瀬 127
Image *Source:* https://en.wikipedia.org/w/index.php?title=File:Mitsuuroko.svg *License:* Public Domain *Contributors:* -Strogoff-, Courcelles, Damian Yerrick, Maxima m, Slady, WTCA, 宇治主水, 2 anonymous edits 127
Image *Source:* https://en.wikipedia.org/w/index.php?title=File:So_clan_mon2.svg *License:* Public Domain *Contributors:* , vectorized by 127
Image *Source:* https://en.wikipedia.org/w/index.php?title=File:Ageha-cho.svg *License:* GNU Free Documentation License *Contributors:* JÚLIO REIS and MISOGI 127
Image *Source:* https://en.wikipedia.org/w/index.php?title=File:Kikuchi_mon2.jpg *License:* Creative Commons Attribution-Sharealike 3.0 *Contributors:* Victorblarsson ....
Image *Source:* https://en.wikipedia.org/w/index.php?title=File:Moko_Shūrai_daki_Gyouyou.svg *License:* Creative Commons Attribution-Sharealike 3.0,2.5,2.0,1.0 *Contributors:* user:Mukai 127
Image *Source:* https://en.wikipedia.org/w/index.php?title=File:Maru_juji.svg *License:* Public Domain *Contributors:* , vectorized by 127
Image *Source:* https://en.wikipedia.org/w/index.php?title=File:Japanese_Crest_Matura_mitu_Hosi.svg *License:* Creative Commons Attribution-Sharealike 3.0,2.5,2.0,1.0 *Contributors:* user:Mukai 127
Image *Source:* https://en.wikipedia.org/w/index.php?title=File:Japanese_crest_narabi_Takanoha.svg *License:* Creative Commons Attribution-Sharealike 3.0,2.5,2.0,1.0 *Contributors:* Mukai 128
Image *Source:* https://en.wikipedia.org/w/index.php?title=File:Japanese_Crest_Hita_Suhama.svg *License:* Creative Commons Attribution-Sharealike 3.0 *Contributors:* User:Mukai 128
Image *Source:* https://en.wikipedia.org/w/index.php?title=File:Hidari_mitsudomoe.svg *License:* GNU Free Documentation License *Contributors:* -Strogoff-, AnonMoos, Benzoyl, BraneJ, Bukk, Courcelles, Los688, Lx 121, MGA73bot2, Reggaeman, Sarang, Sturmgewehr88, Switchercat, Tokorokoko, WTCA, Waldir, 自拍子花子, 4 anonymous edits 128
Figure 51 *Source:* https://en.wikipedia.org/w/index.php?title=File:LetterFromKhubilaiToJapan1266.jpg *License:* Public Domain *Contributors:* Qubilai Qa'an/(transcribed by 東大寺宗性 Soushou (1202-1278)Todai-ji temple, Nara, Japan 130
Figure 52 *Source:* https://en.wikipedia.org/w/index.php?title=File:Genko_Borui_Nishijin_Fukuoka_02.jpg *License:* Creative Commons Attribution-Sharealike 3.0 *Contributors:* User:Momotarou314 131
Figure 53 *Source:* https://en.wikipedia.org/w/index.php?title=File:MokoShurai.jpeg *License:* Public Domain *Contributors:* Kikuchi Yoosai / (of the reproduction) Tokyo National Museum 133
Figure 54 *Source:* https://en.wikipedia.org/w/index.php?title=File:Mōko_Shūrai_Ekotoba_e2.jpg *License:* Public Domain *Contributors:* Usiwakamaru, 魔天動地 134
Figure 55 *Source:* https://en.wikipedia.org/w/index.php?title=File:Mōko_Shūrai_Ekotoba4.JPG *License:* Creative Commons Attribution-Sharealike 3.0 *Contributors:* User:魔天動地 135
Figure 56 *Source:* https://en.wikipedia.org/w/index.php?title=File:Takezaki_suenaga_ekotoba_bourui.jpg *License:* Public Domain *Contributors:* MathieuMD, Momotarou2012, Usiwakamaru, Worldantiques 135

Figure 57 *Source:* https://en.wikipedia.org/w/index.php?title=File:Takezaki_suenaga_ekotoba3.jpg *License:* Public Domain *Contributors:* 竹崎季長 ... 136

Figure 58 *Source:* https://en.wikipedia.org/w/index.php?title=File:Mōko_Shūrai_Ekotoba_e20(2).JPG *License:* Creative Commons Attribution-Sharealike 3.0 *Contributors:* User:震天動地 ... 138

Figure 59 *Source:* https://en.wikipedia.org/w/index.php?title=File:Mooko-SamuraiShips.jpg *License:* Public Domain *Contributors:* Amcaja, Aotake, Kaba, MathieuMD, World Imaging, Yaan ... 139

Figure 60 *Source:* https://en.wikipedia.org/w/index.php?title=File:Mōko_Shūrai_Ekotoba_e17.JPG *License:* Creative Commons Attribution-Sharealike 3.0 *Contributors:* User:震天動地 ... 139

Figure 61 *Source:* https://en.wikipedia.org/w/index.php?title=File:□□□□□□□□□.JPG *License:* Creative Commons Attribution-Sharealike 3.0 *Contributors:* User:震天動地 ... 141

Figure 62 *Source:* https://en.wikipedia.org/w/index.php?title=File:Mooko-SamuraiShips.jpg *License:* Public Domain *Contributors:* Amcaja, Aotake, Kaba, MathieuMD, World Imaging, Yaan ... 142

Figure 63 *Source:* https://en.wikipedia.org/w/index.php?title=File:MokoShuraiE-Kotoba_I.jpg *License:* Public Domain *Contributors:* Fukuda Taika / (of the reproduction) Tokyo National Museum ... 142

Figure 64 *Source:* https://en.wikipedia.org/w/index.php?title=File:MokoShuraiE-Kotoba_III.jpg *License:* Public Domain *Contributors:* Fukuda Taika / (of the reproduction) Tokyo National Museum ... 142

Image *Source:* https://en.wikipedia.org/w/index.php?title=File:Commons-logo.svg *License:* logo *Contributors:* Anomie, Callanecc, CambridgeBayWeather, Jo-Jo Eumerus, RHaworth ... 144

Image *Source:* https://en.wikipedia.org/w/index.php?title=File:Lhasa_Potala.jpg *License:* Creative Commons Zero *Contributors:* René Heise . 145

Image *Source:* https://en.wikipedia.org/w/index.php?title=File:Himalayas-Lhasa10.JPG *License:* Creative Commons Attribution 2.5 *Contributors:* ignat ... 145

Figure 65 *Source:* https://en.wikipedia.org/w/index.php?title=File:MongolEmpire.jpg *License:* Creative Commons Attribution-Sharealike 3.0 *Contributors:* User:Keithpickering ... 148

Figure 66 *Source:* https://en.wikipedia.org/w/index.php?title=File:Yuan_dynasty_and_Tibet.jpg *License:* Creative Commons Attribution-Sharealike 3.0 *Contributors:* Jason22 and Chinyin ... 150

Figure 67 *Source:* https://en.wikipedia.org/w/index.php?title=File:Kalmykia_1720.jpg *License:* Public Domain *Contributors:* Calmouk, David Kernow∼commonswiki, Flamarande∼commonswiki, Frank Schulenburg, Geagea, Khiruge, Latebird, Lotje, Popolon, Sibom ... 153

Image *Source:* https://en.wikipedia.org/w/index.php?title=File:Alex_K_Kyiv_Michael_2.svg *License:* Public Domain *Contributors:* Alex Tora or Alex K in Ukranian and Japanese wiki ... 156

Image *Source:* https://en.wikipedia.org/w/index.php?title=File:Alex_Chernigiv.svg *License:* Public Domain *Contributors:* Alex Tora or Alex K in Ukranian and Japanese wiki ... 156

Image *Source:* https://en.wikipedia.org/w/index.php?title=File:Coat_of_Arms_of_Vladimir_(1781).png *License:* Public Domain *Contributors:* vector-images.com ... 156

Image *Source:* https://en.wikipedia.org/w/index.php?title=File:Alex_K_Halych-Volhynia.svg *License:* Public Domain *Contributors:* = in Ukranian = in Japanese wiki ... 156

Image *Source:* https://en.wikipedia.org/w/index.php?title=File:Nowogród.svg *License:* Creative Commons Attribution-Sharealike 3.0 *Contributors:* J a1 ... 156

Image *Source:* https://en.wikipedia.org/w/index.php?title=File:Symbol_Duchy_of_Ryazan.svg *License:* Creative Commons Zero *Contributors:* User:Лобачев Владимир ... 156

Image *Source:* https://en.wikipedia.org/w/index.php?title=File:Coat_of_Arms_of_the_Polish_Crown.svg *License:* Creative Commons Attribution-Sharealike 2.5 *Contributors:* Bastianow (Bastian) ... 156

Image *Source:* https://en.wikipedia.org/w/index.php?title=File:POL_województwo_dolnośląskie_COA.svg *License:* Public Domain *Contributors:* Poznaniak ... 156

Image *Source:* https://en.wikipedia.org/w/index.php?title=File:Blason_Boheme_couronne.svg *License:* Creative Commons Attribution-Sharealike 3.0 *Contributors:* User:El_Bey_Effendi, User:David Liuzzo, User:El_Bey_Effendi ... 156

Image *Source:* https://en.wikipedia.org/w/index.php?title=File:Moravia_Arms.svg *Contributors:* Ipankonin ... 156

Image *Source:* https://en.wikipedia.org/w/index.php?title=File:Coa_Hungary_Country_History_Bela_III_(1172-1196).svg *License:* Creative Commons Zero *Contributors:* Madboy74. ... 156

Image *Source:* https://en.wikipedia.org/w/index.php?title=File:Crusades_TF.JPG *License:* Public Domain *Contributors:* Roger Davies ... 156

Image *Source:* https://en.wikipedia.org/w/index.php?title=File:Coat_of_arms_of_Croatia_1495.svg *License:* Public Domain *Contributors:* 17:38, 8 March 2014 Goran tek-en DIREKTOR, based on the 1495 coat of arms ... 156

Image *Source:* https://en.wikipedia.org/w/index.php?title=File:Gules_a_fess_argent.svg *License:* Creative Commons Attribution-Sharealike 3.0,2.5,2.0,1.0 *Contributors:* user:Odejea, user:Odejea ... 156

Image *Source:* https://en.wikipedia.org/w/index.php?title=File:Flag_of_the_Second_Bulgarian_Empire.svg *License:* Creative Commons Zero *Contributors:* User:Samhanin ... 156

Image *Source:* https://en.wikipedia.org/w/index.php?title=File:Wappen_Schlesiens.png *License:* Creative Commons Zero *Contributors:* Schläsinger 157

Image *Source:* https://en.wikipedia.org/w/index.php?title=File:POL_województwo_opolskie_COA.svg *License:* Creative Commons Attribution-Sharealike 2.5 *Contributors:* project: Leszek Ołdak, Marian Panic, Bolesław Polnar, vectorization: Poznaniak ... 157

Image *Source:* https://en.wikipedia.org/w/index.php?title=File:Coa_Hungary_Country_History_Béla_IV_(1235-1270).svg *License:* Creative Commons Zero *Contributors:* Madboy74 ... 157

Image *Source:* https://en.wikipedia.org/w/index.php?title=File:Hungary_Arms.svg *Contributors:* Ipankonin ... 157

Figure 68 *Source:* https://en.wikipedia.org/w/index.php?title=File:Suzdal-invasion2.jpg *License:* Public Domain *Contributors:* Adelchi, Anne97432, Berillium, Demidow, Foroa, Mhmrodrigues, Ranveig ... 158

Figure 69 *Source:* https://en.wikipedia.org/w/index.php?title=File:Capture_of_the_Mongol-Tatars_Russian_city.jpg *License:* Public Domain *Contributors:* Aschroet, Berillium, Shakko ... 159

Figure 70 *Source:* https://en.wikipedia.org/w/index.php?title=File:Henryk_Pobozny.jpg *License:* Public Domain *Contributors:* Acoma, Kokodyl, Mathiasrex, Mhmrodrigues, 4 anonymous edits ... 160

Figure 71 *Source:* https://en.wikipedia.org/w/index.php?title=File:HedwigManuscriptLiegnitz_b.jpg *License:* Public Domain *Contributors:* unknown / (of the reproduction) Wroclaw University Library / T. Zoltowska-Huszcza (sorry for ignoring diacritics) ... 161

Figure 72 *Source:* https://en.wikipedia.org/w/index.php?title=File:Battle_of_Mohi_1241.PNG *License:* Public Domain *Contributors:* Anonymous illumination ... 163

Figure 73 *Source:* https://en.wikipedia.org/w/index.php?title=File:Klis_0807_3.jpg *License:* Creative Commons Attribution-Sharealike 3.0 *Contributors:* Roberta F. ... 166

Figure 74 *Source:* https://en.wikipedia.org/w/index.php?title=File:Meczennicy_Sandomierscy.jpg *License:* Public Domain *Contributors:* probably Karol de Provost ... 173

Figure 75 *Source:* https://en.wikipedia.org/w/index.php?title=File:MongolsInHungary1285.jpg *License:* Public Domain *Contributors:* unknown / (of the reproduction) Széchényi National Library, Budapest ... 175

Figure 76 *Source:* https://en.wikipedia.org/w/index.php?title=File:Victory_of_king_Milutin_over_Tatars.jpg *License:* Public Domain *Contributors:* Anastas Jovanović (1817-1899) ... 176

Figure 77 *Source:* https://en.wikipedia.org/w/index.php?title=File:RYAZAN.JPG *License:* Public Domain *Contributors:* Annenkov, Aschroet, Berillium, BotMultichill, MGA73bot2, Maximalist, Shakko, Xardaas ... 177

Figure 78 *Source:* https://en.wikipedia.org/w/index.php?title=File:KIEV1240.jpg *License:* Public Domain *Contributors:* русский летописец 178

Figure 79 *Source:* https://en.wikipedia.org/w/index.php?title=File:Oborona_Kozelska.jpg *License:* Public Domain *Contributors:* Berillium, Il Dottore, Sasha Krotov, Shakko ... 178

Figure 80 *Source:* https://en.wikipedia.org/w/index.php?title=File:Mongols_vladimir.jpg *License:* Public Domain *Contributors:* Bahatur, Berillium, OgreBot 2, Shakko, Spectorman ... 178

Figure 81 *Source:* https://en.wikipedia.org/w/index.php?title=File:Ephrosinia_of_Suzdal.jpg *License:* Creative Commons Attribution-Sharealike 3.0 *Contributors:* user:shakko ... 179

Figure 82 *Source:* https://en.wikipedia.org/w/index.php?title=File:MongolsInHungary1241.jpg *License:* Public Domain *Contributors:* unknown / (of the reproduction) Széchényi National Library, Budapest ... 179

Image *Source:* https://en.wikipedia.org/w/index.php?title=File:Flag_of_Chagatai_khanate.svg *License:* Creative Commons Attribution-Sharealike 3.0 *Contributors:* Barış yolu Peláez, Cwbm (commons), Denniss, History of Persia, Magasjukur2, Sarang, 1 anonymous edits ... 183

Figure 83 *Source:* https://en.wikipedia.org/w/index.php?title=File:Genghis_Khan.jpg *License:* Public Domain *Contributors:* Bogdan, BáthoryPéter, Choufanging, Gabor∼commonswiki, Latebird, Nik Sage, Nilfanion, OsamaK, Rex, Saperaud∼commonswiki, Svdmolen, Un1c0s bot∼commonswiki, Woodledoodledoodle, Yaan, Zolo, 5 anonymous edits ... 185

Figure 84 *Source:* https://en.wikipedia.org/w/index.php?title=File:MongolEmpire.jpg *License:* Creative Commons Attribution-Sharealike 3.0 *Contributors:* User:Keithpickering ... 187

Figure 85 *Source:* https://en.wikipedia.org/w/index.php?title=File:Sultan-Allahudeen-Gherzai.jpg *Contributors:* Beria, BotMultichill, Ekabhishek, Officer, Tryphon, Utcursch, احمد نجيب بيابانی ابراهیمخلل 188
Figure 86 *Source:* https://en.wikipedia.org/w/index.php?title=File:Timur_Exhumed.gif *License:* Creative Commons Attribution 2.5 *Contributors:* Atilin 191
Figure 87 *Source:* https://en.wikipedia.org/w/index.php?title=File:Timur_defeats_the_sultan_of_Delhi.jpg *License:* Public Domain *Contributors:* Zafarnama of Sharaf Al-Din 'Ali Yazdi 191
Figure 88 *Source:* https://en.wikipedia.org/w/index.php?title=File:Babur.jpg *License:* Public Domain *Contributors:* ALE!, Fast track~commonswiki, Gryffindor, Hannah~commonswiki, Jkelly, LX, Officer, Rex, Roland zh, Un1c0s bot~commonswiki 192
Image *Source:* https://en.wikipedia.org/w/index.php?title=File:Symbol_support_vote.svg *License:* Public Domain *Contributors:* Anomie, Fastily, Jo-Jo Eumerus 195
Image *Source:* https://en.wikipedia.org/w/index.php?title=File:Mongol_invasions_of_Burma_(1277-87).png *License:* Public Domain *Contributors:* Hybernator 195
Figure 89 *Source:* https://en.wikipedia.org/w/index.php?title=File:Pagan_Empire_-_Sithu_II.PNG *License:* Creative Commons Attribution-Sharealike 3.0 *Contributors:* User:Hybernator 198
Figure 90 *Source:* https://en.wikipedia.org/w/index.php?title=File:China_11b.jpg *License:* GNU Free Documentation License *Contributors:* User:LiDaobing 198
Figure 91 *Source:* https://en.wikipedia.org/w/index.php?title=File:Bagan,_Burma.jpg *License:* Creative Commons Attribution 2.0 *Contributors:* Corto Maltese 1999 200
Figure 92 *Source:* https://en.wikipedia.org/w/index.php?title=File:Mongol_invasions_of_Burma_(1277-87).png *License:* Public Domain *Contributors:* Hybernator 202
Figure 93 *Source:* https://en.wikipedia.org/w/index.php?title=File:MongolArcher.jpg *License:* Public Domain *Contributors:* Bahatur, BotMultichill, Jann, MGA73bot2, Michele-sama, Pitke, Thib Phil, Алексей03 203
Figure 94 *Source:* https://en.wikipedia.org/w/index.php?title=File:Mongol_warrior_of_Genghis_Khan.jpg *Contributors:* User:Stonnefrety7777 205
Figure 95 *Source:* https://en.wikipedia.org/w/index.php?title=File:YuanEmperorAlbumKhubilaiPortrait.jpg *License:* Public Domain *Contributors:* Anige (also known as Araniko) of Nepal, an astronomer, engineer, painter, and confidant of Kublai Khan 206
Figure 96 *Source:* https://en.wikipedia.org/w/index.php?title=File:Burma_in_1450.png *License:* Creative Commons Attribution-Sharealike 3.0 *Contributors:* Hybernator 209
Image *Source:* https://en.wikipedia.org/w/index.php?title=File:Battle_of_Bach_Dang_(1288).jpg *License:* Public Domain *Contributors:* Jeff G., OgreBot 2, TRMC, Tarchivum, Unserefahne, 鴻雁飛傳奇雜隊 215
Image *Source:* https://en.wikipedia.org/w/index.php?title=File:Flag_of_the_Mongol_Empire_2.svg *License:* Public Domain *Contributors:* Nozomi Kariyasu (creator) and Sj (uploader) 215
Figure 97 *Source:* https://en.wikipedia.org/w/index.php?title=File:YuanEmperorAlbumKhubilaiPortrait.jpg *License:* Public Domain *Contributors:* Anige (also known as Araniko) of Nepal, an astronomer, engineer, painter, and confidant of Kublai Khan 217
Figure 98 *Source:* https://en.wikipedia.org/w/index.php?title=File:Chongquannguyenlan2.svg *License:* Public Domain *Contributors:* Lưu Ly 219
Figure 99 *Source:* https://en.wikipedia.org/w/index.php?title=File:YuanJunk(14thcentury).jpg *License:* Public Domain *Contributors:* User PHG on en.wikipedia 224
Figure 100 *Source:* https://en.wikipedia.org/w/index.php?title=File:Mongol_warrior_of_Genghis_Khan.jpg *Contributors:* User:Stonnefrety7777 228
Figure 101 *Source:* https://en.wikipedia.org/w/index.php?title=File:MongolArcher.jpg *License:* Public Domain *Contributors:* Bahatur, BotMultichill, Jann, MGA73bot2, Michele-sama, Pitke, Thib Phil, Алексей03 229
Figure 102 *Source:* https://en.wikipedia.org/w/index.php?title=File:MongolCavalrymen.jpg *License:* Public Domain *Contributors:* Sayf al-Vāhidī. Herāt. Afghanistan 231
Figure 103 *Source:* https://en.wikipedia.org/w/index.php?title=File:Mongol_hunter_with_tame_cheetah.jpg *License:* Creative Commons Attribution-Sharealike 3.0 *Contributors:* Abujoy, Bahatur, BeatrixBelibaste, BotMultichill, File Upload Bot (Magnus Manske), Gareth, Janbies, MGA73bot2, Michele-sama, OgreBot 2, Richard001, Иван Дулин 233
Figure 104 *Source:* https://en.wikipedia.org/w/index.php?title=File:DiezAlbumsMountedArchers.jpg *License:* Public Domain *Contributors:* unknown / (of the reproduction) Staatsbibliothek Berlin/Schacht 234
Figure 105 *Source:* https://en.wikipedia.org/w/index.php?title=File:Mongol_soldiers_by_Rashid_al-Din_1305.JPG *License:* Public Domain *Contributors:* Rashid al-Din 236
Figure 106 *Source:* https://en.wikipedia.org/w/index.php?title=File:Bagdad1258.jpg *License:* Public Domain *Contributors:* Sayf al-vāhidī et al. 238
Figure 107 *Source:* https://en.wikipedia.org/w/index.php?title=File:□□□□□□.jpg *License:* Creative Commons Attribution-Sharealike 3.0,2.5,2.0,1.0 *Contributors:* Kopiersperre, The real Marcoman, お館さま, そらみみ 239
Figure 108 *Source:* https://en.wikipedia.org/w/index.php?title=File:Vladimir_mongols.jpg *License:* Public Domain *Contributors:* Bagratun, Bahatur, Cplakidas, Mike Rosoft, OgreBot 2, Thib Phil 241
Figure 109 *Source:* https://en.wikipedia.org/w/index.php?title=File:Battle_of_Mohi.svg *License:* Creative Commons Attribution-Share Alike *Contributors:* Alex:D 243

License

Creative Commons Attribution-Share Alike 3.0
//creativecommons.org/licenses/by-sa/3.0/

Index

'Abbas ibn 'Abd al-Muttalib, 102
'Alā' ad-Dīn Muḥammad, 64

Abachi, 215
Abagha, 68
Abaqa Khan, 11, 73
Abaújvár, 165
Abbasid, 70
Abbasid Caliph, 171
Abbasid Caliphate, 67, 69, 101, 102
Abu Said (Ilkhanid dynasty), 77, 190
Academy Award, 53
Acre (city), 69
Afghanistan, 33, 49, 63, 84, 99, 187
Aftermath of Ögedeis death, 167
Age of Empires II: The Age of Kings, 54
Agvaantserengiin Enkhtaivan, 52
A History of the English-Speaking Peoples, 168
A History of Warfare, 264
Ahlat, 10
Ahmad Fanakati, 11
Ahmed Sanjar, 64
Ain Jalut, 69
Ainu people, 129
Ajall Shams al-Din Omar, 10
Aju, 11, 117, 215, 216
Ala al-Din Kayqubad I, 80
Alain Demurger, 108
Alamut, 8, 123
Alamut Castle, 102, 104, 123, 238
Alans, 116, 156, 158
Alauddin Khalji, 184, 188
Aleppo, 10, 68, 69, 74, 82
Alexios I of Trebizond, 80
Alex Man, 53
Alghu, 10, 11
Almaliq, Xinjiang, 2, 64
Al-Mustansir II of Cairo, 68, 70
Al-Mustasim, 9, 68, 101–103, 106
Al-Nasir, 102
Al-Nasir Muhammad, 68
Altai Mountains, 2
Altan Debter, 169

Altan Khan, 152
Altan Khan of the Khalkha, 152
Ambaghai, 19
Ambassador, 124
Ambush, 42
Amdo, 151, 152
Amir Qazaghan, 190
Amu Darya, 96
Ananda Pyissi, 196, 200, 263
Anatolia, 67, 216
Anatolian beyliks, 79
Andrew II of Hungary, 162
Anhui Province, 6
Anju (city), 112
Ankara, 79
An-Nasir, 85
An-Nasir Yusuf, 10, 68, 69
Antichrist, 172
Aoki Ookami to Shiroki Mejika IV: Genghis Khan, 54
Appanage, 149, 164
Aqatai, 215
Arabian Sea, 30
Aral Sea, 97
Archduchy of Austria, 156
Arghun, 73
Arghun Agha, 103
Arghun Aqa, 101
Arigh Khaiya, 218
Arikhgiya, 117, 215
Ariq Böke, 9–11
Armenia, 33
Armenian Kingdom of Cilicia, 7, 67, 82, 101, 103
Armenians in China, 123
Arranged marriage, 21
Arrow, 236
Arslang Tayji, 151
Arthur Purves Phayre, 212
Artillery, 101
Asia, 85
Asia Television, 53
Assassinated, 117
Assassins, 8, 102, 104, 123, 238

Assault, 120
Asud, 116
Ata al-Mulk Juvayni, 33, 97
Ata-Malik Juvayni, 32, 60, 65, 104, 108, 123
Ataqai, 218
Athinkhaya, 196, 208, 213
Atilla the Hun, 40
Attar of Nishapur, 50
Aung San Suu Kyi, 211
Austria, 155
Auxiliaries, 220
Ava Kingdom, 214, 263
Aybak, 9
Ayyubid, 69, 82
Ayyubid dynasty, 10, 67, 68
Azerbaijan, 6, 11, 12, 33, 71

Babur, 50, 184, 192
Bạch Đằng River, 220
Badakhshan, 4
Badr al-Din Lulu, 7, 10
Baekjeong, 112
Bael, 223
Bagan, 197
Baghdad, 9, 49, 50, 69, 70, 85, 101, 102
Bago, Burma, 206
Bahri Mamluks, 69
Baibars, 10, 68, 71
Baibars II, 68
Baidar, 157
Baijiu, 68
Baiju, 7, 9, 80, 101, 103
Bakhkar, 186
Balasaghun, 64
Balkh, 4, 34, 98
Ballista, 87, 238
Balochistan (region), 185
Baltic Sea, 99
Bamian, 98
Bamyan, 5
Banarsi Prasad Saksena, 193
Baoshan Prefecture, 202
Baoshan, Yunnan, 195, 199
Barding, 231
Bashkirs, 162
Batdorj-in Baasanjab, 53
Battering rams, 87
Battle at Blue Waters, 176
Battle of Ain Jalut, 10, 69, 99, 227
Battle of Amroha, 189
Battle of Ankara, 79
Battle of Bạch Đằng (1288), 215, 220
Battle of Baghdad (1258), 49, 69
Battle of Bunei, 132
Battle of Cheoin, 113
Battle of Hermannstadt, 259

Battle of Indus, 5, 99, 184
Battle of Kalka River, 34
Battle of Kili, 188
Battle of Kōan, 137
Battle of Köse Dağ, 7, 68, 79
Battle of Łagów, 173
Battle of Legnica, 7, 158, 160, 167, 235, 259
Battle of Mari, 73
Battle of Marj al-Saffar (1303), 12, 76
Battle of Mohi, 7, 158, 160, 163, 167, 230, 234, 243
Battle of Parwan, 4, 99
Battle of Qatwan, 64
Battle of Samara Bend, 34, 227
Battle of Stary Sącz, 174
Battle of the Kalka River, 5
Battle of the Salween River, 153
Battle of the Sit River, 6, 158
Battle of the Vorskla River, 176
Battle of Wadi al-Khazandar, 12, 74, 75, 227
Battle of Xiangyang, 11, 238
Battle of Yamen, 125
Battle of Yehuling, 3, 28
Battle of Zhongdu, 3
Batu Khan, 5–8, 35, 43, 50, 99, 157, 158
Baurchuk Art Tekin, 64
Bayan of the Baarin, 117
BBC, 60
Bedouin, 70
Behead, 86
Behter, 21
Beijing, 3, 29, 30, 86, 120, 129
Béla IV, 157, 165, 168, 180
Béla IV of Hungary, 160, 175
Belarus, 155
Belgutei, 21
Berke, 8, 10, 11, 71, 72, 157, 171
Berke–Hulagu war, 11
Berke Khan, 99
Berthold Schwarz, 168
Besiegers, 120
Bhamo, 204
Bhera, 184
Biligtü Khan, 115
Biligtü Khan Ayushiridara, 13
Biliton, 224
Bistriţa, 175
Black Sea, 33
Blacksmith, 20
Blackwell Publishing, 79
Blood brother, 22
Blue Horde, 43
Bodonchar Munkhag, 19
Bohemia, 162
Bohemond VI of Antioch, 68, 69
Boleslaus Děpoltic, 7

274

Bolghar, 6
Bonpo, 153
Boorchu, 21, 63, 84
Borjigin, 18–20, 60
Boroldai, 7, 10, 157
Börte, 1, 18, 21, 22, 56
Borts, 233
Boyars, 162
Braşov, 175
Brinal, 190
British Burma, 208
Buda, 164
Buddhism, 27, 113
Buddhist, 186, 190
Buddhists, 11
Bukhara, 4, 10, 32, 50, 93, 104, 202
Bulgar, 5
Bulgaria, 7
Bulgars, 5, 202
Buqa Temür, 9, 103
Buqa-Temür, 101
Bureau of Buddhist and Tibetan Affairs, 11, 150
Büri, 6
Burkhan Khaldun, 1, 2, 20, 39
Burma, 213
Burmese chronicles, 201, 202
Burmese language, 196
Burundai, 173
Buryats, 2
Bushido, 134
Bytom, 173
Byzantine Empire, 71, 80, 83
Byzantine-Mongol alliance, 71

Caffa, 11, 33, 176
Cairo, 69, 70
Caliph, 85
Cambridge University Press, 14
Camel train, 30, 86
Cangue, 21
Capital city, 197
Carpathian Mountains, 160, 164, 175
Carrion, 21
Caspian Sea, 30, 44, 96
Castle, 175
Catapult, 89, 122
Catapults, 65
Category:History of Tibet, 145
Category:History of Turkey, 81
Cathedral, 165
Catholicos, 108
Caucasus, 18, 19, 33, 71, 170
Cavalry, 40, 101, 236
Census, 48

Central Asia, 18, 63, 64, 84, 119, 183, 187, 196, 216
Central Committee, 46
Central Europe, 155
Chabi, 149
Chagaan, 117
Chagatai Khan, 2–5, 7, 10, 18, 22, 40, 43, 53, 63, 71, 84, 95, 187
Chagatai Khanate, 7, 10, 12, 43, 76, 183, 187, 190
Chahar Mongols, 151
Champa, 196, 215, 216, 219, 224
Chao (currency), 10
Charles Oman, 244
Charlton Heston, 52
Cheetah, 233
Chengdu, 9
Chernihiv, 6, 159
Chilaun, 21
Child marriage, 21
Chiliarchy, 114
China, 7–9, 29, 63, 116, 223
China proper, 117, 124
Chinese expedition to Tibet (1720), 153
Chinese historiography, 56
Chinese language, 55, 56
Chinese people, 101, 223
Chinggis Khaan International Airport, 46
Chinzei Bugyō, 130
Choe, 114
Choe Chung-heon, 115
Choe Woo, 111, 112
Choghtu Khong Tayiji, 151
Chogyal, 152
Chokutō, 140
Cholera, 124
Chormaqan, 5, 6, 80, 103, 185
Christianity, 27
Christians, 10
Christmas day, 164
Chungju, 112
Chungnyeol of Goryeo, 115, 131
Chương Dương, 220
Chupan, 77
Chupanid Dynasty, 12
Chu River, 64
Chuy Valley, 64
Cilician Armenia, 69
Circassians, 156
Circuit (administrative division), 199
Circumcision, 28
Citadel of Damascus, 76
Citation needed, 264
CITEREFAndrade2016, 247, 248
CITEREFAtwod2004, 248
CITEREFAtwood2004, 247–249

CITEREFBanarsi Prasad Saksena1992, 262
CITEREFBiran2005, 247
CITEREFKishori Saran Lal1950, 262
CITEREFMote2003, 247
CITEREFPeter Jackson2003, 262
CITEREFSinor1990, 247
CITEREFTwitchett1994, 247–249
CITEREFTwitchett2009, 248, 249
Civilian, 41
Civilization (series), 54
Cizre, 10, 11
Classical Chinese, 130
Climate, 261
Code (law), 40
Coloman of Galicia-Lodomeria, 157
Commander, 26
Commons:Category:Military of Mongolia, 245
Commons:Mongol invasions of Japan, 144
Composite bow, 235
Confederation, 21, 22
Conn Iggulden, 54, 244
Conquest dynasties, 117
Constantinople, 83
Coronation, 17
Counterattack, 42
Count of Jaffa, 251
County of Tripoli, 67
Crimea, 6, 33, 158
Croat, 166
Croatia, 165
Croatia in personal union with Hungary, 165
Croatia in the union with Hungary, 156
Croatia in union with Hungary, 7
Croatian nobility, 165
Crusader Kings 2, 54
Crusader states, 69
Cultural Revolution, 39
Cuman, 33
Cumania, 6
Cumans, 5, 156, 162, 170
Czarna Hańcza, 161
Czech lands, 155

Daidu, 11

Đại Việt, 8, 9, 196, 215, 216, 219

Dalai Lama, 152
Dala township, 204
Dali City, 8, 197
Dali Kingdom, 8, 116, 117, 121, 197, 216
Dalmatia, 160, 164, 165
Damascus, 50, 68, 69, 74, 102
Damxung Town, 149
Dangquka, 8
Daniel of Galicia, 5, 8, 10, 157

Danube, 7, 160, 164
Danylo of Halych, 171
Darqan, 147
Darughachi, 80, 108, 115, 164, 186, 218, 224
David Morgan (historian), 59, 107
David Nicolle, 108
David VI of Georgia, 101
Dazaifu, Fukuoka, 132
D-Day, 136
Deadliest Warrior: Legends, 54
Decapitation, 30
Deel (clothing), 229
Defeat in detail, 87
Dehong Dai and Jingpo Autonomous Prefecture, 195, 196, 199
Dehong Prefecture, 203
Delhi Sultanate, 183, 184, 186
Delüün Boldog, 1, 20
Denis Tomaj, 157
Deshun, 36
Despotate of Epirus, 80
Diaoyu Fortress, 9, 124
Died of wounds, 157
Digital object identifier, 79, 126
Diplomat, 121
Divasar, 190
Division of the Mongol Empire, 19, 222
Dmitry Glukhovsky, 54
DOhsson, 226
Dokuz Khatun, 108, 250
Dominican Order, 162
Douglas Adams, 54
Drigung Monastery, 147
Drikung Kagyu, 11
Drogon Chogyal Phagpa, 146
Drogön Chögyal Phagpa, 8, 10, 12, 149
Dschinghis Khan, 54
Dschinghis Khan (song), 54
Duan Xingzhi, 8, 117
Duchy of Greater Poland, 156
Duchy of Opole, 156
Duchy of Sieradz, 174
Duchy of Silesia, 161
Duke of Masovia, 156
Duke of Silesia, 156, 160
Duwa, 187, 189
Dynasty, 18
Dysentery, 124
Dysentry, 9
Dzungaria, 146
Dzungarian Gate, 92
Dzungar Khanate, 152
Dzungars, 151, 152

Early East Slavs, 157
Early modern warfare, 128

East Asia, 140
Eastern Europe, 155, 216
Egypt, 50, 69
Ejin Horo Banner, 39
Electorate of Saxony, 162
Elege of the Jalayir, 10
Emir, 13
Emperor Aizong of Jin, 6, 117, 121
Emperor Bing of Song, 117, 125
Emperor Duanzong, 117
Emperor Duzong, 117
Emperor Frederick II, 172
Emperor Gong of Song, 117, 125
Emperor Huanzong of Western Xia, 117
Emperor Kameyama, 128
Emperor Lizong, 117
Emperor Mo of Jin, 6, 117
Emperor Mozhu of Western Xia, 5, 117
Emperor of China, 124
Emperor of Japan, 130
Emperor Xiangzong of Western Xia, 3, 4
Emperor Xianzong of Western Xia, 117
Emperor Xuanzong of Jin, 30, 117, 121
Empire of Nicaea, 80, 83
Empire of Trebizond, 80, 82, 176
Empress Gi, 115
Endemic warfare, 21, 47
English, 19, 249
Era of Fragmentation, 145
Ertuğrul, 79
Erzurum, 81
Esztergom, 165
Ethnicity, 41
Euphrates, 10, 73
Euphrosyne Palaiologina (daughter of Michael VIII), 174
Eurasia, 9, 13, 18, 19, 216
Eurasian Steppe, 26
Europe, 12, 19, 155
Europeans in Medieval China, 169
Eurovision Song Contest 1979, 54
Ezhou, 9

Fall of Ruad, 75
Fall of Tripoli (1289), 72
Fanji, 215
Federation of American Societies for Experimental Biology, 253
Feigned retreat, 243, 244
Fengxiang County, 5
Fergana, 4
Ferghana Valley, 92
File:Genghis Khan empire-en.svg, 177
Fire Arrow, 165
Fire lance, 6, 124
First Battle of Homs, 10, 70

First Mongol invasion of Burma, **195**, 213
Flamethrower, 124
F. L. Lucas, 53
Fortresses, 164
Fourth Crusade, 80
Fragmented Poland, 157, 160
Franco-Mongol alliance, 71
Franks, 82
Frederick II, Duke of Austria, 157, 162, 166
Friar Julian, 162
Fujian, 125, 132, 216, 223
Fujisawa, Kanagawa, 136
Fukuda Kaneshige, 128
Fukuoka, Fukuoka, 131
Fülek, 165

Gaesong, 112
Galdan Boshugtu Khan, 152
Galdan Tseren, 152
Galich, Russia, 159
Galician–Volhynian Chronicle, 38
Gallop, 236
Ganden Phodrang, 145
Gandhara, 210
Gangetic plains, 189
Ganghwa Island, 112–114
Gansu, 8, 9, 36
Gansu Corridor, 5
Ganzhou, 35
Gaochang, 64
Gaza City, 10, 69, 74
Gelug, 151
Genghis Khan, 1–5, **17**, 63, 64, 71, 84, 85, 102, 117, 145, 146, 158, 184, 192, 193
Genghis Khan (1950 film), 52
Genghis Khan (1965 film), 52
Genghis Khan (1992 film), 52
Genghis Khan (2004 TV series), 53
Genghis Khan and the Making of the Modern World, 264
Genghis Khan - A Proud Son Of Heaven (1998 film), 52
Genghis Khan (ATV TV series), 53
Genghis Khan Mausoleum, 39
Genghis Khan: To the Ends of the Earth and Sea, 52
Genghis Khan (TVB TV series), 53
Genko Borui, 131
Genoa, 11
Genocide, 19, 49
Geographic coordinate system, 109
George Bailey Sansom, 143
George Coedès, 211
George I of Bulgaria, 174
George V the Brilliant, 176
Georgia (country), 6, 33, 71

Ghazan, 68, 72, 75, 77
Ghazan Khan, 76
Ghazni, 185
Ghiyas-ud-din Baraq, 11, 12
Ghiyath al-Din Tughluq, 184
Ghor, 185
Ghori, 185
Ghōr Province, 183
Ghurid Dynasty, 183
Gibelet, 76
Gilgamesh, 40
Giovanni da Pian del Carpine, 169
Giovanni de Plano Carpini, 50
Giyath al-Din Kaykhusraw II, 80
God, 169
Godan Khan, 145, 147
Gojong of Goryeo, 112–114
Gokenin, 129
Golden Bull of 1242, 165
Golden Horde, 10, 11, 35, 43, 67, 71, 99, 155, 156, 158, 164, 172–174, 177–180
Gongmin of Goryeo, 115
Goryeo, 4–6, 8, 9, 111–113, 127–129
Goryeosa, 131, 144, 255, 256
Go-Toba, 132
Government Palace (Mongolia), 47
Gradec, Zagreb, 165
Graham Chapman, 54
Greater Khorasan, 11, 37, 65, 98, 190
Greater Persia, 101
Great Hungarian Plain, 164, 234
Great Khan, 17, 43, 124, 185, 217
Great Seljuq Empire, 64, 71
Great Wall, 120
Guangdong, 125
Guangzhou, 218
Guerrilla warfare, 168, 218
Gunpowder, 65, 87, 122, 159, 168
Gunpowder warfare, 237
Guo Kan, 101, 103, 108, 117, 122, 237
Guozijian, 11
Gurkhan, 64
Güshi Khan, 151
Guy of Ibelin (died 1304), 76
Guyuan, 119
Güyük Khan, 6, 7, 82, 103, 113, 117, 147, 157, 158, 160, 171
Gwangju, Gyeonggi, 113
Gyeonggi, 112
Gyeongsang, 113
Győr, 165

Hachiun, 21
Hainan, 220
Hakata Bay, 132
Hakata-ku, Fukuoka, 131, 135, 136

Hakozaki Shrine, 135
Halal, 27
Halberd, 231
Halych, 7, 33
Han Chinese, 116, 124, 128, 197, 210, 237
Hanlin, Burma, 197, 206
Hanthawaddy Kingdom, 263
Hao Jing, 10
Harold Lamb, 58, 193
Hasar, 21
Hassan Qarlugh, 185
Hazara people, 49
Heavy cavalry, 84
Hebei, 3
Hechuan, 124
Helan Mountains, 36, 119
Henan, 5, 6, 8
Henry II of Silesia, 161
Henry II the Pious, 7, 157, 160, 235
Henry Yule, 212
Herat, 4, 98, 186
Hethum I, King of Armenia, 68, 69, 82, 101
Hida Nagamoto, 128
Hidzume Castle, 134
High Duke of Poland, 157
Hindukush, 98
Hindu Kush, 4
Hirato Island, 138
Historical money of Tibet, 145
History of Burma, 197
History of European exploration in Tibet, 145
History of Japan, 128
History of Tibet, 145
History of Tibet (1950–present), 145
History of Turkey, 81
History of Tuva, 64
History of Yuan, 131, 223, 255, 264
History (U.S. TV channel), 58
Hmannan Yazawin, 212
Hmong people, 220
Hoelun, 1, 18, 20
Hohhot, 48
Hōjō clan, 127, 129
Hōjō Tokimune, 128, 130
Holdon, 128
Holy Land, 171
Homs, 73
Hong Bok-won, 112, 113
Hong Dagu, 135, 137
Hongirat, 115
Horse archer, 231
Hotula Khan, 19, 60
House of Wisdom, 102, 106
Htin Aung, 211
Huainan, 9
Huguang, 223

Hulagu, 50, 71, 79, 103, 106, 149
Hulagu Khan, 7–11, 49, 101, 102, 122, 171, 184, 186
Hulegu Khan, 86, 89
Hulunbuir, 56
Human uses of horns, 235
Hunan, 220
Hungary, 162, 230
Huochong, 65, 89
Husashi Sashi, 134

Ian Frazier, 109
Iberian Peninsula, 102
Ibn al-Athir, 34
Ibn Battuta, 190
Iekiyo Ryuzoji, 138
Igor de Rachewiltz, 59
Iki Island, 132
Ilkhan, 190
Ilkhanate, 9, 12, 67, 71, 79, 101–103, 149, 169, 183, 190
Il-Khanate, 71
Il-Khanid, 238
IMDb, 60
Imperial Ancestral Temple, 11
Imperial Court in Kyoto, 127
Imperial examination, 150
Imperial Preceptor, 10
Im Yeon, 12
Inalchuq, 4, 30, 63, 84, 86, 93
In antiquity, 124
Indian subcontinent, 85, 183, 184
Individual battles and sieges, 33, 97
Indonesia, 222, 225
Indravarman V, 218
Indus, 31
Indus River, 5
Indus valley, 186
Infantry, 101
Inner Mongolia, 3, 39, 48, 55
In Our Time (radio series), 60
Institute of Muslim Astronomy, 12
Intelligence (information gathering), 26
International Standard Book Number, 13–16, 57–59, 78, 79, 100, 108, 126, 143, 154, 180, 181, 193, 211, 212, 215, 221, 222, 225, 226, 244
International Standard Serial Number, 79
Internet Archive, 58, 59
Invasion of Ryukyu, 140
Inventions in medieval Islam, 120
Investment (military), 102
Iran, 33, 35, 43, 49, 63, 84, 102, 185
Iranian peoples, 50
Iraq, 70, 101, 124
Irbil, 103

Isamu Sashi, 134
Ishiji Jirō, 128
Ishiji Kane, 128
Islam, 27, 77, 190
Islamic Caliphate, 102
Islamic Golden Age, 102
Ismaili, 103, 104
Issyk-Kul, 2
Italian people, 164
Ivailo, 174
Ivan Asen II, 157, 167

Jack Weatherford, 55, 170
Jacques de Molay, 68
Jadaran, 22, 57
Jalairs, 218
Jalairtai, 111, 114
Jalal ad-Din Mingburnu, 4, 5, 31, 63, 84, 184
Jalaluddin Khalji, 187
Jalayirids, 13
Jami al-tawarikh, 25, 26, 36, 49, 59, 118, 231, 236
Jamukha, 1, 2, 22, 23, 25, 56, 57
Janibeg, 176
Jani Beg, 12
Jan Matejko, 160
Japan, 85, 127, 130
Japanese archipelago, 128
Japanese invasions of Korea (1592–98), 140
Java, 222
Jaya Indravarman VI, 215
Jayakatwang, 222, 223
Jean II de Giblet, 76
Jebe, 3–5, 30–33, 42, 63, 64, 84, 92, 117, 157
Jeju Island, 115
Jelme, 21, 25, 63, 84
Jeolla, 113
Jews, 28
Jiangxi, 223
Jia Sidao, 117
Ji Gwang-su, 112
Jin dynasty (1115-1234), 22, 86
Jin dynasty (1115-1234), 2–4, 6, 19, 23, 24, 28, 35, 48, 57, 64, 116–118, 121, 146
Jin dynasty (265–420), 2
Jing River, 5
Jingzhao, 8
Jinsha River, 8
Jochi, 2–5, 18, 22, 25, 26, 31, 40, 43, 56, 63, 64, 71, 84, 92, 158, 159
John Andrew Boyle, 193
John III Doukas Vatatzes, 83
John Keegan, 170, 264
John Man (author), 57
John of Montecorvino, 123
John Wayne, 52

Jōkyū War, 130
Jōryū-Ji, 136
Joseph Needham, 15
JRAS, 78
JSTOR, 79, 126, 212
Junk (ship), 224
Jurchen people, 19, 22, 28, 116
Jurchens, 238
Jurchen script, 24
Juyong Pass, 3

Kabul, 192
Kadampa, 147
Kadan, 6, 7, 157–159, 165, 180
Kaegyong, 114
Kaesong, 112, 113
Kaidu, 12, 187
Kaidu–Kublai war, 12
Kaifeng, 6, 30, 119, 121
Kakatiya, 189
Kamakura, Kanagawa, 136
Kamakura shogunate, 127, 129
Kamikaze (typhoon), 129, 137
Kangxi Emperor, 152, 153
Kara-Khitan, 85
Karakorum, 6, 10, 13, 42, 43, 82, 103, 149, 168, 169, 186
Karamanid, 67
Karamanoğlu Mehmet Bey, 68
Karluks, 3, 64
Karma Kagyu, 149, 151
Karmapa, 149
Karma Pakshi, 2nd Karmapa Lama, 149
Kashgar, 3, 30
Kashmir, 183, 186
Kasur, 188
Katana, 133
Kaykhusraw II, 7
Kayseri, 82
Kazakhstan, 45
Kazakhstani tenge, 45
Kediri Kingdom, 222, 223
Kenchō Suematsu, 48
Keraites, 1, 2, 19, 22, 23, 25, 57
Kerman, 183
Kertanagara, 223
Kertanegara, 222
Khabul Khan, 19
Khagan, 17, 18, 27, 37, 41, 60, 102, 129, 148
Khalji dynasty, 187
Khalka Mongols, 151
Khamag Mongol, 19, 20, 22, 24, 60
Khanate, 19, 30, 43, 189
Khanbaliq, 129
Khan (title), 17, 22, 25, 27, 30, 41, 43
Kharakhorum, 43

Khara-Khoto, 5, 117, 119
Khentii Mountains, 1, 7, 18, 56
Khentii Province, 39
Khereid, 117
Kherlen River, 5, 7, 20
Kheshig, 2, 11, 229
Khitan people, 41, 53, 111, 116
Khitans, 3, 64
Khmer Empire, 196, 197
Khochu, 117
Khokhar, 183, 185
Khongirad, 1, 20, 21
Khoshut, 151
Khoshut Khanate, 146, 151, 152
Khulan (wife of Genghis Khan), 18
Khumar Tegin, 96
Khums, 188
Khuzestan, 49
Khuzistan, 108
Khwarazmian dynasty, 5, 30, 63, 84, 119, 183, 202, 204
Khwarazm-Shah, 103
Khwārazm-Shāh dynasty, 185
Khwarezm, 31
Khwarezmia, 30
Khwarezmian Dynasty, 86
Khwarezmian Empire, 31
Khwarezmid Empire, 37, 57, 65, 85
Khwarezm-Shah, 104
Khwārezm-Shah, 64
Khwarizmian Empire, 64
Kiev, 7, 49, 50, 161
Kievan Rus, 33, 42, 99, 155–157
Kikuchi clan, 127
Kikuchi Takefusa, 128
Kikuchi Yōsai, 133
Killed in action, 68, 111, 117, 157, 196
Kim Bang-gyeong, 128
Kim Chwi-ryeo, 111
Kim Yun-hu, 111, 113
Kingdom of Armenia (Middle Ages), 80
Kingdom of Bohemia, 156
Kingdom of Croatia (925–1102), 155
Kingdom of Croatia (medieval), 165
Kingdom of Dali, 35
Kingdom of Galicia–Volhynia, 156
Kingdom of Georgia, 67, 69, 71, 80, 101, 103
Kingdom of Hungary, 7, 155, 156, 158, 164
Kingdom of Poland (1025–1385), 155, 156
Kingdom of Qocho, 123
King of Kings, 17
Kipchack, 72
Kipchak Khanate, 43, 171
Kipchak people, 33
Kipchaks, 3, 202, 220
Kirman, 185

Kishtwar, 190
Kitbuqa, 10, 68, 69, 101, 104
Klis Fortress, 165, 166
Kłodzko, 162
Knight, 231
Knights of St. John, 168
Knights Templar, 7, 67, 156, 167
Koke Ilge, 101
Kokochu, 23
Komárom, 165
Komoda Beach, 134
Konbaung Dynasty, 214
Köneürgenç, 49
Konya, 82
Konya-Urgench, 33, 96
Konye-Urgench, 37
Korea, 19, 50, 111–113, 127, 128, 135
Korean peninsula, 111–113, 115, 130
Koreans, 128, 130
Korea under Yuan rule, 111
Korechika Togo, 138
Koretoo Togo, 138
Kosher, 28
Köten, 5, 157
Kotony, 163
Kozelsk, 6, 158
Kraków, 173
K. S. Lal, 193
Kuban steppe, 5
Kublai, 74, 121
Kublai Khan, 3, 7–12, 43, 48, 56, 63, 71, 84, 108, 115, 117, 128, 140, 146, 150, 196, 200, 215–217, 219, 220, 222
Kublai Khans Campaigns, 127, 195, 222
Kuchlug, 3, 4, 30, 63
Küchlüg, 64
Kumara Kassapa, 213, 214
Kumbum Monastery, 39
Kunya Urgench, 94
Kuomintang, 39
Kurd, 5
Kuriltai, 160
Kurultai, 2, 5, 7, 10, 17, 25, 27, 57
Kusong, 112
Kutluqshah, 68
Kyaukpyu District, 199
Kyawswa of Pagan, 197, 208
Kyoto, 129, 130
Kypchak, 158
Kyrgyz people, 2
Kyūshū, 127
Kyzyl Kum, 93

Ladislaus IV of Hungary, 168, 175
Lahore, 184, 186
Lake Baikal, 54

Lake Balkhash, 30
Lamellar armor, 231
Laminate, 235
Lancer, 84
Lancers, 231
Langzhong, 8
Latin Empire, 80, 83
Léka, 165
Le Livre des Merveilles, 73
Lesser Armenia, 82
Leszek II the Black, 173
Levant, 67
Lev Gumilev, 69
Lha-bzang Khan, 152
Lhasa, 153, 258
Liangzhou District, 119
Li Anquan, 117, 118
Liaodong, 114
Liao dynasty, 23, 30, 64
Liaoning, 3
Liaoyang, 3
Ligdan Khan, 151
Lincang, 199
Lingua franca, 130
Lingwu, 5, 36, 119
Lintiao, 36
List of medieval Mongolian tribes and clans, 20
List of rulers of Prome, 207
List of rulers of Tibet, 145
Lithuania, 10, 176
Liu Heima, 117, 121
Liupanshan, 36
Lizhou District, 8, 9
Lobsang Gyatso, 5th Dalai Lama, 151
Lobzang Danjin, 153
Looting, 22, 121
Loupsang Danzan, 152
Lozang Gyatso, 5th Dalai Lama, 152
Luan River, 8
Lublin, 161, 173
Luciano Petech, 147, 258
Luc Kwanten, 258
Lurs, 104

Macrohistory, 128
Madura, 223
Maha Sithu of Twinthin, 212
Maha Yazawin, 211
Mahmud Ghazan, 74
Mainland Southeast Asia, 196, 197
Majapahit, 222, 223, 225
Malay Peninsula, 224
Malik, 186
Malik Kafur, 184, 189
Malik Salih, 10
Mamluk, 49, 69, 71, 102, 171, 234

Mamluks, 10, 11
Mamluk Sultanate (Cairo), 67, 68, 85
Manchu, 28
Manchuria, 3, 216
Mandate of Heaven, 129
Mangonel, 98
Manuel Conde, 52
Maragha, 71
Marco Polo, 38, 107, 197, 212
Mardin, 10, 115
Margrave, 157
Margraviate of Moravia, 156
Maria Laskarina, 166
Mar Makikha, 108
Marmot, 21
Martin Stuart-Fox, 212
Mashad, 98
Materiel, 42
Matsura Clan, 127, 138
Matthias Rátót, 157
Mausoleum of Genghis Khan, 39, 52
Ma Yong, 117
Mazandaran, 11
Mazovia, 173
Measuring against the linchpin, 27
Media:GenghisKhan01.ogg, 19
Media:Temujin.ogg, 249
Medieval Crusades, 103
Medieval Hungary, 155
Melayu Kingdom, 223
Melee, 167
Mengu-Timur, 11
Meritocracy, 19, 23, 41, 45
Merkit, 1, 2, 22, 24, 26, 27, 56
Merkits, 2
Merv, 4, 50, 98, 202
Mesopotamia, 102, 107, 108
Metal, 235
Metro 2033 (novel), 54
Michael Prawdin, 164, 252, 260
Michael VIII Palaeologus, 174
Michal Biran, 14
Michiyasu Shiraisi, 135
Michiyasu Shiroishi, 128
Micromanagement, 230
Middle Ages, 244
Middle east, 8, 187
Middle Mongol language, 249
Mieszko II the Fat, 7, 157
Military, 128, 222
Military alliance, 21
Military dictatorship, 115
Military history of China (pre-1911), 27
Military intelligence, 43
Military strategy, 26
Military tactics, 42

Minamoto no Yoriie, 129
Minamoto no Yoshitsune, 48
Mingburnu, 96
Mingghan, 228
Minhaj-i-Siraj, 85, 88
Mitsui Yasunaga, 128
Moko Shurai Ekotoba, 144
Moldavia, 164, 176
Mongke Khan, 168
Möngke Khan, 6–10, 69, 83, 102, 103, 111,
    113, 117, 121, 148, 157, 158, 171, 184,
    186, 215, 216
Mongol, 2, 6, 8, 9, 11, 41, 43, 64, 84, 128, 223,
    233, 234, 239
Mongol Armenia, 6
Mongol Army, 196
Mongol bow, 170, 231
Mongol conquest, 80
Mongol conquest of China, **116**
Mongol conquest of Khwarezmia, 4, 5, **84**
Mongol conquest of the Jin dynasty, 3–6, 18,
    85
Mongol conquest of the Qara Khitai, 3, 4, 18
Mongol conquest of the Song dynasty, 8–11,
    199
Mongol conquest of Western Xia, 2–5, 18
Mongol conquests, 63, 116, 183, 184, 213
Mongol Empire, 1–8, 10, 12, 13, 17–19, 40,
    60, 63, 65, 67, 68, 80, 83–85, 101–103,
    111, 112, 116, 117, 127, 129, 145, 146,
    148, 149, 155–157, 183, 184, 187, 196,
    199, 215–217, 219, 222, 227, 235
Mongol (film), 53
Mongol–Jin War, 118
Mongolia, 4, 5, 7–9, 13, 17, 19, 20, 39, 43, 47,
    48, 64, 80, 83, 146, 216
Mongolian, 19, 249
Mongolian calendar, 47
Mongolian cuisine, 233
Mongolian culture, 45
Mongolian Cyrillic alphabet, 18
Mongolian horse, 229, 231
Mongolian language, 19, 55, 115, 249
Mongolian nobility, 23
Mongolian Peoples Party, 46
Mongolian Peoples Republic, 46
Mongolian script, 47
Mongolian tögrög, 46, 51
Mongol invasion, 168
Mongol invasion (1206–1258), 107
Mongol invasion of Anatolia, 170
Mongol invasion of Central Asia, **63**, 71, 84,
    183
Mongol invasion of East Asia (disambiguation),
    127
Mongol invasion of Europe, 7, 34, 85, **155**

Mongol invasion of Hungary, 51
Mongol invasion of India, 1297-98, 188
Mongol invasion of India, 1303, 189
Mongol invasion of India, 1306, 189
Mongol invasion of Japan, 239
Mongol invasion of Java, **222**
Mongol invasion of Khwarezmia, 18
Mongol invasion of Khwarezmia and Eastern Iran, 119, 238
Mongol invasion of Rus, 6, 230
Mongol invasion of Sindh, 188
Mongol invasion of Vietnam, 227
Mongol invasion of Volga Bulgaria, 5, 6
Mongol invasions, 18, 101, 222
Mongol invasions and conquests, 18, 155, 195, 215
Mongol invasions of Anatolia, **79**
Mongol invasions of Dzurdzuketia, 168
Mongol invasions of Georgia, 6
Mongol invasions of India, **183**
Mongol invasions of Japan, **127**, 218
Mongol invasions of Korea, 6, 8, 9, **111**, 129
Mongol invasions of the Levant, **67**, 234
Mongol invasions of Tibet, 7, 8, 12, **145**
Mongol invasions of Vietnam, 8, 9, 126, 140, **215**
Mongol method of eating, 28
Mongol military tactics and organization, **227**, 252
Mongols, 1–4, 6, 9, 10, 17, 19, 23, 27, 41, 64, 86, 111, 120, 129, 153, 196, 216, 222
Mongol script, 18
Mongol siege of Kaifeng, 6, 30, 121
Moravia, 160–162
Morganatic marriage, 22
Mosonmagyaróvár, 165
Mosul, 7, 10, 11, 70
Motivation, 26
Mottama, 199, 204
Mounted archery, 84, 237
Mstislav III of Kiev, 5, 33, 34, 157
Mstislav II Svyatoslavich, 5, 157
Mstislav Mstislavich, 5, 157
Mstislav the Bold, 33
Mubarak Shah (Chagatai Khan), 7, 10, 11
Mugaku Sogen, 133
Mugan plain, 81
Mughal emperors, 50
Mughal Empire, 50, 184, 192
Muhammad, 102
Muhammad bin Tughluq, 184, 190
Muhammad II of Khwarezm, 4, 30, 63, 65, 84, 85, 102
Muhammad Khan (Ilkhan), 41
Mulay, 76
Multan, 184

Muqali, 3–5, 33, 42, 89, 117
Muslim, 4, 8, 19, 27, 50, 124
Mutiny near Jalore, 188
Mutukan, 5
Myinsaing, 214
Myinsaing Kingdom, 209, 213, 214

Nagahisa Shimazu, 138
Naimans, 2, 22, 24–27, 30, 57, 64
Name and title, 27
Nanzhao, 197
Naphtha, 98
Nara, Nara, 130
Narathihapate, 196, 200, 213
Nasr al-Din (Yunnan), 196, 204, 215, 220
National Geographic (magazine), 60, 253
National League for Democracy, 211
National Palace Museum, 17, 51
Navy, 220
Negübei, 12
Negudar, 187
Negüderi, 188
Neo-Confucian, 150
Neolithic Tibet, 145
Nestorian Christian, 108
Nestorian Christianity, 41
Ngô Quyền, 220
Niccolò and Maffeo Polo, 8, 11, 12
Nikolay Kradin, 58
Ninth Crusade, 70
Nishapur, 4, 50, 98, 202
Nivkh people, 129
Nizari, 102
Nogai Khan, 173, 174
Nomad, 20, 21, 85
Nomadic tribe, 18
Nomukhan, 11
No Right to Die - Chinggis Khaan, 53
North China, 4, 10, 216
Northeast Asia, 18
Northern Yuan dynasty, 1, 13
Novgorod, 50
Novgorod Republic, 156
Novhorod-Siverskyi, 5
Noyan, 188
Noyans, 230
Nusrat Khan Jalesari, 188
Nyingmapa, 153
Nyitra, 165

OCLC, 143, 193

Ögedei, 3, 4, 31, 71, 147, 158
Ögedei Khan, 3–7, 12, 17–19, 22, 33, 40, 43, 44, 63, 71, 80, 84, 95, 103, 111, 112, 117, 148, 167, 169, 184, 185

Oghul Qaimish, 7
Oirats, 2, 38, 115, 146, 151
Old Delhi, 184
Old Uyghur alphabet, 19

Öljaitü, 77

Oljeitu, 68
Olkhunut, 20
Olomouc, 162
Omar Sharif, 52
Onggirat, 22
Ong Khan, 117
Ongud, 2
Onon River, 17, 20, 39
Opus Majus, 168
Orda Khan, 6, 7, 43, 157
Ordos (city), 55
Ordos Loop, 118
Orghana, 7
Orok people, 129
Osman I, 79

Ōtomo clan, 127
Ōtomo Yoriyasu, 128

Otrar, 4, 30, 31, 85, 86
Ottoman Empire, 79
Oxford University Press, 143
Oxus, 32

Pagan Kingdom, 195–197
Pakistan, 184
Pakosław of Sandomierz, 157
Pak Seo, 111
Palaiologos, 83
Palaung people, 199
Pa Laung Self-Administered Zone, 263
Palestine (region), 10, 69
Pamalayu, 223
Pannonhalma, 165
Pannonia, 164, 165
Pannonian plain, 162
Parwan, 99
Pathein, 204
Pat Morita, 52
Patricia Buckley Ebrey, 14
Patron and priest relationship, 146, 150
Pax Mongolica, 41
Pereiaslav-Khmelnytskyi, 6, 159
Persia, 80, 104, 234
Persian Gulf, 30
Persian people, 50, 196
Peshawar, 183, 185
Pest, Hungary, 175
Peter Jackson (historian), 193

Phagmodrupa Dynasty, 145, 149
Phags-pa script, 12
Physician, 122
Piers Anthony, 54
Pincer movement, 31, 219
Pinya Kingdom, 214
Pinyin, 18, 55, 56, 249
Podhale, 174
Podolínec, 174
Poland, 10, 155
Poles, 159, 161
Pope Alexander IV, 173
Population decline, 48
Portal:Tibet, 145
Portal:Turkey, 81
Pozsony, 165
Pre-Imperial Tibet, 145
Prince Godan, 258
Principality of Antioch, 67, 101, 103
Principality of Chernigov, 156
Principality of Kiev, 156, 176
Principality of Ryazan, 156
Prisoner of war, 63, 157
Protecrate, 70
Protectorate, 218
Pskov, 50
Psychological warfare, 240
Pucha Guannu, 117
Punitive expedition, 222
Punjab, 183, 184
Punjab region, 184, 188
Puxian Wannu, 117
Pyay, 204
Pyongan Province, 111

Qaghan, 83
Qalawun, 68
Qara Hülegü, 7
Qara Khitai, 3, 4, 23, 25, 30, 64
Qara Khitai Khanate, 63, 64
Qaraunas, 183, 184, 190
Qasar, 3, 21, 26, 63, 84
Qianlong Emperor, 152
Qing, 146
Qing Dynasty, 152, 153, 237
Qinghai, 152
Qinghai Lake, 151
Qingshui County, 36
Qiu Chuji, 27, 49
Qocho, 2
Quanzhou, 132, 224
Quran, 190
Qutlugh Khwaja, 184, 188
Qutuz, 10, 68

Rab, 165

Race (classification of human beings), 41
Raden Wijaya, 222, 223
Raid (military), 21
Rashid Al-Din, 169
Rashid-al-Din Hamadani, 50, 59, 60, 118, 231
Ravi River, 189
Razadarit, 263
Reconnaissance, 147
Red Guards (Peoples Republic of China), 39
Reghin, 175
Reinforcements, 128
Religious tolerance, 19, 27, 41
René Grousset, 69, 193
Republic of Genoa, 33
Reting Monastery, 7, 147
Reuven Amitai, 78
Richardson, Hugh E, 258
Richard Tyson, 52
Riding and archery, 237
Righteous army, 113
Rinpungpa, 145
River March, 167
Robert Greene (American author), 253
Roger Bacon, 168
Rogerius of Apulia, 164
Rokuhara Tandai, 128
Roman Catholicism in China, 123
Royal Burmese armed forces, 196
Royal Historical Commission of Burma, 212
Rûm, 71
Runan County, 6
Rus people, 159
Russia, 155
Russian languages, 55
Ruthenia, 43
Ryazan, 6, 158
Ryuzoji Clan, 138

Sack of Sandomierz (1260), 10
Safavid dynasty, 252
Saint Margaret of Hungary, 166
Sajó, 164
Sajo River, 160, 165
Sakhalin, 129
Sakya, 8, 145, 147, 150
Sakya Pandita, 145, 147
Salt Range, 183, 185
Samarkand, 4, 31, 32, 49, 184, 202
Sambyeolcho Rebellion, 12, 115
Samgar, 68
Samurai, 127, 136
Sandomierz, 10, 173
Saqsin, 5, 6

Śarīra, 200

Saritai, 111
Sarpay Beikman, 212
Sartaq, 112
Sartaq Khan, 8
Sashi clan, 127, 134
Sashi Husashi, 128
Sashi Isamu, 128
Sashi Nao, 128
Sashi Tōdō, 128
Sawara District, 134
Sawhnit, 214
Sayyid Ajjal Shams al-Din Omar, 201
Scholar, 122
Scimitar, 231, 237
Scorched earth, 219, 234
Scriptures, 113
Sea of Japan, 44
Second Battle of Homs, 73, 74
Second Bulgarian Empire, 156
Second Mongol invasion of Burma, 197, 209, 213
Second Mongol invasion of Hungary, 168
Second Mongol invasion of Poland, 10
Secret History of the Mongols, 55
Sehwan Sharif, 188
Semirechye, 64
Sempad the Constable, 82
Senggum, 24
Seniorate Province, 156
Seppuku, 132
Sergei Bodrov, 53
Setoura beach, 138
Shaanxi, 5
Shah, 30, 32, 85, 87
Sham al-Din Muhammad Kart, 186
Shaman, 26
Shamanism, 23
Shamanism in Mongolia, 149
Shamanist, 171
Shams al-Din Juvayni, 11
Shandong, 5, 10, 11
Shangdu, 10
Shan State, 199
Shan states, 195
Shanxi, 3, 8
Shiban, 157
Shi Chu, 11
Shikhikhutug, 4
Shikken, 129, 130
Shimazu clan, 127
Shimo Mingan, 28
Shin Ditha Pamauk, 207
Shi Tianze, 11, 117, 121
Shivalik Hills, 189
Shogun, 129
Shogunate, 135

Shōni clan, 127
Shōni Kageyasu, 128
Shōni Sukeyoshi, 128
Shōni Tsuneyasu, 128
Shouxian, 6
Shugodai, 134
Sibiu, 259
Sichuan, 8, 11, 121, 146
Siege, 36
Siege engine, 84, 237
Siege of Baghdad (1258), 9, 99, **101**, 122, 242
Siege of Bamyan (1221), 5
Siege of Caizhou, 6, 30, 121
Siege of Chittorgarh (1303), 189
Siege of Diaoyu Castle, 9
Siege of Esztergom (1241), 164
Siege of Kiev (1240), 7, 159
Siege of Kozelsk, 6
Siege of Kuju, 112
Siege of Ryazan, 6
Siege warfare, 26, 42, 87
Sieradz, 173
Silesia, 161
Silistra, 174
Silk, 235
Silk Road, 19, 30, 45, 86
Silvan, Diyarbakır, 10
Silver, 10
Simplified Chinese characters, 18, 56
Sindh, 102, 183, 185, 188
Singhasari, 222
Single combat, 132, 140
Sinuiju, 8
Siri Fort, 189
Sivas, 82
Slavery, 28
Slavs, 34
Small kingdoms, 196
Smolensk, 12
Sō clan, 127, 132
Sodu, 215
Sogetu, 218
Sohara, 134
Soil salination, 107
Song dynasty, 6, 8–11, 18, 35, 44, 108, 119, 149, 196, 197, 216
Son of Heaven, 10
Sopron, 165
Sorghaghtani Beki, 3
Sorkin-shara, 63, 84
Sō Sukekuni, 128
South China, 216
Southeast Asia, 85
Southern Song, 117, 137
Southern Song dynasty, 116
Southwest Asia, 19, 216

Sovereign, 79
Split, Croatia, 166
Srinagar, 186
Stalinist repressions in Mongolia, 50
Stary Sącz, 174
Stefan Uroš II Milutin of Serbia, 175
Stephen G. Haw, 263
Stephen R. Turnbull, 143
Steven Runciman, 79
Stirrup, 232
Subutai, 3–8, 25, 26, 32–34, 42, 63, 84, 95, 117, 119, 122, 157, 158, 217, 229, 240, 243
Successor state, 80
Sudak, 5
Suenaga Takesaki, 138
Suenaga Takezaki, 135
Suicide, 117
Sukekado Hujiwara, 138
Sukekuni So, 134
Sukhothai Kingdom, 213
Sulaiman Shah, 68, 101
Sulisław of Cracow, 7, 157
Sultanate of Rum, 67
Sultanate of Rûm, 80
Sultan of Delhi, 191
Sumatra, 223, 224
Sunitai, 101, 103
Supremacism, 118
Susan Hayward, 52
Suzdal, 6
Suzdalia, 158
Svat Soucek, 107
Syr Darya, 4
Syria, 10, 234
Syria (region), 68
Székely, 175
Székesfehérvár, 165

Tabriz, 12
Tachi, 133
Tagaung, 214
Tagaung, Mandalay, 195, 196, 206
Taghachar, 9
Taglung Monastery, 147
Taipei, 17
Tai peoples, 196, 210
Taira clan, 127
Taira no Kagetaka, 128, 134
Taiwan, 17
Tajik people, 64
Takagi Clan, 138
Takehusa Kikuchi, 134
Takezaki Suenaga, 127, 128
Talabuga, 173, 175
Taldykorgan, 2

Tang dynasty, 197
Tangut people, 28, 146, 147
Tanguts, 24, 238
Tantra, 223
Taoism, 27
Tao River, 8
Taping River, 205
Tarikh-i Jahangushay, 88
Tarmashirin, 184, 190
Tashkent, 192
Tatar, 1, 3, 22, 162
Tatar confederation, 19
Tatars, 1, 2, 19–21, 23, 27, 56, 57
Tatsunokuchi, 136
Tayichiud, 19, 21
Taylor & Francis, 143
Tbilisi, 11
Tekuder, 73
Television Broadcasts Limited, 53
Template:History of Tibet, 145
Template:History of Turkey, 81
Template talk:History of Tibet, 145
Template talk:History of Turkey, 81
Temüge, 7, 21
Temüjin, 1, 2
Temülen, 21
Temür Khan, 140, 208, 213, 221
Temür Khan, Emperor Chengzong of Yuan, 189
Temur Meliq, 84
Tengrism, 23
Tengrist, 27
Terek River, 11
Terken Khatun (wife of Ala ad-Din Tekish), 4, 96
Termez, 4, 32, 98
Thado Minbya, 263
Thant Myint-U, 212
Than Tun, 212, 215
Theben, 167
The Conqueror (film), 52
The Crusades Through Arab Eyes, 78
Theft, 21
The Levant, 234
The Mongol Empire during the reign of Kublai Khan, 71
The New Yorker, 106, 109
Theodore Svetoslav, 174
The Private Life of Genghis Khan, 54
The Secret History of the Mongols, 20, 37, 38, 88, 103
The Travels of Marco Polo, 197, 202
Thihathu, 196, 208, 213
Thihathu of Prome, 207
Thrace, 174
Thunder crash bomb, 6

Thuringia, 162
Tian Shan, 31, 86
Tibet, 8, 11, 12, 57, 146, 148, 151–153, 216
Tibet (1912–1951), 145
Tibetan Buddhism, 8, 151
Tibetan Empire, 145, 197
Tibetan people, 146
Tibet under Qing rule, 145
Tibet under Yuan rule, 145, 146
Tiflis, 103
Tigris, 106
Tigris River, 9, 69, 104
Tihany, 165
Timeline of the Mongol Empire, 1
Timeline of Tibetan history, 145
Timur, 13, 50, 78, 190–192
Tōdai-ji, 130
Toghan (son of Kublai Khan, 215
Togha Temür, 12
Toghon Temür, 140, 190
Toghrul, 1, 2, 20, 22
Tōgō Korechika, 128
Tolui, 3–6, 18, 22, 31, 37, 43, 60, 63, 71, 84, 97, 99, 117
Toluid Civil War, 10, 11
Tomaru Sashi, 134
Tomb of Genghis Khan, 19
Tongguan County, 5, 6
Tony Liu, 53
Toqtamysh, 43
Töregene, 117
Töregene Khatun, 7, 41, 171
Torikai-Gata, 135
Torzhok, 158
Traditional Chinese characters, 18, 56, 207, 249
Trajectory of a projectile, 236
Tran dynasty, 125, 216
Trần dynasty, 8, 215, 216
Trần Hưng Đạo, 215
Trần Nhân Tông, 215, 218
Trần Quang Khải, 215
Transoxania, 89, 122
Transoxiana, 4, 35
Transport, 42
Transylvania, 160, 164, 175
Trần Thái Tông, 9, 215
Trần Thánh Tông, 215, 218
Trần Thừa, 126, 216
Treaty of Aleppo, 67
Trebuchet, 120
Trebuchets, 238
Tribute, 240
Tripitaka Koreana, 113
Trogir, 165
Tsakhiagiin Elbegdorj, 47, 211

Tsangpa, 145, 152
Tsepon W. D. Shakabpa, 154
Tsering Dhondup, 152
Tsewang Arabtan, 152
Tsewang Rabtan, 152
Tsushima Island, 132, 134
Tuban, 224
Tufan, 148
Tughlaq, 190
Tulku, 152
Tümed, 151
Tumen (unit), 30, 33, 157, 184, 228, 242
Turco-Mongol, 192
Turkic languages, 54, 55, 162, 199, 202
Turkic people, 41, 101, 171
Turkic peoples, 11, 45, 50, 64, 104, 116, 171, 196, 197, 202
Turkmen people, 65, 183, 185
Turrell V. Wylie, 147
Tus, Iran, 98
Tuul River, 151
Typhoon, 129, 133

Ugrin Csák, Archbishop of Kalocsa, 157
Uiju, 112

Újhely, 165

U Kala, 211
Ukhaantu Khan, 115
Ukraine, 50, 155
Ulaanbaatar, 20, 46
Ulaghchi, 8
Ulugh Khan, 188
Umayyads, 102
Umi no Nakamichi, 137
Under The Eternal Blue Sky, 52
UNESCO Collection of Representative Works, 59
Unsupported attributions, 107
Upper Burma, 195
Ural River, 5
Urdu, 193
Urgench, 4
Uriyangkhadai, 8, 215
Uryankhadai, 8
Uses of sinew, 235

Ü-Tsang, 151

Uyghur people, 27, 64, 115
Uyghurs, 2, 57
Uzbeg Khan, 174

Vassal, 19, 22, 130, 155
Vassalage, 80, 221

Vassal state, 129
Vasvár, 165
Venice, 8
Veszprém, 165
Viceroy, 69
Vienna, 166
Vietnam, 224
Vietnamese language, 219
Vijaya (Champa), 218
Vladimir, Russia, 49, 158, 241
Vladimir-Suzdal, 7, 156, 157
Voivode, 161
Volga, 162, 202
Volga Bulgars, 34, 156, 227
Volga River, 7
Volodymyr-Volynskyi, 159

Wade–Giles, 18, 207, 249
Wade-Giles, 263
Wallachia, 164
Wang Dechen, 8
Wang Khan, 22, 56
Wanyan Heda, 117
Wanyan Yongji, 117
Wa people, 199
Warangal, 189
Wareru, 204, 213
Warlord, 64
Wa Self-Administered Division, 263
Wasit, 9
Wassaf, 106
Wenceslaus I of Bohemia, 157, 161
Wen County, Gansu, 146
Wen Tianxiang, 117
West Asia, 7
Western Liang (Sixteen Kingdoms), 36
Western Xia, 2, 4, 5, 28, 35, 38, 44, 57, 116, 117, 146, 147
Wettest known locations, 261
White Horde, 43
Wiener Neustadt, 166
Wikipedia:Citation needed, 21, 41, 48, 65, 76, 86, 95–98, 106, 128, 140, 216, 233, 234, 240
Wikipedia:Disputed statement, 240
Wikipedia:Please clarify, 152
Wikipedia:Verifiability, 19, 240
William of Rubruck, 168
William Rubruck, 149
Winston Churchill, 168
Withdrawal (military), 42
Włodzimierz of Cracow, 157
Womens rights, 41
Wonjong, 114
Wonjong of Goryeo, 9, 12, 115, 128
Worlds largest empires, 18

World War II, 140
Wuhai, 118
Wujing Zongyao, 168
Wuwei, Gansu, 119
Wuyuan County, Inner Mongolia, 2
W:zh:二王三恪, 125
W:zh:劉黑馬, 121
W:zh:段興智, 122
W:zh:蕭札剌, 121

Xiangyang, 11
Xiangyang District, Xiangfan, 124
Xiao Zhala, 117, 121
Xindu, 36
Xing Prefecture (Shaanxi), 2, 4
Xining, 36, 39
Xu Heng, 11

Yaan, 9
Yale University Press, 14
Yalu river, 112
Yamashiro Kai, 128
Yam (route), 12, 26, 42
Yanan, 39
Yanda Pyissi, 196, 263
Yangtze, 9
Yangzhou, 221
Yanjing, 121
Yan Shi, 117
Yao people, 220
Yaroslav II of Vladimir, 158
Yassa, 24, 40, 47, 56, 149
Yazathingyan, 196, 208, 213
Yazawin Thit, 212
Yellow River, 2, 5, 36, 118, 121
Yelü Chucai, 41, 53
Yelü Dashi, 64
Yenisei Kyrgyz, 64
Yesugei, 1, 20
Yesügei, 18–20
Yesugen, 18
Yesui, 18
Yesükhei, 56
Yesü Möngke, 7
Yinchuan, 38, 118
Yingchang, 13
Yingjiang County, 201, 203
Yi people, 8, 216
Yongin, 113
Yongzheng Emperor, 152
Yoshmut, 10, 11
Yuan dynasty, 1, 12, 27, 43, 48, 56, 67, 108, 111, 115–117, 124–127, 131, 146, 149, 150, 189, 190, 195, 196, 200, 206, 213, 215–220, 222, 224, 239
Yuan era, 17

Yugur people, 223
Yunnan, 8, 122, 199, 220
Yuri II of Vladimir, 6, 157, 158
Yurt, 21

Zafar Khan (general), 184
Zafar Khan (Indian general), 188
Zagreb, 165
Zagros Mountains, 4
Zawichost, 173
Zen, 134
Zen master, 133
Zhang Hongfan, 117
Zhang Rou, 117
Zhang Shijie, 117
Zhangye, 119
Zhangzhung, 145
Zhao Mengfu, 125
Zhao Yong, 125
Zhongdu, 86

www.ingramcontent.com/pod-product-compliance
Lightning Source LLC
Chambersburg PA
CBHW030527230426
43665CB00010B/793